DIVI

MW00807315

About the Editors

Michael Bergmann is Professor of Philosophy at Purdue University. He has held fellowships from the Social Sciences and Humanities Research Council of Canada and Pew Charitable Trusts. He has published numerous articles in epistemology, metaphysics, and philosophy of religion as well as a book, *Justification without Awareness.*

Michael J. Murray oversees the programs and evaluation departments of the John Templeton Foundation. Before joining the Foundation, he was the Arthur and Katherine Shadek Humanities Professor of Philosophy at Franklin and Marshall College. He is the author or editor of several books including *Nature Red in Tooth and Claw: Theism and the Problem of Animal Suffering* and *The Believing Primate: Scientific, Philosophical, and Theological Reflections on the Origin of Religion* (edited with Jeffrey Schloss).

Michael C. Rea is Professor of Philosophy and Director of the Center for Philosophy of Religion at the University of Notre Dame. He has published numerous articles in metaphysics and the philosophy of religion and is author or editor of several books, including *Analytic Theology: New Essays in the Philosophy of Theology* (edited with Oliver Crisp) and *The Oxford Handbook of Philosophical Theology* (edited with Thomas Flint).

Divine Evil?

The Moral Character of the God of Abraham

Edited by
MICHAEL BERGMANN,
MICHAEL J. MURRAY, AND MICHAEL C. REA

OXFORD
UNIVERSITY PRESS

OXFORD
UNIVERSITY PRESS

Great Clarendon Street, Oxford, OX2 6DP,
United Kingdom

Oxford University Press is a department of the University of Oxford.
It furthers the University's objective of excellence in research, scholarship,
and education by publishing worldwide. Oxford is a registered trade mark of
Oxford University Press in the UK and in certain other countries

First published 2011
First published in paperback 2013

British Library Cataloguing in Publication Data
Data available

Library of Congress Cataloging in Publication Data
Data available

ISBN 978-0-19-957673-9(Hbk.)
ISBN 978-0-19-967185-4 (Pbk.)

Printed in Great Britain by
MPG Books Group, Bodmin and King's Lynn

To our children:
Mayfawny and Sophia Bergmann
Sam, Elise, and Julia Murray
Aaron, Kristina, and Gretchen Rea

Acknowledgements

This volume grew out of a conference sponsored by the Center for Philosophy of Religion at the University of Notre Dame in September 2009. We are grateful to the staff and graduate students involved with the Center for their assistance with that—especially Joyce Zurawski, the Center's Program Coordinator, and Charity Anderson, the graduate assistant who took the lead in managing all of the many details that needed attention while the conference was in session. We are also grateful to the Henkels Lecture Series and the College of Arts and Letters at the University of Notre Dame for their generous financial support, and (again) to Charity Anderson for preparing the manuscript for publication.

Contents

II. PHILOSOPHICAL PERSPECTIVES:
SOLUTIONS PROPOSED

III. THEOLOGICAL PERSPECTIVES

IV. CONCLUDING REMARKS

Notes on Contributors

Gary A. Anderson is Professor of Old Testament/Hebrew Bible, Department of Theology, University of Notre Dame.

Louise Antony is Professor of Philosophy, University of Massachusetts, Amherst.

Michael Bergmann is Professor of Philosophy, Purdue University.

James L. Crenshaw is Robert L. Flowers Professor of Old Testament, Emeritus, Duke University.

Edwin Curley is James B. and Grace J. Nelson Professor, University of Michigan.

Paul Draper is Professor of Philosophy, Purdue University.

Evan Fales is Associate Professor of Philosophy, University of Iowa.

John Hare is Noah Porter Professor of Philosophical Theology, Yale University.

Wes Morriston is Professor of Philosophy, University of Colorado, Boulder.

Mark C. Murphy is Fr. Joseph T. Durkin, SJ Professor of Philosophy, Georgetown University.

Michael J. Murray is Arthur and Katherine Shadek Professor in the Humanities and Philosophy, Franklin and Marshall College.

Alvin Plantinga is John A. O'Brien Professor of Philosophy Emeritus at the University of Notre Dame.

Michael C. Rea is Professor of Philosophy at the University of Notre Dame.

Christopher Seitz is Professor of Biblical Interpretation, Toronto School of Theology, University of Toronto.

Eleonore Stump is Robert J. Henle Professor of Philosophy, St Louis University.

Richard Swinburne is Nolloth Professor of the Philosophy of the Christian Religion, Emeritus, Oxford University.

Peter van Inwagen is John Cardinal O'Hara Professor of Philosophy at the University of Notre Dame.

Howard Wettstein is Professor of Philosophy, University of California, Riverside.

Nicholas Wolterstorff is Noah Porter Professor of Philosophical Theology, Emeritus, Yale University.

Introduction

Adherents of the Abrahamic religions have traditionally held that God is morally perfect and unconditionally deserving of devotion, obedience, love, and worship. The Jewish, Christian, and Islamic scriptures tell us that God is compassionate, merciful, and just. Jesus admonishes his followers to be perfect 'as your heavenly Father is perfect'. The Psalms sing at length of the abundance of God's mercy and forgiveness and the everlastingness of God's loving kindness.

As is well known, however, these same scriptures contain passages that portray God as wrathful, severely punitive, and jealous. Critics furthermore argue that the God of these scriptures commends bigotry, misogyny, and homophobia, condones slavery, and demands the adoption of unjust laws—for example, laws that mandate the death penalty for adultery and rebellion against parents, and laws institutionalizing in various ways the diverse kinds of bigotry and oppression just mentioned.

Troubling passages can be found in all of the sacred texts of three major theistic religions, but the texts of the Hebrew Bible[1] have received somewhat

---

[1] We learned quickly during the beginning stages of assembling this volume that there is no unproblematic term for referring to the texts that we are taking as our focus. To refer to them collectively by the term 'Old Testament' suggests various decisions and biases that we don't intend to take on; but other terms suffer from the same problem. Part of the problem we face is summed up nicely by James Sanders as follows: 'Another problem [arising around the middle of the twentieth century] was what Christians should call the first of their double-testament Bible. Most wanted to drop the sub-title, Old Testament, out of respect for the continuing existence and variety of Judaism . . . Some Christians began to say "Hebrew Bible" instead of Old Testament, but this is clearly inaccurate and inappropriate since "Hebrew Bible," or *Biblia Hebraica*, is a time-honored term for the Jewish tri-partite Bible, the Tanak, and not for the Old Testament (besides there being a few Aramaic portions in it). The unfortunate designation persists even in sophisticated circles despite the fact that the Christian First Testament and the Hebrew Bible are significantly different from one another in shape and even contents. Another suggestion, my own in fact, was to refer to it as the First Christian Testament, but some object to this because it apparently suggests that Jews should have a Second Testament as well. . . . In Jewish institutions it is called simply "Bible" to distinguish it from Talmud and Responsa' (Sanders 2005: 7–8).

Still, 'Hebrew Bible' *is* widely used (even if ill-advisedly) in 'sophisticated circles' to refer neutrally to the books of the Old Testament and Jewish Bible. (The *Oxford Dictionary of World Religions*, for example, says '[t]he Christian Old Testament corresponds to the Hebrew Bible' (Bowker 1997: 147).) Thus, since it is the closest thing to a convenient suitably neutral term that we have found, we are going to persist with that term here. To those who object, we simply say that we understand the problems, have no stake in the debates, and mean to take no substantive

more focused attention in recent years. Perhaps part of the reason for this is that some think, along with Cyril Rodd, that '[t]he Old Testament can easily appear to be the most bloodthirsty of all the sacred scriptures within the great religious traditions' (Rodd 2001: 185). As he puts it, 'the Old Testament *glories* in war' and God is praised therein as a 'man of war' (199, emphasis in original; and Exod. 15: 3). Moreover, God seems in those texts to be portrayed as condoning, commending, and even sometimes commanding human moral atrocities (like slavery, rape, genocide, and child sacrifice) that disturb modern readers to a much greater degree than the more abstract and 'eschatological' threats of death and hellfire that are more readily to be found in the New Testament and Koran.

Again, though, the New Testament and Koran also contain troubling passages—and ones that are troubling in much the same way as the texts of the Hebrew Bible. Thus, we suspect that the greater part of the reason for the focus on the latter texts is that all of those texts, unlike the New Testament and Koran, are treated as divine revelation by Jews and Christians alike, and they are, to a certain extent, treated as revelation by Muslims as well.[2] Problems with the Hebrew Bible texts, therefore, provide the basis for a wider-ranging critique of the Abrahamic religious traditions. Absent some sort of explanation for these problematic passages, then, Jews and Christians, and perhaps Muslims as well, face a hard dilemma: it seems that they must either deny that the problematic texts constitute divine revelation, or they must admit that the God they worship is not even morally decent, much less morally perfect.

There is, of course, nothing new in these criticisms. Theologians in all three traditions have struggled to make sense of the texts that seem to portray God in a morally suspect light. Indeed, as early as the second century CE, something like the very dilemma just mentioned seems to have been clearly seen by Marcion, who rejected the Hebrew Bible because the God portrayed therein seemed to be wrathful, cruel, petty, whimsical, and subject to a variety of other vices.[3] But the problem has taken on new urgency in recent years. Religious extremism has of late had drastic and devastating effects throughout

positions with our choice of terminology. What we are primarily interested in, in any case, are problems in the various texts that *compose* the collections referred to as the Old Testament or the Jewish Bible.

[2] From a Muslim point of view, the Jewish and Christian Bibles *contain* God's revelation, but in corrupted form. The problems, if any, that they will face with problematic Hebrew Bible texts are, therefore, of a somewhat different texture from the problems that Jews and Christians will face (Bowker 1997: 148).

[3] Harnack 1990: chs. 4 and 5, esp. p. 58. On Marcion's view, the Hebrew Bible did reveal the nature of *a* god (the 'creator God'); just not the nature of the eternal and good God revealed in the New Testament, and in Jesus of Nazareth (Wilson 1980: 80–8; 115–17).

the world in the form of terrorist attacks, beheadings, and other atrocities performed in the name of God. In light of this, many unbelievers have decided that the time for polite, private disagreement with religious people has come to an end: if devoted believers can appeal to their religious texts as justifica-tion for horrific acts of violence (or other sorts of egregious misbehavior), then the texts need to be exposed for what they are. Holding back from such criticism so as not to give offence simply encourages more of the same extremely immoral and dangerous behavior.

This line of reasoning has led people like Richard Dawkins, Daniel Dennett, Christopher Hitchens, Sam Harris, Bill Maher, and others who share their concerns to become outspoken critics of religion and of sacred texts like the Bible. The attacks of September 11, 2001 in particular brought religiously motivated violence forcefully and vividly to the attention of the general public. In the wake of those attacks, the so-called 'New Atheists'—whose newness consists primarily in their evangelical fervor—have made much of the apparent fact that, rather than being categorically condemned by the sacred texts of the great theistic religions, violence against God's enemies seems to be condoned and gloried in by them. Thus, Dawkins writes:

> The God of the Old Testament is arguably the most unpleasant character in all fiction [and is] proud of it: A petty, unjust, unforgiving control-freak; a vindictive, blood-thirsty ethnic cleanser; a misogynistic, homophobic, racist, infanticidal, genocidal, filicidal, pestilential, megalomaniacal, sadomasochistic, capriciously malevolent bully. (2006: 51)

Again, Dawkins is hardly the first (or most competent) proponent of this sort of objection. But in the new environment of forceful, blunt, and harsh criticism of the Bible, this old objection demands a direct and satisfying response. How then, *are* we to interpret the morally objectionable passages of the Hebrew Bible? What, then, might theists say in response to the charge that the God of their sacred texts apparently condones and commands moral atrocities?

In September of 2009, precisely these questions took center-stage at a conference entitled 'My Ways Are Not Your Ways: The Moral Character of the God of the Hebrew Bible', organized by the editors of the present volume and hosted by the Center for Philosophy of Religion at the University of Notre Dame. This volume is the product of that conference. The conference was motivated both by the renewed importance of the problem, as just described, and by the sense that, despite its familiarity, there remains a great deal of work to be done towards solving it.

The chapters in this volume fall into four groups: (i) the first three of the eleven main chapters press objections by philosophers to the moral character of God as it is represented in the Hebrew Bible; (ii) the next five offer responses by theistic philosophers to such objections; (iii) the next two after that present additional responses from the perspective of specialists in biblical studies; and (iv) the final chapter provides some general reflections on the conference at which these papers were initially presented. Also included in the volume are commentators' remarks on each chapter (except the last), along with replies by the original authors. Abstracts spelling out the content of each of the eleven main papers in more detail can be found immediately following this Introduction.

Most of the contributors to this volume are philosophers; a few are biblical scholars. In our view, the problems raised by these texts are fundamentally interdisciplinary. On the one hand, they raise distinctively philosophical questions. Under what conditions can one rationally regard a text, oracular pronouncement, religious experience, or whatever as divinely revealed or inspired? Is it coherent to suppose that a morally perfect God issued the troublesome permissions, commendations, and commands found in the Hebrew Bible? If not—if the texts fundamentally misrepresent God at those points—can one still rationally believe that the texts count, in any meaningful sense, as authoritative (or even useful) divine revelation? What duties would a perfectly good and loving God have toward human beings? Could the punishments that God is said to mete out either directly or through the agency of others possibly be just or deserved? And so on. On the other hand, answering these sorts of questions requires a great deal of awareness of and sensitivity to relevant facts about ancient Near Eastern religion and culture, systematic theological considerations, facts about the various traditions of commentary that have grown up around these texts, and other matters of history and textual interpretation—all of which fall squarely under the provenance of theology and biblical studies.

Despite the interdisciplinary character of the questions, however, philosophers have not been rushing to address the issue; and scholars in biblical studies seem (to us, anyway) not to have addressed the crucial philosophical questions with the kind of thoroughness, directness, philosophical sensitivity, and rigor that philosophers of religion might otherwise hope for.[4] Moreover, there has been very little by way of productive interdisciplinary discussion of the topic. The primary goal of the conference, therefore, was to help begin a

---

[4] This seems not just to be an outsider's perspective. Thus, for example, in commenting on the state of discussion within biblical studies on the problem of Old Testament attitudes toward war, Cyril Rodd writes: 'More attention needs to be given to the problems which [these attitudes] raise for the authority of the Old Testament as divine revelation. None of the attempts which have been made to come to terms with the presence of war and the attitudes toward it can be regarded as satisfactory. In the Old Testament war was not only accepted but religion

much-needed interdisciplinary discussion of the morally problematic aspects of the Hebrew Bible, with an eye to encouraging further work on the topic both within our own discipline of philosophy of religion and also within the disciplines of theology and biblical studies.

As noted earlier, abstracts of the chapters in the volume appear immediately after this introductory essay. Thus, for the remainder of the Introduction, rather than discuss the chapters in detail, we shall instead (i) provide a brief sketch of what seem to us to be the main options for addressing the problematic passages in the Hebrew Bible, and (ii) lay out what seem to us, in light of our experience in organizing and attending the conference, to be important areas for further research.

1. OPTIONS FOR ADDRESSING PROBLEMATIC PASSAGES

The troublesome texts under discussion in the present volume—i.e. texts that involve what Eric Siebert (2009) calls *disturbing divine behavior*—vary widely with respect to what makes them troublesome. In some cases, the texts are problematic because they (appear to) contain expressions of divine sentiment that many nowadays think reflect bad moral values. Other texts seem not merely to presuppose divine approval for bad moral values, but to commend or command practices (exterminating entire people groups or commanding a faithful follower—Abraham—to kill and burn his only son upon an altar) which reflect unflinching cruelty and a complete disregard for the negative effects of such commands upon victim and perpetrator alike. Those who reject current moral opinion and embrace the moral values apparently represented in the text might not be concerned about texts of the first sort. However, all believers in the Abrahamic traditions must come to grips with the apparent conflict between passages of the latter sort and the traditional picture of God as maximally loving, merciful, and compassionate. Even if the implicit moral norms are viewed by some as unproblematic, the apparent

commonly justified it and intensified its evil. This view of war is irredeemable.... [Thus] Christians and others who seek a scriptural basis for their ethical decisions are driven to re-examine the source of their moral philosophy. And if this is so with regard to war, how far does it also apply to other aspects of Old Testament ethics?' (2001: 205–6).

On the other hand, it must be noted that the literature is not entirely devoid of detailed treatments of the relevant problems. The most thorough recent treatment is Seibert 2009; but see also, for example, Brueggemann 2009 (discussed in the chapter by Wolterstorff), Craigie 1978, Niditch 1993, and von Rad (1958/1991), all of which deal in various ways with issues of war and violence in the Old Testament.

endorsement of rape, genocide, and child sacrifice must surely be addressed in some fashion.

Many of the chapters collected here focus primarily on texts dealing with the conquest of Canaan and, specifically, the practice of *herem*, or 'the ban'—the devoting of human beings, livestock, and other things to God for wholesale destruction.[5] In what follows we will start by summarizing some of the most natural strategies for dealing with those texts, noting along the way authors in this volume who endorse each of the different strategies. Our goal in doing this is to provide a sort of taxonomy within which to locate the various views defended in this volume. Reflection on this taxonomy will also enable us at the end of the section to construct a more general taxonomy of responses that defenders of the Hebrew Bible might deploy in responding to critics.

To focus our discussion, it will help to have before us an example or two of the problematic texts. Consider the following:

Deuteronomy 20: 10–18 [10] When you draw near to a town to fight against it, offer it terms of peace. [11] If it accepts your terms of peace and surrenders to you, then all the people in it shall serve you at forced labor. [12] If it does not submit to you peacefully, but makes war against you, then you shall besiege it; [13] and when the LORD your God gives it into your hand, you shall put all its males to the sword. [14] You may, however, take as your booty the women, the children, livestock, and everything else in the town, all its spoil. You may enjoy the spoil of your enemies, which the LORD your God has given you. [15] Thus you shall treat all the towns that are very far from you, which are not towns of the nations here. [16] But as for the towns of these peoples that the LORD your God is giving you as an inheritance, you must not let anything that breathes remain alive. [17] You shall annihilate them—the Hittites and the Amorites, the Canaanites and the Perizzites, the Hivites and the Jebusites—just as the LORD your God has commanded, [18] so that they may not teach you to do all the abhorrent things that they do for their gods, and you thus sin against the LORD your God.[6]

In this text, God is portrayed as commanding the enslavement of towns that surrender to the Israelites, and the wholesale slaughter of particular people groups—the Hittites and the Amorites, the Canaanites and the Perizzites, the Hivites and the Jebusites. Elsewhere, as the Israelite army comes face to face with the armies of the Amorites, Perizzites, Hivites, Jebusites, and others, the following is attributed to God:

---

[5] But not all of the chapters deal with this issue. John Hare's contribution, for example, focuses on the issue of animal sacrifice.

[6] Except where otherwise noted, this and all other biblical quotations in this introduction come from the *New Revised Standard Version Bible*, copyright 1989, Division of Christian Education of the National Council of the Churches of Christ in the United States of America.

Joshua 11: 6 And the LORD said to Joshua, 'Do not be afraid of them, for tomorrow at this time I will hand over all of them, slain, to Israel; you shall hamstring their horses, and burn their chariots with fire.'

Modern readers might find this injunction triply problematic. First, it promises the death of the aforementioned people groups without even the suggestion that surrender is an option. Second, the horses who are to be hamstrung have done nothing to deserve such violent treatment. Third, the horses which are to be hamstrung are *already* victims by virtue of having been turned into vehicles of war by the Amorites et al.

In the literature dealing with Israelite war and the practice of *herem*, one finds at least three main strategies for dealing with these problematic texts:

1. Deny that the texts are divinely inspired.

2. Allow that the texts are divinely inspired, but (i) deny that the apparently problematic *commands and permissions* therein were in fact the commands and permissions intended by God, and (ii) identify a morally unproblematic message as the overall divine message of the text.

3. Allow that the texts are divinely inspired and that the apparently problematic commands and permissions were in fact divinely intended, and argue that they are unproblematic because they serve a greater good, or impose just punishments for sin, or are in some other way consistent with God's duties toward human beings and with God's character as perfectly loving and morally perfect.

Within these categories—particularly the latter two—there are obviously many sub-categories. Each also is attended by problems. On this, we shall comment only briefly.

The first strategy is recommended by each of the first three authors in this volume. As noted earlier, it was also (in a way) defended in the second century CE by Marcion of Sinope and by various more recent scholars such as Friederich Delitzsch, Adolf von Harnack, and Hector Avalos.[7] It is tempting to regard this as the 'easy way out' for religious believers.[8] But it raises serious problems for those who want to preserve the view that at least some of the texts in the Jewish and Christian Bibles are divinely inspired. For if one says that some parts of the Hebrew Bible are not divinely inspired, one thereby

---

[7] For references and discussion, see Siebert 2009: 57–8, 64–6. We say 'in a way' in connection with Marcion because, as noted above (n. 3), Marcion did think that the Hebrew Bible was inspired by *a* god, just not by the God revealed in Jesus of Nazareth.

[8] Wes Morriston, who provides comments on the essays by Mark Murphy and Richard Swinburne, is a religious believer who joins the authors of the first three essays in this volume in taking this approach.

undercuts any appeal to the authority of tradition as evidence that other texts are inspired. This is a problem since the authority of tradition is widely taken both to provide evidence for many believers that the texts of the Bible are divinely inspired and to provide a means of correcting or corroborating whatever other criteria individual believers happen to use to determine that a text is divinely inspired. With the authority of tradition undercut, there is no obvious reason for thinking that contemporary believers will be able to arrive at a criterion for detecting divine inspiration that will yield the results that they desire—namely, that the problematic texts are *not* inspired, but other texts in the Hebrew Bible *are*.[9]

The second strategy encompasses a wide variety of more particular strategies. For example, some have argued that the texts are not to be understood as literal historical accounts, but rather are to be viewed as typological or allegorical narrative.[10] One suggestion along these lines is that the message of our example text above from Deuteronomy is *not* that God really, at some point in history, ordered the complete destruction of the Amorites et al., but rather that God wants *readers of the text* (represented by Israel) utterly to destroy sin in their lives (represented by the Amorites et al.).

Others argue that the relevant texts are stylized and heavily perspectival histories—accurate perhaps in broad outline but not in fine detail. Thus, for example, Walter Brueggemann argues that the most we can reasonably believe God to have authorized in the conquest narratives is the hamstringing of horses and the destruction of chariots—horses and chariots being symbols of monarchical power and oppression. The attribution to God (implicit or otherwise) of more extensive permissions or commands was simply the result of Israel's leaders interpreting oracles or other putative modes of revelation in light of their own preconceptions, biases, fallible memories of the words of Moses and of the liberation from Egypt recorded in Exodus, and fallible understanding of what is right and good.[11] On his view, the overall message we are to take from the texts is that God stands firmly on the side of the weak and oppressed, over against the powerful and oppressive.

Along similar lines, still others note that the preponderance of scholarship favors the conclusion that, in fact, 'the Canaanites were not eliminated' and so perhaps the command to practice *herem* was, like many other laws, 'not intended to be enforced [but rather was] promulgated to indicate the moral

---

[9] For related discussion, see Crisp 2009 and Sundberg 1975.

[10] This was a common approach to biblical interpretation for early Christian interpreters. (See Kugel 2007: esp. 17–19.) For its application to the 'conquest' texts, see e.g. Origen, *Homilies on Joshua* 1.3. See also Siebert 2009: 60–4, and the chapters by Swinburne and Seitz in the present volume.

[11] See especially Brueggemann 2009: 26–40. Cf. also Eichrodt 1961: 282–6.

and social priorities of the lawgiver' (Goldingay 1987: 164).[12] On this view, the command to put the Canaanites under the ban 'may, then, be a statement of an attitude to be taken toward Canaanite religion rather than a military policy to be implemented' (Goldingay 1987: 164) against the Canaanite people themselves. If this is correct, then (again) the *problematic* command was never issued; rather, proper interpretation of the text, together with attention to genre and relevant facts of history, reveals that the *actual* command was more benign and the narratives *taken at face value* misrepresent to the untrained modern eye what actually took place.[13]

Here too, however, there are serious difficulties for the traditional theist. For on all of these views, the *plain sense* of the text radically misrepresents what actually took place and what God actually intended to communicate to readers. On some of the views in question, this is because the texts contain a mixture of accurate and inaccurate reporting that is left to us, generations after the fact, to sort out. On other views it is because the texts are of a genre (allegory, stylized quasi-history, etc.) for which the standards of accuracy involve something other than straightforward conformity with the historical facts. Either way, what we have in these texts is not obviously what we would expect from material that is supposed to be both inspired by God, and revelatory of God's nature and personality.

To see the problem more vividly, suppose the older children in a family tell the younger children horrifying stories about how their father severely beats them for unmannerly behavior; and suppose they also tell stories according to which the father insisted that they be willing to sell themselves into prostitution in order to help pay the family bills. Now imagine the older kids later saying, 'Our stories weren't meant to be taken as "history". Their basic message is that good manners and helping to pull one's own weight in the family are important to our father. We simply exaggerated a lot to make the point.' Most of us would think that, on the assumption that *some* of the younger kids *might* believe the stories just as they are told, what the older kids have done here is utterly appalling. And matters are made worse, not better, by the supposition that the father himself inspired or otherwise authorized

---

[12] See also McKeating 1979 (cited by Goldingay in partial support of the claim about 'many other laws'), which argues that the severe sanctions against adultery were probably rarely, if ever, carried out, and that their real function was more to establish certain ideals of behavior—i.e. to convey the ideal that adultery is *really bad* and not to be tolerated—rather than to define the standard penalty for transgressors.

[13] Discussion of the historicity of the conquest narratives and of the practice of *herem* may be found in several of the sources we have already cited (as well as the essays by Anderson, Wolterstorff, and Seitz in this volume), but a good starting place is von Rad 1958/1991: esp. ch. 2.

the telling of those stories as his 'revelation' to his younger children. No decent father would do such a thing. But if that is right, then, we might wonder, why think that God would allow something apparently similar to go on in the revealed narratives of the Hebrew Bible?

The third strategy, unlike the others, concedes that God did indeed issue the problematic commands and permissions, but seeks to justify them somehow. One prominent version of this strategy takes its cues from the texts themselves and maintains that God commanded the destruction of the Canaanite peoples to punish the sins of those nations and to prevent the Israelites from becoming corrupted by them.[14] The sins of the Canaanites are reported to include institutionalized child sacrifice, aberrant sexual practices, and many other vicious behaviors.[15] Critics of this strategy, however, argue that we have no reason to believe that the Canaanites were substantially worse than their neighbors (including the Israelites) and, even if they were, the punishment that is being meted out—which includes the destruction of innocent children and the hamstringing of horses—goes beyond what could possibly be deserved (cf. Rodd 2001: 199).

On other variants of this third strategy, the problematic commands and permissions are justified by greater goods that they are supposed to yield. Perhaps the slaughter of the Canaanite peoples served the purpose of bringing about the triumph of order (in some sense) over chaos.[16] Perhaps it spared the Canaanites from suffering the bad effects of allowing their souls to become more deeply corrupted by their own sinfulness.[17] Of course, it isn't very easy to see how the destruction of Canaanite *children* and the hamstringing of their horses would serve purposes like these. Indeed, it is hard to see how such things might serve any good purpose at all. But one might respond to this further worry by insisting that, for all we know, the commands served unknown goods that *do* benefit the sufferers but that only someone intimately acquainted with the lives of the Canaanites and their children could appreciate.[18]

Lastly, one might unpack this third strategy by arguing that the problematic commands and permissions are *automatically* justified because God has no

---

[14] For discussion of this view, see, in particular, the chapters by Anderson, Seitz, Stump, and Wolterstorff in the present volume. See also Craigie 1978, Kaiser 1983: 267–8, and Niditch 1993: ch. 2.

[15] See Kaiser 1983: 268, discussed in Rodd 2001: 199.

[16] This view is defended by P. D. Hanson (1987).

[17] This is a line taken by Gleason Archer, discussed in Siebert 2009: 77–8. Eleonore Stump also proposes it for consideration in her contribution to this volume.

[18] 'Unknown goods' responses are considered and discussed in the essays by Edwin Curley, Mark Murphy, and Eleonore Stump (as well as in some of the comments and replies). There are

duties toward the people who would be victimized by those commands. This might be because God has no duties toward people generally, or it might be because certain features of God's relationship to (say) the Canaanites make it the case that God has no duties toward *them* (even if he does have duties toward, say, the Israelites).[19] One concern with this view, however, is that it appears simply to appeal to a 'technicality' to absolve God of responsibility for the victimization of the Canaanites. One is still left wondering how the command to practice *herem* could possibly be consistent with other divine attributes such as being perfectly loving and merciful.[20]

We have now finished canvassing what we take to be some of the most obvious strategies for responding to the passages dealing with *herem*. We turn now to a more general taxonomy of strategies for dealing with morally troubling passages in biblical texts.

In light of the foregoing, it seems that the options are fairly straightforward. With respect to any morally problematic text, we will face, broadly speaking, two questions:[21]

I. Is there some explanation that mitigates the problem while remaining consistent with the claim that the text is divinely inspired and to be interpreted at face value?

II. Can the text plausibly be assigned some meaning other than the 'face-value meaning' and still be regarded as divinely inspired?

Answering 'yes' to the first question but not the second will push us in the direction of a generalized version of Strategy 3 above; answering 'yes' to the second but not the first will push us in the direction of a generalized version of Strategy 2.

---

various reasons why the goods in question might be 'unknown' to us. It might be that we (unlike God) are wholly unacquainted with them; or it might be that we (unlike God) lack the cognitive capacity to see how (e.g.) the destruction of Canaanite children contributes to them; or it might be that, although we are acquainted with the relevant goods (as such) and able in principle to understand how they are connected with the evils reported in Scripture, we simply don't have enough information about the people experiencing those evils to see how their experiences contribute to their good. Curley seems primarily to object to appeals to goods that are supposed to be unknown for the first two reasons. In her contribution to this volume, Eleonore Stump suggests simply that the relevant goods might be unknown for reasons of the third sort. The unknown goods response can also be employed to address some of the concerns raised about Strategy 2. Cf. Peter van Inwagen's comments on the essay by Edwin Curley.

[19] This line of reasoning is developed in the chapter by Mark Murphy.

[20] Murphy is aware of this concern (see pp. 166–7, below).

[21] Note that both questions speak of the 'face-value' meaning of a text—we don't mean to suppose that this is unproblematic.

For some passages, the answer to both questions might be 'yes': there might be multiple interpretive options, and perhaps even multiple meanings. The view that biblical texts have multiple meanings was widely accepted among ancient commentators, and it was also endorsed by patristic and medieval commentators.[22] Proponents of Strategy 2 are, in effect, those who think that what we would naturally identify as the 'plain meaning' simply can't be one of the *divinely intended* meanings, due to the absence of a plausible justifying explanation. But it's not out of the question that one might find some such explanation *and* retain the multiple meanings view and thus find oneself with an overabundance of resources for handling some troublesome passage.

Alternatively, one might answer both questions negatively. In that case, the remaining options seem to be fourfold:

(i) deny that the text is divinely inspired,
(ii) deny that God was (or is) perfectly good,
(iii) retain all of the beliefs that one initially brought to the text and declare its presence in a divinely inspired book to be a mystery,
(iv) (try to) revise one's own moral values, intuitions, or whatever in light of the text.

Option (i), obviously, is just Strategy 1 above. Option (ii) rejects perfect-being theology, attributing to God moral error and, as it is sometimes developed, moral growth.[23] Option (iii) simply gives up on trying to deal with the problematic passages. Option (iv) is characterized in some traditions as the uniquely pious response, since it ostensibly treats scripture as authoritative over 'mere human reason' and moral intuition rather than vice versa. But others will regard this feature of it as a vice rather than a virtue.[24]

---

[22] Kugel 2007: ch. 1. See also Stump 1989.

[23] Cf. Howard Wettstein's contribution to the present volume.

[24] One hazard with option (iv) is that, in trying to be pious by revising our moral intuitions so that they accord with portrayals of God that conflict with them, we run the risk of another sort of impiety—namely, believing evil things about God. Thus, for example, in a sermon entitled 'Justice', George MacDonald writes: 'To say on the authority of the Bible that God does a thing no honourable man would do, is to lie against God; to say that it is therefore right, is to lie against the very spirit of God. To uphold a lie for God's sake is to be against God, not for him ... While his child could not see the rectitude of a thing, he would infinitely rather, even if the thing were right, have him say, God could not do that thing, than have him believe that he did it' (MacDonald 1989: 116–17).

2. AREAS FOR FUTURE RESEARCH

We noted near the beginning of this chapter that the questions that take center-stage in this volume are clearly interdisciplinary. Our hope is that our sketch of ways of dealing with problematic texts has helped to drive home that conclusion. Successfully executing any of the above strategies will require sensitivity both to matters in which philosophers are expert and to matters in which biblical scholars and theologians are expert. The contributors to this volume took the work of interdisciplinary engagement on this topic well down the road. But, unsurprisingly, more work is yet to be done. In some cases, the need for additional effort became apparent even in the question and answer periods during the conference.[25] As the event progressed conversations among presenters and attendees made it clear that this topic is fertile soil indeed.

In the closing portion of this Introduction we would like to take the opportunity to highlight four areas of inquiry to which, in our view, *philosophers* working on this topic need to pay more attention. (We mostly leave it to biblical scholars and theologians reading this volume to determine for themselves the areas to which their respective disciplines need to pay greater attention.) These are: (1) the variety and character of ancient Near Eastern literary styles, (2) relevant facts about ancient Near Eastern cultures, (3) the role played by *interpretive traditions* in shaping the meaning of these texts for the relevant religious communities, and (4) the different theories about the nature of divine inspiration and revelation and about the authority of both scripture and tradition. We shall discuss each in turn.

1. Ancient Near Eastern literary styles. Imagine a time 500 years from now. English is a dead language. The overwhelming volume of material published since its death has elbowed out English literature from the curriculum to the point where students have no acquaintance with it at all. An ambitious graduate student in history labors to learn the language and decides to use her newfound linguistic skill to undertake a study of the genre of historical narrative in the twentieth century. She decides to focus on the historical methodology deployed by history books that begin with the words 'Once upon a time...'

It is clear to us why this dissertation is doomed to failure. Books that start out with the words 'Once upon a time...' are not historical texts, they are

---

[25] Videos of the conference sessions, including the question and answer periods, are presently available at the following website: http://www.nd.edu/~cprelig/conferences/video/my_ways/.

fiction. The student's lack of basic understanding of English narrative styles has misled her into thinking that the words 'Once upon a time' signal what they indeed would seem to signal on a literal reading: that at some time in the past the events recounted really took place.

Awareness of this sort is keenly relevant for scholars who wish to explore the topics raised in this volume since it might be the case that apparently historical narratives were neither intended to be understood as such nor likely to be read as such. It was common, for example, for royal chroniclers in the ancient Near East to construct narratives with only partial grounding in actual historical events for the purpose of inspiring the nation in the face of adversity, shoring up claims of political authority on the part of the ruling class, and so on.[26] As a result, when we look at the narratives purportedly recording the destruction of the Amalekites, or of the prophets of Baal in their encounter with Elijah, it is important to know just what the author intended to convey and how readers were likely to understand them. Were they reporting or condoning genocide or murder, or were those accounts intended, and understood, to be wholly incidental to the point of the narrative?

2. Ancient Near Eastern cultures. In addition to a working knowledge of ancient Near Eastern literary styles, future philosophical work on this topic may need to pay increasingly close attention to details about ancient Near Eastern culture. It should come as no surprise, of course, that information about culturally ingrained beliefs, attitudes, practices, and norms in ancient Near Eastern people groups might have an impact on how we interpret biblical texts. But it is perhaps less obvious that such information might help to solve some of the particular problems with which the present volume deals. After all, the question in view here is whether an omniscient and wholly good God could command or allow the sorts of things that these narratives report. The only standards that are relevant to assessing the goodness or badness, the permissibility or impermissibility of such things, are the absolute standards of moral goodness and rightness. Members of ancient Near Eastern cultural groups might not have endorsed or been aware of such standards. But that will not have any relevance to the theological lessons that we can and must draw from the text. Or so it might seem.

Biblical scholars treating these texts tend to see the matter differently. Peter Craigie (1978), for example, in an appendix devoted to a discussion of the 'cultural and religious environment of Israel's wars' notes that some scholars think that the degree to which Israelite war practices and ideologies resembled

---

[26] For a broad ranging discussion of this issue see Seibert 2009: 132–44 and 175–6.

those of their neighbors makes a direct difference in how we view the character of the God of Israel.[27] Walter Brueggemann (2009) and John Goldingay (1987), as we have already seen, think that attention to various features of ancient Israelite culture (specifically, the ways in which legal penalties tended to be viewed and enforced, and the ways in which divine commands tended to be discovered and delivered) make a difference in our understanding of the nature and function of some of the problematic divine commands in the Hebrew Bible and, consequently, in our understanding of the God who purportedly issued them. Susan Niditch (1993) devotes her entire study of war in the Hebrew Bible to a discussion of the different ideologies of war in the biblical texts, partly with an eye to showing that 'the history of attitudes toward war in ancient Israel is a complex one involving multiplicity, overlap, and self-contradiction' (154). If she is right, and if the 'multiplicity, overlap, and self-contradiction' is both present in the Hebrew Bible and reconcilable with the claim that the Bible is divinely inspired (both controversial claims, of course), then, again, attention to these sorts of cultural facts will be highly relevant to our overall understanding and evaluation of various problematic texts.

Reflection on the sorts of examples just mentioned should make it clear that the extent to which attention to facts about ancient Near Eastern culture might be helpful will vary with one's views about the nature and function of divine commands, about how God's commands are disclosed to the people of God, and about the nature of divine revelation and inspiration. For some who work on these issues, texts can sensibly be viewed as divinely inspired and commands can sensibly (even if only loosely) be attributed to God even if the views they embody are heavily colored by the author/reporter's own (false) beliefs, values, and perspectives on things. If views like this are defensible, then attention to beliefs, attitudes, and so on that were prevalent in ancient Near Eastern cultures will be absolutely vital to our understanding of what our problematic texts are *really telling us* about God's actual values and commands.

---

[27] Often what is at issue is the question whether God's commands to the Israelites represent some sort of 'accommodation' to deeply entrenched views and practices, or a kind of improvement on such practices, or neither. Perhaps these particular lines of inquiry are not entirely helpful. After all, one might naturally object that a God who issues commands that *accommodate* or only *slightly improve* upon deeply entrenched homicidal, genocidal, misogynistic, or homophobic beliefs and practices (to name just a few) still seems to be very far from morally perfect. At the same time, however, it is not clear that a morally perfect God would not engage in progressive revelation of moral truth. Nor is it clear that these lines of inquiry are the only ones that might be opened up by attention to similarities and differences between the beliefs and practices of the ancient Israelites and those of their neighbors.

Other background assumptions might likewise heighten the relevance of attention to ancient Near Eastern cultures. According to John Hare (2007: 270), for example, God's commands don't necessarily reflect God's will. One who shares this assumption might then follow Hare in offering something like the following answer to worries about God's commanding Abraham to sacrifice his son:

Perhaps...Abraham already thought he should be willing to make this sacrifice (because it was in line with surrounding culture), and God showed him the evil of this by telling him to go ahead, taking him to the very brink, and then forbidding it. (269)

The claim that God might command things that in fact God does not will (and, indeed, rightly abhors) will, of course, be controversial. But we are not here recommending Hare's solution. Rather, our point (again) is just that various strategies for addressing particular problematic passages in scripture will turn in part on facts about ancient Near Eastern cultures, and philosophers dealing with these passages may have to pay closer attention to such facts.

3. The relevance of interpretive traditions. In commenting on the narrative in which Abraham is commanded to sacrifice Isaac, Evan Fales discusses whether or not Abraham might have been in a position to think that sacrificing Isaac was permissible because it was a necessary step towards some outweighing good. On this he says: '[T]he story gives us—and Abraham— no reason whatever to think that Isaac's sacrifice will engender more good than ill or that it's a necessary condition for an optimal outcome: on the contrary, what Abraham must accept is not only the expected loss of his son, but God's vacating his prior promise to provide Abraham, through Isaac, with descendants numerous as the stars' (this volume, p. 104).

If one considers only the immediately surrounding context of the passage, such a claim might seem plausible. But when one considers the full account of Abraham to this point in Genesis, the verdict is far less clear. Monotheists in the Abrahamic traditions have often cast God's relationship with Abraham up to this point as one in which God is training the 'father of a great nation' to display faithfulness and obedience. In doing so, however, God sometimes asks Abraham to do things that, from Abraham's limited vantage point, seem wrongheaded and unworkable. Many theists have held that the aim was not to encourage Abraham towards recklessness, but rather to encourage him to obey God even when he could not see how following the command will yield greater goods. Thus, in those cases in which Abraham trusts God and obeys divine commands, things *go well.* And when Abraham weighs the practical consequences of following a divine command and subsequently refuses to obey (for example, ignoring God's promise that he would have a son through his barren and post-menopausal wife, choosing instead to take his reproductive fortunes into his own hands) things turn out quite badly.

In the narrative in question, God asks Abraham to sacrifice his son. Assuming that Abraham (inculpably, and perhaps in accord with beliefs prevalent in his culture) does not think such a command to be immoral, what ought his reaction to be? Much of the theological tradition has argued that while Abraham could see as well as anyone that sacrificing one's childless son is a bad way to maximize offspring through that son, Abraham also knew that God brought great goods from seeming impossibility in the past. So having read the narrative to this point, one could easily imagine Abraham reasoning as follows:[28] 'Sacrificing my son seems like a patently counter-productive way to realize the promise of giving me a son through whom I will have descendents as numerous as the sand on the seashore. On the other hand, every time I have reasoned through the practical consequences of following a divine command and decided to act contrary to it as a result, things have gone very badly. Thus, I should obey.'

The point here is not to argue that Fales's reading is incorrect. (More would have to be said in order to establish that conclusion.) Rather, the point is just that one's interpretation of the text, or of the God portrayed in the text, can be influenced dramatically both by attention to relevant theological traditions and by a patient attempt to read the text charitably. This is part of the reason why traditional theists are not as quick to dismiss narratives like this as suborning immoral patterns of thought and behavior. Instead, their first inclination is to look at the text with greater care and sensitivity, often relying on the resources of their theological interpretive tradition, to see how the account might fit naturally into a larger narrative which provides us with important theological insights. As future scholarship on this topic develops, cultivating theological sensitivity and subtlety of this sort will be urgently demanded.

That said, however, it is important to note (as some biblical scholars seem not to) that the mere existence of an interpretive tradition that helps to make sense of the text does not *automatically* solve the problems *we* face with the texts. For the fact is, ancient interpreters often interpreted texts very differently from how we interpret them. They saw non-literal meanings where many of us would not; they saw foreshadowing and prediction where many of

---

[28] The issue of the historical reality both of Abraham and of the narratives detailed in Genesis concerning Abraham does not matter for the point being made here. All that matters is that a careful reader of these narratives would sensibly believe that Abraham, whether real or mythic, ought to reason as we describe here.

us would not; they interpreted texts in light of other texts that we would regard as wholly irrelevant; sometimes they seem to go too far in the attempt to understand characters in the text charitably; and so on.[29] In some cases, of course, we can simply *learn* from the ancient interpreters, viewing them as valuably supplementing or correcting our own readings of the texts. But in other cases we might find that we cannot follow where they are trying to lead because their interpretations rest on principles that we (rightly or wrongly) take to be entirely wrongheaded. In those cases, the existence of an interpretive tradition that makes sense of the text will be of no use to us, for, in our view, the tradition will be misguided.

4. *Theories about biblical inspiration, divine revelation, and the authority of scripture and tradition.* One thing that becomes clear on perusing the chapters in this volume is that there are various ways of understanding what it means to say a text is divinely inspired or revealed, or that the Bible is God's authoritative word. These different ways of understanding biblical inspiration, divine revelation, and scriptural authority, in turn, lead people to bring different expectations and interpretive principles to the text. Some, for example, seem to expect that a divinely revealed text would be one whose message is generally clear even to very unsophisticated readers (an assumption shared by many among both devoted religious believers and non-religious critics). This expectation does not rule out non-literal interpretations of particular passages, but it does lead to interpretive principles that reject literal meanings only when the presence of non-literal speech is very clearly signaled by the text (through signals that *modern* readers and ancient readers alike would readily recognize). Others think that 'obvious falsity' is a cue to the presence of non-literal speech or of accommodation to human presuppositions, so that, other things being equal, if a passage would be saying something obviously false under a literal interpretation, then the literal content of the passage is not part of the message that God intended to communicate.[30] This principle is, in turn, apparently grounded in two further suppositions, which some share and others don't: (i) that divine revelation would be free from error and (ii) that only some of what seems to be the 'literal content' of a divinely inspired text would actually be authoritative, or normative, for religious faith and practice. And, of course, these claims are but a small handful of the sorts of expectations, assumptions, and interpretive principles that people bring to the text based on their preconceived notions about divine inspiration, revelation, and biblical authority.

---

[29] For a variety of examples, see (e.g.) Kugel 2007: ch. 1 and Enns 2008: ch. 4. See also Louise Antony's reply to Eleonore Stump in Chapter 1 of the present volume.

[30] Cf. Swinburne 2007.

Thus, when one tries to identify problems for religious traditions that view a particular text as divine revelation, one must first ask difficult questions about what it means to say that a text is divinely inspired or that it is or contains divine revelation; and one must then go on to ask hard questions about what we should expect from such a text. For it is only in light of answers to these questions—whether arrived at via careful philosophical reflection or simply taken for granted—that we can make judgments about the rationality of viewing the text as the revelation of an all-knowing and morally perfect being.

This concludes our brief sketch of areas to which we think philosophers dealing with the problematic texts under consideration in this volume need to pay more attention. In providing this sketch, we have tried, among other things, to highlight some of the complexity involved in biblical interpretation and to note some of the diverse views that people might hold not only about interpretation but also about divine revelation, scriptural authority, and other matters. We are keenly aware that in doing this we have glossed over and ignored a wide variety of additional issues and alternatives—ones that would become clear with greater attention to matters in the philosophy of language, hermeneutics, moral epistemology, the epistemology of religious belief (including the belief that a text is divinely inspired), and so on. But our omissions in this regard only serve to underscore our basic point: dealing with these texts and either raising or rebutting objections against them in a philosophically and theologically responsible manner is a far more complicated task than many of us have recognized or been willing to admit. More conversation needs to take place between philosophers, theologians, and biblical scholars; and it is our hope that this volume will go some distance toward promoting such conversation.

REFERENCES

Archer, Gleason L. 1982. *New International Encyclopedia of Bible Difficulties*. Grand Rapids, Mich.: Zondervan.

Bowker, John (ed.). 1997. *Oxford Dictionary of World Religions*. Oxford: Oxford University Press.

Brueggemann, Walter. 2009. *Divine Presence Amid Violence: Contextualizing the Book of Joshua*. Eugene, Ore.: Cascade Books.

Craigie, Peter. 1978. *The Problem of War in the Old Testament*. Grand Rapids, Mich.: Eerdmanns.

Crisp, Thomas. 2009. 'On Believing that the Scriptures are Divinely Inspired', in Oliver D. Crisp and Michael Rea (eds.), *Analytic Theology: New Essays in the Philosophy of Theology*. Oxford: Oxford University Press, 187–213.

Dawkins, Richard. 2006. *The God Delusion*. Boston: Houghton Mifflin Co.

Eichrodt, Walter. 1961. *Theology of the Old Testament*, vol. i, trans. J. A. Baker. Philadelphia: Westminster Press.

Enns, Peter. 2008. *Inspiration and Incarnation*. Grand Rapids, Mich.: Baker.

Goldingay, John. 1987. *Theological Diversity and the Authority of the Old Testament*. Grand Rapids, Mich.: Eerdmanns.

Hanson, Paul D. 1987. 'War, Peace, and Justice in Early Israel', *Bible Review*, 3: 32–45.

Hare, John. 2007. *God and Morality: A Philosophical History*. Malden, Mass.: Blackwell Publishing.

Harnack, Adolf von. 1990. *Marcion: The Gospel of the Alien God*, trans. J. E. Steely and L. Bierma. Durham: Labyrinth.

Kaiser, Walter. 1983. *Toward Old Testament Ethics*. Grand Rapids, Mich.: Zondervan.

Kugel, James. 2007. *How to Read the Bible*. New York: Free Press.

MacDonald, George. 1989. *Unspoken Sermons: Series Three*. Eureka, Calif.: J. Joseph Flynn Rare Books.

MacKay, Peter. 1973. *Violence: Right or Wrong?* Waco, Tex.: Word Books.

McKeating, Henry. 1979. 'Sanctions against Adultery in Ancient Israelite Society, with Some Reflections on Methodology in the Study of Old Testament Ethics', *Journal for the Study of the Old Testament*, 11: 57–72.

Niditch, Susan. 1993. *War in the Hebrew Bible: A Study in the Ethics of Violence*. New York: Oxford University Press.

Rad, Gerhard von. 1958/1991. *Holy War in Ancient Israel*, trans. and ed. Marva Dawn. Grand Rapids, Mich.: Eerdmanns.

Rea, Michael (ed.). 2009. *Oxford Readings in Philosophical Theology*, ii: *Providence, Scripture, and Resurrection*. Oxford: Oxford University Press.

Rodd, Cyril. 2001. *Glimpses of a Strange Land: Studies in Old Testament Ethics*. Edinburgh: T. & T. Clark.

Sanders, James. 2005. *Torah and Canon*, 2nd edn. Eugene, Ore: Cascade Books.

Seibert, Eric. 2009. *Disturbing Divine Behavior: Troubling Old Testament Images of God*. Minneapolis: Fortress Press.

Stump, Eleonore. 1989. 'Visits to the Sepulcher and Biblical Exegesis', *Faith and Philosophy*, 6: 353–77. Reprinted in Rea 2009.

Sundberg, Albert, Jr. 1975. 'The Bible Canon and the Christian Doctrine of Inspiration', *Interpretation*, 29: 352–71. Reprinted in Rea 2009.

Swinburne, Richard. 2007. *Revelation: From Metaphor to Analogy*, 2nd edn. Oxford: Clarendon Press.

Wilson, Robert Smith. 1980. *Marcion: A Study of a Second-Century Heretic*. London: James Clarke & Company Limited.

Chapter Abstracts

CHAPTER 1: LOUISE ANTONY, DOES GOD LOVE US?

God is often conceived as a loving Father. It's argued in this chapter, however, that he is anything but. The God of the Hebrew Bible is far more concerned with his own glorification than with the well-being of his human 'children'. Indeed, his actions would constitute child abuse if perpetrated by a human parent. The author supports this indictment primarily through a close reading of the story of the Fall: in his relations with Adam and Eve, Yahweh's attitudes, motives, and methods contrast with those of the genuinely loving parent depicted in a parallel tale of prohibition and disobedience, the contemporary children's story *Heckedy Peg*. Corroborating evidence is drawn from narratives throughout the Hebrew Bible, including the story of the binding of Isaac and the testing of Job.

CHAPTER 2: EDWIN CURLEY, THE GOD OF ABRAHAM, ISAAC, AND JACOB

This chapter argues that the moral character of God, as portrayed in the scriptures he is supposed to have inspired, is a reasonable test of the claim that those scriptures convey a divine revelation. The Christian scriptures (the 'Old' Testament *and* the New) fail the test. They frequently represent God as authorizing bad conduct. He commands child sacrifice and genocide. He permits slavery and rape. This is only a partial list of passages which make it incredible that the morally perfect being of Christian theology could have inspired the Bible. Also problematic: the Bible contradicts itself about how God will treat his creatures after death, sometimes denying an afterlife, sometimes affirming it; when it affirms an afterlife, it threatens those who do not believe with eternal punishment. Better to give up the hypothesis of divine inspiration than to corrupt our moral thinking by trying to defend the indefensible.

CHAPTER 3: EVAN FALES, SATANIC VERSES: MORAL CHAOS IN HOLY WRIT

According to John Locke, true revelation must conform to our divinely infused moral understanding. I argue that apologetic explanations of the morally 'difficult' passages in scripture fail, unless one resorts to a voluntaristic divine command theory. Special attention is given to the Mosaic Law, the war against Midian, child sacrifice, divine punishments, and the *herem* against Canaan. It is further argued that Christian soteriology, especially the doctrine of vicarious atonement, is psychologically pernicious and morally indefensible. Among apologetic strategies considered and rebuffed are: dispensationalism, allegorical and interpolative interpretations, denial of the historicity of genocidal wars, demonization of Israel's enemies and other attempts to make the literal text morally palatable, and teleological suspension of the ethical. The price for each of these is interpretive implausibility or moral compromise. Locke's criterion condemns much of scripture as false revelation. Sociologically informed readings of scripture provide better explanations for these passages.

CHAPTER 4: JOHN HARE, ANIMAL SACRIFICES

In the Hebrew scriptures God is represented as requiring a sacrificial system involving the deaths of many thousands of animals every year as a way to produce atonement for sin. This system is taken up in the Christian scriptures as one of the most important ways to understand the death of Christ. But could a morally good God set up a system by which individuals are released from divine punishment for what they have done wrong because an animal or some other human being is killed? This does not seem to fit with our ideas either of individual accountability for wrongdoing or of the value of animal life. The chapter discusses these issues.

CHAPTER 5: MARK C. MURPHY, GOD BEYOND JUSTICE

Suppose that one aimed to call into question the moral goodness of the God of the Old Testament by appeal to God's command to destroy Jericho (Josh. 6: 16–21). In this chapter, it is argued that the only plausible way to do so would be to show that, by issuing that command, God *acted wrongly with respect to* the Jerichoites in issuing that command; and it is also argued that, for reasons brought forward by defenders of skeptical theism, the only way to show that God so acted wrongly with respect to the Jerichoites is to show that God's issuing that command *wronged* the Jerichoites. It is then shown that we have good reason to think that, by nature, it is not possible for God to wrong the Jerichoites, for God and humans do not naturally share a dikaiological order.

CHAPTER 6: ELEONORE STUMP, THE PROBLEM OF EVIL AND THE HISTORY OF PEOPLES: THINK AMALEK

This chapter discusses the problem of evil as it is raised by the story in the Hebrew Bible in which God commands Israelites to slaughter the Amalekites, and possible defenses or theodicies as regards that story. One way to deal with this story is to reject it as non-veridical, either by claiming that it should not be taken as part of divine revelation or by interpreting it to say something other than its literal meaning. This chapter adopts a different approach. It partially describes a putatively possible world which is very similar to the actual world, including the existence of evil, but in which the central claims of Christianity are also true. The chapter then investigates, as a thought experiment, whether the story of the slaughter of the Amalekites could be literally true in a world of that sort. The chapter argues that it could.

CHAPTER 7: RICHARD SWINBURNE, WHAT DOES THE OLD TESTAMENT MEAN?

When the Christian Church took over the Old Testament, it did so on the understanding that some of it should be understood in non-literal ways. Origen and then Gregory of Nyssa and Augustine developed a doctrine which Augustine summarized as 'Whatever there is in the Word of God that cannot, when taken literally, be referred either to purity of life or soundness of doctrine, you may set down as metaphorical.' And he applied this so as to reinterpret not merely passages which seemed inconsistent with Christian doctrine or moral teaching but also passages which seemed inconsistent with the supposed scientific truths established by contemporary Greek science. This tradition influenced much biblical interpretation until the Reformation and should lead us to interpret the Bible in the light of modern science. The meaning of any text depends on its context. The Bible is a patchwork of passages from different centuries. Only the whole Bible, and so any passage understood in that context, can claim full truth and full divine inspiration.

CHAPTER 8: NICHOLAS WOLTERSTORFF, READING JOSHUA

This chapter offers an interpretation of the stories of extermination to be found in the Old Testament book of Joshua. The author considers two interpretations which take the stories more or less at face value, the contemporary interpretation by the Old Testament scholar Walter Brueggemann, and the traditional interpretation by John Calvin. The author then argues that there are compelling internal reasons for not taking the stories at face value. The book is to be read as a hyperbolic and highly metaphorical celebration of Joshua as Israel's leader. The author concludes by reflecting on whether stylized celebrations of the deeds of admired leaders can play a positive role in the modern world.

CHAPTER 9: GARY ANDERSON, WHAT ABOUT THE CANAANITES?

This chapter begins with a significant moral problem raised by the book of Joshua: Is there any way to justify the Israelites' seizing of the land of another people (in this instance the Canaanites)? I discuss some of the historical issues involved (archeology shows that the conquest as described did not happen) but spend most of my time with the texts themselves. I begin by articulating the unique relationship Israel has to her land. I then turn to the way in which Gen. 15 sets the canonical framework for reading the book of Joshua. In brief, God is justified in evicting the Canaanites because of their sinful behavior that has gone on for centuries. God will use the same moral principles to judge Israel later in the biblical narrative.

CHAPTER 10: CHRISTOPHER SEITZ, CANON AND CONQUEST: THE CHARACTER OF THE GOD OF THE HEBREW BIBLE

Form-Critical and later Canonical Reading taught that texts make sense only when one attends properly to genre and to larger theological patterns in the literature, within which difficult issues like the treatment of the Canaanites must be assessed. This chapter seeks to read the Bible canonically. It questions the existence of something like a neutral 'Hebrew Bible' independent of Jewish tradition, on the one hand, or of a two-testament Christian Bible with its own history of interpretation, on the other. God's character is not something the Bible seeks to justify, but rather to depict truthfully.

CHAPTER 11: HOWARD WETTSTEIN, GOD'S STRUGGLES

This chapter takes issue with something fundamental in the overall outlook of many of the contributors to the volume. It sketches a traditional religious approach that nevertheless agrees with the critics on the ethical awfulness of some of what the Hebrew Bible attributes to God. The approach draws its inspiration from Jewish tradition, and focuses special attention on the *Akedah* and the book of Job, stories that present extreme challenges to the conception of God as ethically perfect. These stories, it is argued, have great religious power and meaning, which is not to say that we understand God's role in them, his attitude towards his beloved, what he allows, commands, mandates. The chapter ends with some speculations about what we might make of God's treatment of Abraham and Job.

Part I

Philosophical Perspectives

Problems Presented

1

Does God Love Us?

Louise Antony

I'd like to begin by telling you a children's story. The story is called *Heckedy Peg*.[1]

A mother lives in a modest house with her seven children. One day she must go to market, and leave the children at home. She gives them very specific instructions how to behave while she is gone: they are not to touch the fire, and they are not to open the door to strangers. She promises to bring each of them a treat of their choosing. One picks butter, another pudding, and so on.

After the mother leaves, the children play quietly until they hear a knock on the door. Ignoring their mother's instructions, the children open the door. It's an old woman, with a cart. 'I'm Heckedy Peg; I've lost my leg,' she says. 'Please bring me a lighted straw from the fire, so that I may light my pipe.' The children, remembering their mother's rule, are reluctant, but Heckedy Peg shows them an enormous sack of gold she's carrying in her cart, and promises that it will be theirs if they do as she asks. So the children bring her the burning straw. But as soon as her pipe is lit, each child is transformed into a piece of food. The wicked Heckedy Peg gathers them all into her wagon and makes off to her house to enjoy her feast.

Meanwhile, the poor mother returns home to find all her children gone, and is desolate. A small bird sees her crying and tells her what has happened. The mother immediately sets off to rescue her children.

The mother finally finds the evil woman's cabin, and tricks Heckedy Peg into admitting her. Heckedy Peg gives the poor mother one chance to save her children: she must guess which child has been turned into which piece of food. The clever mother realizes that she can recognize each child by the treat they requested from the market: the child that wanted butter is the bread, and so on. The children are restored. Gathering them safely around her, the

---

[1] The following is my paraphrase. Wood and Wood 1987.

mother chases the wicked woman out of town. Heckedy Peg is never heard from again.

You'll perhaps have noticed a parallel between this tale and another, very well-known story, one which, according to a familiar interpretation, also concerns a loving parent and his disobedient children. I am speaking, of course, of the story of Adam and Eve and the Fall (Gen. 2: 4–3). As in *Heckedy Peg*, a parent (God) warns his children (Adam and Eve) not to do something. As in *Heckedy Peg*, a tempter (the serpent) gets the children to disobey the parent. And as in *Heckedy Peg*, disaster ensues. Within this overall similarity, however, the stories differ enormously, as we will soon see. *Heckedy Peg* celebrates the valor of maternal love; Genesis exhibits the power of a tyrant.

The figure of God as a loving Father is ubiquitous in Christian writings and teachings, but it is also a common trope in the Hebrew Bible. (Deut. 32: 6, Mal. 2: 10, Exod. 4: 20, 2 Sam. 7: 11–14). The story of the Fall is convention-ally read against this metaphorical background. God creates Adam and Eve in an expression of profound love, just as human parents (ideally) conceive or adopt children as a way of sharing and enlarging their love for each other. God intends for his human children to live with him in a state of perfect spiritual happiness, but, like headstrong adolescents, Adam and Eve squander his gift, and must face the consequences. Adam and Eve's sin, according to this reading, is as much a sin of ingratitude as a sin of hubris. Not content with the extraordinary bounty God has bestowed upon them, Adam and Eve grasp greedily for the single thing that God, in his wisdom, has withheld from them.

But did Adam and Eve really sin? Disobedience is only morally wrong if the flouted authority is legitimate. And parental authority is only legitimate if the parent in question is a *good* parent. God, I submit, is a terrible parent. He is, in fact, an abusive parent. God does not love his children, and anyone who suggests that we ought to love *him* is displaying the psychology of an abused child.

I propose to support my indictment primarily by means of a close reading of Genesis 2: 4–3. When we compare the divine parent to the valiant mother in *Heckedy Peg*, stark contrasts emerge at every point. In attitudes, motives, methods, and reactions, God is the antithesis of a good parent. Although I'll be focusing on the story of the Fall, I'll draw corroborating evidence from narratives throughout the Hebrew Bible. The overall picture is quite consis-tent: God is far more concerned with his own glorification than with the well-being of his human 'children'. And that's putting it mildly.

Before turning to the texts, let me say a little more about parents, children, obedience, and love. My own particular view of parental authority derives from a more general account of authority *per se* that I developed in collaboration with Rebecca Hanrahan (Hanrahan and Antony 2005: 59–79). On our account, authority is a relation among persons that arises (or is created) as a way of fulfilling certain social functions. The legitimacy of any form of authority depends upon the satisfaction of some set of substantive grounding conditions, conditions determined by the particular social functions to which that form of authority is geared. Some of these grounding conditions are empirical, and pertain to the specific competencies required for the furthering of the relevant social goal. But importantly, some of these grounding conditions are normative. At a minimum, two things must be true: first, the social goal at which the system of authority is aimed must be a morally legitimate one, and second, individuals authorized by that system must themselves be aiming at that morally legitimate goal. The satisfaction of these (and potentially other, more specific conditions) constitutes the *normative ground* of an individual's authority.

The morally legitimate aim of the institution of parenthood is the nurturing of children; hence, commitment to the well-being of one's children is the *normative ground* of one's authority over them. Children are not their parents' property, to use as the parents wish. Neither are they slaves. Children are rational-agents-in-the-making, and a parent's role is to guide and support that process of becoming, to provide the child with the physical, emotional, and psychological prerequisites for moral autonomy in adulthood. The legitimacy of parental authority derives from, and is contingent upon, the parent's fulfilling this role to a reasonably high degree. Correlatively, children are only morally obliged to obey a parent if the parent' authority *is* legitimate, that is, only if the parent possesses and acts upon a genuine regard for the children's well-being.

I thus reject the view that a parent has a *natural* right to control her children, that children owe their parents loyalty and obedience simply because their parents are causally responsible for the children's existence. But that is not the crucial point. The main argument of this chapter depends only on the assumption that parental authority is not *unconditional*, whatever its original basis. I trust that everyone will grant this much: that abusive or negligent parents forfeit legitimate authority over their children, that they lose any moral right to expect deference or obedience from their children, even if, as is sadly often the case, they are still quite capable of compelling it. If this assumption is granted, and if I show, as I mean to, that the God of the Hebrew Bible is both negligent and abusive, it will follow that we, his children, owe him nothing.

I raise these considerations in order to forestall an objection that may have occurred to some people, namely, that my account of authority could at best apply only to *human* authorities. God's authority, the objection would run, is entirely different from the human variety. God's authority is certainly not dependent on social practices, even if human authority is.

While I would welcome the opportunity to show that Hanrahan's and my account is fully general, there is no need for me to do that here. Since my argument in this chapter depends only on the assumption that legitimate authority can be *lost*, the objection would have to be that God's authority, unlike human authority, is *absolute*. Now perhaps some people find this plausible, but I think that it would be an astonishing position to take, and a particularly strange one to take for a participant at this conference. To maintain that God's authority is unconditional is to say that there is *nothing* God could do to us, his children, which would be morally illegitimate. It would be to cede to God the moral right to do anything at all. (If God is alive, everything is permitted?) If such a right is asserted at the outset, the question whether 'his ways are our ways' becomes idle. It simply wouldn't matter. *Our* way is to protect our children, love them, and value them. If his way is rather to endanger them, ignore them, or casually destroy them, what of it?

Finally, a few notes about love. I ask in my title if God *loves* us. But perhaps this is not the right question; perhaps I should just ask directly whether God has any legitimate authority over us. What is the connection, anyway, between adequate parenting and love?

Parenthood is a demanding job. Those of us who have taken it on would probably all attest that we would not be able to do it if it were not for love. While it is conceivable that a person could parent a child adequately without loving him, this probably doesn't happen often in the real world. As several philosophers have pointed out,[2] a sense of duty takes one only so far. Children's needs, especially at first, are intense, non-negotiable, and virtually unlimited. Caring for infants and small children is physically exhausting, and often emotionally draining. Love helps us keep going. But love does more than motivate; it deeply structures our behavior. Perhaps a child need not *be loved* in order to thrive; but he at least needs to *feel loved*. Because children's needs are emotional and psychological as well as physical, adequate parenting requires modes of attention and response—subtleties of expression, gesture, touch, tone of voice—that none but the most skilled human actor would find possible to feign. Love makes the right responses largely automatic.

But still, suppose that, despite all these challenges, a parent did manage to care adequately for a child without loving him—wouldn't that parent's authority be legitimate? And wouldn't the child be morally obliged to respect it? If so, then perhaps God is *this* kind of parent—a parent who is a good parent, despite not loving his children. After all, it seems that God would not *need* love in the way we human beings do. He faces none of the difficulties in

---

[2] Baier 1987; Ruddick 1989/1995; Williams 1981.

discharging his moral duties that we face (of course, it may just be *easier* to deal with a colicky baby in the middle of the night if you don't have a body that needs sleep), and so would not require the emotional backup system provided to us by love. It might even be suggested that it is inappropriate in any case to speak of 'love' in connection with God. If parental love functions in the way I've suggested it does, then perhaps it is an essentially human emotion, tied to a specifically human inventory of demands and means. In any case, if the foregoing analysis is correct, then the mere fact that God does not 'love' Adam and Eve would not be enough to relieve the two of filial duty. The issue would turn entirely on the adequacy of God's parenting.

In the human case, we allow that even good parents will sometimes do the wrong thing: sometimes out of ignorance, sometimes out of ineptitude, sometimes out of anger, sometimes out of weakness. These errors, if they are minor and infrequent, do not undermine human parental authority; human parents are, after all, *only human*. Divine parental authority, however, is quite a different matter. Precisely because God is *not* subject to the various infirmities that handicap human parents, he would have no excuse for exhibiting the shortcomings we are forced to tolerate in ourselves. He is never overtired, overworked, or ill. We need not forgive him for losing his temper, neglecting our needs, or putting his own interests ahead of ours. We cannot expect our *human* parents to be perfect, as our therapists keep telling us, but we certainly can expect *God* to be.

How then, does God measure up? Appallingly. Not only is God not a perfect parent, he fails dismally relative even to the minimal standards we set for ourselves. To see this, let's turn, finally, to the texts.

Heckedy Peg portrays a happy and harmonious family. The mother presides over the household, but everyone pitches in to help make the home clean and comfortable. The children's chores seem appropriate to their ages, and the children have ample time for play. In Genesis, the picture is quite different. There's no indication that God and his two human creatures form a 'family' of any sort. On the contrary, God seems to have created Adam to be a worker, or rather, since there appears to be no question of securing Adam's consent to the arrangement, a slave. God, the text tells us, simply needs a gardener:

when no plant of the field was yet in the earth and no herb of the field had yet sprung up—for the Lord God had not caused it to rain upon the earth, and there was no one to till the ground . . . (Gen. 2: 5–6)[3]

---

[3] All quotations will be from the *New Revised Standard Version*, unless otherwise noted. Italics indicate my emphasis.

God took the man and placed him in the Garden of Eden, to work it and keep it. (Gen. 2: 15)

His purpose in creating this 'child' is purely instrumental. The only time God shows even an appearance of concern for Adam's needs is at Gen. 2: 18, when he observes that 'It is not good that man be alone.' But that appearance is dispelled in the very next clause: 'I will make him *a helper* (KJ: 'help meet') corresponding to him.' Eve, in short, is created not to relieve Adam's loneliness, but to help him carry out his preordained duties.

Both stories involve prohibitions. In *Heckedy Peg*, the mother's restrictions—no touching fire, no talking to strangers—are motivated entirely by concern for her children's safety, and represent eminently sensible precautions against real and very serious dangers. But it's very hard to find any similarly sound rationale for God's commandment to Adam and Eve.

There is, first of all, nothing in the text to suggest that God is thinking about Adam's safety when he issues his commandment. Context suggests quite the reverse. The injunction comes just after we've been reminded that Adam has a job to do: he was placed in the garden 'to till it and to keep it' or, as the Art Scrolls translation has it, to 'work it and *guard it*'. Adam is meant to be protect*or*, not protect*ee*. Secondly, it's not clear there *are* any dangers in Eden that Adam needs protecting *from*. The wording of God's commandment may suggest that he is warning Adam about a tree in the garden that bears poisonous fruit: ' . . . of the tree of the knowledge of good and evil you shall not eat, for in the day that you eat of it you shall die' (Gen. 2: 17–18). But if the tree is really that dangerous, why isn't it called 'The Tree of Death' or 'The Tree of Vomitous Berries?' Why does its very *name* suggest that it is salutary? Subsequent events, moreover, appear to confirm that the tree is not *inherently* dangerous. Whatever depredations Adam and Eve suffer because of their disobedience, food poisoning is not among them. They do not *literally* 'die' 'in the day' that they eat the fruit.

Some interpreters will challenge my reading here. The word 'die', they'll say, must be understood in an extended or metaphorical way, as meaning something like 'become mortal'.[4] Perhaps Adam and Eve were originally *im*mortal, and became *subject to* death by eating the fruit. This interpretation would allow us to acquit God of the charge of lying, but it has little support in the text. We are never told that God planned for Adam to live forever, and the early imagery of mortality (Gen. 3: 7) suggests that Adam was doomed to die all along.

---

[4] See Kugel 2007: 49–50.

But suppose the tree was really dangerous. This would hardly vindicate God's parenting style. It would make the warning reasonable, but it would also raise a new question: if the tree has the power to kill, why did God create it in the first place? The mother in *Heckedy Peg* did not introduce danger into her children's environment, and she lacked the power to eliminate it. But God can do anything. Why would he deliberately place within easy reach of his inexperienced children an appealing object that poses a mortal danger? A human parent would be judged criminally negligent for such behavior. Even unrelated adults can be held liable if a child suffers injuries in connection with an 'attractive nuisance' on their property.[5]

And speaking of hazards in the garden . . . Whatever is true about the tree, there is, according to conventional interpretations, at least one other thing in the garden that is definitely dangerous. The serpent, tradition says, is evil, bent on destroying Adam and Eve's relationship with their loving Father. Yet God never mentions this creature to Adam, never warns him that there's a liar afoot who'll try to trick him into disobedience. Why not? The mother in *Heckedy Peg* realizes that there are evil people around, eager to take advantage of naive and open-hearted children. Why doesn't God at least warn Adam *not to speak to strangers?*

Of course, one could interpret God's words differently, not as a warning about a dangerous object, but as a threat: *eat that fruit, and I'll kill you.* I don't think this is right, but not because such a monstrous proclamation would be out of character. Elsewhere, God shows himself quite willing to punish a single act of disobedience with the ultimate sanction. When Lot's wife is fleeing the inferno of Sodom, she disobeys an order not to look back, and is turned into a pillar of salt (Gen. 19: 23). Aaron's sons, set to perform the first sacrifice in the 'tent of worship' (which God has demanded the Israelites construct while they are wandering in the desert), commit some breach of protocol, and are incinerated on the spot. (Lev. 10: 1–3). During the transportation of the Ark to Baalejudah by cart, one of the drivers, Uzzah, reaches out to steady the Ark when the motion of one of the oxen threatens to dislodge it. For his troubles, God strikes him dead (2 Sam. 6: 6).[6] Indeed, the only thing that would be unusual about God's threatening Adam with death would be the advance notice. My reason for rejecting the threat interpretation of Gen. 3: 16–17 is that it doesn't fit the rest of the text. If God had been threatening Adam with death, why didn't he kill Adam as soon as the forbidden fruit was eaten? God does punish Adam and Eve for their

---

[5] See http://definitions.uslegal.com/a/attractive-nuisance/.
[6] Thanks to Evan Fales for pointing out this passage.

transgression, but the penalties are far less harsh than death. And as we know from the examples above, God is not soft-hearted.

As a parent, God is not looking good. If the commandment is a warning, he's a liar; if it's a threat, he's a bully. But warning or threat, we still don't know the purpose of the prohibition. If it's not to keep Adam safe, what's it for? An answer given by many interpreters is that God issues the prohibition in order to *test* Adam, to see if he's obedient. There's a great deal to say about this suggestion.

One might think that the hypothesis that God is testing Adam at least answers the question why God put a dangerous tree in the garden. But while it might explain the *presence* of the tree, it cannot adequately explain its lethality. If God merely needed a prop for a learning exercise, he could have used a benign species: 'Stay away from the mulberry bush!' But if the tree is really dangerous, we must once again question God's motives as a parent. I cannot see how there could be *any* legitimate parental purpose that such a 'test' might serve that would not be undercut by the peril of the test itself. Imagine this: a parent, worried about adulterated Halloween candy, makes a rule that her child cannot eat anything until he has brought it home for inspection. The parent is worried, however, that the child will be too tempted by the goodies in the bag to obey the rule. She doesn't want to deprive the child of the fun of trick-or-treating if she doesn't have to, so she decides to do a little experiment, to see if the child can be trusted. She employs a confederate, someone the child doesn't know, to offer him some candy, so she can observe what happens. Perhaps such an experiment would be reasonable— *but only if the test candy isn't poisoned.*

The 'testing' hypothesis might also seem to explain, at once, both the presence of the serpent and God's failure to warn Adam about him. The idea would be that God *intended* for Adam (or Eve) to encounter the tempter—the snake is part of the plan. But this 'rationale' runs into the same problem I described above. If the serpent is really evil, and if there is a substantial risk that Adam and Eve will succumb, then there's no difference between the 'test' and the danger that's supposed to make the test necessary. The parent in my scenario does not enlist a child murderer as her confederate.

Suppose, though, that the tree and the serpent are benign. Would the 'test' be legitimate in that case? Given that God clearly intends to punish his children if they fail the test, I think not. If God somehow engineered the encounter between Eve and the serpent, he was engaging in *entrapment*. The reason that entrapment is wrong when human police do it is that it *increases the likelihood that a crime will be committed.* If laws are just, then violations are *ipso facto* bad. The point of 'stings' is to arrest people who are *anyway* engaged in criminal activity, not to generate criminal activity that would not otherwise have occurred. We human beings all have our breaking points, and it is unjust for people in authority to push until they find them.

Another point: God, should he choose to engage in this kind of entrapment, has significantly more resources at his disposal than do mere human beings. While human beings must rely on fallible empirical knowledge about what people are likely to do in the circumstances they have arranged, God can control minds. Theodicies to the contrary notwithstanding, the God of the Hebrew Bible has no scruples against directly manipulating his creatures' 'free will', even if the 'actions' his puppet subsequently performs carry formidable punishments. Pharaoh, recall, tried repeatedly to free the Israelites, and even to repent of his own misdeeds, but God kept 'hardening his heart'. God did this to occasion the administration of ever more monstrous plagues, all so that 'the Egyptians may know that I *am* the Lord' (Gen. 14: 5).

It is particularly chilling to think of a parent entrapping a child. Part of the responsibility of a parent is to *shield* her child from temptation until the child develops the resources to resist it. Good human parents make rules that conduce to their children's well-being, and so are distressed when their rules are broken. They do not test the limits of their children's forbearance, nor contrive opportunities to punish their children. The difference between God's attitude toward his disobedient children and the mother's toward hers demonstrates the perversity of God's priorities.

The mother in *Heckedy Peg* understands that her children are *children*. She realizes that they may not appreciate how dangerous it could be to disobey her. As it happens, the petitioner who approaches them seems completely harmless, and offers an inducement their mother's instructions did not anticipate. The children are taken in, and disaster ensues. When the mother discovers their disobedience and its consequences, her first—indeed her only— thought is for her children. How can she get them back? Not until the children are rescued does she begin to think about blame or punishment—and then her ire falls, not on the disobedient children, but on Heckedy Peg, the powerful adult who is the actual agent of the crisis. She, not the children, has committed a crime, and she, fittingly, is the one who must be banished from village society.

God, however, takes no account of his children's position and limitations. Adam and Eve, although physically mature, appear to be psychological and intellectual infants. They have no knowledge of the world, and no experience to tell them who to trust. They lack 'knowledge of good and evil', and so presumably cannot apprehend any *duty* to God (even if they are in fact morally bound to obey him, which I doubt). The serpent, who approaches Eve either at God's behest or at his sufferance, gives Eve a *reason* to want to eat the fruit, and a reason, moreover, that makes sense of God's otherwise baffling prohibition. How is Eve supposed to know who is lying?

When God discovers that Adam and Eve have disobeyed him, his response is brutal. Even though he doesn't kill them (as, perhaps, he had threatened to do), he does impose life sentences: Adam must toil, and Eve must bear her children in pain. Then, to prevent further disruption within his domain, God throws the children out of their home.

This last act—banishment—is simply the culmination of what has been only the first episode in a long and consistent story of neglect and abuse. The Hebrew Bible records on nearly every page divine behavior that meets the legal definition of 'child maltreatment':

... any ... act or failure to act, on the part of a parent or caretaker ... which results in death, serious physical or emotional harm, sexual abuse or exploitation, or an act or failure to act which presents an imminent risk of serious harm.[7]

The law recognizes four categories of mistreatment: neglect, physical abuse, psychological abuse, and sexual abuse. God commits crimes in at least three of them.[8] In his dealings with Adam and Eve, as we've seen, God is guilty of at least three counts of *neglect*: 'inadequate supervision', 'substantial inattention to the child's need for affection', and 'expulsion from the home'.[9]

The instances of *physical abuse*—'the infliction of physical injury' and 'over-discipline or corporal punishment'—are too numerous to detail in full. Corporal punishment is about the only form of discipline God ever employs, and he is never stinting. He routinely wipes out entire populations who have displeased him (e.g. Gen. 6: 13ff. and Gen. 18: 20ff). Being 'Chosen' is no protection. When some of the sojourning Israelites accept the invitation of Moabite women to join in their worship of the god Baal, God visits upon them a lethal plague, killing 24,000 people (Num. 25: 1–9). The right to torment Jews, however, is one of God's prerogatives, so nations whose leaders have the audacity to trouble his Chosen People are slaughtered wholesale: Egyptians, Amalekites, Canaanites, and so forth. In the case of the Amalekites, the offense is never forgotten, and punishment is revisited on descendants many generations distant from the original offenders (Deut. 25: 18–19).

---

[7] Child Abuse Prevention and Treatment Act (CAPTA), amendments of 1996, reauthorized by the Keeping Children and Families Safe Act of 2003. See http://www.libraryindex.com/pages/1365/Child-Abuse-Problem-Definition-CAPTA-DEFINES-FOUR-MAIN-TYPES-CHILD-MALTREATMENT.html.

[8] I believe that forcing your child to mutilate his genitals as a condition of your continued protection would probably count as sexual abuse, but I am not going to press this point.

[9] CAPTA.

God's true excellence, however, lies in the area of *psychological abuse*: 'acts or omissions ... that have caused, or could cause, serious behavioral, cognitive, emotional, or mental disorders.'[10] Although this crime is defined in terms of effects on the child, the law does not always require authorities to wait until the child has already been harmed before taking action against a psychologically abusive parent:

In some instances of emotional child abuse, the acts of parents or other caregivers alone, without any harm yet evident in the child's behavior or condition, are sufficient to warrant the intervention of child protective services. For example, the parents or caregivers may use extreme or bizarre forms of punishment, such as confinement of a child in a dark closet.[11]

'Confinement in a dark closet' would seem like a day at the beach to some of God's children. We've certainly seen extreme punishment in the story of Adam and Eve, but there are plenty of other examples. The Israelites, newly freed from slavery and wandering in a foreign desert, express apprehension when scouts report a formidable enemy ahead. For this brief lapse in faith, God threatens to destroy his 'Chosen People' with a plague. They're spared only through the intercession of Moses, who gets the sentence reduced to lifelong exile from the promised land (Num. 14: 2–24). Moses, however, soon becomes the victim himself of an extreme punishment: he, too, is denied entry to Canaan because he has the temerity to *strike* a rock God told him to *speak to* (Num. 20: 12). The plagues visited upon the Egyptians provide examples of punishments both extreme *and* bizarre: a river of blood, selective darkness, and the slaughter of first-born children, not to mention frogs and locusts (Exod. 7–11). For sheer weirdness, though, you can't beat the case of 'Snow-white Miriam'. When Moses' faithful sister dares to criticize her brother's choice of wife, God strikes her with leprosy, turning her 'as white as snow' (Num. 12: 10).

God's overall approach to discipline, evidenced both in his acts and in his commandments to human parents, closely matches that of human child abusers. Human parents who mistreat their children characteristically employ what M. L. Hoffman calls the 'power-assertive' mode of discipline, a style that 'provides the child no rationale for altering his or her behavior other than to avoid punitive consequences' (1994: 26–8). God almost never explains to his children *why* he demands of them the things he does. (The commandment to Adam in the garden is one of the few exceptions, but one that may turn out to prove the rule.) Having created beings with the power of reason, God

---

[10] Ibid.
[11] Ibid.

perversely withholds *reasons*, and delights in setting tests of loyalty that require his children to flout logic, prudence, and sometimes even his own laws.

The most notorious of these arbitrary tests is, of course, God's command to Abraham to sacrifice his son Isaac. This is a monstrous and utterly outrageous order. A human parent who required a child to do anything like this—say, to kill a beloved pet—would be judged sociopathic. And it is not only Abraham who is tortured. Imagine Isaac's terror as he realizes what his father has in mind. Imagine Sarah's horror when she learns what Abraham has set out to do. (According to the medieval Jewish commentator Rashi, Sarah actually dies from the shock (Zlotowitz 1989: 116 n. 2).) Beyond the sheer sadism of God's order, there is the horror of the fact that this parent is *pleased* that his child is so terrified of him that he is willing to commit murder, and to murder his own child, the atrocity compounded by Abraham's abrogation of his own parental duty.

What does this order tell Abraham about the status of God's own law? Abraham, of course, never saw the Ten Commandments, but we know, from God's displeasure with Cain, that God expected human beings to know that they were not to kill each other. But why not? God apparently wants Abraham to know that rules are only rules *because God says so*—if God changes his mind, then the rules change, too. God is evidently very happy that Abraham is a divine-command theorist of the crudest sort: he simply identifies the good with what God wants. This is not the meta-ethical perspective that human parents want to encourage in their children. We want our children to internalize the bases of moral judgment, and not just to do what we say because we say it. We want them to become morally independent of us. God's plan for Abraham is clearly different: Abraham is to be allowed no moral judgment of his own. The story of the *Akedah* would have been *marginally* more palatable if Abraham had refused God, and *that* pleased him.

The fact that God expected Abraham to respond so reflexively to an order that contravened such a weighty and intuitively obvious moral rule as 'don't murder' suggests that God's laws really do have a degree of moral arbitrariness to them, that he doesn't so much care whether murder occurs as he cares about whether the murder is *authorized*. This suggestion is supported by God's reaction to some world-class wrongdoing on the part of one of his favorites, King David. David commits two sins for which death was the mandated punishment—adultery and murder (with the cuckolded husband the victim). God, through his prophet Nathan, lets David know that he's quite displeased. Once David admits his guilt, Nathan reports that God has 'put away his sin', and vacated the death sentence. But not quite all is forgiven.

Nevertheless, because by this deed you have utterly scorned the Lord, the child that is born to you shall die. (2 Sam. 12: 14)

Adultery and murder are one thing; dissing the Lord is *serious*.[12]

Abusive human parents are also overly concerned with their children's deference. Abusive fathers, in particular, 'tend to be very controlling of their children', and

demand respect and unconditional love. They are insecure and are constantly looking for signs of defiance or disrespect.... An abusive father has a sense of entitlement, expecting his children to do as he says. (Scott and Crooks 2004)

God could hardly fit the profile more exactly. He is constantly demanding tribute from his children, tribute that must be paid in highly specific ways. Of his Ten Commandments, the first four set out the Israelites' duties to God, while the latter six concern relations among the Israelites themselves. This apparent parity is misleading, however. Commandments Five through Ten are expounded concisely, one verse per commandment, whereas the first four require a total of nine verses. The elaboration of the human-oriented laws occupies an additional two and a half chapters, and focuses largely on the proper punishment for violations. (There are a mere eleven verses that mandate anything that might be recognized as charity or sympathy (Exod. 23: 1–11).) After that, it's all about God again, with a full five chapters devoted to the details of worship: the proper objects and materials for offerings, the dimensions, materials, manner of construction, and furnishings for two holy structures, the individuals authorized to offer sacrifices, the clothes they should wear and the procedures they should follow (Exod. 20–32). The requirements involve enormous volumes of gold, silver, precious stones, luxury fibers, and exotic woods—only the best for God!

God is infuriated by anything that he construes as a sign of disrespect, and like the stereotypical abusive father described above, he sees such signs nearly everywhere. Consider again the incident of Moses' striking the rock, described at Num. 20: 7–13. The Israelites have been complaining about the lack of water. Moses appeals to God, and God commands him to 'command the rock' to 'yield its waters'.[13] Moses *strikes* the rock instead of *speaking to* the rock. This, in God's mind, is an act of flagrant insubordination. But a less narcissistic parent might well have seen the matter in a different light. Moses might have *misunderstood* God; he might have thought that 'command' was a generic term covering *any* way of indicating to the rock what it was to do. After all, this was not the first time that God had empowered Moses to draw water from a rock. Early on in their sojourn, when the Israelites had just

---

[12] Note, too, that God punishes *David* by killing a perfectly innocent party. The injustice of this, as well as the completely instrumental treatment of the baby, are perfectly typical of God's approach to justice.

[13] The Hebrew word is 'דברתם' (dibartem) which literally means (I am told) 'speak to'.

reached Rephidim, they also complained of thirst, and Moses also appealed to God for relief, just as he would later, at Kadesh. Here are the instructions God gave Moses at that time:

take in your hand the staff with which you struck the Nile, and go. I will be standing there in front of you on the rock at Horeb. Strike the rock, and water will come out of it, so that the people may drink. (Exod. 17: 5–6)

Not only does God explicitly tell Moses to *strike* the rock on this occasion, He makes a point of reminding Moses that the staff he's to use is the same one as the staff he used to *strike* the Nile.[14] Surely Moses could be forgiven for inferring that the *staff* was the instrument God had given him for dealing with water, and that *striking things with it* was the proper mode of employment. Supposing now that God had some serious reason for wanting Moses to use his voice rather than his staff on this new occasion in Kadesh, he might have realized that Moses would be expecting to do what he had always done in the past, namely, use the staff, and taken care to emphasize the difference in the procedure. Even if this thought didn't occur to God beforehand (although he is supposed to be omniscient), he ought surely to have considered it in retrospect, once Moses struck the rock. Given Moses' past experience, God might have at least allowed that Moses had simply made a mistake about what God wanted him to do—that he had just failed to appreciate the significance of a small novelty in the wording of God's commandment.[15]

Of course, insolence is not Moses' only crime. If there's anything that gets God angrier than disrespect, it's *loss of face*. God is obsessed with his reputation, both within and outside of the nation of Israel. Moses, therefore, compounds his sin by performing the insubordinate act *in public*, and it is for this that God bars him from entering Canaan: 'Because you did not trust in me, *to show my holiness before the eyes of the Israelites*' (Num. 20: 12). God's anxiety about his image frequently overcomes his wrath at more primary transgressions. Moses understands this: when God threatens to destroy the ever-complaining Israelites, Moses persuades him to relent by appealing to his vanity—what will people think?

Then the Egyptians will hear of it, for in your might you brought up this people from among them, and they will tell the inhabitants of this land. . . . Now if you kill this people all at one time, then the nations who have heard about you will say, 'It is

---

[14] The Hebrew word, used in both places, is 'הכית' (hikitah).

[15] To be fair, I must acknowledge that scholars doubt that these stories are records of distinct incidents. According to Friedman, the story in Numbers is a retelling by P, the 'priestly writer', of the earlier E story recounted in Genesis (Friedman 1987/1997: 197–201). But both Jewish and Christian traditions take there to have been two separate incidents.

because the Lord was not able to bring this people into the land he swore to give them that he has slaughtered them in the wilderness.' (Num. 14: 13–15)

God's preoccupation with his reputation pushes him to what one hopes is the nadir of sadism when he turns the faithful Job into a laboratory animal for use in a repellent experiment.[16] The text tells us quite frankly why Job is tortured. Satan[17] has been taunting God, alleging that Job is only loyal to God because God has caused things to go well for him.

But stretch out Your hand and hurt everything he has, and then see if he does not curse You to Your face. (Job 1: 11)

God takes the bait, and sets out to prove to Satan that Job is perfectly abject, that he will remain loyal to God—will still *fear* him, at any rate—no matter how great his misery. Satan is granted permission to do whatever he likes to Job, short of personal injury. Job passes this test, despite the loss of his ten children, their spouses, and countless servants, not to mention all his livestock and property. But Satan is unsatisfied, so God modifies his one proviso and allows Satan to afflict Job with physical pain.

Once again, this 'display behavior' of God's has a parallel in the behavior of abusive human parents, especially abusive fathers. 'Some fathers maltreat their children because they feel that they have to show others that they are doing a good job as parents' (Scott and Crooks 2004).

The connection I'm drawing between God's approach to discipline and that of abusive parents is not casual or idle. Scripture is potent; many people rely on the Bible for moral guidance in all their affairs. Those who look to the Hebrew Bible for lessons in child-rearing will find a brutal and unloving model of parent–child relations that celebrates raw parental power and assigns no importance to the child's own experience or point of view. Parents who are inclined to use violence to control their children can easily find scriptural support for their behavior, both in the stories of God's treatment of human beings, and in passages like Deuteronomy 21: 18–20 and Proverbs 13: 24. It is hardly surprising, then, that parents who identify as 'fundamentalists' or 'literalists' are significantly more likely than other parents to hit their children, to have more inappropriate expectations of their children, and to show less empathy toward their children's needs.[18] Several popular

---

[16] I hope it goes without saying that it would have been wrong to treat an *actual* laboratory animal this way, too.

[17] Kugel points out that this character is not yet 'Satan' as we know him. He is rather one of the 'sons of God', or as Kugel puts it, 'heavenly attendants'. He is less a devil, and more a devil's advocate. (Kugel 2007: 638. Cf. Pagels 1996/1995.)

[18] See studies cited in Grille 2005.

fundamentalist parenting guides recommend the regular use of corporal punishment, with complete subjugation as the goal: 'The spanking should be painful . . . and should last until the child's will is broken' (Wiehe 1990: 173–87). And fundamentalist churches have made headlines for advocating the use of a specially manufactured 'rod' in disciplining their children:

Parents who belong to the Bethel Baptist Church in El Sobrante are told in no uncertain terms: Spank your children or oppose God's will.

The church, which also runs the 200-student Bethel Christian Academy, discourages parents from using their hands and recommends using a 'rod' or flexible stick to swat children until their will is broken. But an eight-panel church pamphlet with corporal punishment instructions does caution against using instruments such as hairbrushes, cords or 2-by-4s.

'Corporal punishment is not something you do to the child, it's something you do for the child,' said Bethel Pastor David Sutton, who wrote the pamphlet. 'Your goal as a parent is to correct the child or get him back on the right path.'

Parents who do not practice corporal punishment are depriving their children of the only method God says produces wisdom and they risk directly opposing God's will, according to the pamphlet. If parents do use corporal punishment, they also should use other methods of discipline such as time-outs and restrictions on activities, Buchanan said.

But the church directs parents to spank for all disobedience, because *all other methods are not designed by God.* (Geluardi and Wetzel 2007. My emphasis)

I want to be clear that I am not trying to indict *religion* as a cause of child abuse. I would be remiss if I failed to mention that there are several religious organizations working actively to oppose such perspectives as those of Bethel Academy, which they regard as hateful and 'ungodly'.[19] The problem, however, is that Bethel parents are the ones who seem to have read the texts: parental tyranny is all too 'godly'. What exactly are the literalists supposed to have gotten wrong? It would no doubt make an interesting project—and certainly a challenging one—to construct an apologetic 'interpretation' of the text, to remake God into a humane and loving Father. Moral judgment is non-monotonic; the addition of detail can always reverse the ethical valence. It's imaginable, then, that some set of interpolations to the stories I've been discussing could even redeem God. But what would be the point? If we all agree that beating, banishment, and death are not acceptable tools for disciplining children, let us acknowledge that we have come to know this despite, and not because of, scripture.

---

[19] For example: Christians for Nonviolent Parenting: http://www.nospank.net/cnpindex. htm.

I'd like to conclude by answering, finally, the main question I raised about the story in Genesis 2 and 3: what was the purpose of the prohibition? I think we can find a clear and simple answer in the text, once we give up the interpretive constraint that God must turn out to be good.

The key, I think, is the serpent. His counterpart in the children's story is the character Heckedy Peg. She is clearly depicted as someone up to no good. We see that she has grotesquely selfish reasons for deceiving the children, and for inducing them to violate their mother's rules: she wants to eat them. The serpent, on the other hand is not so clearly evil. He is never characterized as such: the Hebrew word used to describe him is ערום (*arum*), which careful English translations render as 'subtle' (KJ), 'crafty' (NRSV), or 'cunning' (ArtScrolls).[20] Although each of these English terms can carry negative connotations, they can also carry positive ones. We are given no hint as to *why* the serpent would want to mislead Adam and Eve; he appears to have nothing to gain from getting the two human beings to disobey God.[21]

Most significantly: the serpent *does not* mislead Adam and Eve. Heckedy Peg is a liar—the story makes this clear. She promises the children she will give them gold if they do what she asks, but we see that this was never her intention. In contrast, every detail in Genesis, if taken at face value, testifies that the serpent tells the truth. Everything the serpent tells Eve turns out to be true: Adam and Eve do *not* die when they eat the forbidden fruit, they *do* gain knowledge, and, tellingly, God *is* worried about their becoming 'like him'. The serpent's explanation of God's motives is spot-on: God is trying to preserve a divine prerogative, to keep his gardeners away from the source of his most valuable power. God later admits as much:

Then the Lord God said, 'See, the man has become like one of us, knowing good and evil; and now, he might reach out his hand and take also from the tree of life, and eat, and live for ever.' (Gen. 3: 22–3)

The serpent's view makes sense to Eve, and her own observations add further proof.

---

[20] Brown, Driver, and Briggs, in their *A Hebrew and English Lexicon of the Old Testament*, include 'sensible' among the English synonyms for the Hebrew word. The nominal form of the word, ערמה, is used with this positive meaning throughout Proverbs. (Thanks to Ed Curley for this point.)

[21] Jack Miles takes very seriously the idea that the serpent is not evil, and points out that the serpent could be, for all the text tells us, God's rival. See Miles 1996. Campbell (1964/1978) reports that serpent-gods, as well as powerful trees connected with life, health, and knowledge, are extremely common in Mesopotamian myths.

So when the woman saw that the tree was good for food, and that it was a delight to the eyes, and that the tree was to be desired to make one wise, she took of its fruit and ate . . . (Gen. 3: 6)

The Tree's name, as I've already noted, seems an additional clue for the reader, and may have also been one for Eve.

What about the effects of eating from the Tree? We learn that Adam and Eve do undergo some kind of shift in epistemic power. Their 'eyes . . . were opened, and they realized they were naked' (Gen. 2: 7). Conventional interpretations read this passage as saying that Adam and Eve realized that they had done something wrong, that the subsequent 'covering' is an act of shame. But this reading is hardly mandated by the text. Here's an alternative reading. Perhaps the new epistemic power Adam and Eve have acquired is the power to see the normative dimension of things. Perhaps they now apprehend that they are not merely animals, that they are moral as well as natural beings. Natural conditions, like nakedness, have now acquired meaning, clothing signifies their new status. Perhaps they suppose, as the serpent does, that this new power is so valuable that getting it is worth risking everything, worth incurring the wrath of the most powerful Being in the universe. Perhaps it is.

Comments on 'Does God Love Us?'

Eleonore Stump

In her chapter Louise Antony has issued an indictment of God. He is 'a terrible parent'; he is psychologically and physically abusive to human beings. He is a liar or a bully. He commits crimes against human beings. He is a sociopath. He is merciless. He is sadistic. And so on. Her chapter is the answer to the question that is the chapter's title: 'Does God Love Us?' Certainly not, is Antony's answer. What's more, she says, 'Anyone who suggests that we ought to love *him* is displaying the psychology of an abused child.' (30)

Her evidence for her thesis that God does not love us is a concatenation of readings and interpretations of stories in the Hebrew Bible. She begins with her interpretation of the story of Adam and Eve in Genesis, and she interweaves that interpretation with a variety of shorter or longer interpretations of many other stories, including the stories of Noah's flood, the destruction of Sodom and Gomorrah, the binding of Isaac, the suffering of Job, the plagues on Egypt, the Ten Commandments, various episodes involving Moses, the slaughter of the Amalekites, and various episodes involving David. In each of these cases, she gives her reading of the text and her interpretation of the story as she reads the text. In the process, she relies on earlier philosophical work of her own on legitimate authority, duties to parents, and other related issues. On this basis, she argues that, as portrayed by each of the stories, God should be disdained and repudiated. The summing of her interpretations of all the stories is meant to give a damning picture of God.

I want to begin by saying that in very many things I agree with Antony. Here is a partial, not a complete, list of those things.

I agree that not all authority is legitimate and that not all disobedience is bad. No good person is more concerned with his own glorification than with the well-being of his children. Children are not the property of their parents, and certain kinds of acts and practices on the part of parents vitiate some or even all of the obligations children typically owe their parents. *Mutatis mutandis*, these points also apply to God. It is not true in the case of God that God has a right to do anything at all to human beings or that anything

God does counts as good just because it is God who does it. It is not right for a parent, even a divine parent, to treat other human beings unjustly in any way, including entrapment, lying, bullying, physical brutality, or psychological cruelty. And, in general, it is not right for any person, even a divine person, to use a human being just as a means to some other end with no care for that human being's own well-being.

In addition, I share Antony's affect about these things. Abuse of children is loathsome, in my view; cruelty to human persons of any age is too. It's worth being passionate about these things, as Antony obviously is.

Finally, I also share with Antony some interest in a certain kind of methodology. I think, as she also seems to think, that philosophers can benefit from bringing stories into their philosophical reflections. In my view—but this may be going further than Antony wants to go—stories have something to contribute that cannot be gotten without the stories. Sometimes it is helpful to employ on issues in philosophy a methodology combining ordinary philosophical techniques with the study of narratives.

Where I disagree with Antony is first in her use of such a methodology and then in the conclusions she draws as she uses that methodology. I think that I also disagree with the thesis she takes to be supported by these conclusions, although I am not sure about this because I am not entirely sure what that thesis is. If its scope is modified as I think it needs to be, then in fact I agree with the thesis of her chapter; but I disagree with her about what that thesis implies.

Let me begin with Anthony's use of the methodology that brings stories into philosophical reflections.

Philosophical work, especially in the analytic tradition, commonly has a certain sort of tight order to it because it is structured around arguments; philosophical discussion typically proceeds in an orderly way designed to try to command agreement. By contrast, interpretations of narratives—for that matter, interpretations of people and their actions—do not admit of rigorous argument. We can definitively rule some interpretations out, but it is hard to make a compelling argument that only *this* interpretation is right. Even a carefully supported interpretation of narratives is, in effect, only a recommendation to look at a text in a certain way. It invites readers to consider that text and ask themselves whether after all they do not see the text in the way the interpretation recommends. Interpretations present, suggest, offer, and invite; unlike philosophical arguments, they cannot attempt to compel. Because this is so, it is especially important in presenting an interpretation of a text to consider alternative readings. To support one interpretation is to support it over others. But then those others need to be canvassed, and something needs to be done to show why they are to be rejected.

Furthermore, the interpretation of narratives is itself an art. For narratives, as for philosophy, there is an expertise and a community of scholars in whom that expertise is vested. Although communal expertise can certainly be mistaken, it is not generally wise to jettison it wholesale. It represents the results of many minds working in community over a considerable period of time. This is the case for the study of narratives just as it is for the study of philosophy. In the case of narratives, one thing this communal expertise typically gives us is a plethora of interpretations of a text. It shows us the range of interpretations possible as regards that text, and so it makes us more thoughtful and more sophisticated in our interpretation of that text. It also shows us what needs to be done to support a particular interpretation of a text. It helps us understand what interpretations need to be argued against if one particular interpretation is to be put forward as the right one.

These remarks apply to narrative texts in our own culture and language, but they are especially pertinent when the narratives in question are written in a language very different from our own and stem from a culture very different from our own. In the case of such texts, even before the difficulties of interpreting the text, there is the difficulty of finding the right reading of it. Just understanding what a line means can take considerable expertise. For such texts, the work of generations of linguists, historians, and literary scholars can yield insight into readings and interpretations that would be hard to come by otherwise. Think of a Greek tragedy such as Sophocles' *Philoctetes* or a Chinese novel such as *Dream of the Red Chamber*, and you see the point. In the case of the stories in the Hebrew Bible, the texts have been studied for centuries by some of the best minds in the Jewish and Christian traditions; and many of the commentaries of those scholars, with their philological and literary competences, are still available to us. As far as that goes, the Hebrew biblical texts in question are still very much under discussion today, not only by historical biblical scholars and literary critics but even by philosophers, even by analytic philosophers. I myself have written extensively on some of them.[1]

Finally, many ancient and contemporary studies make clear to us that the Hebrew biblical narratives in particular have neutron-star density. For example, Eric Auerbach has famously contrasted the narratives of the Hebrew Bible with the narratives of Homer, to bring out the biblical narrative's ability to convey an enormous amount with a tiny bit of detail (1953). The noted literary scholar Robert Alter has made contemporary readers aware of what can be done with the Hebrew narratives when their detail is unfolded by

---

[1] See, for example, Stump 2010.

someone trained in the analysis of narratives and attentive to the nuances of ancient Hebrew poetry and prose.[2]

These considerations highlight the problematic character of Antony's attempt to bring narratives into philosophical reflection. She runs through many biblical stories in short space with scant attention to the details of the text. She gives little consideration of alternative interpretations. And she avails herself of very little of the vast communal expertise that has been devoted to both the reading and the interpretation of these narratives by scholars from different disciplines, times, and world-views. What is needed for employing well a methodology combining philosophy and ancient Hebrew biblical narratives is missing in her chapter, in my view.

I also disagree with the conclusions Antony draws as she employs this methodology. In the case of the stories Anthony canvasses, very many of the available commentaries read and interpret the narratives differently from the way Antony does, and I do not find her readings of the texts or her interpretations of the readings she provides compelling.

Sometimes the issue has to do with the way in which Antony reads a line. To take just one small example, consider the line about the creation of Adam that in the translation Antony uses is rendered into English this way: 'there was no one to till the ground.' Commenting on this line, Antony says that

> God seems to have created Adam to be a worker, or rather, since there appears to be no question of securing Adam's consent to the arrangement, a slave. God, the text tells us, simply needs a gardener.

Although Antony is confident about what the text tells us, in fact other readings are possible. The traditional Jewish commentary, the Bereshith Rabbah, reads the same line very differently. The word Antony takes to refer to gardening can have connotations of religious worship or service, and the commentary in the Bereshith Rabbah highlights this sense of the word. It reads the line as commenting that there was as yet no human being to engage in religious service of God. It recognizes that the biblical text seems to imply that human beings were created for work, but it emphasizes that work in religious service of God is a blessing for human beings. In interpreting the biblical line at issue, the commentator says, 'Happy is the man whose toil is in the Torah!' (Midrash Rabbah. Bereshith 103).

Whatever one may think about the reading that the Bereshith Rabbah gives to the biblical line, it ought at least to call to our attention that the biblical line can be read in highly various ways. It is hasty to suppose, as Antony does, that

---

[2] See, for example, Alter 1991.

this line, or any line in an ancient Hebrew narrative, wears its meaning on its sleeve. For my part, I do not find Antony's reading of this line persuasive.

A similar point applies to Antony's interpretations of her readings of the stories. About the story of the creation of Eve, Antony notes the line in which, on the reading Antony provides, God says about Adam, 'I will make him a helper...corresponding to him.' Based on her reading of this line, Antony interprets the story of the creation of Eve this way: 'Eve...is created not to relieve Adam's loneliness, but to help him carry out his preordained duties.'

A different interpretation of the same story is given by Robert Alter, in his highly influential study of biblical narrative. Alter calls attention to the fact that between this statement of God's and the actual creation of Eve, there is the episode of Adam's naming of the animals. Alter comments,

The contrast between mateless man calling names to a mute world of mated creatures is brought out by a finesse of syntax not reproducible in translation. Verse 20 actually tells us that man gave names 'to all cattle...to birds...to beast...to the man,' momentarily seeming to place Adam in an anaphoric prepositional series with all living creatures. This incipient construal is then reversed by the verb 'did not find', which sets man in opposition to all that has preceded. (1991: 30)

Having noted these nuances of the prose, Alter argues that one point of the episode of the naming of the animals is to elicit from Adam an awareness of his loneliness right before the creation of Eve. And Alter calls attention to the fact that, in the narrative, the first thing Adam does after the creation of Eve is to name her, so that, by highlighting Adam's use of language in naming, the narrative connects the episode of the creation of Eve with the episode of the naming of the animals. On Alter's interpretation, the loneliness of Adam and Eve's creation to assuage that loneliness is central to the story of the creation of Eve.

For my part, I find Alter's reading much more compelling than Antony's. And, in general, by contrast with the alternative readings and interpretations I know, I do not find Antony's construals of the stories plausible. So I don't accept the particular conclusions Antony draws from her use of the methodology that interweaves philosophy and narrative any more than I accept the way in which she uses that methodology.

Finally, there is the question of the thesis that Antony means her work in this chapter to support. The title of her chapter is a question, 'Does God Love Us?', and her chapter is meant to be a resounding negative answer to the question. But since the chapter focuses just on some narratives in the Hebrew Bible, it is hard not to suppose that her thesis has to be much narrower than the title suggests. To take just one example of a Christian philosopher whose work I know well, Aquinas supposes that God loves human beings. But this view is not one that emerges for Aquinas on the basis of his interpretations of stories in the Hebrew Bible. On the contrary, he gives philosophical arguments for this view. His case is made, *inter alia*, on the basis of metaphysical considerations having to do with goodness and being. Nothing in Antony's chapter is so much as germane to arguments such as these for taking God to be loving.

So even if we grant Antony all she wants in this chapter, as I have been unwilling to do, her chapter does not constitute an argument for the claim that God does not love human beings. The title of Antony's chapter would be more accurate if it were phrased this way: 'Does the God of the narratives in the Hebrew Bible love us?' But even this version of the title wouldn't be quite right. That is because the biblical narratives canvassed by Antony admit of multiple interpretations. On at least some of those interpretations, the texts support the claim that God loves human beings. Since Antony has not considered such interpretations, it is too strong to claim that her chapter makes a case that the God of the Hebrew Bible's narratives does not love human beings. The title of her chapter would therefore be correct only if it were something like this: 'Does the God of the Hebrew Bible's narratives, as I read and interpret those narratives, love us?'

At most, then, what Antony is entitled to claim is that her chapter shows that the God of her readings and interpretations does not love human beings. And in this thesis she seems to me entirely right. The God who emerges from her readings and interpretations is cruel and evil, as she says, more worthy of human hatred than of human love. So if we take Antony's thesis in this highly circumscribed way, then I agree with it.

But now there remains a question about what this thesis shows. What follows from this thesis? I take it that Antony supposes her thesis shows something to the detriment of at least two of the major monotheisms. But, of course, this is not the only conclusion possible. Another possible conclusion is that Antony's interpretations of the narratives in the Hebrew Bible are mistaken. Antony has argued that the God of her readings and interpretations is unloving. But she has not argued for her readings and interpretations. And so although she has shown that two things are incompatible—her readings and interpretations, on the one hand, and the claim that the God of the stories is loving, on the other—she has not given arguments to show which of these two incompatible things ought to be rejected. On the evidence available to me, including the evidence of the alternative interpretations of the narratives, I would not hesitate to choose her interpretations as the thing to be rejected.

Here, then, is where I think we are left. The thing Antony finds worthy of excoriation, I do too. And so do most other interpreters in the mainstream of Jewish and Christian commentary on these stories. The God who emerges from her interpretations is not one they accept; the God they worship is not the God Antony is concerned to repudiate. That is at least in part because their readings and interpretations of the stories are very different from hers, and so is the God whose nature is illuminated by their interpretations. Consequently, in the thesis of her chapter, if it is suitably circumscribed, Antony is not at odds with Jewish or Christian thought but actually solidly in the mainstream of it: the God of her readings and interpretations is not loving and is not worthy of love or worship in return.

Reply to Stump

Louise Antony

I'd like to thank Professor Stump for her comments, and I'd like to say immediately how appreciative I am of her clearly heartfelt endorsements of the moral principles to which I appealed in my chapter. From my perspective, consensus on central ethical matters is all that's needed—no matter if we disagree on ontology.

Stump takes me to task for presenting a—this is my word, not hers—superficial reading of Genesis. I have assumed that the text 'wears its meaning on its sleeve', when in fact there are layers and layers of meaning within the biblical narratives.

Just understanding what a line means can take considerable expertise. For such texts, the work of generations of linguists, historians, and literary scholars can yield insight into readings and interpretations that would be hard to come by otherwise. (49)

My failure to consider alternative interpretations sharply limits the interest of my indictment. Stump agrees that the God of my interpretations 'is not loving and is not worthy of love or worship in return', but insists that this is not the God who emerges from erudite and theologically informed readings from 'interpreters in the mainstream of Jewish and Christian commentary', and thus not the God they worship.

I can offer no defense against Stump's challenges to my 'scholarship'. But I do not claim to have produced a scholarly interpretation of the ancient texts I discuss. I hope only to have produced a respectable instance of what my college English professors used to call a 'close reading'—a careful attempt to draw out a coherent meaning from a rich and complex literary object, preserving as much as possible of the plain meaning of the words that constitute it. So I'm fully prepared to learn that other—better, more defensible—interpretations exist.

Still, I wonder: how different can these interpretations be from mine, and still be *interpretations*, rather than inventions? Mustn't they be constrained at least by what is straightforwardly asserted in the text? If not, then anything goes. Consider the following passage:

And it came to pass, when Israel dwelt in that land, that Reuben went and lay with Bil'hah his father's concubine: and Israel heard it. (Gen. 35: 22)

This passage appears to describe the son of a patriarch committing an act of adultery,[1] a grievous sin. The Talmud, however, disagrees: 'whoever says Reuben sinned is mistaken' (Shabbos, 55b). Why? Well, in order to properly understand the passage, one needs the following background: Rachel, Jacob's favorite wife, had just died. In Reuben's opinion, Jacob's favor should have passed to Leah, Jacob's first wife and Reuben's mother. But Jacob instead moved in with Rachel's maidservant, Bil'hah. To defend his mother's honor, Reuben entered Bil'hah's tent and removed his father's belongings (Scherman 1989: xvii–lvii).

But if this is what happened—and none of it is in the text—then why did the passage say that Jacob '*lay* with Bil'hah?' Here's why, according to the Talmud:

for a person of Reuben's stature to tamper with his father's privacy, to interfere in the personal life of the patriarch Jacob, was a gross, coarse act. By the standard of behavior expected of a Reuben, such an indiscretion is tantamount to adultery and the Torah so labels it.

This is composition, not interpretation. The reading is constrained far more by external ideas about what the text 'must' mean than it is by the words actually on the page.

But even allowing broad interpretive license, I have trouble imagining how scholarship is going to eliminate the enormous moral problems posed by so many of the biblical stories. According to the text: God ordered Abraham to slaughter his son. God hardened Pharaoh's heart. God permitted Satan to torture Job. God killed indiscriminately, and ordered others to kill indiscriminately. Over and over and over. Stump identifies one point in my reading of Gen. 2–3 at which scholarship might make a difference, but if so, it would affect only a minor clause in my multi-count indictment. I would have liked to hear the full response.

Sound interpretations generally identify and take account of broad themes. God's indifference to the lives and suffering of non-Israelites, and his frequent disregard even for his own 'Chosen People' is a *theme*. I'm not basing my case on an isolated example, or a nuance in a single phrase. The evidence is all over the place. If the Bible were simply a piece of literature, no interpreter would suggest that God loved his creatures, just as no interpreter of Shakespeare would suggest that Hamlet is a bold man of action.

---

[1] Bil'hah was a concubine, not a wife, but still counted legally as a married woman.

One final point. If, as Stump suggests, extensive scholarship is necessary in order to understand the meaning of the Bible, how can this text serve as a guide for ordinary people, people who cannot devote their lives to the study of these texts, nor even to the study of their own religious traditions? The fact that a large number of parents who practice corporal punishment, including some who are clearly abusers, *can* and *do* point to the Hebrew Bible to justify their actions shows at least that misinterpretation is widespread. And so I pose an additional, final ethical challenge: why would a benevolent God 'reveal' himself in so obscure a way that one needs a Ph.D. to understand him?

REFERENCES

Alter, Robert. 1991. *The Art of Biblical Narrative*. New York: Basic Books.

Auerbach Eric. 1953. *Mimesis: The Representation of Reality in Western Literature*. Princeton: Princeton University Press. Repr. 2003.

Baier, Annette C. 1987. 'The Need for More than Justice', *Canadian Journal of Philosophy*, Supp. Vol. 13.

Campbell, Joseph. 1964/1978. *The Masks of God: Occidental Mythology*. Harmondsworth: Penguin Books.

Friedman, Richard Elliot. 1987/1997. *Who Wrote the Bible?* New York: HarperCollins.

Grille, Robin. 2005. *Parenting for a Peaceful World*. Woollahra: Longueville Media.

Hanrahan, Rebecca Roman, and Antony, Louise. 2005. 'Because I Said So: Toward a Feminist Theory of Authority', *Hypatia*, 20/4: 59–79.

Hoffman, M. L. 1994. 'Discipline and Internalization', *Developmental Psychology*, 30/1: 26–8.

Kugel, James. 2007. *How to Read the Bible: A Guide to Scripture, Then and Now*. New York: Free Press/Simon and Schuster.

Midrash Rabbah. Bereshith. New York: Soncino Press, 1983.

Miles, Jack. 1996. *God: A Biography*. New York: Vintage Books/Random House.

Pagels, Elaine. 1996/1995. *The Origin of Satan*. New York: Vintage Books/Random House.

Ruddick, Sara. 1989/1995. *Maternal Thinking: Toward a Politics of Peace*. Boston: Beacon Press.

Scherman, Rabbi Nosson. 1989. 'An Overview: Ruth and the Seeds of Mashiach', in Rabbi Meir Zlotowitz (trans. and annot.), *The Book of Ruth*. Artscroll Tanach Series. Brooklyn, NY: Mesorah Publications.

Scott, Katreena L., and Crooks, Claire V. 2004. 'Effecting Change in Maltreating Fathers: Critical Principles for Intervention Planning', *Clinical Psychology: Science and Practice*, 11/1.

Stump, Eleonore. 2010. *Wandering in Darkness: Narrative and the Problem of Suffering*. Oxford: Oxford University Press.

Wiehe, V. R. 1990. 'Religious Influence on Parental Attitudes toward the Use of Corporal Punishment', *Journal of Family Violence*, 5/2: 173–87.

Williams, Bernard. 1981. 'Moral Luck', in *Moral Luck*. Cambridge: Cambridge University Press.

Wood, Audrey, and Wood, Don. 1987. *Heckedy Peg*. Orlando, Fla.: Harcourt, Brace & Co.

Zlotowitz, Rabbi Meir (trans. and annot.). 1989. *The Family Chumash: Bereishis (Genesis). Introductions, Translations and Concise Commentary with Haftarahs.*, trans. and annotated by Artscroll Tanach Series. Brooklyn, NY: Mesorah Publication.

2

The God of Abraham, Isaac, and Jacob

Edwin Curley

I thank the organizers of this conference for inviting me to speak on behalf of those who reject the God of the Bible. It's an honor to be thought worthy of this task, particularly when so many have been called to defend the biblical God, and so few have been chosen to make the case against him.[1]

The question before us is whether the moral character of God, as presented in the Bible, is a compelling objection to the Christian view that the Bible is the inspired word of a god possessing all the perfections Christian philosophers commonly ascribe to their God. I say it is. And I offer the following argument for that conclusion. Consider this principle:

1. If a passage in the Bible reports that God, or someone purporting to speak on behalf of God, has told someone to do something clearly wrong, then we ought to dismiss the claim of that passage to report accurately the kind of demand God is apt to make on his creatures.

This proposition has, not only the support of eminent authority,[2] but also the support of reason. Suppose God is the perfectly good being Christian

---

I'm indebted to Martti Nissinen, Pamela Barmash, Wes Morriston, Evan Fales, Michael Murray, Michael Bergmann, and Michael Rea for their comments on earlier versions of this chapter, and to the Institute for Advanced Study in Princeton for the research time which helped me to write it.

[1] I don't, of course, wish to suggest that there is anything unfair about the conference arrangements. I know the organizers had their reasons for the disparity in numbers between believers and non-believers. It's so easy to make moral objections to the God of the Bible and there is such variety in the responses defenders of Christian theism make. But the critics do bear a heavy burden if a small number are expected to anticipate and respond to all the main lines of defense. There are so many objections to make, so many possible replies to consider, and the space allowed for discussion is so short.

[2] Cf. Swinburne (1992: 86): 'The content [of the purported revelation] must, as far as we can judge by independent evidence, be true. The evidence that it is true will be, first, that none of the prophet's teaching is evidently false. His teaching on morality, for example, must not involve his telling men that they ought to do what is evidently morally wrong—the prophet who commends cheating and child torture can be dismissed straight away.' In the second edition of his book,

philosophical theology typically says he is.[3] Would such a being command his creatures to do something clearly wrong? Or would he permit a work through which he was revealing himself to mankind to mislead us about the kind of thing he was apt to command, misguiding us about what it is right to do? One might hope that the answer to these questions would be an unequivocal 'no'. But then we confront the fact that:

2. Genesis 22 reports that one day God told Abraham to sacrifice his son, Isaac, and to make a burnt offering of him.

If we then judge that

3. child sacrifice is clearly wrong,

we quickly get to the conclusion that:

4. we ought to dismiss the claim of Genesis 22 to report accurately the kind of demand God is apt to make on his creatures.

This looks like a valid argument. So far as I can see, the premises are true. (2) is clearly indisputable. If I were a Christian theist, I don't think I'd want to dispute (1). So I suppose the defenders of Christian theism will have to challenge (3), if they dispute anything. We'll consider later some grounds on which they might do that. But first I note that some Christian philosophers have been willing to accept the conclusion of this argument and to dismiss the claim that Genesis 22 accurately reports a command God gave to Abraham.

This is the way Robert Adams solves what he calls 'Abraham's dilemma', the quandary which would have been generated if Abraham had believed the following three propositions:

(i) If God commands me to do something, it is not morally wrong for me to do it;
(ii) God commands me to kill my son; and
(iii) It is morally wrong for me to kill my son.

Certainly these three propositions are inconsistent with one another. Any pair of them entails the denial of the third. So it's not possible for all three propositions to be true. Whether the biblical Abraham believed both (i) and (iii) may be unclear. If he acted from fear of God, as the usual translation of Genesis suggests, he may not have given much thought to the moral issues

---

Swinburne took a similar position, but, perhaps anticipating the kind of objections which might be made to his earlier proposition, stated it more guardedly: 'If [a candidate revelation] tells us that rape and lying, murder and theft (without exceptional divine permission), are good, then that is a good reason for supposing the candidate revelation not to be a genuine one' (2007: 110).

[3] Of many possible examples I cite two: Swinburne 1993: 1; and Plantinga 2000: vii.

his situation raised. But clearly he is presented as believing (ii), and Adams thinks that's the proposition he ought to have rejected, no matter how strong the evidence for it was.[4] He appeals to Jeremiah as supporting his claim that the biblical God never commanded any such thing. Jeremiah has God say that

The people of Judah have done evil in my sight, says the LORD; they have set their abominations in the house that is called by my name, defiling it. And they go on building the high place of Topheth . . . to burn their sons and their daughters in the fire—which I did not command, nor did it come into my mind.[5]

Of course, as Adams acknowledges, Ezekiel contradicts Jeremiah on this point. Though he shares Jeremiah's disapproval of child sacrifice, Ezekiel does not deny that God commanded it. And he represents God as making the rather startling admission that:

I gave them statutes that were not good and ordinances by which they could not live. I defiled them through their very gifts, in their offering up all their firstborn, in order that I might horrify them, so that they might know that I am the LORD. (20: 25–6)[6]

Adams follows Jeremiah in preference to Ezekiel. I applaud the fundamental decency which moves him to resist the idea that he could be bound to obey a God who might have commanded him to kill one of his children. But I have not been able to grasp the principle on which he prefers the one prophet to the other—unless it is that, faced with a contradiction in scripture, we must always prefer the passage which shows God in a better light, as judged by our present moral standards. No doubt that's an interpretive principle many believers use, but it does diminish the value of scripture as an independent moral authority.[7]

---

[4] See Adams 1999: 284, where he quotes with approval Kant's statement that 'Abraham should have replied to this supposedly divine voice: "That I ought not to kill my good son is quite certain. But that you, this apparition, are God—of that I am not certain, and never can be, not even if this voice rings down to me from (visible) heaven."' (See Kant 1996: 283 n.)

[5] 7: 30–1. Unless otherwise noted, I cite the Bible from the *New Revised Standard Version*, as given in Metzger and Murphy 1991.

[6] The NJPS translation of this text reads: 'I gave them laws which were not good, and rules by which they could not live. When they set aside every first issue of the womb, I defiled them by their very gifts—that I might render them desolate, that they might know that I am the LORD' (NJPS 1999). The reference to laws commanding the sacrifice of the first-born appears to be an allusion to Exodus 22: 'The firstborn of your sons you shall give to me. You shall do the same with your oxen and with your sheep . . .' (vss. 29–30). The interpretation of these and similar verses is controversial, but Levenson 1995 argues forcefully that at a certain stage Israel did practice child sacrifice.

[7] In his paper for this conference, Nicholas Wolterstorff quoted Augustine's embrace of an analogous principle: 'We must show the way to find out whether a phrase is literal or figurative. And the way is certainly as follows: Whatever there is in the word of God that cannot, when taken literally, be referred either to purity of life or soundness of doctrine, you may set down as figurative' (*De doctrina Christiana*, III, 10, 14). Wolterstorff notes that the Jewish exegetical tradition has also followed this policy. Maimonides' discussion of the eternity of the world (in

Rejecting the Genesis narrative has not, historically, been a popular solution to this problem. In the Christian tradition, Abraham has generally been celebrated for his unquestioning faith in God, and that faith has been understood as a faith that in the end he would not really have to lose his son. Abraham trusted the promise God made to him, which would be threatened if Isaac were permanently lost. He must have thought that God didn't really mean it. And as Genesis tells the story, he was right about that. Abraham may not have anticipated the precise manner of his son's restoration, may not have guessed that God would stay his hand at the last moment. But he did have faith that somehow God would work things out, that a true sacrifice was not really required. If necessary, God could raise Isaac from the dead.[8] But if Abraham believed that he was not really being asked to sacrifice his son, why does God reward him so profusely for his willingness to do so? Even if God does not have foreknowledge of Abraham's future decisions, he must know his intentions at the moment when he intervenes. So he claims, when he says to Abraham: 'Now I know that you fear God, since you have not withheld your son, your only son, from me.'[9] The story does not make sense if Abraham thinks he is just going through the motions of a sacrifice.[10]

One reason this Christian reading of Genesis 22 has been so popular may be that the price to be paid for taking Adams's way out is just too high. If the Bible often reports that God has commanded things which seem clearly wrong, things perhaps just as horrifying as the command to sacrifice Isaac, then taking that route will require us to reject much of what the Bible tells us about God's moral nature, and concede that it is not a reliable source of information about that. But if the Bible is seriously misleading about God's moral nature, it cannot be the word of a perfectly good God. If God is perfectly good, he would not seriously mislead us about his moral nature. Or so we might naturally think.[11]

Guide of the Perplexed II, 25) illustrates this. Those tempted by such principles should read Spinoza's critique of Maimonides in ch. 7 of his *Theological-Political Treatise*.

[8] So speculates the author of the letter to the Hebrews, 11: 17–19.

[9] Gen. 22: 11 suggests that this line is spoken by 'an angel of the Lord', but the use of the first person pronoun—'since you have not withheld your son . . . from *me*'—makes sense only if the speaker is God, not merely a divine messenger. This is common in the Genesis narrative. Cf. 16: 7, 13.

[10] Levenson makes the point forcefully: 'No interpretation of the aqedah can be adequate if it fails to reckon with the point made explicit here [in Gen. 22: 16–18]: Abraham will have his multitudes of descendants only because he was willing to sacrifice the son who is destined to beget them. Any construal of the text that minimizes that willingness misses the point.' Cf. Levenson 1995: 13, and 125–6.

[11] Since the Christians I talk to about these matters often insist that they are not fundamentalists, it's worth emphasizing that I am not assuming that a defender of scripture must be a fundamentalist. All I assume is that she must think that if scripture is the word of God, it cannot

Here's a variation on this argument, using the premise that

5. If a passage in the Bible reports that God, or someone purporting to speak
   on behalf of God, has given someone permission to do something clearly
   wrong, then we ought to dismiss the claim of that passage to report
   accurately the kind of action God is apt to permit his creatures to do.

We might then note that

6. Exodus 21 gives the Israelites permission to sell their daughters into
   slavery, provided they follow certain rules,

and add that

7. selling your daughter into slavery is clearly wrong.

If we accept that moral judgment, we seem forced to conclude that

8. we ought to dismiss the claim of Exodus 21 to report accurately the kind of
   action God is apt to permit his creatures to do.

We now have two patterns of argument, both apparently valid, both apparently
having, in the instances given, true premises, and both leading to the conclusion that certain passages in the Bible cannot be trusted to have reported
accurately the sorts of thing God is apt to authorize his followers to do.

If these patterns of argument can be replicated in numerous instances, with
different examples of actions which ought not to be commanded or permitted,
and if God is the morally perfect being he is supposed to be, then the Bible is quite
unreliable as a source of information about God's commands and permissions.
If it was written under divine inspiration, God must have wanted to mislead
us, either about his moral nature, or about the difference between right and
wrong. But that cannot be. So the Bible was not written under divine inspiration.

It's not difficult to find further examples. It's a hard call, trying to decide
what the worst commands in scripture are, but probably the passages most
troubling to modern readers are those which command genocide. Some may
resist the application of the term 'genocidal' to any command in the Bible, but
if we accept the *OED*'s definition of 'genocide' as 'the deliberate and systematic extermination of an ethnic or national group', it's hard to deny its
accuracy. The Bible repeatedly represents God as commanding the people of
Israel to 'utterly destroy' the nations they conquer.

When the LORD your God brings you into the land that you are about to enter and
occupy, and he clears away many nations before you . . . and the LORD your God gives

be seriously misleading about such important matters as the moral nature of God, the commands and permissions he might give, and the way he might treat his creatures.

them over to you and you defeat them, you must utterly destroy them. Make no covenant with them, and show them no mercy.[12]

That passage from Deuteronomy is only one example of God's being represented in the Bible as having given a genocidal command.[13]

Sometimes these passages are quite chilling in the details they give about what it means to 'utterly destroy' a people. Later God makes a distinction between two different kinds of conquered peoples. If the people live in a distant town, and agree to submit to Israelite rule, they're to be spared—enslaved, but not killed (Deut. 20: 10–11). If the people in the distant town resist, then all the men must be put to the sword. But the women, children, and livestock may be spared, taken as booty, to be 'enjoyed' by the conquering Israelites (Deut. 20: 12–14). The people who live in nearby towns are not so lucky. God commands that in those towns nothing which breathes be left alive (Deut. 20: 16). In some of the passages where complete extermination is prescribed, God makes it quite explicit that not even infants are to be spared (1 Sam. 15: 3).

So in this one chapter of Deuteronomy we have God authorizing the enslavement of some captive peoples, the killing of others (including non-combatants), and the appropriation, for the victors' sexual pleasure, of whatever women are permitted to survive. If you think I'm reading too much into the use of the word 'enjoy' here, consider the following passage:

When you go out to war against your enemies, and the LORD your God hands them over to you, and you take them captive, suppose you see among the captives a beautiful woman whom you desire and want to marry, and so you bring her home to your house; she shall shave her head, pare her nails, discard her captive's garb, and shall remain in your house a full month, mourning her father and mother; after that you may go in to her and be her husband, and she shall be your wife. But if you are not satisfied with her, you shall let her go free and not sell her for money. You must not treat her as a slave, since you have dishonored her.[14]

Nothing is said here about the woman's *consenting* to become the man's 'wife'[15]—her consent is clearly not considered important. The NRSV transla-

---

[12] Deut. 7: 1–2. The NJPS translation reads: 'When the LORD your God brings you to the land you are about to enter and possess, and He dislodges many nations before you . . . and the LORD your God delivers them to you and you defeat them, you must doom them to destruction: grant them no terms and give them no quarter.'

[13] Other examples may be found in Deut. 3: 2–7; 20: 1–20; Josh. 6: 15–21; and 1 Sam. 15: 3.

[14] Deut. 21: 10–14. In Num. 31: 17–18, 35, it is 'the young girls who have not known a man by sleeping with him' who are to be spared so that they may become the victors' 'wives'.

[15] I put the terms 'wife' and 'husband' in scare quotes in this passage, because it does not seem that these Canaanite women were granted much in the way of rights in this relationship. But apparently it is unclear what rights even Israelite women had in their marriages. From Deut. 24: 1 we learn that Israelite law gave husbands the right to divorce their wives if they found

tion, which I've been treating as my default version, euphemizes when it says that the man has 'dishonored' her. The NJPS translation brings out more clearly the fact that the intercourse is forced: 'you are not to sell her, because *you have had your will of her.*' The verb here is the same one used in Genesis 34: 2 for the rape of Dinah.

So Deuteronomy grants the Israelite warriors permission to rape the Canaanite women they take captive (or at least the ones they find beautiful). If the woman fails to please her 'husband', he is not permitted to sell her into slavery. This may, for all I know, be an improvement on the customs of other countries in the ancient Near East. He is required to 'release' her, like a fish which is too small to keep. But the situation of a woman 'set free' in an alien nation, after her family, and, indeed, her whole culture, have been destroyed, could not have been pleasant. The interests of Canaanite women are evidently not of much concern to the God of Deuteronomy.

Nowadays critical biblical scholars inform us that the stories told in Joshua about the conquest of Canaan describe events which probably never occurred. As Professor Anderson puts it: they 'are not historical records of what really happened, but after-the-fact literary fictions'.[16] If the genocide did not occur, or at least not with the thoroughness the texts brag of,[17] we may doubt whether any genocidal commands occurred either. But what matters is not whether these things happened, but whether, if there were a God of the kind the biblical narrative describes, he would deserve our unconditional love, honor, and obedience. It is an unpleasant fact that the Bible presents for our worship a god whom it pictures as being capable of issuing such commands— and expects us to love him, honor him, and obey him anyway. If he did not issue any such commands, the Bible is seriously misleading about his moral nature.

Some of you may now be getting impatient, and saying to yourself: 'All right, we know all about that. We know that the God of the Bible commanded child sacrifice and genocide, and gave permission for slavery and rape, and did many other things which might seem embarrassing to a twenty-first-century Christian. We knew all about these things long before the "New Atheists" began making such a fuss about them. So we don't need to be told about that. We have our ways of defending God against these charges, which

---

'something objectionable' about them. We do not now know how much of a limitation this might have been. See the *Anchor Bible Dictionary*, art. on 'Divorce'.

[16] Anderson, Ch. 9 below. For a similar account of the conquest of Canaan, see Kugel 2007: ch. 22.

[17] e.g. in Num. 21: 1–3; Deut. 2: 30–5, 3: 3–7; Josh. 6: 17–21, 10: 28, and 11: 10–11.

don't require us to deny that God said what the Bible says he said. What we want to see is whether you have any objection to our defenses which we might need to reply to.'

You will see that I'm under no illusions about my role in this conference. It's not to represent a point of view which Christian philosophers might ultimately be persuaded to accept. It's to be a sparring partner, who can help the faithful work out their best defense against old criticisms which have acquired a new urgency now that the events of 9–11 have freed the critics of religiously based ethics to become more vocal. I accept this role. But that seems to me all the more reason to insist that we appreciate how many truly appalling passages there are in the Bible—and not just in the Hebrew Bible either, but also in those scriptures which Christians refer to as the 'New Testament'. Christians should not be complacent about the moral superiority of their scriptures to those of the Jews, as I shall try to show before I'm done. We've already seen one example of the importance of numbers, in our discussion of the binding of Isaac. If the command to sacrifice Isaac were an isolated case, then it might not be too damaging to admit that on one occasion the Bible attributes to God a command he never gave, and never would have dreamed of giving, particularly if we can find passages in the Bible in which God is represented as saying that he never, ever, would have commanded such a thing. But if the Bible repeatedly attributes appalling commands to God, then the accuracy of the text cannot be denied without raising serious questions about its claim to speak for God. We shall see further examples of the importance of numbers as we proceed.

But first let's consider a reply some might wish to make about the binding of Isaac: 'Look,' it may be said,

the reason Adams got in trouble about the binding of Isaac is that he was too squeamish. He's constructed a modified version of divine command theory, according to which divine commands obligate only if they are the commands of a loving God.[18] He can't bring himself to admit that it would be right to practice cruelty for its own sake if God commanded it. So when confronted with a biblical narrative in which God gives what seems to be a very cruel command, a command too hard to reconcile with the loving nature he believes God must have, his only option is to deny the data.

But as you've shown, that way out, if followed consistently, leads to too much skepticism about the accuracy of the biblical record. The proper course is to embrace a more robust version of divine command theory. God's sovereignty entails that whatever he commands is just, no matter what the specific content of the command. If there were moral restrictions on his conduct—things justice required him not to do—that could only be because he was subject to the will of a higher authority. But

---

[18] e.g. in the essays on this topic included in Adams 1987.

there is no higher being who has the authority to command him to do anything. So we must overcome our squeamishness and admit that all these things you find so offensive—child sacrifice, genocide, slavery, rape, and whatever other embarrassments you may bring up—are right, whenever God either commands them or permits them.[19]

I do not claim that my robust version of divine command theory, and the version formulated by Adams, are the only ones available. There are many different ways of developing voluntarism. All I claim is that a theory of this kind will be sufficient to justify any embarrassing commands scripture may have to offer. That is its great strength, from the point of view of a defender of the faith. That may also be its great weakness, from anyone's point of view: there is nothing, in or out of scripture, it cannot justify. That may make it too brutal for many contemporary stomachs.[20]

A literary comparison may help us see why. Let's concede, for the sake of the argument, that someone who creates something has, in virtue of that fact, the right to destroy it. As Job says, 'The Lord gave and the Lord has taken away. Blessed be the name of the Lord' (Job 1: 21). So God, having given Isaac life in the first place, has the right to take away Isaac's life whenever he pleases. Still, it's one thing to take a life and quite another to command someone else to take the same life, particularly when the someone else would normally have a special duty to care for the person to be killed and, what's more, loves that person deeply. Part of what makes the story of Abraham and Isaac seem so cruel is that God commands *the father* to kill his own son, a son whom the text insists that he loves. In William Styron's novel *Sophie's Choice*, a doctor at Auschwitz forces a young mother to decide which of her two children will live and which will go to the gas chamber. If the doctor had simply wanted one of the children to die, he could have killed the child himself, or ordered someone else to do it. But that would not have been enough for him; he wanted to

---

[19] In his comments on Evan Fales's chapter in this volume, Professor Plantinga seemed to endorse a pretty robust version of divine command theory. For a good discussion of some of the problems, see Morriston 2009: 1–19.

[20] But here's a line of argument not dependent on the moral revulsion most people feel when they think, in concrete terms, about the idea that there is no class of actions which can be ruled out as clearly wrong. There are biblical texts most easily interpreted by a robust version of divine command theory. In Curley 2002 I argued that the book of Job was one. But there are other texts inconsistent with a robust version of divine command theory. In Curley 2004 I argued that a robust version of divine command theory would be inconsistent with the biblical notion of a covenant between God and man, according to which God makes promises to the people of Israel by which he is subsequently bound. I contend that the book of Job, consistently with its embrace of divine command theory, rejects covenant theology. Any robust divine command theory must reject the idea that God can make promises by which he is subsequently bound.

make the mother complicit in her child's death by deciding which one would die. I say: sadistic bastard. How horrible for the child, to die in the knowledge that her mother has chosen her to die! How horrible for the mother, not only to have to make that choice, but to know that her child died with the knowledge that she had done so! At the end of the novel, Sophie, unable to live with her guilt, commits suicide.

Is God a sadistic bastard? Or does he merely play one in the Bible? Commanding Abraham to roast his dead son's flesh does seem a gratuitously nasty touch. Even the Nazi doctor did not go that far. But perhaps we should be grateful that God did not go farther. After all, he did not, as the story has come down to us, add the command: 'Before you reduce your son's flesh to a pile of ashes, cut out his liver, and fry it up for supper. Have it with some fava beans, and a nice Chianti.' The details of this hypothetical command may be anachronistic, but its possibility can hardly be excluded on any version of divine command theory robust enough to justify genocide. Nor does cannibalism seem to be outside the range of things the God of the Hebrew Bible might command. When the people of Jerusalem offended God by offering up worship to Baal, he was perfectly willing to threaten to 'make them eat the flesh of their sons and the flesh of their daughters' (Jer. 19: 9). Perhaps some mystery is concealed in these words. But 'it's a mystery' is such a handy answer to so many objections that we must be careful not to overuse it.

The organizers of this conference selected as its motto a line from Isaiah (55: 8) which reads: 'My ways are not your ways.' I suppose that verse may have appealed to them because they were thinking something like this. God is a being of infinite power, knowledge, and goodness. We, on the other hand, are finite human beings, whose power, knowledge, and goodness are extremely limited. God, then, is so far above us that we cannot always understand the reasons for his actions, which may be exceedingly complex. Sometimes he does things which seem to us wrong, even deeply repugnant to our moral sensibilities. But the gap between his intellect and ours gives us good grounds for doubting our judgment in those cases. Insofar as we have good reasons for believing that a God having the traditional perfections exists, we must also believe that he had morally sufficient reasons for everything he did, and that there must have been special circumstances which justified his actions in the cases which disturb us, reasons inscrutable to us, but intelligible to an infinite intellect. I'll call this *the Higher Ways Objection*. It seems to be the kind of line skeptical theists are inclined to like.[21]

---

[21] By a 'skeptical theist' I understand someone who holds the view, formulated initially in response to Rowe's evidential version of the problem of evil, that we do not know enough about good and evil to make even a probabilistic judgment about whether the existence of widespread,

That passage in Isaiah might seem congenial to skeptical theism, but I do not think it supports the view that it is a defect in our understanding which prevents us from appreciating the higher morality which sanctions genocide. In context these lines are part of a call to repentance, which seeks to provide the wicked with a motive for repentance by assuring them that God's way is unlike that of men in this: if a sinner truly repents his sins and amends his conduct, God will forgive him. Men aren't always so forgiving. This is one of those passages in which the God of the Bible appears in an attractive moral light. We humans do not forgive as often as we should. But though it may be difficult in particular cases to know whether forgiveness is appropriate, and there may be legitimate differences of opinion about whether the existing circumstances justify it, most of us have no difficulty understanding that we would often be following a better path if we were more forgiving than we are. Thankfully, most of us do have some difficulty understanding that we would be following a better path if we committed child sacrifice, or genocide, or rape.

I don't suppose the organizers of this conference want to rest anything on that passage in Isaiah. They just thought those familiar lines could be used as a convenient way of summing up a very different point, which was philosophically plausible independently of any passage in scripture: that it's presumptuous of us to draw negative inferences about God's moral character from what scripture tells us about his actions. This may seem an attractively modest position considered in the abstract. But it does raise questions: how are we to judge God's moral character if not from his actions? Don't we need to make some judgments about God's moral character—his veracity, for example—if we are to believe what he tells us in those scriptures which are supposed to be his word? And more specifically: is this moral skepticism defensible when we consider concretely what it entails, given the scriptural record of God's commands and permissions? Do we really want to hold that child sacrifice is not clearly wrong? or that genocide is not clearly wrong? or that selling your

intense, and undeserved suffering is a good reason for rejecting God's existence. As Michael Bergmann explains (Bergmann 2001: 278–96), the skeptical theist's theism is 'just the traditional monotheistic view that there exists an omniscient, omnipotent and perfectly good being'. He is not skeptical about that. He *is* skeptical about our knowledge of values, whether the possible goods and evils we know are representative of the possible goods and evils there are, and what the entailment relations between these possible goods and evils are.

Without conceding that skeptical theism is an adequate response to Rowe's version of the problem of evil, I would argue that it faces special difficulties when extended to what David Lewis (2007) called 'Divine Evil'. We must know enough about good and evil to make some judgment about God's moral character—specifically, his veracity—if we are to assume that his having revealed something to us in the Bible is evidence of its truth.

daughter into slavery is not clearly wrong? or that raping women whom you've taken captive in war is not clearly wrong?

I would not want to have to defend an affirmative answer to *all* these questions, to say that in *none* of these cases is it clear what the right thing to do is. If these things are not clearly wrong, what is? Here again, the numbers matter. Must the skeptical theist be a total skeptic about morality? It may be argued that it's *possible* that our moral intuitions are mistaken, or 'wrongly shaped by current and misguided fashion'.[22] I suppose that anything is possible in the world of the theist. But if our moral intuitions are so systematically mistaken, about so many things, even about things which seem so very clear, we cannot put all the blame on fashion. In the case of child sacrifice, at least, the condemnation is not a matter of current fashion, but goes back to the days of Jeremiah and Ezekiel.

I doubt that someone who takes the line I'm considering here will want to embrace total moral skepticism. I suspect he will probably want to hold that *some* things are clearly right and others clearly wrong. For example, the Bible represents God as commanding us to love our neighbors as ourselves. Even a skeptical theist will probably grant that loving our neighbors is clearly right. But suppose he does. Can he coherently add that, though we must, of course, love our neighbors, for all we know it may be right to kill them? or that for all we know it might be all right to kill the men and rape their women?

I would have thought not. But one of the organizers of this conference offered me such a defense, in the case, not of raping the Canaanite women, but of attempting to exterminate the whole Canaanite community. I should stress that when Professor Bergmann sent me this reasoning, he made it clear that he did not endorse it. He was just presenting it as a line of thought I ought to consider. It goes like this:[23]

---

[22] Michael Bergmann suggested this possibility in comments he gave me on a draft of my paper submitted in June, though he offered it as a general consideration to keep in mind when relying on moral intuitions as evidence, not as a response to specific moral intuitions against, e.g., rape or genocide. He assures me he doesn't think those are due to mistaken current fashion. The context was a question about whether our moral intuitions about the immorality of conduct commanded or permitted by the biblical God were sufficient by themselves to override any historical evidence in favor of the divine inspiration of scripture. My view about that is that while the historical evidence might in principle be sufficient to persuade us that a supernatural being had inspired the biblical authors to write what they did, the immorality of the conduct commanded or permitted would be an overwhelming objection to regarding that being as the perfectly good God of Christian philosophical theology.

[23] The numbered paragraphs are drawn from Bergmann's comments on my June draft paper. I've paraphrased for the sake of brevity, but Bergmann has assured me that my paraphrase did not misrepresent what he wrote. The emphases are mine. Michael Rea also thought that this line should be considered, though he didn't endorse it either.

(¶1) Could a perfectly loving God decide to destroy *a single person*, whom he loves deeply, but *whose behavior has been persistently immoral*? That seems epistemically possible and coherent. Although God is represented as loving and merciful, not always punishing people as they deserve, he does sometimes punish by killing. It seems that that could be both just and consistent with perfect love and goodness.

(¶2) Now consider a hypothetical community most of whose members have engaged in similar wrongdoing for generations. Suppose God decides to destroy *only those members of the community who have persistently done wrong*. If a perfectly loving, good, and merciful God could kill one person for this reason, it seems he could also kill *all the guilty members of the community*. Does it matter that they are all of the same race? It seems not, since God isn't targeting them for their race but for their wrongdoing.

I would concede the point made in the first paragraph, but I'm dubious about the move from a single wicked person to all the wicked people. It does invite the question: 'What about God's mercy? If God is merciful, won't he sometimes spare those who deserve punishment?' It may be replied that God can exercise his mercy outside the hypothetical community. But then it does seem that the wicked people in this community are not being punished only for their wrongdoing, but also for their membership in the community. God will sometimes be merciful to people outside the community, but never to people inside it. The really problematic moves, however, are yet to come.

(¶3) Now compare the case imagined in ¶2 with the genocides in recent history. Do such cases seem morally on a par? No. The genocides of recent history were motivated by foolish hate, racism, and power-grabbing. God's killing the guilty members of our hypothetical community is motivated by his love for the members of that community and his love of what is right and just. The two kinds of killing are very different, one motivated wickedly and the other purely. And this despite very similar results: the death of most of the people in a single community. Thus, it seems that the term 'genocide' is not a good one, since it runs together two very different kinds of mass killing.

(¶4) Of course, the case described above, where God targets only the guilty, isn't the sort of case we have in the Bible. In the Bible we have God commanding the killing of the innocent (children and infants) along with the guilty. Thus, the real problems are that (a) innocents get killed along with the guilty, and (b) God doesn't do the killing himself but gets humans to do the killing. As for (a), one has to think about what sense it makes to bring harm to entire communities for the sins of the majority of their members. It's clear that the innocent members are not guilty and deserving of punishment.[24] But is it clear that it is unjust for them to be killed along with the guilty? Is it clear that it is always morally inappropriate for all members of a group to

---

[24] This is a concession to modernism worth noting. Compare the passage from Augustine quoted by Professor Seitz in his chapter: 'One should not at all think it a horrible cruelty that

be harmed because of the wrongdoing of the majority of its members, even though not all members of the group have done wrong? If this is not clear, then it's not so clear that (a) is an insurmountable problem. The problem with (b) is that it can cause psychological damage to those who do the killing; it also presents temptations to do the killings from impure motives (not with the love and mercy and desire for justice that, presumably, would motivate God if he did the killings). In light of that, is it coherent to think a loving God could command humans to do the killings for him? If God can do the killing himself in a loving and righteous way, is it contrary to his nature to ask humans to do it (presumably in that same way)? Here again, it's not so clear.

Thus endeth the (hypothetical) skeptical theist's rebuttal. I can see why the actual skeptical theist who sent me the defense here summarized might not want to endorse it.

First, it's understandable that a Christian might want to avoid calling the command to utterly destroy the Canaanites genocidal. It's such an ugly word. But that's just what genocide is: the systematic extermination of an ethnic or national group. We don't commonly make the motive for the extermination part of the definition. And the reason is not far to seek: it's pretty hard to imagine a good reason for trying to kill all the members of an ethnic group, including the children, including even infants. Unless we're committed to defending scripture at its worst, we don't have much need to try to distinguish good genocide (the kind God commanded) from bad genocide (the kind Hitler and Pol Pot commanded).

Secondly, this attempt to find a good motive for the Israelite genocide is no more convincing than the rationale offered in the Bible. 'God so loved the Canaanites that he ordered the Israelites to utterly destroy them.' 'God so loved justice that he ordered the innocent to be slaughtered along with the guilty.' Perhaps it's unkind to put these thoughts in such Orwellian terms. Perhaps it would be more in keeping with academic etiquette to cloak the thought in the decent obscurity of philosophical jargon: 'It's epistemically possible that God ordered the Israelites to destroy the Canaanites out of love for the Canaanites' and 'It's epistemically possible that God ordered the

---

Joshua did not leave anyone alive in those cities that fell, for God himself had ordered this. However, whoever for this reason thinks that God himself must be cruel, and does not wish to believe then that the true God was the author of the Old Testament, judges as perversely about the works of God as he does about the sins of human beings. Such people do not know what each person ought to suffer. Consequently, they think it a great evil when that which is about to fall is thrown down, and when mortals die.' *Questions on Joshua* 16. So even the Canaanite infants deserved to suffer. Augustine accepts a doctrine of the universality of sin which has deep roots both in the Hebrew Bible and in the Christian scriptures. On this, cf. the *Anchor Bible Dictionary*, art. 'Sin, Sinners'. See also the analysis in Brown 2000: 390–9.

Israelites to destroy the innocent along with the guilty out of a love of justice.'
But isn't this just to give lip service to the ideas that we must love our
neighbors and love justice? We are enjoined to love these things, but we
can't say with any certainty what these injunctions require of us by way of
concrete actions. For all we know, loving our neighbor might require us to kill
our neighbor.[25]

Not that the Bible's justification for the slaughter is much better. God does
not make a mystery of the reason for his genocidal commands. He says that
the Canaanites must die because if they are allowed to live, they will seduce
the Israelites into accepting their idolatrous religious practices.[26] This official
justification calls for them to be killed to protect Israelite religion, not to
punish their own wickedness, much less out of some strange belief that this is
the loving thing to do. We can understand why the priests and prophets who
told us what the will of God was would have regarded protecting Israelite
religion as a goal worth the sacrifice of many Canaanite lives. But just as the
claim that justice requires the death of the Canaanite children founders on the
fact that the innocent are to be killed along with the guilty, so the claim that
the protection of Israelite religion requires their death founders on the fact
that the children pose no real threat to Israelite religion. They did not imbibe
the worship of Ba'al with their mothers' milk. And that's just the official

---

[25] Here's a question for the skeptical theist. When we say that it's epistemically possible that
God acted out of love when he commanded the Israelites to destroy the Canaanites, what we
mean, presumably, is that nothing we know precludes us from reaching that conclusion. But can
we make a rough estimate of the probability of the conclusion? Is it, say, less than 0.01? is it in a
range between 0.01 and 0.1? Is it greater than 0.1, but less than 0.5? Or is our uncertainty so great
that we can't make even a rough estimate—so that for all we know the probability might be
quite high?

[26] This is the dominant justification. See Deut. 7: 4, 16; 20: 18; and Exod. 23: 23–4, 32–3; 34:
11–16. Sometimes the Bible does appeal to Canaanite wickedness, but this is not typical. Two of
the organizers (Murray and Bergmann) suggested in comments on my June draft that these
might not be God's only reasons, or even his best reasons, for ordering the slaughter. Perhaps we
could not understand his best reasons. 'If not, can we conclude that we can see that God's
reasons are bad ones (given that we don't know that we have them all before our minds)?'
(Bergmann).

The problem is that when someone in authority gives a command or permission, and cites a
reason for that authorization, the person thus authorized will naturally take that reason to be a
sufficient ground for similar action in similar circumstances in the future. If I permit a student
to take extra time on an exam because she has a learning disability, I cannot fairly refuse to
generalize the permission to later exams (or other students) unless there is some difference in
the circumstances. If God could not adequately explain his reasons for commanding the
Israelites to destroy the Canaanites, he ought to have said that, and made it clear that the
combination of command and reason given in that case should not be regarded as setting a
precedent for future, apparently similar situations. Laws need to be clear if they are to guide
action responsibly. This is one difficulty about trying to transfer the argumentative strategies of
skeptical theism from the evidential problem of evil to the problem of divine evil.

justification. We get a hint that less respectable motives may have been in play when we read that the people in distant towns are to be spared *provided they agree to submit to Israelite rule.* But of course no one here was motivated by a desire for power, especially not the priests and prophets.

Much of this hypothetical argument in defense of the Israelite genocide is conducted by asking rhetorical questions. I have no objection in principle to playing the Rhetorical Question Game. I've done it myself in this chapter. But when we are on the receiving end of such questions, we must always ask whether they should really receive the answer they're intended to receive. 'Is it clear', my hypothetical opponent asks, 'that it's unjust to kill the innocent along with the guilty?' The intended answer may be 'no', but I want to say: 'Yes, it's quite clear.' If anything in morality is clear, that's clear. And this, happily enough, is one of those cases where we can quote the Bible against itself. In the early days Moses proclaimed that God was a jealous God, who would 'punish the children for the iniquity of the parents, to the third and fourth generation of those who reject me'.[27] The biblical tradition treats Moses as the greatest of the prophets, the one to whom God spoke more clearly than he did to any other.[28] But I suggest that on this issue the later prophets had a better grasp of right and wrong. Ezekiel recognized and corrected the injustice of the rules Moses ascribed to God:

The person who sins shall die. A child shall not suffer for the iniquity of a parent, nor a parent suffer for the iniquity of a child. The righteousness of the righteous shall be his own, and the wickedness of the wicked shall be his own. (18: 20)

This discrepancy between Moses' teachings and Ezekiel's is easy to understand if we regard the Bible as a merely human text, which may ascribe to God different views at different times, as the people of Israel gradually develop a more adequate sense of justice. It is very hard to understand on the assumption that the Bible is the inspired word of a morally perfect God, whose moral character does not change.

This mention of moral progress brings me to my final point. The organizers of this conference have designated its subject as 'the character of the God of the *Hebrew* Bible'. This focus on the Hebrew Bible may suggest that that's where the problems lie, not in the specifically Christian scriptures, where God is represented as being kinder, gentler, and more loving than he is in the Hebrew Bible, where he is so prone to anger and vengeance. There may be

---

[27] This is Exod. 20: 5. The language in Deut. 5: 9 is the same.
[28] See Deut. 34: 10 and Num. 12: 6–8.

some basis for this Christian stereotype, but in many ways it's unfair. I've noted that there are signs of moral progress within the Hebrew Bible, mentioning as examples the rejection, by some of the later prophets, of child sacrifice and vicarious punishment. (It would be sad if skeptical theists were to undo the moral clarity the prophets achieved about those issues.) Here I'll add those wonderful lines in Micah:

> What does the LORD require of you
> But to do justice, and to love kindness,
> And to walk humbly with your God.[29]

We might wish that everything in the Bible were consistent with that teaching.

These are a sample of the signs of moral progress we might find within the Hebrew Bible.[30] There are also signs of moral progress when we move from the Hebrew Bible to the Christian scriptures. The Hebrew Bible prescribed the death penalty for adultery.[31] Adultery is surely wrong, but this penalty is absurdly severe. This is a frequent problem in the Law of Moses, and a strong reason for our questions about the moral character of the God who is supposed to be the ultimate source of that law.[32] So it's refreshing when Jesus, challenged to say what should be done with a woman taken in adultery, is reported as replying: 'Let anyone who is without sin among you be the first

---

[29] 6: 8. In the NJPS translation this verse reads: 'He has told you, O man, what is good, And what the LORD requires of you: Only to do justice, And to love goodness, And to walk modestly with your God.'

[30] In a similar spirit we might mention Amos 5: 21–4, Hos. 6: 6, and Isa. 2: 2–4. But recognizing signs of moral progress in the Bible is problematic if you're committed to the idea that scripture is the word of a God whose moral character does not change.

[31] For example, in Lev. 20: 10 and Deut. 22: 22. Neither of these passages specifies death *by stoning*, a penalty which Deut. 22: 23–4 prescribes for the special case where the woman is a virgin, engaged to be married. All three passages prescribe the penalties they invoke for both the man and the woman.

[32] Let's stipulate that striking your father or mother, or cursing them, are wrongs. Still the death penalty prescribed for these offenses in Exod. 21: 15, 17, is excessive. In other cases I would say that the problem is, not that an excessive penalty is prescribed for conduct which deserves some penalty, but that any penalty at all is prescribed for conduct which deserves none. That would be my view of the prohibition on same-sex relations in Lev. 18: 22, and the death penalty prescribed for witchcraft in Lev. 20: 27 and Exod. 22: 18. One unfortunate feature of religiously based moralities is that they tend to preserve, as if carved in stone, the prejudices and superstitions of a barbarous stage of human development, and to cloak these prejudices and superstitions in the mantle of divine authorization. We can see this easily enough when the religion is that of another culture, like Islam. It's harder to see when the religion is that of our own culture. When this results in futile attempts to ban children's novels, it is merely ridiculous. When it results in the deaths of harmless old women and the denial of equal rights to decent citizens, it is worse. It is tragic.

to throw a stone at her.'[33] I hesitate to endorse the proposition that only those without sin have moral standing to inflict punishment on sinners, as this passage might seem to suggest. The legal system would collapse if we followed that rule. But it does seem salutary for those who are charged with inflicting punishment to be mindful of their own faults. We might be more forgiving if we were. This is a lesson we might have learned from Isaiah, and so perhaps not an entirely happy example to support the idea that the Christian scriptures show moral progress when compared with the Hebrew Bible. But the concreteness of this passage, the compassion it seems to show for human weakness, and the explicitness with which it rejects the Law of Moses may have combined to help make it a more effective piece of moral teaching. One might wish Jesus had always spoken in that spirit.

A clearer example of moral progress, perhaps, is the gradual change in the interpretation of the Mosaic Law that we should love our neighbors as ourselves. When that law was promulgated in Leviticus, the term 'neighbor' seems to have been intended to cover only fellow Israelites.[34] Over time it came to be understood as covering the whole human race. It may be unclear whether Jesus or Paul deserves the credit for this transformation.[35] But whoever deserves the credit, and whatever the motivations for it, the change was real, important, and on the whole, I think, beneficial, even if it makes this particular commandment much harder to follow—strains, really, against the nature God is supposed to have given us. We find it much easier to love family and friends than other members of our culture with whom we have no special relationship, much less members of other cultures.

All this is to the good. But later is not always better. Some of the changes we see in the Christian scriptures are for the worse, from a moral point of view. Consider the doctrine of the afterlife. There is not much about the afterlife in the Hebrew Bible, and what there is, is mostly inconsistent with Christian views. To deal briefly with a complex subject, some passages simply deny that there is an afterlife;[36] other passages affirm a kind of afterlife, but not one Christians would recognize as theirs. They do not make a distinction between

---

[33] John 8: 7. We might wish we had better evidence that Jesus actually said this. As is now well known, this oft-quoted story does not appear in the oldest MSS of that gospel, but seems to have been added at a later date.

[34] Lev. 19: 17–18. Here I follow Wright 2009: 235, who cites Orlinsky 1974: 83. Cf. the commentary on this in the *New Oxford Annotated Bible*.

[35] Wright's *Evolution of God* argues plausibly that it belongs properly to Paul. See 2009: 257–61, 264–87.

[36] So in Ecclesiastes we read: 'The fate of humans and the fate of animals is the same; as one dies, so dies the other. They all have the same breath, and humans have no advantage over the animals; for all is vanity' (3: 19).

the righteous and the wicked, and they do not make anyone's afterlife seem very attractive. The locus of this afterlife is generally called Sheol, and pictured as 'a land of gloom and deep darkness' (Job 10: 21), to which all go, no matter what they have done in this life (Job 3: 13–19).[37]

Now the specifically Christian scriptures are, in some respects, tolerably clear about the way God will treat us after death. There will be an afterlife for everyone, which may be either wonderful or awful. Those who find favor with God will enjoy eternal bliss; those who don't will suffer eternal torment. I use the vague phrase 'those who find favor with God' to accommodate the fact that the Christian scriptures are not clear about how we achieve salvation (if it is something we can achieve). Sometimes they suggest that we can achieve salvation through loving our neighbors and obeying God's law; sometimes they suggest that we can do nothing to achieve it on our own, but must depend on God's grace, and the gift of faith, which may or may not be granted.[38]

However that unclarity is resolved, the Christian doctrine of the afterlife presents a problem for our assessment of God's moral nature for at least two reasons. First, there is the familiar question: how can it be just to condemn anyone, on whatever grounds, to eternal punishment? The evil of even the worst sin is finite. How can it deserve infinite punishment? I know what's commonly said about this: because God is infinitely good, any act contrary to his will must be infinitely evil, and hence, deserve infinite punishment. But this is question-begging in a context in which God's goodness is at issue. And the evil of an act should be judged by the harm it does, not the status of the person it offends.

Secondly, there is the question why, if God revealed himself to man through both the Hebrew Bible and the Christian scriptures, he should have sent such different messages about the afterlife in these two texts. Surely he did not change his mind about our treatment between the two different sets of

---

[37] Commenting on Job 14: 10–12, Marvin Pope writes: 'Again . . . Job expresses the standard OT view, shared by his friends. There is no afterlife worthy of the name. The torpor of the shades in the netherworld cannot be regarded as life' (1985: 107). The main exception to this generalization, Dan. 12: 1–2, is atypical of the Hebrew Bible, late, and under suspicion of showing foreign influence.

[38] I count the following passages as favoring salvation by works: Mark 10: 17 ff. Cf. Matt. 16: 27–8, 19: 16 ff., Luke 18: 18 ff. I count the following passages as favoring salvation by faith: John 3: 16, 18; John 3: 36, 5: 23–4, 14: 6, Acts 4: 8–12, 10: 43; Rom. 3: 21–6, 5: 12–21; Eph. 2: 12, 1 John 2: 22–3; 4: 3; 5: 12; 2 John 9. At Christian funerals one hears much talk of the Christian hope of immortality, as if this were an unequivocal blessing. But if Christian exclusivism is correct—and there's much scriptural evidence for it—most of God's children will not qualify for this blessing. For non-Christians who find Christianity incredible, the Christian doctrine of an afterlife, reserved for the faithful, is not good news, but a threat.

revelations. But if he didn't, why did he conceal from the people of Israel the momentous nature of the choice they faced? Wouldn't giving them false information about how he intended to treat them after death count as deceiving them about his moral nature?

The doctrine of eternal punishment is not only indefensible in itself, but also the cause of much subsequent mischief. Christianity, unlike Judaism, is a proselytizing religion. It bids us to love our neighbors as ourselves, and tells us that all our fellow human beings are our neighbors. It also tells us that there can be no greater good for a human being than to be saved, no greater evil than to be damned, and that the way to achieve salvation and avoid damnation is to have faith in Jesus. It may not be consistent about saying that faith is the one thing necessary for salvation, but it says that often enough that it will be seriously misleading about God's moral nature if this is not true.

Some Christians may hold—perhaps some skeptical theists would say this—that we don't know enough about good and evil to know what specific actions love requires of us. But that's a recent and rather dubious view. It's far more plausible to hold, and historically, I think, most Christians have held, that love requires a genuine concern for and endeavor to promote the well-being of those we love. This seems like a nice feature of Christianity, until we realize that its combination with exclusivism—with the doctrine that belief in Jesus is necessary for salvation—provides us with a seductive argument for using force if necessary, including torture and killing, to bring our fellow men to the correct faith. The prospect of achieving infinite goods and avoiding infinite evils seems to justify any amount of temporal suffering, so long as it's finite, as Pascal emphasized. Too often this best of motives has led people to employ the worst of means.[39]

In the earliest days of Christianity, when it was a persecuted minority in the Roman Empire, Christians favored religious liberty. Once they got power, once the emperor became a Christian, that changed. For centuries Christian churches which had access to political power persecuted heretics, mounted crusades, conducted inquisitions, and attempted to forcibly convert Jews, Muslims, and the indigenous peoples of the New World. When the Reformation challenged the power of Rome, the resulting wars of religion killed thousands of people. And the new Protestant Churches fought not only the Roman Church, but also other Protestant denominations. No doubt the

---

[39] Augustine seems to have been the first to develop this line of thought, though he stopped short of recommending torture and killing. See his Letters 93 and 185. For Aquinas' endorsement and extension of the argument, see his *Summa theologiae* II–II, Qu. 10–13.

religious rationales given for torturing and killing people who did not believe as the dominant Church believed were often a cover for less respectable motives. But religion was there to provide the cover. God is love, the Christians tell us. But his followers have shed a lot of blood spreading that message.[40] With this history, it would be more seemly if Christian theists directed their skepticism against the proposition that scripture is the word of God, and left alone the proposition that it is wrong to kill the innocent.

---

[40] For an illustration of how this worked in one place, see Clendinnen 2003.

Comments on 'The God of Abraham, Isaac, and Jacob'

Peter van Inwagen

I can discuss only a very few of the points raised in Ed's splendid chapter. (And I do think it's a splendid chapter: it's a splendid presentation of a certain line of argument—by far the best I've seen.) This is an uncomfortable position for me to be in because there are about ten-paragraphs-worth of things I want to say about almost every paragraph in the chapter. And yet my reply must not be ten times as long as the chapter. (It can, in fact, be only about three-tenths as long.) For example, I positively *itch* to reply at length to Ed's treatment of the story of God's command to Abraham to sacrifice Isaac, and to go on and on about what he says about the moral qualities of God as he is represented in the New Testament. But I must not scratch that itch. I am going to try to do only one thing, and that is to reconcile two propositions, both of which I accept:

At many places in the Hebrew Bible, God is represented as commanding things that are indisputably morally wrong (genocide, for example).

The Bible is, throughout, and in every passage, the inspired Word of God—of a God who is an omniscient and morally perfect being.

I cannot attempt to present a full and adequate discussion of what I mean by the words I have used to state the second proposition. But I will say this much: that proposition entails the following proposition:

God wants there to be such a thing as the Bible—that is, a set of writings that play the role that the Hebrew and Greek Scriptures have played in the history of Israel and the Church; and the wording of the various books of the Bible is (more or less) the way God wants it to be.

A more exact statement of my purpose in these comments is this: I will attempt to reconcile the first proposition with the proposition I have said the second entails. (And that very imperfectly: I cannot say nearly enough to do this adequately in these brief comments.) My attempt at reconciliation is just that: mine. I speak for no other Christian, much less for any Jew. My intention, moreover, is not to give a theologically correct account of the nature of biblical inspiration—for the simple reason that it has not been given to me to know what the true nature of biblical inspiration is. What I shall do is to tell a story about God and the Bible that I contend is a true story *for all anyone knows*—given that there is a personal God who acts in history— a story according to which both propositions are true. (That is to say, I propose to do something analogous to what students of the argument from evil call 'presenting a defense'.)

My 'defense' will make use of some ideas that are remarkably similar to the ideas contained in the following passage in Ed's paper:

This discrepancy between Moses' teachings and Ezekiel's is easy to understand if we regard the Bible as a . . . human text, which may ascribe to God different views at different times, as the people of Israel gradually develop a more adequate sense of justice. (73)

You will see that I have omitted a single word from this passage: I have dropped the word 'merely' from the phrase 'merely human text'. Whether the Bible is a *merely* human text or not, it is certainly a *human* text: every single word of it was written by human beings, each of whom was, necessarily, like Spinoza and Kant and Ed and myself, a product of a certain time and a certain culture. (The concrete humanity of the authors of the various books of the Hebrew Bible is on striking display in every page—to a much greater extent than the humanity of, say, Spinoza or Kant is displayed in the pages of their books.) And these times and cultures varied, and the world-views that they imposed on the authors of the various books of the Bible varied with them.

The Latin singular 'biblia' ('the Bible') is of course an adaptation of the Greek plural 'ta biblia'—'the books'. Leaving aside the later Christian additions to (what Christians regard as) the canon, we may speak of this collection of books (in Belloc's words, 'That great mass of Jewish folklore, poetry and traditional popular history and proverbial wisdom which we call the Old Testament') as the Jews' own story of the Covenant that, as they believed, they had entered into with God, a story told from many points of view. According to Exodus, God said to Moses:

Behold, I make a covenant. Before all your people I will do marvels, such as have not been wrought in all the earth or in any nation; and all the people among whom you are shall see the work of the Lord; for it is a terrible thing that I will do with you. (34: 10, RSV)

The Old Testament—'the Old Covenant'—as Christians call the Hebrew Bible, is the story of the 'terrible thing' God did with the Jews. It is a story of a long and painful process of straightening the crooked timber of

humanity—a process that never produced (and was never intended to produce) 'perfectly straight' people, but which produced a people who began to
be straight enough to be aware of how crooked they still were (and perhaps
more aware than was entirely good for them of how much more crooked than
they 'the Nations' were). One part of that straightening was a training in a
new morality. (And not simply the *proclamation* of a new morality. It's easy to
say, 'Now, children, I want you all to share.' *Getting* the children to share is a
more demanding task.)

Critics of the morality of the God of the Hebrew Bible rarely ask themselves
what the source of the morality from whose perspective they present their
criticism is. A few years ago, I watched with great pleasure the HBO production called 'Rome'. The final disk of the DVD version of 'Rome' includes
interviews with some of the people involved in the production of the program. In one interview, someone or other was asked in what ways he thought
the Romans were like us and unlike us. He replied that they were remarkably
like us in most ways, but that there was one way in which they were very
different from us: in their extreme brutality—in both their willingness to
commit brutal acts and in their indifference to the pervasive, entrenched
brutality of their world. When he was asked whether he could explain why
we and the Romans were so different in this respect, he did not quite answer
by saying 'Christianity is what made the difference'—I don't think he could
have brought himself to say that—but he did identify 'Judaeo-Christian
morality' as the source of the difference. And that was a very good answer.
The morality of almost everyone in Western Europe and the anglophone
countries today (if that person is not a criminal or a sociopath) is either the
morality that the Hebrew Bible was tending toward or some revised, edited
version of that morality. Almost every atheist (in Western Europe and the
anglophone countries), however committed he or she may be to atheism,
accepts some modified version of what Judaeo-Christian morality teaches
about how human beings ought to treat other human beings. And even the
modifications are generally achieved by using one part of that morality to
attack some other part. (For example, by attempting to turn the principle
'don't make other people unhappy' against Judaeo-Christian sexual morality.)

The morality to which critics of the moral character of the God of the Bible
appeal is a gift to the world from Israel and the Church and is by no means
self-evident. I don't think that many missionaries have heard anything resem-
bling the following from those whom they were attempting to convert: 'Hey—
it says here, "But of the cities of these people, which the Lord thy God doth
give thee for an inheritance, thou shalt save alive nothing that breatheth . . .
thou shalt utterly destroy them." That's *awful*. How can you expect us to
worship such a God?' And the reason they haven't heard that is that most

people in most times and at most places would see nothing but good sense in that command. Most people have taken it for granted that when a tribe or nation moves into new territory it will kill those of the previous inhabitants that it does not enslave. That's what people do—the Old Common Morality says—and they'd be crazy to do otherwise. And the authors of Deuteronomy saw nothing wrong with that policy, either. Whether they lived during the reign of King Josiah or during the Exile, whether they were editing and expanding older written material with Mosaic roots or composing the book with no sources but oral tradition (and their own political interests), they didn't hesitate to represent God as commanding what we call genocide because they were typical human beings, and typical human beings see nothing wrong with genocide. After all, that's what the authors of Deuteronomy would have commanded if *they* had been God.

The Hebrew Bible, the multi-perspectival history of the Covenant, is, as I have said, a human document, or a little library of human documents. It is, among other things, a history of a people 'gradually developing a more adequate sense of justice'. It is, among other things, the story of a people being trained in a new and unobvious morality. It is a history of a gradual straightening of crooked timber under the hand of a master joiner. It presents readers of the Bible with 'snapshots' of people at various stages in the straightening process: that's the kind of history it is, and it's that kind of history because that's the kind of history God wanted it to be.

'But then how can we turn to the Bible for moral guidance?' Well, if you turn to the Bible for moral guidance, you mustn't treat it as an essay intended to present a system of morals, as a book like Spinoza's *Ethic* or *The Critique of Practical Reason*. Spinoza and Kant could influence the thoughts and beliefs of their readers only by saying things, only by putting forward propositions and arguments for those readers to consider. God (who is in one sense the author of the Bible) is under no such limitation. He can reach into you and touch your heart and guide your thoughts. And—the Church's promise is—he will do this when you read the Bible. He will be present within you and will guide you through its pages, highlighting this passage, awakening your critical capacities when you read that one, creating in your mind a sense that 'this passage is not addressed to my condition' when you read a third. He will, moreover, guide you to passages he particularly wants you to read: *tolle lege*. And, if you encounter difficulties in the text, he will lead you to people—the Doctors of the Church or your Aunt Alice—who will help you to resolve them.

All this is true *provided* you are willing to be transformed by submitting yourself to the will of God. If you come to the Bible with preconceived moral notions (say, that slavery is morally permissible) looking for 'proof texts', you will not only get no moral truth out of it, but you will almost certainly do yourself positive moral harm. But if you have submitted yourself to God's will and if you read—say—that God has commanded that the children be punished for the sins of the fathers, your reaction will be along these lines: 'Yes, that's what seemed self-evidently true to the Hebrews once, that it was right to punish the children for the sins of the fathers, and that that was therefore what God would have told their ancestors to do; with God's help, we now know better. And their descendants came to know better. This was the mindset that God was leading the Hebrews out of. This is what—with God's help—the author of Ezekiel knew that the authors of the Pentateuch did not know.'

'Well, why didn't God just *tell* the Hebrews that it was wrong to behave in certain ways?—that genocide, for example, was just wrong? Why didn't God, instead of *guiding* them to a new and better morality, just *tell them at the outset* what that "better" morality was?' Well, perhaps he did—and perhaps he didn't. I don't know. I wasn't there. And neither were the authors of Deuteronomy and Joshua (I mean the writers responsible for the final wording of those books). But think about the question using this model. You are a schoolteacher who is renowned for having taught the large, strong children in your class not to bully the small, weak ones. Did you begin by *telling* the large, strong ones not to bully the small, weak ones—or by asking them how *they'd* like to be the victims of bullying? Maybe you did and maybe you didn't. But if you did, it didn't do much good, not by itself. If you did, your *saying* things to them was only a very small part of your success in getting them to stop their bullying.

'But if God is a morally perfect being, why did he create human beings in such a way that one of their cultures could be made a little better than the (appalling) moral norm only by being subjected to centuries of painful moral training?' That's not our topic. That's the problem of evil, or one strand of it. Here I will remark only that the question rests on a false presupposition, one that is analogous to the false presupposition of the question, 'If the Athenians were such wonderful architects, why did they make the Parthenon without any roof?'

'Why has God presented the story of the Covenant from many incompatible points of view—including points of view that incorporate horrible (if typically human) moral error? Why didn't he produce a nice coherent history, and one that represents a morally correct point of view throughout?' I confess I don't know. But I can guess, and I think that my guess is true—or an important part of the truth—for all anyone knows. Since I'm presenting only a 'defense', a guess that is right for all anyone knows is as good for my purposes as the no doubt unknowable truth.

The Bible has been a remarkably effective document—as believing Jews and Christians judge effectiveness. As Professor Dawkins might say, the Bible (or the set of religious practices grounded in the belief that that document is the Word of God) has been a very efficient 'meme', a meme that—history demonstrates—is very good at persisting through historical time and spreading itself about in geographical space. That's something that missionaries know. The Bible has not been translated into more languages than any other book *only* because missionary societies believe it to be the inspired word of God; another important part of the explanation is that missionaries know from experience that the Bible is one of their most effective tools. They know that those to whom they preach 'take to it' with very little prompting or preparation. They know that it captures their attention. They know that people of most cultures will listen to the words of the cloud of witnesses who speak to them across the millennia from its pages. And quite possibly—who is in a position to deny this?—a version of, or a replacement for, the Bible that a secular reader of our culture would find more appealing (or less appalling) than the actual Bible would have little meaning for the peoples of most times and most cultures.

Reply to van Inwagen

Edwin Curley

I thank Peter for the compliment he paid me when he said my chapter is the best presentation he's seen of a certain line of argument. It's a slightly ambiguous compliment, perhaps; but I take it as a compliment, and I return the compliment. He's made the best reply to that line of argument that I've seen. I have, however, had some problems understanding precisely what his reply is. So in my response I'll restate my argument in a way designed to make our agreements and disagreements more perspicuous, relying partly on conversations we had at the conference after our session and subsequent email exchanges.

Think of my argument as a *reductio ad absurdum* which starts from the following propositions:

1. God is a supremely perfect being, who possesses all perfections, including moral perfection.
2. The Bible is the inspired word of God.
3. In many places the Bible represents God as authorizing—that is, either commanding or giving permission for—conduct which is clearly morally wrong.

The first two propositions are standard assumptions of contemporary Christian theism. Peter explicitly accepts (2), saying that the Bible is, *throughout, and in every passage*, the inspired Word of God. He doesn't say explicitly that God possesses *all* perfections, but I expect that he would also accept (1). He does say that God is omniscient and morally perfect. Perhaps that's all I need.

In my chapter I argued at some length for proposition (3). In his comments Peter seemed to grant that (3) is true, though in conversation after our session he did express some reservations about that concession. I'll come to those reservations later, but for now simply note that he does not attempt to cast doubt on the wrongness of genocide, or child sacrifice, or slavery, or rape. That seems to me all to the good.

Now I had thought: if (1) and (2) are true, if the Bible is the inspired word of a supremely perfect God, it must follow that

4. The Bible does not seriously misrepresent God's moral nature by repeat-edly portraying him as authorizing conduct he did not authorize.

And I imagined that Peter would accept this proposition also. In his comments he says it follows from the divine inspiration of the Bible that

... the wording of the various books of the Bible is (*more or less*) the way God wants it to be. (79)

The phrase I've italicized does allow for some distortion of God's revelation by the humans who transmitted it; but the passage quoted looks like a concession of (4). Could an omniscient and morally perfect being be even 'more or less' satisfied with the wording of a book he inspired—think it 'good enough'—if it seriously misrepresented his moral nature? I thought not, but this is an issue to which we shall have to return.

If (3) and (4) are true—if the Bible repeatedly represents God as authoriz-ing conduct which is clearly morally wrong, and if it doesn't seriously misrepresent God's moral nature by repeatedly portraying him as authorizing conduct he didn't authorize—it follows that

5. God did repeatedly authorize conduct which was clearly morally wrong.

But that, I thought, would be incompatible with God's moral perfection. I thought it followed from (1) that

6. God would never authorize conduct which is clearly morally wrong.

(6) contradicts (5). If we are to avoid this contradiction, we must hold that there is a mistake somewhere in this reasoning, either in the initial assump-tions or in one of the inferences made from those assumptions.

I thought—and continue to think—that the weakest link in the argument is the assumption that the Bible is the inspired word of God. But I've had some difficulty deciding what Peter would think is wrong with the argument. Since he seemed willing, in his comments, to grant (3), it seemed to me that he must either reject the inference of (4) from (1) and (2), or the inference of (6) from (1). When I initially replied to his comments at the conference, I guessed he would accept (4) and (5), and reject (6). He would say that, in spite of his moral perfection, God did repeatedly authorize conduct which is clearly morally wrong. That seemed to me a pretty unattractive position, but I thought that was what he was committed to.

I was wrong. After our session Peter told me that he would accept (6), and reject (4) and (5), granting that the Bible does seriously misrepresent God's moral nature by repeatedly portraying him as authorizing conduct he did not authorize. And perhaps—in the absence of a disambiguation he said it required—he would also reject (3). It wasn't that he wanted to question the wrongness of child sacrifice, genocide, slavery, rape, and the other acts God is represented as authorizing. But he did think the notion of representation was ambiguous. In what follows I summarize what I take his position to be.

Peter does not accept much of modern biblical scholarship. But he does accept this much: the authors or editors who were responsible for putting the books of the Bible into the form in which we have them were working at a date much later than that of the events their narratives describe; in part, no doubt, they were seriously trying to tell the history of their people as well as they could, given the limitations of their sources; but they were doing so without much evidence that a modern historian would regard as reliable, and without a modern historian's scruples about evidence; in part they may simply have been passing on stories which had come down to them, perhaps from earlier writers, perhaps from an oral tradition, without necessarily intending to present those stories as historically accurate;[1] and in part, they may also have taken the liberty of making some things up, simply because they thought this was how things must have happened.

Although Peter takes the Bible to be divinely inspired, he does not think it is an accurate account of the history of the people of Israel, or even of God's dealings with his people. The most divine inspiration entails is that at certain stages of their history the people *thought* God had dealt with them in the way their sacred books said he had. It's accurate as a representation of their representations of God, but not as a representation of the way God actually acted. The fact that God, an omniscient and morally perfect being, inspired a Bible in which he is represented as authorizing certain kinds of conduct, is no guarantee that he did authorize such conduct.

Peter's idea is that in the Hebrew Bible God is showing us the gradual development, under his guidance, of a new morality among the Jews—and he is doing this by representing successive stages in the development of their moral consciousness. Although his moral perfection entails that he would not have *authorized* conduct of the kinds I discussed in my chapter, it does not entail that he would not have *allowed people to think he had authorized* such conduct. For all we know, this might have suited his purposes. It's possible that he thought the timber of humanity so crooked that the only way—or perhaps, the best way—but at least a morally acceptable way—to straighten it

---

[1] This might, for example, be suggested by such phenomena as the two versions of the creation story we find in Genesis 1–3, or the two versions of a story in which Abraham, visiting a foreign country, attempts to pass his wife off as his sister (in Gen. 12 and 20).

would be to apparently accept the morality most people find natural, and then gradually wean them away from that. If people typically see nothing wrong with genocide, there's no point in simply telling them that genocide is wrong. Let them think for a while that it is right. Then reach into them, touch their hearts, and guide their thoughts, till they see that the way they ought to act is often different from the way the Bible teaches them to act.

I think this is a fair summary of Peter's position. He definitely holds that God did not authorize all the kinds of conduct the biblical narratives represent him as authorizing. And he definitely holds that if we take the divine inspiration of the Bible to guarantee its accuracy in such matters, we are making a mistake. I suppose he would grant that for centuries readers of the Bible have made that mistake. So over the course of history God's revealed word has misled most of its readers about his moral nature. He would insist that *we cannot know* why God would have allowed this to happen. But we can tell a story about how such a deception *might* have played a legitimate role in our moral education, a story which has the virtue of being, if not true, then at least not demonstrably false. The epistemic possibility that this story is true allows us to see that the three propositions with which we started are consistent. We cannot infer from God's moral perfection and his inspiration of the Bible that he would not permit the authors whom he inspired to mislead us about what he wanted us to do.

I do not know whether Peter's co-religionists will welcome this defense of God's honor. They might think that there is no significant moral difference between authorizing bad conduct and encouraging a general belief that you have authorized bad conduct. They might also think that whatever else the idea of divine inspiration might imply, it ought at least to imply that God would not mislead us about how he wants us to behave. They might think that Peter's 'just-so story' assumes limitations on God's nature inconsistent with his theology. An omnipotent God does not, they might think, have to choose between merely proclaiming a new morality and accepting the old morality provisionally, as a means of getting us to see its wrongness. Human teachers face severe limitations on their power to impart moral lessons to their students. But God has resources human teachers don't have—offers of wonderful rewards, and threats of horrible punishments—all backed by an unfailing ability to know whether his students have transgressed. If the biblical narrative has any credibility at all, God does not think making these offers and threats interferes with human freedom.

But these are criticisms I should leave for Peter's co-religionists to make, if they wish to. The right thing for me to do, I think, is to accept gratefully the concession he has made. Once you grant that a text inspired by God may not be a reliable source of moral guidance, that scripture might frequently mislead us about the kinds of conduct a morally perfect being would authorize, then the whole idea of the Bible as a divinely inspired text becomes much less dangerous. What concerns non-believers most about the Christian belief that their scriptures are divinely inspired is the apparent implication that, as the word of a morally perfect being, its commands and prohibitions deserve unconditional obedience. If Peter's understanding of divine inspiration became general, I think it would diminish the moral authority of scripture. In some respects that might be unfortunate. Sometimes the Christian scriptures have very good things to say. But in other respects it would be a blessing. In the enterprise of encouraging a critical attitude towards the teachings of scripture, I seem to have found an unexpected ally in my commentator.

Unfortunately, I cannot end this response on such an agreeable note. Peter claims that 'the morality to which critics of the moral character of the God of the Bible appeal is a gift to the world from Israel and the Church', as if we in the Western tradition had learned nothing about morality from the ancient Greeks and Romans, and as if many of the better parts of Judaeo-Christian morality had not been developed independently in other traditions. Peter may believe that those of us who criticize biblical morality got all our moral insights from the biblical tradition. I can't.

REFERENCES

Adams, Robert. 1987. *The Virtue of Faith.* Oxford: Oxford University Press.

——1999. *Finite and Infinite Goods: A Framework for Ethics.* Oxford: Oxford University Press.

Bergmann, Michael. 2001. 'Skeptical Theism and Rowe's New Evidential Argument from Evil', *Noûs*, 35: 278–96.

Brown, Peter. 2000. *Augustine of Hippo: A Biography,* new edn. Berkeley and Los Angeles: University of California Press.

Clendinnen, Inga. 2003. *Ambivalent Conquests: Maya and Spaniard in Yucatan, 1517–1570,* 2nd edn. Cambridge: Cambridge University Press.

Curley, Edwin. 2002. 'Maimonides, Spinoza and the Book of Job', in Heidi Ravven and Lenn Goodman (eds.), *Jewish Themes in Spinoza's Philosophy.* Albany, NY: SUNY Press.

——2004. 'The Covenant with God in Hobbes' *Leviathan*', in Tom Sorell and Luc Foisneau (eds.), *Leviathan after 350 Years.* Oxford: Clarendon Press.

NJPS. 1999. *NJPS Hebrew–English Tanakh: The Traditional Hebrew Text and the New JPS translation,* 2nd edn. Philadelphia: The Jewish Publication Society.

Kant, Immanuel. 1996. *Conflict of the Faculties,* in *Religion and Rational Theology,* ed. Allen Wood and George di Giovanni. Cambridge: Cambridge University Press.

Kugel, James. 2007. *How to Read the Bible: A Guide to Scripture, Then and Now.* New York: Free Press/Simon and Schuster.

Levenson, Jon. 1995. *The Death and Resurrection of the Beloved Son: The Transformation of Child Sacrifice in Judaism and Christianity.* New Haven: Yale University Press.

Lewis, David. 2007. 'Divine Evil', in Louise Antony (ed.), *Philosophers without Gods.* Oxford: Oxford University Press, 231–42.

Metzger, Bruce, and Murphy, Roland (eds.). 1991. *New Oxford Annotated Bible.* Oxford: Oxford University Press.

Morriston, Wes. 2009. 'What if God Commanded Something Terrible? A Worry for Divine-Command Metaethics', *Religious Studies,* 45: 1–19.

Orlinsky, Harry. 1974. *Essays in Biblical Culture and Bible Translation.* New York: Ktav.

Plantinga, Alvin. 2000. *Warranted Christian Belief.* Oxford: Oxford University Press.

Pope, Marvin. 1985. *Job: A New Translation, with Introduction and Commentary.* New Haven: Anchor Bible.

Swinburne, Richard. 1992. *Revelation: From Metaphor to Analogy.* Oxford: Clarendon Press.

——1993. *The Coherence of Theism,* rev. edn. Oxford: Clarendon Press.

——2007. *Revelation: From Metaphor to Analogy.* 2nd edn. Oxford: Oxford University Press.

Wright, Robert. 2009. *The Evolution of God.* Boston: Little, Brown.

3

Satanic Verses:

Moral Chaos in Holy Writ

Evan Fales

According to tradition, we may know moral truths in two ways: by reason and by faith. Reason teaches the natural law, a moral code ordained by God who made us rational; faith apprehends God's will through revelation. God evidently wished to make double-sure that the recipients of His image would know right from wrong. The moral law is a deliverance of His essentially impeccable reason. Thereby the medieval theologians solved the Euthyphro dilemma by going between its horns: the moral law is neither sovereign over God nor an arbitrary creation of his will. It lies at the heart of God's very essence.

1. GETTING A LOCK ON REVELATION

John Locke must have had this tradition in mind when he remarked that one test of the genuineness of revelation is whether it conforms to the moral law. Locke's remark is nevertheless surprising, for as we will see, it, and the tradition that informs it, run hard up against a barrier Locke must have been aware of, a barrier that forces Christians and Jews, as disciples of the Book, apparently to grasp one horn of the Euthyphro dilemma, namely divine command theory.

Writing on faith and reason, Locke enunciates several principles that constrain the reach of faith. Locke (like Aquinas before him) understands faith as trusting someone's testimony—in particular God's testimony—on matters not otherwise knowable (Locke 1959: bk. IV, ch. XVIII, p. 416).

Thanks are owed to Michael Bergmann, Ed Curley, Wes Morriston, and Michael Rea for valuable advice.

Faith...is the assent to any proposition, not thus made out by the deductions of reason, but upon the credit of the proposer, as coming from God, in some extraordinary way of communication. This way of discovering truths to men, we call *revelation*.

Locke sees a problem here. Receiving testimony from other people, we must exercise a caution consistent with the recognition that they are not always competent or sincere. We are ordinarily able to identify those others and, if the testimony be doubtful, examine their credentials. In revelatory experiences, the credentials of the original source, if divine, are impeccable. But the source of the revelation is not so easily identified. Was that still, small voice in the night God? Or the devil? Or whisperings of an overheated imagination? Locke's design is to show that certain principles constrain our judgments of authenticity. The guiding thought is that to be credible, a revelation must have an identifiable content that must not overthrow 'sense and reason'.

Now this matters to Locke because the original recipients of a revelation, presumably taught by God, could have no better assurance (either from independent evidence for it or knowledge that it came from God) than could be afforded by their use of sense and reason. To privilege their cognitive faculties over our own (having no reason to suppose ours defective) would be to call radically into question the reliability of ours, and thus to abandon hope that we can reach the truth in such matters (or indeed any knowledge at all).

Locke is relying upon the principle that nothing gives the early followers of Jesus authority in doctrinal matters—sufficient authority to subvert our own fundamental sources of justification—save authority conferred by God Himself. But how to determine whether God has spoken? That requires evidence; and here no one has any recourse but to her natural faculties. There is no more damning evidence than that the content of a revelation be epistemically refractory.[1] Such a 'revelation' undermines its own authority.

How we can tell that a *non*-refractory revelation is genuine? Regarding that, Locke's appeal is traditional: we look to signs; and he goes on to argue that, by their number and quality, the miracles recorded in the New Testament secure the unique place of the gospels as authoritative revelation (Locke 2000: 114–17).

In making that appeal within the constraints of his epistemic criteria, Locke marches straight down a path that arrives at Hume's reflections on testimonial evidence for miracles. But that's not the only irony in Locke's argument. For, as mentioned, Locke invokes also a *moral* criterion in distinguishing revelatory wheat from chaff. No revelation

---

[1] One such case, for Locke, was the doctrine of the real presence, which (I presume) Locke took to contradict sense because the wafer has no sensible properties suggesting the body of Christ, and reason because one and the same body could not be fully present in many wafers at the same time.

can be looked on to be divine, that delivers any thing derogating from the honour of the one, only, true, invisible God or inconsistent with natural religion and the rules of morality: because God having discovered to men the unity and majesty of his eternal godhead, and the truths of natural religion and morality, by the light of reason, he cannot be supposed to back the contrary by revelation; for that would be to destroy the evidence and the use of reason, without which men cannot be able to distinguish divine revelation from diabolical imposture. (Locke 2000: 118)

That brings us, however, to the barrier I mentioned above.

2. STONE

It seems, on its face, that scripture *does* teach morally repugnant things about God. There are, for starters, legal statutes whose rigors should cause even the most stout-hearted moralist to blanch. These include strict proscriptions against male homosexuality, fornication and adultery, witchcraft, and filial impiety. The penalty was execution by stoning.[2]

I confess some uncertainty respecting the immorality of witchcraft; still, infidelity (whether marital or not) is a severe transgression, almost always a reprehensible violation of trust.[3] But death by stoning? And such a penalty for cursing one's parents and homosexual acts—indeed, *any* penalty for the latter—is morally indefensible.

Suppose one essayed a defense; how might it go? One line is to emphasize how much *better*—more humane—the Jewish Law allegedly was than the laws of contemporary ancient Near Eastern societies. That argument is historically suspect, if only because documentary evidence is so sparse. But it's infirm in any case. Why should a divinely guided Israel be merely *better* than its neighbors? Why, say, should it countenance slavery—even if a more *humane* form of slavery?

A second argument suggests that God had to teach an Israel so fallen, so influenced by immoral practices of surrounding cultures, that God had no choice but to 'tone down' His moral demands. But that does not ring true to YHWH's personality at all. What's more, it makes Him out to be a compromiser (or relativist?), at least pragmatically. Besides, Israel went to extraordinary lengths to separate itself, socially and culturally, from tribal neighbors.[4]

---

[2] For sexual codes see Lev. 20: 10–11 and Deut. 22: 13–14; for wizardry, Lev. 20: 27.

[3] Except perhaps when—as seems commonly enough to have been the case (cf. Gen. 29: 16–27; Deut. 22: 28–9; Josh. 15: 16–18; Judges 21)—marriage was a coerced and loveless affair.

[4] Intermarriage was forbidden. Kasrut restrictions (e.g. Lev. 11; Exod. 34: 26, Deut. 14: 21) prevented the sharing of meals. And see Lev. 18.

Could it be, nevertheless, that God's harsher laws were justified _in the circumstances_—that cultural insensitivities blind _us_ to good reasons for God's dispensation for Israel? That's a hard case to make.[5] Indeed, it's not difficult to specify behaviors that are immoral no matter the cultural context. We can agree, surely, that rape and genocide are such acts. But then so is capital punishment for homosexuality, adultery, and disrespect for parents. Indeed, of the Ten Commandments, six carry the death penalty for infraction—including the making of graven images.[6] And the punishments with which God threatens Israel for defection from this stringent covenant are too grotesque to bear enumeration.[7]

Of course, maybe Israel was just _mistaken_ in thinking God to have commanded these things. Maybe they were not only a stiff-necked people, but hard of hearing as well. Perhaps God didn't intend Israel to follow these morally rebarbative statutes after all. That's an eminently reasonable suggestion. But the cost of accepting it to the inspirational integrity of the Tanak is heavy. Wouldn't God have made clear to Moses His will in _these_ matters—considering especially all the grief Israel suffered for straying, at least in its self-understanding, from the Law? If the Bible isn't to be trusted concerning the Law, what confidence are we to repose in it?[8]

3. TERROR TIME

The indigestible parts of the Law are not the only apologetical nightmare presented by the Bible. There is also a long list of particular actions allegedly accepted, commanded, or done by God, that appear violently immoral. I cannot even begin to catalogue the 'horrors', as I shall call them, of the NT, to say nothing of the Old, which implicates God in (among other things) rape, incest, genocide, child sacrifice, and the killing of the innocent to punish

---

[5] Theists (including ancient Israelites) regularly have no compunctions about accusing pagan societies of immorality, without regard to 'mitigating circumstances'.

[6] Commandments 1–4, 6, and 7: cf. Exod. 22: 20, Deut. 13: 1–11, 2 Chron. 15: 13 for 1, Exod. 32: 27 for 2, Lev. 24: 16 for 3, Exod. 31: 14–15, 35: 2 for 4, Exod. 21: 12, Lev. 24: 17 for 6, and Lev. 20: 10, Deut. 5: 18 for 7). For commandments 5 and 8, it was death in certain cases (see Lev. 20: 9, Matt. 15: 4, and Deut. 21: 18 for 5; Exod. 21: 16 for 8).

[7] Deut. 28: 17–68, Lev. 26: 14–39.

[8] At the cost of loosening our grip on just what moral injunctions God _does_ command, we can hold the Laws to be subject to interpretation. Unsurprisingly, there is within Judaism a long halachic tradition—no doubt as ancient as the laws themselves—of doing exactly that. The complexities go far beyond any hope of proper discussion here. But you can't turn a sow's ear into a silk purse.

the guilty.[9] In the New, Jesus stridently opposes family unity, and God kills a man and wife for cheating on a promised gift to the Church.[10]

A sensible reading of the Tanakic genocidal texts is that they reflect no divine mandates, but rather the convenient rationalizations of a nascent, insurgent Israelite nation, seeking to define itself and its place in history through campaigns of conquest—seeking, as men always have, power, wealth, and territory. This is plausible: what better justification than to cloak perfidy in the mantle of divine approval? Why should we expect from a repeatedly wayward Israel anything less? But what are the consequences? If that is plausible, surely it is also plausible that Israel's self-understanding—inherited by Christianity[11]—as a people specially chosen by God, is equally a self-justifying rationalization, one available to defend virtually any transgression, so long as directed against outsiders.

Clearly, a proper discussion of the horrors would have to tackle some hard, and complex, questions of interpretation of relevant texts: questions about authorship, date of composition, redaction history, language, *sitz im Leben*, etc.—and require discussion within the larger context in which the passages appear. That would entail nothing less than a book—or several; here, I am unavoidably forced to pluck examples from the text, largely ignoring hermeneutical issues. Still, it is hard to see how interpretive maneuvers can remove

---

[9] *Rape*: arguably Gen. 30: 3, 30: 9–18; Deut. 20: 10–14, 21: 10–14, 22: 28–9; Num. 31; the extraordinary story at Judges 19: 22–21: 25; 2 Sam. 12: 11–14. *Incest*: Gen. 4: 17, 5: 6, 19: 32–6, 20: 11–12. *Killing of the innocent*: numerous cases, e.g. plagues sent as punishment for an individual's sins. Three dramatic examples are Exod. 7: 14–11, 2 Sam. 12: 7–20, and 24 (cf. Gen. 13: 16 and esp. Exod. 30: 11–16). The Exodus story implies that the Egyptians *would have been spared*, but for the fact that God 'hardened Pharaoh's heart' so that His 'wonders may be multiplied in the land of Egypt' (11: 9). *Child sacrifice*: most transfixing, the *Akedah*, Gen. 22. This story must be understood in the light of the Passover story; see Exod. 13: 13–16 and 22: 29. More difficult is the sacrifice of Jepthah's daughter, Judg. 11 (and cf. 2 Kgs. 3: 27; also Lev. 27: 28). Child sacrifice appears to be proscribed by Lev. 18: 21, 20: 1–5; Deut. 12: 31 (and cf. Jer. 7: 30–3, 32: 35), but there are complications. As standardly translated, these passages proscribe sacrifices to Molech, god of Ammon. But the 'Molech' translation is disputed. Levenson (1993: ch. 2) supports it; Stager and Wolff (1984: 31–51) have challenged it, arguing that the sacrifices buried in the Tophet were offered to YHWH. Either way, Judges 11 remains a fishbone stuck in the exegete's throat. More endearing, perhaps, are God's human frailties, such as a short fuse that on occasion needs the steadying hand of human reason to calm it; see e.g. Gen. 18: 20–33; Exod. 32: 10–14.

[10] For anti-family sentiments, see especially Matt. 8: 21–2 and 10: 34 and Luke 14: 25; other passages include Matt. 12: 46–50/Luke 8: 19–21 and John 2: 4. Other morally problematic teachings include Luke 19: 27 and Matt. 5: 39, which raises difficult questions, including apparent incompatibility with Matt. 21: 12–13; and Luke 13: 1–5 and John 9: 1–3 (cf. Job 42: 7, Isa. 45: 7, Lam. 3: 38, and Amos 3: 6).

[11] Christianity was, much more than Judaism, a proselytizing, 'universal' religion, but equally one in which only the saved are justified (Rom. 8: 30).

the stench of moral outrage without sacrificing much that Christians typically hold dear.

To indicate the sort of question we face, let me indulge, with all due apologies, in a modern-day fantasy to help fix intuitions. The scene is contemporary America. Mormons, ever eager to bring others into the fold, decide to use their married women to engineer a hostile but wily religious takeover of Southern Baptists. Mormon women being cleverly seductive, and Baptist men being, as they regularly claim, prone to sins of the flesh, the plot begins to succeed. And (as Baptists tell the tale) the Lord's response is, first, to wipe out 24,000 Baptists by visiting upon them a rabies epidemic; and second, to incite the remaining Baptists to rise up and engage in wholesale slaughter of the Mormons, reserving only their virgin daughters to be raised as breeding stock. What judgment shall we render? Were the story true, what should we think of the Baptists' Lord? And if false, what would it nevertheless tell us about the moral sensibilities of Baptists, or the likelihood that they understand the will of a morally perfect God?

With these considerations in mind, let's turn to the slaughter of the Midianites, recounted in Num. 25 and 31. They provide Moses with safe harbor when, having killed a man, he flees Egypt. Jethro, Midian's priest, gives Moses his daughter Zipporah in marriage. But when Israel encamps with them en route to Canaan, it's held against the Midianites that their comely maidens begin dating good Jewish boys, thereby apparently fueling divided religious loyalties (between YHWH and Baal of Peor). It's hard to tell whether the more serious sin is miscegenation or its alleged consequence, apostasy.[12] The immediate result is bloodshed,[13] and a plague that kills 24,000 Israelites. That is not revenge enough: God ultimately orders the slaughter of all Midianites except—with palpable irony—the Midianite maidens, who are to be taken as concubines:[14]

---

[12] On the sin of miscegenation, see Kugel (2007: chapter on Dinah), and Num. 12, Gen. 34: 25–9, Deut. 20: 10–14, Deut. 7: 3–6 and Gen. 24: 1 and 28: 1.

[13] YHWH orders Moses to slaughter all Jewish apostates. When Zimri, a Jewish lad, shows up at the tent of the meeting with his Midianite lassie Cozbi, Pinehas, a Jewish stalwart, fetches his spear and runs both of them through (Num. 25). According to ancient legend, Pinehas never dies. He resurfaces, however, several centuries later as the prophet Elijah (Kugel 2007: 533–5). Elijah also knew a thing or two about chastisement, judging by the actions of his disciple and 'doppelganger' Elisha, directly upon inheriting Elijah's mantle: when some boys make the mistake of inciting him (calling him a 'baldhead'), he summons a pair of she-bears, which 'tare' (KJV) forty-two of the boys (2 Kgs. 2: 23–4). As anyone, I'm sure, who has been torn by a bear and lived to tell about it can testify, this is not an experience easily outdone in the chastisement department. And that's an ordinary bear—not a she-bear inspired by the Holy Ghost.

[14] Judg. 6: 11 appears to contradict the Numbers account; there the Midianites not only still exist, but are strong enough to offer a severe threat to Israel. But historicity is irrelevant. My

They warred against Midian, as the Lord commanded Moses, and slew every male . . . And the people of Israel took captive the women of Midian and their little ones . . . and all their cities . . . they burned with fire. . . . Moses said to them, 'Have you let all the women live? Behold, these caused the people of Israel, by the counsel of Balaam, to act treacherously against the Lord in the matter of Peor, and so the plague came upon the congregation of the Lord. Now, therefore, kill every male among the little ones, and kill every woman who has known man by lying with him. But all the young girls who have not known man by lying with him, keep alive for yourselves. (Num. 31: 7–18)

Let us pray.[15]

It's hard to know what to make of such morally horrific depictions of Yahweh, with which many books of the Tanak are saturated. I cannot conceive of any defensible apologetic strategy that exonerates Yahweh, short of denial that these stories, and presumably by extension much of the context in which they are imbedded, fall short of divine inspiration.[16]

---

point concerns what the story has to teach us about ancient Israel's understanding of its god's moral character. In fact the Pinehas precedent has lived on. In 1984, talk-show host Alan Berg of Denver (ironically in part because he was Jewish) was assassinated by the Pinehas Priesthood, a group of Christian Identity thugs who modeled their zeal upon that of Pinehas of old.

[15] She is 14 years old. She has, perhaps, laughing eyes and a cheerful heart. Astonished, she watches the stranger slaughter her father, then her mother and her little brother. He sheathes his bloodied sword. Then he unsheathes . . . May Baal-Peor, the god of Midian, have mercy upon you, my child.

Might some comfort be derived from Deut. 21:10–11? Suppose, contrary to all expectations, every soldier knew, and religiously observed, the commandment to keep the woman captive for a month and only then to take her sexually (no mention, conveniently, of the woman's consent; only of the man's 'delight'). Will Christians permit themselves a collective sigh of relief?

And so, purity of worship, if not purity of bloodline, was for a time restored to Israel. At what price? Look into the eyes of the daughters of Midian, and you will see no balm in Gilead that can heal their wounds.

[16] There is nevertheless no dearth of Christian attempts at justification. On the Midianites, see, e.g., the proposals of apologist Glenn Miller (2001), who suggests that the Israelite action against Midian was provoked by a devious plot to have Midianite wives seduce Israelite men, and so effect apostasy. Moreover, Israel spared only *really small* Midianite girls, to be raised as their own and used to replace the sizeable population lost to the plague.

Let's be generous and call Miller's effort an exercise in creative hermeneutics. The irony is that it utterly fails to fulfill its mission. Imagine that his fantasy is correct: the Midianites viciously plotted to use their women to subvert Israel's religion. *Would that justify Yahweh's response?* Return to my Mormon/Baptist fantasy. Does it help the case if, à la Miller but not the Numbers text, the Lord allowed only the sparing of their 5-year-old daughters, to be raised as breeding stock? Is this Miller's idea of a just and fair response?

The irony is compounded by the significant evidence in the Tanak of Yahweh's original home having been in the region of Midian—and of Moses first having learned to worship him there. Yahweh may originally have been a Midianite god. (The memory appears in some of the most ancient poetry of the Tanak; see Deut. 33: 2, Judg. 5: 4–5, Hab. 3: 3, Ps. 68: 8–9; and see Cross 1973: 86 n. 17 and Kugel 2007: 424–8 for a discussion of the evidence. Scholars recognized the implications already in the nineteenth century.)

It won't do at all to suggest that, as is likely, the genocidal invasion of Canaan didn't really occur with such ferocity and success. For the attribution of the genocidal commandments to Yahweh betokens a religious sensibility impossible to square with the view that Israel was in intimate and comprehending concourse with an impeccable god. If they were not, *even on matters as critical as this*, what are we to think of their other theological claims? And why, *knowing as He must have*, what calamitous mischief later-day Jews and Christians would justify by citing such passages[17] (to say nothing of the *mea culpa* of Mt. 27:25, also historically doubtful); why would a loving God permit such language to be preserved for posterity in Holy Writ?

Richard Swinburne defends adoption of the Tanak into Christian canon by the early Fathers on the grounds that, troubled as they were by these things, they found figurative interpretations of the offending passages. But this, besides significantly oversimplifying early Christian attitudes, is irrelevant. Even granting (as I do not) that by understanding the horrors of the Tanak allegorically,[18] the early Church was able to wash its hands of moral complicity, there remains the point that these passages (also ones from the NT) have been used, with effect and color of reason, to justify slavery, crusades, pogroms, witch-hunts, the treatment of women and children as near-chattel, and much other evil. Any reasonably astute human being could have foreseen this. So, therefore, could God have.

One snare that bedevils the apologete who takes the stories of Israel's genocidal warfare against not only Midian but most of the tribes of Canaan more or less at face value is loss of moral bearings. To take just one modern example,[19] consider William Craig's response to the difficulties posed by the

---

One of the liabilities of the strategy Miller adopts is that it seduces Christians into abandoning their moral compass entirely in the very process of trying to rescue Yahweh's. There is some irony therefore in the fact that Miller's tactic forces him tacitly to appeal to a moral standard, by which to judge an interpretation, that is independent of scripture. Even if scripture contains morally congenial commandments, the exegete has antecedently to determine which passages reflect acceptable moral principles, and are therefore to be taken at face value, and which are to be reworked because they do not.

But in practice, this exercise regularly fails to find a morally unobjectionable reading in any case, and in the process interpolates or mangles the text. The resulting apologetic interpretations are often exegetically indefensible. Of course, the fact that Miller fails doesn't establish the impossibility of successful maneuvers along these lines. But what, realistically, are the prospects?

[17] See e.g. Craigie 1978 for brief discussion of such uses of the Tanak.

[18] Often fancifully; even some early Fathers took exception to Origen's interpretive methods on these grounds. Augustine, for one, didn't think that the Tanak was merely referring to spiritual warfare against 'powers'.

[19] For others, see n. 13 and Paul Copan's recent effort (2008: 8–37), incisively criticized by Wes Morriston (2009: 7–26). John Calvin (1855: 97), whose own hands were stained with innocent blood, says: ' . . . indiscriminate and promiscuous slaughter [of Canaanites], making no distinc-

divine command to treat most Canaanite peoples as *herem*, to be wiped out (Deut. 7: 1–2).[20] Craig offers these mitigating considerations:

1. The adult Canaanites deserved to be slaughtered, because their culture was 'debauched and cruel', engaged in temple prostitution and child sacrifice.

2. Moral duties derive from divine commands; since God does not issue commands to Himself, He violates no duty in demanding the lives of the Canaanites. He has the right to take anyone's life whenever He sees fit.

3. It is morally permissible (indeed obligatory) for human beings (e.g. Israelite soldiers; Abraham) to obey God by committing what ordinarily would be murder, but ceases to be murder if God commands it.[21]

4. God was justified in utterly destroying the Canaanites by the need to remove from Israel the temptation to follow Canaanite ways. Indeed, the slaughter of Canaan's children 'served as a shattering, tangible illustration of Israel's being set exclusively apart for God'.[22]

5. The apparent injustice of slaughtering children is removed when we consider that God, extending His grace to them, could provide for them a heavenly home, so that death was no tragedy but a great benefit to them.

I'll discuss these points in order:

1*. There is historical evidence that some Canaanites did engage in one practice Craig mentions,[23] though for Israel to level such accusations

---

tion of age or sex, but including alike women and children, the aged and decrepit, might seem an inhuman massacre, had it not been executed by the command of God. But as he . . . had justly doomed those nations to destruction, this puts an end to all discussion.' Augustine is an ancient example, if one is wanted. Apropos Josh. 11: 11–12 he says: 'One should not at all think it a horrible cruelty that Joshua did not leave anyone alive in those circumstances . . . for God himself had ordered this. However, whoever for this reason thinks that God himself must be cruel and does not wish to believe that the true God was the author of the Old Testament, judges as perversely about the works of God as he does about the sins of human beings. Such people do not know what each person ought to suffer' (*Questions on Joshua 16*: see Franke 2005: 67). An illuminating case for ancient apologetics is the sacrifice of Jepthah's daughter (Judges 11): here even Origen appeals to a poisoned morality; see Franke 2005: 137–40.

[20] I am citing Craig (2007). This is a website, and Craig is writing for a popular audience, not scholars. So much the worse. The classic study of Israelite warfare, von Rad (1991), is not concerned with the moral issue.

[21] So, too, Eugene Merrill in Gundry 2003: 93: 'The issue, then, cannot be whether genocide is intrinsically good or evil—its sanction by a holy God settles that question.'

[22] This is a popular maneuver. See, e.g., Merrill ibid. 71 and 85. Merrill also gives reason (1) above. And Tremper Longman, ibid. 173–4: ' . . . the Bible does not understand the destruction of the men, women, and children of these cities as a slaughter of innocents. They are all part of an inherently wicked culture that, if allowed to live, would morally and theologically pollute the people of Israel.'

[23] e.g. Stager and Wolff 1984.

sounds like the pot calling the kettle black. No matter: the question is whether the Canaanites collectively deserved extinction on that basis, and whether each and every adult Canaanite deserved the fate of death. And that is utterly implausible; a contemporary equivalent would be George Bush's rationale for the invasion of Iraq *had he further averred that all Iraqis deserved to be slaughtered.* A principle of collective responsibility that reaches such a conclusion condemns itself.

2*. Craig accepts a 'voluntarist' version of the divine command theory of moral obligation. I take that to be a *reductio* of the view. And, indeed, Craig seems uncomfortable with its implications; thus he reverts to asking whether it would be consistent with God's good nature to command genocide. Hence the attempt to justify the slaughter. But

3*. Which is it? Is the Israelite genocide (and e.g. Abraham's binding of Isaac) justified by the very fact that God has commanded these things, or must God have (morally) competent reasons for doing so? Or: did God command murder?

4*. God wishes to provide Israel with *Lebensraum,* so He leads them into a land of temptation—and removes the temptation by commanding the elimination of the land's inhabitants. It seems not to have succeeded very well, if we judge by repeated subsequent prophetic condemnations of Israel. But, after the events of the Exodus, did the Israelites (if they were corrigible at all) really need, at the expense of innocents, another 'shattering' demonstration that they were a people set apart?

5*. Either cultural determinism is true, in which case the Canaanite children could not have been held responsible for growing into corrupt adult Canaanites, or else it's false—in which case God could have provided them with guidance and opportunity to transform Canaanite culture. Killing children in horrific ways, then making it up to them in heaven, is unjust in the same way that kidnapping and maiming an innocent person, to achieve some extraneous end, and then 'making it up' to her would be. The rationale that the children must be killed because they would have grown into sinful adults is all too reminiscent of the rationale given by the wife of the US commissioner of immigration in 1939 for rejecting a bill to provide temporary haven in the USA for 20,000 Jewish children from Germany: 'twenty thousand charming children would all too soon grow into twenty thousand ugly adults.' The bill was defeated in Congress.[24]

---

[24] See, e.g., Medoff 2003.

I, for one, find Craig's justification of the *herem* against Canaan altogether chilling.[25]

Christians—especially those attracted to dispensationalism—may find some comfort in thinking that the morally chaotic Tanak is superseded by the NT. They should not rest easy. I have already alluded briefly to some unsavory aspects of NT moral teaching. Moreover, dispensationalism is itself a view that is difficult to defend; there is no plausible reason why God could not have, and should not have, taught Israel at least the fundamental moral truths from the beginning.[26] Furthermore, even early Christian moral qualms about the Tanak do nothing to mitigate the problematic status of the Tanak as an expression of God's will, or the fact that Christians gave material support to propagating it.

4. ATONEMENT

Focusing blame on the Tanak also runs the risk of violating one of Jesus' wiser teachings, namely not to seek to remove the mote from our neighbor's eye before extracting the beam from our own. Surely, the Tanakic horrors are no mote. But the Christian story of salvation contains much that's not free from moral danger.

At the core of Christian soteriology lie four doctrines, textually supported by the NT and deeply rooted in Judaism, that are morally incoherent, psychologically demoralizing, and practically dysfunctional:[27] the doctrines of

---

[25] Equally heartwarming are other apologetic maneuvers, of which, for good measure, here are a few:

1. 'It is not only those who were subject to Yahweh war but all human beings who deserved annihilation, since by virtue of [original?] sin all stand in opposition to God's holiness.'—Daniel Gard in Gundry 2003: 103. Longman (ibid. 185) agrees; cf. Craig's (2) above.

2. '... in actuality the revelation of Jesus in the New Testament is no less violent than the revelation of God in the Old Testament.'—Longman, ibid. 58–9; also 60 and 185. Gard, ibid. 56, concurs. So far from vindicating the Old Testament, of course, this condemns the New.

3. Skeptical theism: 'There simply comes a point in [*sic*] which human reason must bow to the divine and recognize his ways are truly not ours...'—Gard, ibid. 55; also Merrill, ibid. 93, and Longman, ibid. 108, 202–3. This amounts to an admission that other defenses don't pass muster. The marauding Assyrians—or the modern Turks when they slaughtered Armenians—could have turned such a theology to good account.

[26] Though changing times call for changing applications of those truths, that does nothing to ameliorate the outrage of the moral violations attributed to Yahweh in the Tanak.

[27] Mainstream Christian soteriology can be morally debilitating because it teaches that (a) we are helpless sinners—even our best efforts, our best works, are as filthy rags (cf. Isa. 64: 6), (b) we cannot by our own efforts atone for our sins, and (c) if we give ourselves to Christ, we will

Christian exclusivism, of eternal damnation, of original sin, and of vicarious atonement.[28] I'll focus my brief remarks here upon vicarious atonement.

Substitution theories of vicarious atonement must do three things: explain how sin creates an obligation that is transferable—can be met on one's behalf by someone else—explain why that debt is beyond the sinner's means to pay, and explain how the cross can discharge that obligation.

All such theories founder, as I see it, upon two rocks: the moral impossibility of justly transferring punishment and thereby extinguishing culpability, and the notion that the voluntary death of a uniquely good (even divine) individual can somehow satisfy the debt.

As David Lewis points out (1997), even atheists swallow penal substitution where someone pays a court-imposed fine for another. But intuitions about satisfaction of a *legal* penalty do not match those regarding *moral* guilt. If a sinner owes more than he can repay, or deserves punishment, and simple forgiveness won't answer because it doesn't 'take the sin seriously' or view the sinner as 'properly responsible', God's paying the debt does so even less; and however poignant the sacrifice of another on our behalf, we should be mortified to accept that offer. Would it not *compound* our guilt?

The other popular theme in modern atonement theories is exemplarist.[29] Theories in which Christ as moral exemplar is central face two different difficulties: they can't explain at all, in the face of the evident failure of Christians to achieve moral superiority over others, how Jesus makes an incomparable contribution to our sanctification; and they can't explain why Jesus' example is somehow necessary—or why that example must include death on the cross.

The cross might be thought *causally* necessary to bring about the change of heart that transforms the sinner from rebel to penitent. But that psychological claim is not borne out by reality. Sincere remorse, and desire to make amends for an acknowledged offense, are capacities human beings often exercise

---

nevertheless be saved. How much more seriously will we regard our temptations to err, if we rather believe that (a) we have the power to do right rather than wrong, (b) we generally have the ability to atone when we do wrong, and (c) we therefore have the obligation to atone fully if we sin?

[28] The Tanakic roots of this doctrine of atonement lie, first and foremost, in the *Akedah* and the Passover story, and in the rituals associated with Yom Kippur. (Seldom noticed is that some ancient MSS of Matt. 27 give the name of the criminal released to the mob as Jesus Barabbas; i.e. Jesus the Son of the Father: arguably in parallel to Lev. 16. This detail, which suggests for Barabbas the role of scapegoat, dovetails intimately with little-noticed aspects of the Judas motif—a matter too tangential to pursue here. For the framework within which it can be pursued, see Fales 2005a: 307–48. The resulting conception of vicarious atonement is more morally coherent, but comes at a price: it's not congruent with modern understandings of Christian soteriology.) But see also Isa. 53. Some of these Jewish/Christian ideas may reflect the influence of Assyrian kingship ideology; see Parpola 1999.

[29] e.g. Eleonore Stump, Philip Quinn, Marilyn Adams, and Robin Collins.

without prompting. Jews certainly do not imagine that they need Jesus to put themselves into this frame of mind toward God; they have Yom Kippur. I see no reason to think their repentance less sincere, or less morally adequate, than Christians'.

The doctrine of vicarious atonement can certainly be distinguished from the horrors of the Tanak, though I believe its baneful effects upon the moral psychology of Christians can easily be underestimated.[30] At the least, a Testament that portrays God as offering human beings salvation exclusively by as morally impenetrable a mechanism as the cross offers a portrait of a God who appears not morally up to speed.[31]

Given the absence, to my knowledge, of evidence showing that Christians, taken collectively, are ethically superior to non-Christians, and given the apparent incoherence of the Christian view of atonement, it's hard to see what is morally attractive about Christian soteriology. What sensible story can be told about the moral consequences of sin to show that we owe God something both beyond our capacity to repay, and for which only the Passion could make amends? The cross mediates between divine love and justice only by divine self-immolation and adding one more sin to Israel's already long list. The central moral feature of sin is moral responsibility; that is not something that can be transferred to another. Were I offered the salvation of the cross, I would respectfully decline. I should take more seriously Paul's

---

[30] At least the following popular aspects of Christian soteriology seem likely to impair moral maturity: (1) the notion that human beings are, morally, as little children in God's eyes, utterly powerless against sin and incapable through their own efforts to acquire virtue or atone for past wrongs; (2) the notion that a sincere admission of guilt and submission to Christ wipes the slate clean; (3) the notion that this is so even if the conversion occurs only at the end of life; (4) the notion that we are utterly unworthy of God's love; (5) the notion that what makes one's fellow human beings worthy of love is just that God loves them; and (6) the notion that, however careless our stewardship of the world, God will see it all made right in the end. It's hard to resist the impression that the salvation nailed to the cross encourages in many—even ratifies—moral cowardice.

[31] The very existence of enduring debate within Christian theology over how vicarious atonement can be understood is itself a problem. The mere fact of theoretical disagreement about something does not by itself impugn its existence, but there are different cases. There is ongoing disagreement over how quantum uncertainty is to be understood, but the facts that make uncertainty a feature of the micro-world are so well established that any theory must account for it. There is also disagreement over whether we possess (libertarian) free will. However, the arguments over how that kind of freedom is even to be understood raise doubts over the intelligibility of the notion; we ought on those grounds alone to be less than certain that we have it. Vicarious atonement resembles the second case, not the first. The 'feeling' of freedom is sometimes appealed to by libertarians; similarly, Christians often claim a 'feeling' of having been saved. But feelings of freedom and salvation are distinct from the actual things, and don't count for much as an argument. So, even setting aside serious questions about the historicity of the Crucifixion and the alleged Resurrection, we have a priori grounds to doubt the doctrine of vicarious atonement. For further discussion of atonement, see Fales (2005b).

trenchant advice to the Philippians, to 'work out your own salvation with fear and trembling' (Phil. 2: 12).

5. FATHER ABRAHAM

Rachels (1971) argues that worship is incompatible with human moral autonomy; hence, no being is worthy of worship. Responding to Rachels, Quinn brings matters to a head by proposing that a theist can rationally believe it more likely that she's been commanded by God to perform an apparently heinous action A, than that A is morally forbidden (1975). When God told Abraham to sacrifice his son Isaac, Abraham might have had sufficient evidence to justify belief that God had indeed so commanded, even if that meant taking an innocent life.

Two things are initially striking about this response. First, Quinn appeals to utilitarian considerations to explain how killing Isaac might after all be justified. Yet, it takes a strong consequentialist spine to resist accepting a deontological judgment of wrongness in such a case. What's worse, the story gives us—and Abraham—no reason whatever to think that Isaac's sacrifice will engender more good than ill or that it's a necessary condition for an optimal outcome: on the contrary, what Abraham must accept is not only the expected loss of his son, but God's vacating his prior promise to provide Abraham, through Isaac, with descendants numerous as the stars. Even setting all that aside, it's at least jarring to find a theist suggesting a utilitarian solution to the problem. Christians have good reason to abjure utilitarianism.

The second striking feature is that Quinn's response makes a much stronger claim than his argument requires. For Abraham need not have any reasons so strong as to require overthrowing the moral principle not to murder, to discover a justification for obeying God. All that's required is (a) that this moral principle is defeasible, and imposes only a prima facie duty, and (b) that this duty is overridden by a duty to obey God. Of course, Abraham must wonder why *God* would command something that overrides a strong prima facie moral duty. But whatever God's reasons are, it's not obvious that they entail God's being committed to abrogating the Sixth Commandment.

Suppose Abraham could *know*—did *in fact* know—that God had commanded the sacrifice of Isaac. Would he then be morally obligated to do it? Could his obligation to God override his duty not to kill? One might suppose so, if one thought that obedience to God is an indefeasible moral duty. But why should we suppose that? I can think of two possibilities: (1) that we have an absolute duty of obedience to the one who created us; and (2) that a strong ('voluntarist') divine command theory is true (one that fully endorses the claim that God is free to command whatever actions it is logically and physically possible for human beings to perform, and that the rightness of an action consists in nothing beyond conformity to God's command). A strong DCT should be unpalatable to all morally sensitive Christians who are mindful of its consequences and fully aware of the biblical horrors.[32]

But the same consequences follow from the view that, even if moral norms generally are grounded in something other than the divine will, obedience to that will trumps any other conflicting moral demand. What could be the basis for such a claim? What grounds an absolute duty to obey one's creator? It could not be—on pain of begging the question at issue—that God commands such indefeasible obedience. Nor is it at all apparent how else such a claim could be supported, except on the independent assumption that God always commands what is right: which is, again, precisely at issue in the *Akedah* and other horrors.

However, there remains a possibility. Perhaps Abraham's duty to obey God is not an ethical duty, but a *religious* duty, where religious duties are *sui generis*, and not a species of ethical duty. Quinn himself suggests this possibility; it may be implicit in Kierkegaard's (or more carefully, Johannes de Silentio's) notion of the teleological suspension of the ethical. Now the possibility that there may be religious duties distinct from ethical ones is not particularly hard to grasp (perhaps, for Jews, the duty not to wear clothing of mixed linen and wool would be such a duty); but that there could be religious duties that conflict with, and supersede, ethical duties is difficult to understand. It appears flatly to conflict with the traditional view that God is *essentially* good. And, indeed, Johannes de Silentio is reduced to silence by Abraham's deed. He does not pretend to understand the Knight of Faith; neither, in the end, do I.

Yet Abraham—as Kierkegaard circles around him—appears to be an attractive figure. We cannot take our eyes off of him. What we should make of this I am not sure; it would however provoke a prolonged meditation. What I will say is this: Kierkegaard affects us because of his seriousness, his honesty,

---

[32] Strong DCT, as a general theory of moral obligation, comes a-cropper also on the question of what grounds the duty to obey God's commands. 'Because God commands us to obey' generates an obvious, and vicious, regress. Adams (2002: ch. 12) holds that moral obligation 'consists in' one's having been commanded by God, but it would be wrong to disobey only if God is good. That raises questions about what goodness consists in; but here I note only that Adams, unlike Quinn, believes Abraham was wrong to think he was under a divine command. One wishes Adams had offered his reflections upon what that might imply about Abraham, to say nothing of the many other biblical personae who took themselves to be under morally rebarbative divine commission. See Quinn 1981: 49–66.

and the depth of his psychological insights. His efforts to plumb Abraham's depths therefore deserve respect, even if the biblical text remains silent, and even if de Silentio's Abraham may have little connection to the figure the author of Gen. 22 wanted to portray.[33]

Kierkegaard moves us so powerfully in *Fear and Trembling*, not only because of his extraordinary skill as a writer and seriousness as a thinker, but because of the depth of the tragic sensibility with which he faces the human condition. But it is in Abraham really a kind of inversion of the tragic. The tragic hero suffers social or corporeal shipwreck because he will stop at nothing in his defiance of a morally unjust divine order. The Knight of Faith risks moral chaos because he will stop at nothing to obey the decrees of an incomprehensible God.

The great figures of the ancient tragedies were heroic because they rebelled against an unjust fate decreed by the gods. The tragedy of Abraham is ... that he does not rebel.

6. REVELATION LOCKED OUT

It is surprising, then, that Locke should advocate, in defense of scripture, a necessary condition on revelation that he must have known much of the Bible could not meet. Locke is not alone in his failure to draw the correct conclusion. Among evangelicals in this country, it is increasingly popular to level the charge that atheists are unable to offer any objective grounding for their moral convictions and that, even if collectively they are as moral as Christians, they must concede that no society could function without a divinely sanctioned moral code. These claims are, at best, terribly ironic. They are also demonstrably false.

One response to the difficulty, not uncommon during the Enlightenment, was to 'edit' the sacred text, gerrymandering away the moral repugnancies. But that is not only artificial from a literary perspective; it damages too much of the text.[34] Much more fruitful, if what interests us is an explanation of how the books of the Bible were written, is a sociological perspective. My remarks

---

[33] I believe it's possible to ameliorate the moral repugnance of the story of the binding of Isaac by situating it properly within its cultural and historical context. But doing so deprives it of all its existential depth, and of any meaning it might have for us in our own time. That is a great sacrifice.

[34] Another is to insist upon the integrity of the text, arguing from overwhelming independent evidence for its revelatory status that our moral scruples must be overridden. I suspect that many Christians *do* think that, but I cannot imagine what such evidence could be.

have engaged the kind of Jewish and Christian tradition that sees God in His heaven inspiring specially chosen individuals to communicate His will. But instead, one can approach the texts as cultural artifacts of an ancient tribal people who were deeply concerned to forge and perpetuate their sense of political identity by means of stories of origin and destiny, stories that served to express, and justify, the legitimacy of their social order and (in Israel's case) their right to a specified territory.

Such an approach not only helps us to understand the moral failures of the Tanak and the NT, but permits us to situate our understanding within the broad context of ANE culture and, ultimately, human nature at large. We can thereby understand the demonization of enemies, the exaggeration of battle casualties, and the cloak of divine favor that attends home-team success, as well as the serious wrestling with questions of morality and social order.[35] Of course, this explanatory strategy can be fleshed out in many different ways, but I believe it can help us understand difficult cases. For example, the sociological approach makes it possible to explain how Jesus could have sensibly preached both love of enemies and hatred ($\mu\iota\sigma\acute{\epsilon}\omega$, Luke 14: 26) of one's family, a disparity that has produced some tortured Christian inter-pretations. But such an approach can hardly avoid rendering implausible the view that the Bible is divinely inspired. Where does this leave those unwilling to abandon that doctrine?

The believer can, to be sure, retreat at this point to a strong divine command theory, and preserve the sanctity of scripture by deeming the horrors of the Bible to be righteous simply by virtue of their conformity with God's will. But the price of this rescue is high. It requires abdicating the moral high ground from which Christian apologetes have traditionally at-tacked pagan religions. More importantly, it makes the pursuit of faith an essentially tragic enterprise. Like Father Abraham, we are forced to sacrifice to it our deepest moral convictions and feelings. That price is too high.

7. KADDISH AVELIM

I have offered an argument from the moral knowledge we share to the conclusion that any sacred text that is morally depraved is either no genuine revelation at all, or reveals the character of a god unworthy of worship. Such a god is moreover not merely unworthy of worship, but deserving of moral

---

[35] It also helps us to understand the different 'layers' of the tradition, as it was shaped and reshaped by succeeding generations to address their evolving concerns.

censure. We have a duty to repudiate such a god. A salvation purchased at the cost of complicity in the deeds of such a god is not a salvation that conscience can abide.

The Jewish prayer of mourning makes no mention of the dead; it sings praise of life and Lord. I have chosen instead to name the dead, who still cry from the earth: the men and maidens of Midian, the tortured soul of Isaac, the daughter and son of Jepthah and David, upon whom memory has bestowed no names, the Canaanite babes laid waste in war. Let them be remembered against the god of the Bible.

Who is this Lord who swaggers across the firmament?—who lectures Job on his puniness to evade the one confession He owes: that, tempted by Satan, He has sinned against Job? Who loves whom He will love and hates whom He will hate? He is not a God I hope to know. I prefer to think the heavens vast and void.

Comments on 'Satanic Verses:
Moral Chaos in Holy Writ'

Alvin Plantinga

Evan Fales offers 'an argument from the moral knowledge we share to the conclusion that any sacred text that is morally depraved is either no genuine revelation at all, or reveals the character of a god unworthy of worship. Such a god is moreover not merely unworthy of worship, but deserving of moral censure. We have a duty to repudiate such a god.' (107–8) This, though impassioned, is pretty abstract; a Christian might agree. But Fales means to go further. He argues or at any rate suggests that Christians who accept the Bible, including the Old Testament, as divine revelation do take as revelation a sacred text that is morally depraved and do worship a God unworthy of worship. In failing to repudiate—a fortiori, in worshiping—such a god, they are themselves immoral. This is strong stuff. Fales himself strikes a defiant pose: 'who is this Lord that swaggers across the firmament?' (108) 'The tragedy of Abraham is . . . that he does not rebel.' (106) Is this heroically Promethian? Or is it foolish hubris?

In the process of making his argument, Fales starts many hares, and addresses several main topics: (1) John Locke on revelation, (2) Old Testament passages where God is represented as commanding actions that seem prima facie immoral, (3) the nature of divine atonement, and (4) the story of Abraham and Isaac as seen through the eyes of Kierkegaard. As he says, to treat any one of these topics properly would require a book. In my fifteen minutes, I won't be able to comment on all four of these, and will restrict myself to (2) and (3).

1. OLD TESTAMENT 'HORRORS'?

People who believe (as I do) that scripture is divinely inspired can have a problem or perplexity with Old Testament passages according to which God commands actions that are apparently immoral. Fales settles on the account (Numbers 25, 31) of the battle between the Israelites and the Midianites. Says Fales, 'God ultimately orders the slaughter of all Midianites except—with palpable irony—the Midianite maidens, who are to be taken as concubines.' (96) Here Fales is engaging in creative hermeneutics; God is not depicted as commanding what Fales says. What he does command is to 'harass the Midianites and defeat them' (NRSV) (Num. 25) and (to Moses) 'Avenge the Israelites on the Midianites; afterwards you shall be gathered to your people' (Num. 31). Nothing in those divine commands about raping Midianite maidens or killing everyone.

No matter; there are other passages that might serve his purposes somewhat better. For example, in Deuteronomy 7 Moses tells the Israelites

When the Lord your God has delivered them over to you and you have defeated them, then you must destroy them totally. Make no treaty with them and show them no mercy. Do not intermarry with them. Do not give your daughters to their sons or take their daughters for your sons, for they will turn your sons away from following me to serve other gods . . . This is what you are to do to them: Break down their altars, smash their sacred stones, cut down their Asherah poles and burn their idols in the fire.

Later in the same speech Moses says:

. . . in the cities of the nations the Lord your God is giving you as an inheritance, do not leave alive anything that breathes. Completely destroy them . . . Otherwise, they will teach you to follow all the detestable things they do in worshiping their gods, and you will sin against the Lord your God. (20: 16, 18)

In 1 Sam. 15: 1 ff., Samuel says to King Saul,

I am the one the Lord sent to anoint you king over his people Israel; so listen now to the message from the Lord. This is what the Lord Almighty says: 'I will punish the Amalekites for what they did to Israel when they waylaid them as they came up from Egypt. . . . Do not spare them; put to death men and women, children and infants, cattle and sheep, camels and donkeys'

Of course these passages don't specifically add that Moses and Samuel were in fact correct in what they attribute to God—were they, perhaps, engaging in a little creative hermeneutics of their own? But perhaps we are to understand that they were correct. If so, the command to put to death everyone, including non-combatants, women, children, infants, and even livestock, certainly strikes us as excessive. Why would a perfectly good God command a thing like that?

Such passages can constitute a perplexity for both Christians and Jews; I'll look at the matter from a Christian perspective. There are fundamentally two ways to respond to this difficulty. First, take the passages at face value: God did issue these commands, and had good reason to do so. And second, take it that God did not in fact issue those commands. The first is perhaps the majority Christian response. God really did command the things Moses and Samuel say he commanded, his reasons being the ones mentioned in the text: to punish the Canaanites for gross wickedness and to prevent the Israelites from being misled into their detestable practices. If we find a problem here, so this account would go, it is our initial inclination to think these commands unworthy of God that is at fault. Maybe death as such isn't as horrifying as we ordinarily think. *We* are commanded not to kill (except in special circumstances); and hence it is wrong (except in those circumstances) for us to kill; but of course the same does not go for God. Furthermore, we all die anyway; we are all under a death sentence; how bad is it to die earlier rather than later? And on the other side: how bad is the moral and spiritual corruption, blasphemy, infant sacrifice, temple prostitution, and the like attributed to the Canaanites? Maybe it is worse, even much worse, than we think. (Earlier Christians may have been closer to the truth than we are presently inclined to think.) If so, perhaps God's sentence upon these people is perfectly just. What about the infants and children? Perhaps, as William Craig says, they are spared a life of degradation and sin. Furthermore, Christians, of course, believe that our earthly career is a mere infinitesimal initial segment of our whole life; perhaps the suffering of these children is recompensed a thousand fold.

Considerations such as these are perfectly sensible, and have been what millions of Christians have taken to be no more than the sober truth. Still, the response has its problems. We are commanded by Jesus Christ to love the Lord with all our heart, soul, mind, and strength, and our neighbor as ourselves. How would God's commanding the Israelites to exterminate the Amalekites fit in with that? So consider the second alternative: denying that God did in fact issue that command. A common but unsatisfactory version: think of the New Testament as superseding the Old, and in practice ignore the Old Testament except for, e.g., Genesis, Psalms, and the prophets. Another possibility: follow Old Testament scholar Richard Hess and others in supposing that phrases like 'put to death men, women, children, infants, cattle, etc.' were not used and are not intended literally: they are to be understood more like 'Knock his block off!'; 'Hand him his head!' 'Kill the Ump!' Another version: follow some of the Church Fathers in proposing allegorical interpretations of these passages: they are really about spiritual warfare.

Still another possibility: of course we don't take all of scripture at face value; when Jesus tells the parable of the rich man and Lazarus, we don't suppose it's really possible to yell back and forth between heaven and hell. That's not what's being taught. The same goes for the book of Job; my guess is we are not being taught that there actually was a person who underwent all of Job's misadventures. Sometimes it's far from easy to see what is being taught;

according to Paul, 'I fill up in my own person what is lacking in Christ's afflictions . . . ' (Col. 1: 24). But is there anything lacking in Christ's afflictions? How are we to understand this? In these cases we suppose that the relevant portion is indeed divinely inspired, but we don't know how to understand it. We can think something similar with respect to these puzzling passages under consideration: they are indeed divinely inspired, but it's not clear to us what we are to learn from them. While we understand the main lines of the story in which they are embedded (the Jews' being God's chosen people, and ultimately the vehicle for the introduction of the divine scheme for redemption) we don't know what to make of these particular passages or how they fit in.

Each of these is a sensible way to think about these passages; each is an epistemic possibility. Still, none may seem completely satisfactory; each has its perplexities. How should Christians respond? I mentioned Job earlier on; his story is relevant here. Job is afflicted; he has no idea why. He complains that God is unjust to him; he wants to go to court with God to get this thing straightened out. At the end of the story, however, God shows himself to Job, pointing out among other things that Job's not seeing what reason God has for permitting Job to suffer is not grounds for thinking God doesn't have a good reason:

Who is this that darkens counsel by words without knowledge? . . . Where were you when I laid the foundations of the earth? . . . when the morning stars sang together and all the heavenly beings shouted for joy? (Job 38: 1–7)

Job sees the point, and the storm in his soul is quieted. He still doesn't know why God has permitted him to be afflicted, but he knows that God, being God, must indeed have a good reason.

The same goes for Christians and the puzzling passages we are thinking about—only Christians know something Job didn't. Christians know about the overwhelming divine love revealed in the saga of incarnation and atonement. The divine son of God became human, suffered, and died so that we human beings, we who had turned our backs upon God, could be restored to fellowship with him. God the father, the first being of the universe, the creator of all else, loved the world so much that he was willing to allow his son to undergo suffering, humiliation, and death so that human beings could be restored to fellowship with him. God the son was willing to undergo the suffering and the pain and humiliation heaped upon him in his death on the cross so that sinners could be at one with God. This story of atonement is the greatest story ever told, indeed, the greatest story that *could* be told, a story by virtue of which alpha, the actual world, is among the best possible worlds.[1]

---

[1] See Plantinga 2004.

So we are perplexed about those OT passages: did God really command something like genocide? But then we recall the love revealed in the incarnation and atonement, and we see that whatever God did, he must indeed have a good reason, even if we can't see what the reason is.

2. ATONEMENT

This brings us to my second topic: the Christian teaching of atonement. Of course there are various theories of atonement: the ransom theory, the satisfaction theory, the exemplar theory, and still others, with variations on each. I suppose most Christians have accepted some version of a satisfaction theory, and many have thought in terms of a substitutionary or vicarious atonement, often connected with punishment or a penalty: Christ suffered the penalty due sinful human beings. Fales raises familiar questions: how can one person be justly punished for the transgressions of another? And how can the death of Jesus Christ satisfy the debt incurred by human sin? Says Fales, '... however poignant the sacrifice of another on our behalf, we should be mortified to accept that offer'. (102) Here my moral intuitions differ very substantially from his; though I am or aim to be mortified by my sin, and am therefore mortified that my sin has occasioned Christ's sacrifice, I am or aim to be maximally delighted to accept that gracious offer and maximally grateful for the reconciliation it provides.

As for these objections, here there may be less than meets the eye. True: at the human level perhaps the punishment due my sin can't (ordinarily) be rightly inflicted on someone else, even if that someone else voluntarily accepts it. But suppose I sin against someone *A* and someone else *B* offers to accept the penalty properly accruing to me. Suppose furthermore, *A* agrees to this arrangement and considers that amends have properly been made. This would be somewhat weird, and perhaps morally questionable, but not obviously out of the question from a moral point of view. Furthermore, the reason it is questionable is that it really isn't up to *A* whether or not I am guilty; his holding or failing to hold me guilty doesn't determine whether or not I *am* guilty; there is another party to the transaction, namely the moral law. But when we add that the injured person is God himself, things drastically change. First, there is the difference in status between God and us; we are persons and God is a person, but the moral constraints on interactions between human persons don't all carry over to moral constraints on interactions between God and human persons. God is not just another exceptionally impressive human being.

And second, as most Christians see things, God himself is the origin of moral constraints. It is his will, his commands or approvals, that determine what is right and wrong, morally acceptable or morally objectionable. Moral obligation is established by his commands to his (morally aware) creatures. Of course not every command constitutes a moral obligation for every creature; God can issue special commands in special circumstances, for example to Abraham or Moses.

What about moral constraints on God himself? Presumably God does not issue commands to himself. Divine command would be the source of moral constraints on his creatures, but not on God himself; this would be an important difference between God and his creatures. So what about constraints on, for example, the sort of divine/human interaction we are considering? Here what counts is what God approves or disapproves. If God considers human beings guilty because of the sins they commit, then human beings are indeed guilty. If God approves, as no doubt he does, of his accepting the sacrifice of his son on the cross as a propitiation for human sin, then that arrangement is morally impeccable. If God is willing to accept the death of Jesus Christ, the second person of the Trinity, as restoring the moral balance, then indeed the death of the second person of the Trinity restores the moral balance.

What about intuitions to the contrary? I suggest first that these arise from considering God just one more specially talented human being, a sort of *Übermensch*. Further, there is no guarantee that our moral intuitions are entirely accurate. Earlier generations found sexual sin more appalling than we do; we find intolerance, racial or otherwise, more appalling than they did. Human moral intuitions differ and conflict; we aren't all right. This doesn't mean that we can't trust our intuitions, or that we have any moral alternative to acting in accord with them: but it does mean that we have to be open to the possibility that some of them aren't entirely accurate. The same goes for our intuitions about what God would and wouldn't do.[2]

---

[2] Serious thanks are due Ann Siebels, Brian Boeninger, Josh Rasmussen, Kenny Boyce, Matt Lee, and Nate King.

Reply to Plantinga

Evan Fales

I thank Alvin Plantinga for his thoughtful and characteristically forthright response. About those hares I started: I did also have it in mind to bag 'em and boil 'em. I'll respond to Plantinga by giving further brief chase to three of them.

1. Plantinga accuses me of 'creative hermeneutics'—a charge that carries a certain sting. Have I strayed outside the Word? Far be it from me. Recall Deut. 21:10: attractive women captured in war may be 'taken to wife' after a month's respite to mourn loss of family.[1] (Indeed it was Mike Bergmann who presciently urged me to take explicit account of this law in a footnote.) Well, suppose, improbably, that every Israelite soldier carried in his heart that commandment's imperative for a thirty-day delay. How is that not license to rape? Counterfactuals with impossible antecedents are bad customers. But everything I know about Al makes me morally certain of this one: were he God, he would never have dreamed of commanding Israel's soldiers as Yahweh commanded them.

Plantinga's own creativity is at least a match for mine. He flirts with Craig's justification for the slaughter of Canaanite children, but ignores my responses to Craig (and also the fact that an afterlife is alien to the world of the Pentateuch, and hence to Israel's understanding of the moral implications of the *herem*). Concerning Job, he elides the fact that, though *Job* is left in the dark, the text actually *tells* us what God's motive was.

2. Because I said I would reject Old Testament morality and the Christian plan of salvation, Plantinga describes me as condemning the moral judgment

---

[1] More precisely, my reasons for supposing God to have willed this treatment of Midianite maidens are four: (a) Deut. 21:10 is a general divine ordinance respecting treatment of captured women. (b) The fate of the maidens is consistent with the harshness of Yahweh's commands respecting defeated enemies generally. (c) Even though Moses' instructions at Num. 31:15–18 are not explicitly referred back to a divine command, it is hard to think they were at odds with His will. On those rare occasions when Moses strays from Yahweh's directions, Yahweh whacks him hard—cf. Exod. 4:24, Num. 20:11/Deut. 32:51–2. (d) But this time, so far from reprimanding Moses, Yahweh gives Moses and Eleazar detailed directions concerning the distribution of the 'booty' of 32,000 Midianite maidens among the Israelite men (Num. 31:26–7). The only sensible conclusion is that Yahweh intended the forced concubinage of the Midianite girls.

of Christians. But that's not what I meant to do. Regarding the offer of salvation by the cross, I took care to assert only that I would find it morally indefensible for me to accept it. I do not pronounce this judgment on Christians, for I'm really unsure how they see the matter. Theologically, of course, they themselves have been unsure how to see the matter.

Regarding the Tanakic horrors, I did mean to say that *if* the God of Abraham is the god *I* see revealed in those texts, then we have a duty to reject him. But I don't think Plantinga would disagree with that. The differences lie, I trust, in our estimates of Yahweh's character; and I remain baffled by Christian apologetical strategies. (I can't help but think that thoughtful Christians are torn between the urge to apologetics, and the urge to shrink from the Bible horrors, certainly from translating their apparent lessons into daily action. But I can't speak for them. If there are Christians who whole-heartedly accept the horrors as models of righteousness, then I think they are walking on the dark side.)

3. Plantinga adopts the reasonable posture that the dismaying passages in the Bible need to be interpreted against the backdrop of our knowledge of the divine love revealed in the incarnation and atonement. I will say more about this interpretive stance in my comments on Professor Seitz's chapter. For the moment, I will have to let the following remark about the story of the cross suffice.

First, and to be sure, I don't think the Passion actually happened; indeed, I don't even think the gospel writers meant to be asserting that it did; but reading the story the way Plantinga reads it does reveal a fundamental difference in moral emotions and intuitions. At the risk of oversimplification, one may say that Plantinga finds in the Passion narrative the most wondrous story imaginable, wondrous enough to furnish the makings of a theodicy (Plantinga 2004), whereas I find its soteriology quite appalling. Ivan asks Alyosha whether he would accept a Kingdom of Heaven built upon the unexpiated tears of one innocent child. Alyosha's answer is mine—even if the victim is adult and suffers voluntarily. I do not know how to build a bridge of understanding across this chasm in moral intuitions; but I remain committed to the attempt.

REFERENCES

Adams, Robert. 2002. *Finite and Infinite Goods: A Framework for Ethics.* Oxford: Oxford University Press.

Calvin, John. 1855. *Commentaries on the Book of Joshua*, trans. Henry Beveridge. Edinburgh: Calvin Translation Society.

Copan, Paul. 2008. 'Is Yahweh a Moral Monster? The New Atheists and Old Testament Ethics', *Philosophia Christi*, 10/1: 8–37.

Craig, William. 2007. 'Slaughter of the Canaanites', at *Reasonable Faith*, http://www.reasonablefaith.org/site/News2?page=NewsArticle&id=5767.

Craigie, Peter. 1978. *The Problem of War in the Old Testament.* Grand Rapids, Mich.: William B. Eerdmans.

Cross, Frank M. 1973. *Canaanite Myth and Hebrew Epic.* Cambridge, Mass.: Harvard University Press.

Fales, E. 2005a. 'Taming the Tehom: The Sign of Jonah in Matthew', in Robert M. Price and Jeffrey Jay Lowder (eds.), *The Empty Tomb: Jesus Beyond the Grave.* Amherst, NY: Prometheus.

——2005b. 'Despair, Optimism, and Rebellion', at http://www.infidels.org/library/modern/evan_fales/despair.html.

Franke, John R. 2005. *Ancient Christian Commentary on Scripture*, iv: *Old Testament, Joshua, Judges, Ruth, 1–2 Samuel.* Downers Grove, Ill.: Intervarsity.

Gundry, Stanley N. 2003. *Show Them No Mercy: 4 Views on God and Canaanite Genocide.* Grand Rapids, Mich.: Zondervan.

Kugel, James. 2007. *How to Read the Bible: A Guide to Scripture Then and Now.* New York: Free Press.

Levenson, Jon D. 1993. *The Death and Resurrection of the Beloved Son: The Transformation of Child Sacrifice in Judaism and Christianity.* New Haven: Yale University Press.

Lewis, David. 1997. 'Do We Believe in Penal Substitution?', reprinted in M. C. Rea (ed.), *Oxford Readings in Moral Theology*, i: *Trinity, Incarnation, and Atonement.* Oxford: Oxford University Press, 2009.

Locke, John. 1959. *An Essay Concerning Human Understanding*, ed. Alexander Campbell Fraser. New York: Dover.

——2000. *A Discourse of Miracles*, reprinted in John Earman, *Hume's Abject Failure.* New York: Oxford University Press.

Medoff, R. 2003. http://www.aish.com/holocaust/issues/Kristallnacht_And_The_Worlds_Response.asp.

Miller, Glenn. 2001. 'What About God's Cruelty Against the Midianites?', http://www.christian-thinktank.com/midian.html.

Morriston, Wes. 2009. 'Did God Command Genocide? A Problem for the Biblical Inerrantist', *Philosophia Christi*, 11: 7–26.

Parpola, Simo. 1999. 'Sons of God: The Ideology of Assyrian Kingship', *Archaeology Odissy Archives*, Dec.; online at http://www.gatewaystobabylon.com/introduction/sonsofgod.htm.

Plantinga, Alvin. 2004. 'Supralapsarianism, or "O Felix Culpa"', in Peter van Inwagen (ed.), *Christian Faith and the Problem of Evil*. Grand Rapids, Mich.: Eerdmans, 1–25.

Quinn, Philip L. 1975. 'Religious Obedience and Moral Autonomy', *Religious Studies* 11: 265–81. Reprinted in Paul Helm (ed.), *Divine Commands and Morality*. Oxford: Oxford University Press, 1981.

Rachels, James. 1991. 'God and Moral Autonomy', *Religious Studies* 7: 325–37. Reprinted in *Can Ethics Provide Answers? and Other Essays in Moral Philosophy*. Lanham, Md.: Rowman & Littlefield, 1997.

Stager, L. E., and Wolff, S. R. 1984. 'Child Sacrifice at Carthage: Religious Rite or Population Control?', *Biblical Archaeology Review*, 10/1: 31–51.

von Rad, G. 1991. *Holy War in Ancient Israel*, trans. from the 3rd edn. by Marva J. Dawn. Grand Rapids, Mich.: William B. Eerdmans. 1st edn. 1958.

Part II

Philosophical Perspectives

Solutions Presented

4

Animal Sacrifices

John Hare

In this chapter I am going to reflect as a moral philosopher on the topic of animal sacrifices in the Hebrew scriptures. Because the central ethical criticism of animal sacrifices is that they are 'violence, vengeance, and victimage' against animals, I want to start with a section on the more general treatment of non-human animals that we find in the Hebrew scriptures, in order to give some context.[1] I will then spend most of my time on the sacrificial system. I will end with some brief remarks about the place of ritual and its relation to metaphor.

I should say immediately that I am neither a Bible scholar nor an anthropologist. I will not try to speak intelligently about the order of composition of the relevant texts, or about the cross-cultural similarities and dissimilarities that lie behind various theories about the origin of sacrifice in human culture. In particular I am not going to pass judgment on the relative priority of the priestly materials in Leviticus 1–16 and the Holiness Code in Leviticus 17–26.[2] I am also not going to comment on the question of whether there is some 'origin' of sacrifice that can be validly postulated cross-culturally, and from which the practices described in Leviticus are descended. In my own work I have written about the notion of what I call 'a moral gap' between us and God and the notion of what I call 'evaluative transfer'. I want to expand on these ideas, talking about a holiness gap rather than a moral gap. But

I am grateful to Baruch J. Schwartz, Gary Anderson, Joel Baden, Matthew C. Halteman, Michael Bergmann, and Michael Murray for very helpful comments on earlier drafts.

[1] Hamerton-Kelly 1994: 18–19: The temple is a place of 'violence, vengeance, and victimage'. See also Robins 1998: 296: 'Sacrifice is . . . impossible in ethical terms, insofar as it is abhorrent.' See also Mason 1993: 244 and 263, who analyses sacrifice in terms of 'dominionism—a view of the world that places animals, nature, and Others on a ladder or hierarchy of being'. He takes animals to be the most potent representative of nature, and so 'the bloody animal sacrifices of old impressed the masses and heightened the prestige of a god, its temple, and its priests'.

[2] See Klawans 2006b: 49–50, who says that because these texts formed a unit post-biblically, 'The priestly traditions of the Pentateuch need to be studied as a whole, regardless of the history of their component parts.'

I want to begin by acknowledging that philosophers sometimes have a tin ear for nuances and ambiguities in biblical texts, and that we often do not know the relevant social-scientific literature. This kind of thing is almost inevitable in cross-disciplinary work. I have observed that biblical scholars and social scientists sometimes make use of philosophical ideas, without knowing the contemporary discussions of them within the discipline of philosophy. I think we have to try to be patient with each other about this, and learn what we can.

First, then, some general points about how non-human animals are viewed, especially in Genesis and in the prophets. Those who have grown up in a carnivorous culture like our own, who assume that their diet is perfectly consistent with God's will for their lives, are sometimes surprised to discover that Genesis describes the original state in which we were created in terms of unrestricted vegetarianism, and the prophets pick this up in their description of the eventual state towards which we are headed. I am not here trying to talk about the historical or scientific accuracy of these pictures, but about the stories on their own terms, in as far as we can discern this. On the third day God created the plants and trees, and then, on the sixth day God created both land animals and humans, and gave to both the animals and the humans every seed-bearing plant on the face of the whole earth and every tree that has fruit with seed in it, to be theirs for food (Gen. 1: 11–30). God also gave dominion to humans over the fish and birds and land animals. It is a matter of controversy just what the Hebrew translated 'dominion' means, but it certainly does not mean that humans are to eat the other animals. Perhaps it means that humans have stewardship over the other animals.[3] In the account in Genesis 2, what Adam actually does with the birds and animals is to name them. The best-known description of our vegetarian destination is in Isaiah 11, where the wolf will live with the lamb, the leopard will lie down with the goat, and the lion will eat straw like the ox, and 'they will neither harm nor destroy on all my holy mountain'. There is a similar picture in Hosea (2: 18), who looks forward to the day when God will make a covenant on behalf of Israel with the wild beasts, the birds of the air, and the things that creep on the earth, and will break bow and sword and weapon of war and sweep them off the earth, so that all living creatures may lie down without fear.[4]

This description of a peaceable kingdom is foreshadowed symbolically in a number of places, of which I will mention two. The first is the ark, into which

---

[3] One discussion from an 'animal-friendly' point of view is Scully 2002. See also Cohen 1989.

[4] See also Amos 9: 14, 'I will restore the fortunes of my people Israel, and they shall rebuild the ruined cities and inhabit them; they shall plant vineyards and drink their wine, and they shall make gardens and eat their fruit.'

the animals go in 'seven' (or 'seven pairs') 'of every kind of clean animal, a male and its mate, two of every kind of unclean animals, a male and its mate, and also seven of every kind of bird, male and female, to keep their various kinds alive throughout the earth' (Gen. 7: 2–3). Note that the distinction between clean and unclean animals seems to presuppose some kind of purity code.[5] There are some puzzles here, but I said I was not going to talk about dates of composition. Note that all carnivorous animals are unclean. The fact that they eat the forbidden blood of other animals may not be the reason why God forbids us to eat them, but the prohibitions to them and to us are consistent. This picture of the ark and the human responsibility for it has proved fruitful for the ecology movement, as a picture of our present condition. Planet earth can be seen as an ark. When the flood is over, God makes a covenant with every living creature, symbolized by the rainbow, and this universal scope of the covenant is repeated three times in Genesis 9. The second foreshadowing is the picture of the promised land, given to the people of Israel wandering in the desert, as described in Deuteronomy 8: 6–9. It will be a good land, a land with streams and pools of water, a land with wheat and barley, vines and fig trees, pomegranates, olive oil and honey, a land where bread will not be scarce and they will lack nothing. There is no description of abundant livestock or game.[6]

I anticipate that you will object that God *does* give permission to eat meat, after the flood. 'Everything that lives and moves will be food for you. Just as I gave you the green plants, I now give you everything' (Gen. 9: 3). But this permission comes in the context of a prescription of capital punishment for humans who shed blood, for which God will require an accounting. And God also demands an accounting from every *animal* of the eating of meat with its lifeblood still in it. My suggestion, then, is that both provisions, both meat eating and capital punishment, are God's so-to-speak second best, a divine concession.[7] The best situation, the one at our origin and at our destination, is one where we do not kill each other, animals do not kill each other, and we do not kill animals for meat. I do not know that this is a correct account of the

---

[5] Gen. 7: 14–15 has 'two-by-two' for *all* animals, not making the distinction.

[6] This could be simply because there is not much game (or because it was not of primary interest to an agricultural economy), not because there is game which is deliberately omitted from the description. In general, the account of a vegetarian origin and destination, and its influence on the various forms of sacrifice, is controversial amongst scholars. It is present in Milgrom 1991, and in various 'animal-friendly' writers such as Webb 1998. But it is disputed by, for example, Schwartz 1996. The texts we are immediately concerned with in Leviticus do not refer to a vegetarian origin or destination, and give no sign that sacrifice is supposed to stop at any point.

[7] Milgrom 1991: 705.

permission to Noah, but it seems plausible. Note that even though permission is given to eat flesh, it is not given to eat blood, 'which is the life of it'.[8] That is to say, there is a distinction between the flesh of the animal and its life, to which humans still have obligation. We do not have to identify life with blood to make this distinction. Animals are not *merely* meat to be consumed, even if we are conceded permission to eat this meat. It would be possible to be a dualist about the subject of this obligation, and to talk about animal soul in a dualist manner, separate from animal body. But this text suggests a non-dualist thought, that the life of the animal is tied up intimately with its materiality, but it is not identical with the flesh that we eat.[9] In any case, whether materialist or not, the point is that the animal is seen here as a subject, a being with whom a covenant could be had, and to whom one could have obligations.[10] It is harder for those of us who no longer live in agrarian/pastoralist societies to see animals as subjects in this way just because we no longer live with animals on a regular basis.

The sacrificial system as described in Leviticus should be understood against the background of a society in many ways unlike the urban society of the New Testament. The people of Israel kept animals, which they considered part of their households. I will give two examples of this. It is not a controversial point, I think, but it is helpful in distinguishing the treatment of non-human animals in the Hebrew scriptures from the treatment in, for example, the letters of Paul (e.g. 1 Cor. 9: 9). The first example is the story that Nathan told to David about the poor man's lamb ('It used to eat of his meager fare, and drink from his cup, and lie in his bosom, and it was like a daughter to him', 2 Sam. 12: 6 NRSV), which was stolen and slaughtered by a rich man, prompting David to reply, 'As the Lord lives, the man who has done this deserves to die; he shall restore (i.e. pay for) the lamb fourfold, because he did this thing, and because he had no pity.' Second is the example of Jonah, who reluctantly preached to the Ninevites, and the king proclaimed a fast,

---

[8] Presumably 'eat' blood, because what is forbidden is eating the meat with the blood still in it. Note that this whole narrative presumes the legitimacy of sacrifice, since Noah 'offered burned offerings on the altar and the Lord smelled a sweet savor' (Gen. 8: 20–1). The blood is presumably the life-force in part because if you drain it out, the animal dies. The Levitical codes mandate pouring out the blood at the altar, which can be interpreted as a way of returning the blood to God.

[9] It may be that there is a similar distinction in the New Testament between flesh (*sarx*) and body (*soma*). It is the body and not the flesh that is resurrected.

[10] See Klawans 2006a: 66: 'We will do well to think of animals as subjects, and not as objects. Some are likely to assume that because Israelites performed animal sacrifice, they must have despised or at least objectified the animals they offered. We will proceed with a different assumption: in order to understand what it meant for them to sacrifice, we must first understand what it meant for them to act as their animals' shepherds.'

saying, 'Let neither man nor beast, herd nor flock, taste any thing: let them not feed, nor drink water: But let man and beast be covered with sackcloth and cry mightily unto God: yea, let them turn every one from his evil way, and from the violence that is in their hands.' The book ends with God's rebuke to Jonah, 'And should not I spare Nineveh, that great city, wherein are more than six-score thousand persons that cannot discern between their right hand and their left; and also much cattle?' (Jonah 3: 7–9, 4: 11 KJV). In Jonah, if the household is destroyed, so are the animals; they perish or are saved together. Finally, an examination of the non-sacrificial laws about the treatment of animals provides various examples of compassion, e.g. the prohibition on yoking together an ox and an ass, presumably because the differences between the pair might cause difficulties for the weaker of the two (Deut. 22: 10), the prohibition on slaughtering mother cattle with their young on the same day (Lev. 22: 28), and the requirement to help one's donkey, or the animal of another, to stand when it has fallen under a heavy load (Deut. 22: 1–4). Taken together with similar cases, the rabbinic principle is generated of *tzaar baalei chayim*, literally 'pain of a living being', which phrase is not in the Bible, but is a Talmudic expression of the biblically imposed duty to relieve the suffering of all living beings (Cohn-Sherbok 2006).

If this is the background for how non-human animals are viewed, how are we to take the prescriptions for animal sacrifice? In speaking to this question, I will use two ideas from my own previous work. I mentioned them at the beginning of this chapter, namely the moral gap or what I am going to call in this chapter 'the holiness gap', and the idea of evaluative transfer. The moral gap is the gap between God's moral demand of us, and our natural capacities to comply with that demand. By 'natural capacities' I mean the capacities we are born with and naturally develop. My claim has been that the demand is too high for us by our natural capacities, and that it is incoherent to hold ourselves to a standard we are not able to meet. The principle here is that 'ought' implies 'can', which should be understood as holding that if it is not the case that we can, then the question of whether we ought does not properly arise. For the present topic I need to widen the discussion to include both moral offences and offences against ritual purity. God sets up the standard as holiness, 'Be ye holy even as I am holy', though this has to be understood without the implication that we are actually to become God. The gap structure has three parts to it. There is the demand, and our inadequate capacities and performance, and then there is the being that is seen as the source of the demand. It is interesting that in Western moral philosophy this structure is seen in Immanuel Kant, who says throughout his corpus that we have to recognize our duties as God's commands, and in many post-Kantian secular systems where the third part of the structure is named as 'the point of view of the universe' or 'an impartial observer' or 'the archangel' or 'persons behind the veil of ignorance'.[11] Within Christianity the story is that the third part of the structure, the holy being, intervenes to change the second part of the structure, our capacities and performance, so that they become adequate to the first part of the structure, the demand. I want to suggest that this story also lies behind the sacrificial system in the Hebrew scriptures, and indeed that is where Christianity got it.[12]

The other idea I want to mention is that of evaluative transfer. Again, I will start with Kant, who objects to penal substitutionary accounts of atonement that guilt is not a transmissible liability, that could be transferred, like a financial debt, from one person to another.[13] I think he is wrong about this, and I have argued this in more detail elsewhere (Hare 1996: 248–56). He is objecting to Christian accounts of the death of Christ as taking the penalty for our sin, but the same objection could be made about accounts of atoning animal sacrifice in terms of penal substitution. I want to distinguish, in what follows, between the 'scapegoat', which is not really a sacrifice at all, and sacrifices proper, where these involve the direct killing of an animal. But it is certainly hard to see how one could transfer sins onto a goat. I want to defend the idea that with shame (taking this as a generic notion with both objective and subjective components, and taking guilt for sin as one part of it) it is intelligible that one person could be ashamed of what another person has done. This is what I call 'evaluative transfer', and it is made possible by certain kinds of identification, or partial mergers of identity. A spouse can be proud of what his spouse has done, or a mother of what her child has done. I lived this past year in Kalamazoo, Michigan, and observed how when Michigan State was in the national basketball quarter-finals, having beaten two number one seeds, the governor and even our Presbyterian minister, who never talked about sports in church, said that in this time of economic difficulty we had all been made proud and lifted up by their victory. While this kind of identification is not always healthy, and can indeed be pathological, I think that the possibility of this kind of evaluative transfer lies within most of the relationships that make life worth living. The transfer works because the individuals involved are parts of a larger whole, for example a family or a state. I am going to suggest that the fact that the animal is seen as part of the household of the

---

[11] These ideas are in Henry Sidgwick, Richard Brandt, R. M. Hare, and John Rawls.

[12] This is not to say that atonement is the only, or even the most important, function of the sacrifice system. See Anderson 1992: 878–9.

[13] Kant, *Religion within the Bounds of Mere Reason*, 6: 72.

person offering the atoning sacrifice is a key to making the sacrifice intelligible in the context in which such sacrifices were offered.[14]

I will now describe very briefly a few different models for what is going on in animal sacrifices and sacrificial offerings, and I will end up focusing on three of them. It is possible for a single practice to have multiple levels of meaning, or to be 'multivalent', and sacrifices already form a group of practices (many of them not concerned with atonement at all).[15] On the other hand, some of these models are inconsistent with each other, and are articulated as such. I am going to give preference to models that aim to capture the self-understanding of those who engaged in the practice. Capturing this is very difficult, because the texts, while describing the practice in some detail (though still with notable gaps), say very little about *why* people are to do the things that are prescribed. But I mean to lay aside models that say that whatever the practitioners may have *thought* they were doing, they were in fact doing something quite different. This preference comes from a more general principle of interpretation, which certainly needs more defense than I am going to try to give it, that one should *start* with trying to understand what people do and say in terms of what they think they are doing and saying; only then should one go on, if one is so-minded, to attribute some practice to self-deception or bad faith.[16] I am not denying that there is self-deception and bad faith in much social practice, but the task of exposing it needs to come after the slow and patient unfolding of what the participants (in this case, especially the priests) take themselves to be doing. Even if this were not true generally, it would be true for the discussion of the understanding of God's character revealed in the Hebrew scriptures.

This is all very abstract, and it will be clearer if I give a couple of examples of what I am laying aside (just a couple; this is not intended as an exhaustive list). I am not going to talk about the theory of sacrifice in which humans

[14] This is true even though the animal can be purchased for the purpose of the sacrifice, and does not have to have been raised by the offerer. The animal becomes part of the offerer's household just by being bought.

[15] Anderson 1992: 871 says that sacrifice is a 'multivalent entity'. This point is made eloquently in relation to the Christian doctrine of atonement by Gunton 1989.

[16] See Davidson 1984: 27: 'It must be possible, of course, for the speaker of one language to construct a theory of meaning for the speaker of another, though in this case the empirical test of the correctness of the theory will no longer be trivial. As before, the aim of the theory will be an infinite correlation of sentences alike in truth. But this time the theory-builder must not be assumed to have direct insight into likely equivalences between his own tongue and the alien. What he must do is find out, however he can, what sentences the alien holds true in his own tongue (or better, to what degree he holds them true). The linguist will then attempt to construct a characterization of truth-for-the-alien which yields, so far as possible, a mapping of sentences held true (or false) by the alien on to sentences held true (or false) by the linguist.'

participate by eating the sacrifice of the animal as a *totem*, representing both the god and the tribe, and so experience a communion between the tribe and the god.[17] Evidence for a totemic sense of the animal in the priestly writings is weak, and, most importantly, there is the blood prohibition linked with the principle that the life is in the blood, and the blood is not consumed. The theory of sacrifice as pre-moral magic has been very influential, but it relies on a quasi-Hegelian evolutionist methodology that posits a development of religion from magic to ethics, as in the following quotation about the purity code, 'The irrationality of laws of uncleanness, from the standpoint of spiritual religion or even of the higher heathenism, is so manifest, that they must necessarily be looked on as having survived from an earlier form of faith and society' (Robertson Smith 1927: 449). My suggestion is going to be that this distinction is problematic, and that we can already find ethical concern linked inseparably with the sacrificial system itself and the holiness code more generally.[18]

My second example is the model of sacrifice as a channel or 'shunt' of violence (Girard 1977). The idea is that there is 'an original murder', caused by our ancestors' 'mimetic desire' (the desire for what another person already has, and so the killing of the other to get it). The victim's family and friends then retaliate, and the resulting cycle of reciprocal violence intensifies until it reaches a crisis, in which the community spontaneously channels all blame and all violence onto a single, arbitrarily chosen, victim, the human scapegoat. This ends the cycle of violence, but produces a new one, in which the community re-enacts the event by a secondary substitution, using an animal that will not itself generate the cycle of revenge. The story ends with Christ's sacrifice, a 'sacrifice to end sacrifice', which ends sacrifice by exposing in the open the violence that produces it. Again, I do not want to claim that there is no 'original murder', though it is hard to see what kind of evidence for it there could be. I also agree that animal sacrifice is presented, as in the story of the binding of Isaac, as a replacement for human sacrifice in the surrounding cultures. My point is just that the analysis of sacrifice as a violence-shunt does not fit the self-understanding of the priestly sacrificial texts in the Pentateuch. The model assumes that sacrifice works by concealing its true origin and nature, which is criminal violence. 'In order to be genuine, in order to exist as a social reality, as a stabilized viewpoint on some act of collective violence, scapegoating must remain non-conscious. The persecutors do not realize that

---

[17] The theory of totemic communion is found in Robertson Smith 1927. The fact that sacrifices were performed at the covenant ratification in Exodus 24 does not mean that this one-time event sets the rationale for all subsequent sacrifices.

[18] The case for this kind of integration in the purity code is powerfully made by Douglas 1966.

they chose their victim for inadequate reasons, or perhaps for no reason at all, more or less at random.'[19] As with the previous model, there is a strongly evolutionist structure here, in which animal sacrifice is a primitive and finally failed attempt to do what systems of justice are eventually developed to do, namely to end cycles of violent revenge.

By contrast with these models I am laying aside are three models of sacrifice that attempt to understand the system in its own terms: sacrifice is (1) an imitation of God, (2) an attempt to attract and maintain the presence of God, and (3) an expiation of ritual impurity and sin. I will spend most time on the last of these, but I want to say something about the first two first, where I am following the treatment by Jonathan Klawans I have already referred to. Unfortunately, he seems uneasy with expiation, as in the following quotation, 'Another value of the approach suggested here is that we can understand the aspects of sacrificial ritual discussed above without recourse to scapegoating, substitution, or even expiation. Indeed, the daily burnt offering in particular can well be understood as morally neutral—there are not necessarily innocent victims here any more than there are guilty priests.'[20] His position is best understood as giving priority to the productive aspects of sacrifice (the first two models) over the reparative (the third), rather than trying to eliminate the third. But there is certainly no inconsistency among these three models, and no need to choose a priority between them. Indeed, I will suggest that the three are mutually needed for intelligibility.

The first model is that in the preparation for and the act of sacrifice, human beings become more like God. God tells us we are to become more like God, though we do not actually become God. We cease work on the Sabbath because God ceased work on the seventh day, and in that way we become more like God. Less familiarly, the construction of the tabernacle and then of the temple together with their implements resembles God's work in creation (Levenson 1988). Most importantly, the central text of the entire Holiness Code is 'Be ye holy as I am holy' (Lev. 11: 44–5; 19: 2; 20: 7, 26).

This command presents us with a problem, however, what I called at the beginning a 'holiness gap' between us and God. In Leviticus there are especially two kinds of things that separate human beings from God, ritual impurity and sin. Ritual impurity occurs through natural processes and substances, such as birth, death, bodily flows, certain animal carcasses, and human corpses. The

[19] Girard 1987: 78. The theory claims to find 'confirmation precisely in the fact that what [it] reveals is not actually articulated straight-forwardly in these rituals and myths' (Klawans 2006b: 24).

[20] Klawans 2001: 151. But he goes on to say that 'it certainly cannot be denied that a number of sacrificial rituals described in *Leviticus* are expiatory', 156, and he is elsewhere willing to talk about expiation, e.g. Klawans 2002.

effect is temporary, contagious defilement of persons and objects, and the resolution is ritual purification, including sacrifices (but also, e.g., washing). Sin also contaminates, especially idolatry, sexual transgressions, and bloodshed. The effect is long-lasting contamination of sinners, land, and sanctuary, and the resolution is atonement or punishment (and ultimately, exile).[21] Most of the kinds of ritual impurity reside in two differences we have from God, death and sex: God does not die and God does not have sexual congress. In the case of both impurity and sin, God provides the means for us to satisfy God's command, for example by sacrifice and atonement. This is the gap structure as I described it earlier. Gap structures can present circularity problems. In order to enter the holy place where God dwells, to carry out these means of remedy, a person has to be holy.[22] This does not give rise, however, to the same difficulty of circularity we find in some versions of Christianity, what Kant calls 'Spener's problem' after the famous pietist, 'The end of religious instruction must be to make us *other* human beings and not merely better human beings (as if we were already good but only negligent about the degree of our goodness).'[23] For there is not here the problem of original sin, which affects us all in our fundamental allegiance, and which would prevent our becoming holy by human means so as to enter the holy place to receive God's assistance.

How do we imitate God by sacrificing? The central metaphor that is here enacted is the metaphor of God as our shepherd (Ps. 23, Ps. 95: 7, Isa. 40: 11, Ezek. 34: 15–16), which we can connect with the thought that 'The Lord kills and brings to life' (1 Sam. 2: 6 ESV, Deut. 32: 39). The domestication of animals involves selective breeding, so that the gentled and useful animal is actually different in biological type from the original wild animal. The Levitical law forbidding killing an animal and its children on the same day shows that the shepherd or herdsman keeps track of the lineage lines (Lev. 22: 26–8). The shepherd then provides for the feeding and safety of the animals, as God 'makes me lie down in green pastures', and then selects which of the animals to present for sacrifice, since these animals have to be without blemish. The offerer of the animal kills it and flays it and cuts it up (and the killing is not itself a ritual act).[24] The priest then distributes the flesh and, separately, the blood, and consumes the flesh, either by burning it, or eating it. There is a picture in the language sometimes used by Leviticus of the sacrifice as a meal in which God is

[21] Klawans 2006b: 54–6. But see also Schwartz 1995a.
[22] See Hubert and Mauss 1964: 20, 'All that touches upon the gods must be divine; the sacrificer is obliged to become a god himself in order to be capable of acting upon them.' In terms of the Hebrew cult, 'become a god' is an overstatement.
[23] Kant, 1798/1996, 7: 97.
[24] Perhaps the cutting up is like God 'examining the kidneys and heart' (Jer. 11: 20, 17: 10, compare Lev. 3: 4, 10, 15), but the analogy is here weaker.

given the meat to eat through the smoke that rises to heaven, or through the fire that consumes the sacrifice (compare the story of Elijah at Mt. Carmel, where 'the fire of the Lord fell and consumed the burnt sacrifice', 1 Kgs. 18: 38 KJV, but also Lev. 9: 24).[25] The sacrifices are described as God's food (Lev. 3: 11), and the Lord smells a sweet savor (Lev. 1: 9 and elsewhere, see also the altar as a table at Ezek. 41: 22 and Mal. 1: 7). It is controversial how large a role is played by the idea of God eating the animal.[26] This is denied, for example at Psalm 50: 13. For my present point, all that is necessary is that our treatment of animals is said to be *like* God's treatment of us in our breeding, looking after, selecting, and killing. The idea is that the birthing and feeding and killing are all parts of the overall caring that the shepherd does, just as God brings both to life and death within God's providential care. The shepherd's care is consistent with the animal's destination as food. But my present point is that the sacrificer does not consume the blood, just as God does not consume us, though bringing us to death. The sacrificer does not consume the blood or the life, but only the body of the animal. The blood is returned to God. This will be the beginning of an answer to what I take to be the central puzzle about the sacrifice system from an ethical point of view. If the problem to be solved is the damage done to the relation with God by sin (for example murder) or impurity associated with death (and sex), how does *killing* something solve it?[27] How is this consistent with the covenant idea of Genesis 9? I will return to this, when I come to the third model, namely expiation.

The second model is that in certain sacrifices and offerings the participants attract and maintain the presence of God. This is linked closely to the first idea, since it gives us one central motivation for the first idea, namely that the presence of God abides with those who are like God. The concern to maintain the divine presence dwelling in the midst of Israel is pervasive, for example at the end of Leviticus (26: 11–12 NJPS): 'I will establish my abode in your midst, and I will not spurn you. I will be ever present in your midst: I will be your God, and you shall be my people.' The tabernacle is the place of meeting, from which God spoke to Moses in the first verse of Leviticus. God subsequently stays because God delights in the sacrifices and offerings. The

[25] The theory of sacrifice in terms of a kind of commercial return, food for favor, is found in Plato's *Euthyphro* at 14c, and also in Tylor 1873.

[26] Milgrom 1991: 440 says, about the idea that the Israelites thought they were sustaining their God, 'these words, objects and mores are only *fossilized vestiges* from a dim past, which shows no life in the Bible'.

[27] Klawans suggests (2001: 146–7) that it is illuminating to see that the death of the animal is a *controlled* death, whereas the contact associated with impurity is, often, uncontrolled. But there are many uncontrolled contacts that do not render impure, and there are controlled contacts which do render impure.

consequences of God's leaving would be disaster for the people. In Haggai and Zechariah, the consequences of the absence of the presence of God are extended to the whole land, which lies under a kind of curse of unfruitfulness (Hag. 1: 5–6, 10–11) while the temple lies in ruins.[28]

It is true that there is a prophetic critique of sacrifices, and as I said I am not commenting here on the relative chronology of different texts. Jeremiah (7: 22 ESV) reports God saying, 'For in the day that I brought them out of the land of Egypt, I did not speak to your fathers or command them concerning burnt offerings and sacrifices.'[29] Hosea (6: 6) has God saying, 'For I desire steadfast love and not sacrifice, the knowledge of God, rather than burnt offerings.'[30] Micah (6: 6–8) asks, 'Will the Lord be pleased with thousands of rams?' and answers that the Lord commands 'to do justice, love kindness and walk humbly with your God'. It is significant, however, that Psalm 51: 16–17, which may actually have been recited during sacrifices, already says of God, 'You do not want me to bring sacrifices; you do not desire burnt offerings; True sacrifice to God is a contrite spirit; God, you will not despise a contrite and crushed heart.' (NJPS) It has been disputed in the secondary literature whether the prophetic critique envisages a replacement of the sacrifice system, or merely an insistence that the outward cult be accompanied with inward devotion and obedience. Earlier biblical scholarship tended to what I called before 'the evolutionist view' that Israel developed out of magic into ethics, and the prophetic critique was taken as a sign of the transition to 'the ideal of a religion wholly based on moral fellowship between God and man, and in which sacrificial worship was at best an irrelevance, and at worst an offence' (Skinner 1922: 182). In the current literature this view has been largely abandoned, in favor of the second view, that 'sacrifice, at its best, was an expression of homage and obedience to Yahweh. It was an expression which he ordained. Such homage and dedication, if genuine, would be shown by a life lived in daily obedience to his moral requirements as well as the ritual ones. In other words, it was the way of life of the person who offered the sacrifice that Yahweh looked at, not merely the sacrifice itself.'[31] If this is right, it gives us something to add to the list of what attracts and maintains the presence of God; in addition to giving to God something of material value, we can give a sacrificial spirit, or a broken and contrite heart.

---

[28] See Anderson 1987: 91–126.
[29] Compare Amos (5: 25), who asks, 'Was it sacrifices and offerings you brought to me forty years in the wilderness?'
[30] Compare Isa. 1: 10–17, Hag. 2: 10–19.
[31] Lucas 1995: 72. See also Schwartz 1995b, on Lev. 4: 14, 'Atonement in P is possible only when the realization of wrongdoing and the feeling of guilt move the offender to remorse and to an active desire to rid the sanctuary of the resulting contamination.'

This brings us to the third model, that in sacrificing, God gives us a way to repair the breach with God caused by our ritual impurity and our sin. I will start with the idea that the person offering the sacrifice lays his hands on the sacrificial animal. This gesture has been variously interpreted. Two proposed meanings in particular are relevant to this chapter. The gesture might mean simply that the animal belongs to the person offering the sacrifice, or, more ambitiously, the gesture might mean that the person transfers sin or guilt onto the animal.[32] On my suggestion, we do not need to choose between these alternatives, for those cases where atonement for sin is the purpose. (Many sacrifices did not have atonement in view.) Because the animal is seen as part of, or a member of, the offerer's household, there is already the basis for an evaluative transfer to occur. Note, however, that the identification is only partial, and this allows a combination that is typical of relations where one party represents another. An ambassador represents her country, but when she signs a document it is both true that we do not sign it (she does it instead of us) and that we are committed by her signature. Christian doctrine is familiar with this thought in one traditional account of Christ's sacrifice. Paul says in 2 Corinthians 5: 14 (NIV), 'For Christ's love compels us, because we are convinced that one died for all, and therefore all died.' The 'therefore' is puzzling. It looks as though Paul is saying that Christ died instead of us (*huper*, which might mean also 'on behalf of') and therefore we died as well. We should understand that Christ is the *primary* sufferer in his death, and in this sense he died for us. But because he incorporates us into him, we become the *secondary* sufferers, sharing in his death, and therefore in its fruits of reconciliation with God. This idea belongs with some understandings of atonement in the New Testament, but also, I claim, in the Hebrew scriptures.[33] To be sure, there is a difference between the case of the animal and the case of the ambassador or of Christ. The ambassador and Christ consent to the identification, and it is not clear what consent would mean for the animal.[34] Consent is not, in general, necessary for evaluative transfer. A child can be ashamed of what a parent does, even if the child at no point

---

[32] This first interpretation can be found in e.g. Milgrom 1991: 151–2, and Levine 1989: 6. The second interpretation can be found in Gerstenberger 1996: 26, 29. An intermediate possibility is raised by Wenham 1995: 79–80, that the gesture means not merely ownership, but identification. See Leach 1976: 89, 'The plain implication is that, in some metaphysical sense, the victim is a vicarious substitution for the donor himself.'

[33] One argument strategy for this chapter would have been to defend the substitutionary view of atonement in the New Testament (as I do in Hare 1996: chs. 8–10) and then argue back to Leviticus. But the focus of the present conference is on the Hebrew scriptures and not the New Testament.

[34] See Patton 2006 who discusses cross-cultural indications that the victims of sacrifice are often regarded as willing.

consented to being born of her parents. But consent *is* necessary for evaluative transfer to lead to justified vicarious or substitutionary punishment. So I am not claiming in this chapter that animal sacrifice is now morally permissible, or that it should be reinstituted if the temple were rebuilt. But I am trying to make the practice of sacrifice less alien by relating it to ideas that I think we can understand, in particular the holiness gap and evaluative transfer. If we ask, why did God prescribe this system if it was not supposed to be permanent, I think Maimonides gives us a good answer. He took the same position, that God was not *now* commanding the sacrifice system, even for the hypothetical situation in which the temple was rebuilt. He says, 'It was in accordance with the wisdom and plan of God, as displayed in the whole Creation, that He did not command us to give up and to discontinue all these manners of service; for to obey such a commandment would have been contrary to the nature of man, who generally cleaves to that to which he is used. . . . [God] transferred to His service that which had formerly served as a worship of created beings' (Maimonides 1956: 322–7). In other words, God temporarily allowed the continuance of the familiar sacrificial form of worship, but diverted it away from idols and from human sacrifice.

The laying on of hands is different in the case of the scapegoat, which on the day of atonement is sent into the wilderness. For a start, Aaron places *both* of his hands on the animal's head and confesses over it the sins of the Israelites. It is probable that 'the two-handed rite identifies the scapegoat as the recipient of the sins, while the one-handed rite in sacrifice identifies the animal as belonging to the offerer' (Wright 1987: 17). The 'scapegoat' is not sacrificed, but sent off into the wilderness. But it is related to the sacrifices in the temple, because the sins that are transferred are seen as defiling the sanctuary, and so as needing to be sent off for disposal so that the sacrifices in the temple can take place. Since the scapegoat is not a sacrifice, its function is not to take the consequences of the sins that are transferred, just to take those sins away.

Now we can return to what I called the central puzzle about the sacrifice system from an ethical point of view; how is *killing* something supposed to help with sin and impurity? I said that the blood prohibition starts to give us an answer. The key text is Leviticus 17: 11, where God says, 'As for the life of the flesh it is in the blood. It is I who have assigned it to you upon the altar to ransom your lives. For it is the blood that ransoms by means of life.'[35] Of the

---

[35] This is Jacob Milgrom's translation, Milgrom 1981: 706–7. Milgrom, however, takes the teaching here as applying only to the *selamim* ('peace') offerings. Both Klawans and Wenham (2006: 82, and see Anderson 1992: 879–80) disagree with this restriction, and I will follow them, and take the role of the blood to be the same in the other relevant sacrifices. See Schwartz 1995b,

three parts of this verse, the first and the third form a reversed pair: life/blood: blood/life, and this suggests that the life is the same in both cases, namely the life of the animal. God assigns to this life a ransoming function.[36] Here the word for 'atone' (*kipper*) taking the object 'life' is probably to be linked with 'ransom your lives' (*koper napso*) elsewhere (Exod. 30: 12, Num. 35: 31–3). Milgrom says, 'The Israelites have become liable to death before God and the purpose of the sacrificial blood is "to ransom your lives".' Once this ransom-killing has occurred, the blood can be used for decontamination of the sacred places. 'Blood, as life, is what purges the sanctuary. It nullifies, overpowers, and absorbs the Israelites' impurities that adhere to the sanctuary, thereby allowing the divine presence to remain and Israel to survive.' The puzzle was how killing, or causing another death, could remove sin or impurity, itself associated with death. The key is the separation between death and blood. Blood can cleanse because it is the principle, not of death, but of life. This is, I grant, a strange idea. Heraclitus mocks the idea of blood sacrifices (*Diels*, 5), 'Those who are polluted with blood purify themselves with blood in vain, as if someone who stepped in mud should try to wash himself with mud.' But Heraclitus has not seen the key conceptual point, which is that the blood for the Israelites is not, like mud, just a repetition of the offence, namely dirt.[37] The animal is a subject, just as the offerer is a subject. They both have lives, represented in this symbol system by their blood, and to these lives both animals and humans have covenantal obligations. The lives of other humans and animals do not belong to us, and have to be returned to God. But after the animal's life, in this symbol system, is taken by God as a ransom instead of the life of the animal's owner, its blood can be used in purification, because of the separation between death and blood.

How much of this can we still use, ethically? Not all of it, because the identification of life principle and blood is now problematic. Our blood system is no more intimately tied to our life than any other organic system.

---

on Lev. 1: 4, 'Heb. "kipper," often translated "atone," has two meanings in P: "decontaminate [the sacred precincts] of sin or defilement" and "serve as ransom or payment [for one's life]". The latter seems to be intended here; that is why it is mentioned along with the hand-laying ritual: The moment ownership of the animal is transferred to the deity, it is accepted as payment, i.e. as a substitute for the worshipper himself.'

[36] Leviticus 17 has a formal structure that emphasizes the centrality of this idea. See Schwartz 1991: 34–66, esp. 46–7. The chapter ascends in intensity in its five paragraphs to the third, and then descends from it. The third paragraph has three verses, and the central verse has three sections. The idea is located in the middle section of the middle verse of the middle paragraph.

[37] Milgrom points out (1981: 706) that this postulate of the life force residing in the blood is unique to Israel amongst its neighbors. The blood prohibition is probably a deliberate opposition to the prevailing practices of Israel's environment, and it is prescribed not only for Israel, but to Noah and so to all human beings.

Moreover, evaluative transfer does not justify punishment of a non-consent-ing substitute. There are other elements involved in the sacrificial system that need ethical discussion. To give just one example, there is the idea that God's leaving a building would produce infertile land. I am not going to try to list these elements. But within the domain of the treatment of animals, there are also positive elements. We *can* use the idea that there is an animal life, to which we have obligation. Indeed, there is something a bit odd about us now looking back at ancient Israel and condemning their treatment of animals as 'violence, vengeance, and victimage'. We are the masters of cruelty to animals. There is nothing in ancient Israel like our factory farming of chickens and veal calves, and nothing like our 'sacrifice', the technical term, of hundreds of thousands of animals caused serious pain for research by the cosmetics industry. The relative condemnation belongs the other way round. It is we in the last hundred years who have commodified and objectified other animals, reducing them to mere meat for our consumption and tools for our research. I could wax eloquent here, but I will resist. Ancient Israel retained a sense of connection with their domestic animals, as subjects in their own right. When it killed them, it did so relatively humanely. The rules for ritual slaughter, though not in the Bible, are in the Talmud, and 'this traditional procedure was intended to cause animals the least pain possible, in accord with the Jewish principle of *tsa'ar ba'alei chayim*. . . . For millennia the Jewish method of slaughter was the least painful form of animal killing until this century' (Cohn-Sherbok 2006: 86). At least in Leviticus 17 (though not in Deuteronomy 12) eating of slaughtered domestic animals was restricted to animals offered at the temple, so that the eating of meat (in any case much less than ours) was reduced. Finally, if I have been right about evaluative transfer, the Israelites used animals for a high office, to represent them before God, and symbolized this by the laying on of hands. All of these aspects belong on the positive side of the ledger, but I am not claiming that they justify animal sacrifices. My goal in this chapter has been merely to make the sacrifice system more intelligible.

I said I would end by talking briefly about the place of ritual and its relation to metaphor. There is not time to do this well, but the sacrifice texts make an important contribution to our understanding of this topic, and I did not want to omit it completely. I have talked about the sacrifices 'enacting metaphor', and I want to say a word or two about what this means. There are two kinds of priority I mean to deny. First there is the priority in meaning of what is said as opposed to what is done. It is tempting to think that when we say that the blood cleanses the altar, there is some linguistic item here that explains, as a necessary intermediate, how an action could have meaning. I am not denying here that there is a proposition that is meant. But I am denying that we have privileged access to that proposition through some sequence of words accessible to us, and that without such a sequence actions cannot have meaning. On the contrary, it may be that the action is the most direct form of access that we have. Actions are often much richer than the sequence of words that inadequately describe them. Meaning can be, as I said at the beginning, multivalent, and the different layers of meaning and their interrelation may be more closely captured in doing than in saying. The second kind of priority that I want to deny is the priority of the literal to the metaphorical. This is an independent point, which could be made just about linguistic items, without bringing in non-linguistic action at all. Consider again the idea of blood cleansing the altar. It is tempting to think this is *just* a metaphor, as though we could describe what is really going on less fancifully in some purely literal form of words. But what would that literal form of words be? Milgrom says that the blood 'nullifies, overpowers, and absorbs' the impurity. But 'absorbs' and 'overpowers' are both metaphors already, and 'nullifies', if it just means 'makes into nothing', does not explain how this is supposed to occur, which is just what we wanted help with. In cases like this, we find that metaphor is basic and inescapable, that we cannot get behind it to something 'literal' that is what is really meant. There is a great deal more to be said here. But I want to end with the suggestion that the Hebrew sacrificial rites give us an important example for understanding worship. Here Kant is surprisingly good. 'Yet for the human being the invisible needs to be represented through something visible (sensible), indeed what is more, it must be accompanied by the visible for the sake of worship and, though intellectual, made as it were an object of intuition according to a certain analogy.'[38] If we are now going to use animals in particular in our worship, as visible representations, we need to do it in a better way than by killing them; but we can learn from ancient sacrificial practice the role of enacted metaphor in worship, as well as the ideas I referred to earlier of the subjecthood of animals, their moral importance as more than just potential meat, and the covenantal relation they bear to us and to God.

---

[38] Kant, *Religion within the Bounds of Mere Reason*, 6: 192.

Comments on 'Animal Sacrifices'

James L. Crenshaw

John Hare's rationale for the priestly writer's understanding of animal sacrifice rests on three pillars: (1) animals were a part of the Israelite household, (2) the holiness gap that separates humans and God was overcome by evaluative transfer, the sacrificed animal taking the place of its owner, and (3) sacrifice worked because it enabled mortals to imitate God, to attract and maintain divine presence, and to expiate impurity and sin. Despite my appreciation for the clarity of his argument, I wish to offer a different interpretation of the evidence adduced to support these three points.

1. THE FIRST PILLAR

'Animals were a part of the Israelite household.' Hare's comment that the point is not controversial is a colossal overstatement. His conclusion is based on four things: (1) Nathan's juridical parable; (2) the concern for cattle expressed in the book of Jonah; (3) humane treatment of domestic animals in Deuteronomy; and (4) the Talmudic principle of *zar ba'ale hayim*.

If Hare hopes to discover the priestly writer's perspective, why appeal to prophetic literature to establish a priestly presupposition? If the aim is to describe the general understanding of sacrifice in Israel, the net must be wide enough to include wisdom literature, especially Job and Qoheleth. Moreover, neither goal can be achieved without attention to genre, which provides clues to subtle nuances.

What of Nathan's parable? Rhetoric crafted to indict without provoking uncontrolled anger can hardly provide accurate information about the relationship between an owner and domestic animals. The juridical parable, despite its misfit, exposes greed that hides under the cloak of hospitality. The fanciful image of a lamb reposing in Bathsheba's bosom is transparently aimed at the emotions. It must not be read literally (Simon 1967; McCarter Jr. 1984).

What about the story of Jonah? Repentant animals and notorious people of Nineveh, a personified ship, an ambiguous message of five Hebrew words, a fish capable of swallowing a human and disgorging him alive and well after three days, a petulant prophet, a magical bush—these belong to satire and fables, not to historical fact.[1]

Deuteronomy's concern for the well-being of animals, more humane than that found elsewhere in the Hebrew scriptures, does not represent the usual view in Israel, certainly not the priestly (Weinfeld 1972). And the Talmudic concept of easing the pain of animals, too late to provide evidence for the priestly author's perspective, merely reflects the continuing influence of those who believed that all God's creatures deserve humane treatment.

How about Hare's supporting arguments: that God's original intent was for humans to become vegetarians, that eating meat was a divine concession, a 'second best', and that authors of utopian descriptions in the Hebrew scriptures imagine a return to the original state, foreshadowed by Noah's ark and the description of the land of promise?

I share Hare's view that the story of Adam and Eve probably implies that the mythical pair were vegetarians, but I do not think the conflicting traditions about the animals entering Noah's ark imply an equation of Urzeit und Endzeit. Nor do I believe that the prophetic pictures of a coming paradise imply vegetarianism. All three texts, Amos 9: 13–14 (to which may be compared Joel 3: 18), Hosea 2: 20, and Isaiah 11: 6–9, emphasize human security, not vegetarianism. The focus is not on animals except to stress the taming of wild beasts to ensure the safety of people.

Naturally, utopian visions varied with the socio-economic context of the authors. At least one post-biblical account imagines the killing of the chaos monster Leviathan and serving it at a banquet in the '*olam haba*', the world to come.[2]

If we widen the net to include the book of Job, what was the real animal kingdom like? The divine speeches describe a world of red tooth and claw and label it God's original creation. In this world, as opposed to fantasy, predation is the rule, and humans are pushed to the outer edges far from the central position they think they occupy. Furthermore, in the folktale, Job's three friends offer sacrifices that by no stretch of the imagination belonged to

---

[1] Sasson 1990: 234–7 nicely exposes the ambiguity in the Hebrew word *nehpaket*, 'overturned' or 'turned around' (destroyed or repentant).

[2] Ben Zvi 2006 treats the fertile imagination of canonical prophets.

their households.[3] The same can be said of Abraham, who according to Gen. 22: 13 offered up a ram that had become entangled in a bush on top of Mt. Moriah (Crenshaw 2008: 9–29), and of Solomon, reputed to have sacrificed a thousand burnt offerings at Gibeon. As members of his household, such a huge number of animals would match the number of his wives. Fiction has replaced fact here.

Selective breeding of animals changes their 'biological type', according to Hare. The wild beast may be gentler and useful to humans, but domestication does not alter genetic makeup. When provoked, or for no explicable reason, such creatures can revert to their natural proclivities, as some people at zoos and elsewhere have learned to their dismay.

No examination of sacrifice in the Hebrew scriptures is complete without raising the issue of human sacrifice (Levenson 1993). Like so much else, it linked Israel with her closest neighbors. The divine imperative in Exod. 22: 29b remains a haunting reminder that all first-born sons were to be sacrificed to YHWH, an idea that survived as late as the eighth century when Micah pondered the extent of God's requirement for human rectitude. The prophet Ezekiel even tries to justify this demand as a means of horrifying the nation Israel (20: 26). This practice of sacrificing first-born sons may have been largely abandoned by the time of the priestly author, but it must not be passed over in silence.

2. HARE'S SECOND PILLAR

'The holiness gap is overcome by evaluative transfer.' Kant's famous moral gap is here changed to one of holiness, while his denial of the transferability of guilt is rejected. In my view, the so-called moral gap is a product of theodicy; it functions to exonerate the deity by shifting blame to humans, thought to be willful sinners deserving the disasters encountered as finite creatures (Crenshaw 1992: 444–7; Laato and de Moor 2003; Penchansky and Redditt 2000). This unrealistic view derives from a Deuteronomistic concept of reward and punishment; it underlies virtually the entire canon but is most noticeable in sacred historiography.

The moral gap rests more on Christian dogma than on the actual literary construct of YHWH in the Hebrew scriptures (Crenshaw 2001; Miles 1995). A strong case can be made for a reverse moral gap, humans being more moral

---

[3] Newsom 1996 and Balentine 2006 demonstrate the richness of current research on the book of Job.

than the actual depiction of YHWH. That is exactly what Abraham and Job did, and the story line proves them justified in doing so. I have discussed the dark side of YHWH at some length elsewhere (Crenshaw 2005). For now, I will only say that YHWH's constant petulance, need for praise, and bloodlust set the bar extremely low.

What about a holiness gap? In the priestly source the deity mandates holiness, a demand impossible to meet. Through evaluative transfer, sacrifice removes the gap between God's demand and the natural capacity of humans. Here the theory becomes a bit tricky. Two factors make it work, according to Hare. The blood of the sacrificed animal, its life, belongs to God, and humans transfer guilt to the animal by laying a hand (or hands) on it to symbolize the transfer. Having taught at Duke University, a mecca for college basketball, for over twenty years, I understand Hare's explanation of positive transfer of value, but guilt is another thing. In this regard, I follow Kant. I cannot see how the blood of animals takes the place of that of humans. Viewing animals as subjects is commendable, but transferring guilt is another matter. Hare's belief that the Christian view of Jesus' atoning death derives from Hebrew scriptures needs further elaboration, especially in light of the minimal role of the suffering servant in the New Testament.

I accept Hare's rejection of a totemic understanding of sacrifice and of 'shunt violence' à la René Girard. The former, too evolutionist, rests on a magical view; the latter attaches a finality to Christ's death not borne out in history. In reality, that death merely accentuates the cycle of violence rather than bringing it to an end by exposing cruelty for all to see.

Was YHWH immune to sex? The canonical witness to a residual belief in Yahweh's sexuality has been reinforced by evidence discovered at Elephantine, Khirbet 'el Qom, and Kuntillet 'Ajrud. Although debatable, one can associate YHWH with sexuality from the following: the verb *qana* in the sense of begetting in Eve's exclamation, 'I've gotten a boy with YHWH's help', the epithet *qoneh samayim wa'arets*, and the erotically charged language about the relationship between YHWH and *Hokma* in Prov. 8: 22–31 (Terrien 1985; Keel 2007). Against that background, the prophetic language about YHWH's marriages in Hosea and Ezekiel, although metaphorical, makes sense.

What about the claim that all humans are burdened with original sin? In my view, the Hebrew scriptures do not support such a flawed nature as the result of the first transgression. Not until Sirach, Second Esdras, and Second Baruch is the sin of the first couple said to be passed on to succeeding generations. Although some Tanna spoke of lingering guilt after what they believed to be a sexual union between Eve and the serpent, they suggested that the flood took it away, and after the idolatrous worship of the golden calf, the Sinaitic legislation cleared the slate again.

3. THE THIRD PILLAR

'Sacrifice provided a means of imitating God, bringing near the divine presence, and expiating impurity and guilt.' Hare emphasizes the metaphor of divine shepherd who selects, breeds, and kills sheep; in the process, Hare evokes the idea of providence. It is strange providence indeed that kills.

Cross-cultural analysis shows that Egyptian texts frequently apply the language of shepherd to the gods. As one might expect, the metaphor was common throughout the ancient Near East, especially in literature reflecting on the deity's laxity in caring for his or her own. Amazingly, Death is even called a shepherd. There is, however, a significant difference between humans and the divine shepherd. Whereas God kills and brings to life, human beings can only kill. The effort to imitate God therefore aborts, despite a pure conscience and obedient intent.

Does sacrifice attract and maintain divine presence? Biblical authors held competing views about the possibility of bringing God near, nicely illustrated by the ark of the covenant, a palladium of war and symbol of divine presence, and the tent of meeting, a testimony to a distant God who comes when choosing to do so. Divine presence was dangerous even for near-saints. For the biblical Job, YHWH's presence was torture, yet ironically sought in vain. For Qoheleth, Elohim was too remote to bother with mortals except when provoked. According to Jeremiah, even genuine repentance did not assure divine forgiveness (14: 19–15: 9). Presence, therefore, was problematic to many in Israel.

Leviticus 26 graphically illustrates the ethical ramifications of relying on a canonical text for guidance. The high-flown rhetoric of chasing enemies who outnumber you ten to one reflects a wild imagination, but that is nothing compared to what is attributed to God: making Israelites starve so they will eat their own children. Such divine presence is not a desideratum.

Hare's positive spin on sacrifice as an expiation rests on a magical under-standing of ritual akin to omen literature from Mesopotamia. It is not clear to me precisely how he thinks spilling the blood of an animal removed impurity and guilt, that is, accidental and willful transgression. For the priestly writer, as Hare recognizes, God feasted on the burnt offering and found pleasure in the aroma, anthropomorphisms that do not sit well with moderns. But did anyone other than priests, who had much to gain, really think so highly of sacrifices? Clearly, opinions were divided, as he acknowledges.[4]

---

[4] Tiemeyer 2006 does not view the criticism as rejection but as renewal and reform.

Hare's closing remarks on ethics ring true. Metaphor is superior to a literal reading of sacrifice, action to any sequence of explanatory words. And humans need symbolic action to express the inexpressible. It is the genius of myth that it does not give voice to the truth conveyed (Fishbane 2003). While modern slaughter of animals for human consumption and other uses makes ancient Israel appear more merciful than we, does killing animals for divine consumption render the act any less objectionable, even if the animal was thought of as subject?

To conclude, applying the adjective 'good' to the deity portrayed in the Hebrew scriptures requires a redefinition of the word 'good'. As normally used, it does not fit one who required the killing of animals to exonerate human guilt.

Reply to Crenshaw

John Hare

I am grateful to James Crenshaw for his comments, which have been helpful. I will take the three points in the same order. The first point is about animals being regarded as part of the household. I gave a number of examples of this, though I did not take it to be a point that needed defending. I could have added that archeologists reconstruct the ancient Israelite domicile with animals on the ground level, and people sleeping on top.[1] The examples I used were designed to make a conceptual claim, not a historical one. It is not relevant to this whether Nathan's parable is to be taken literally, or whether, when we consider its genre, we see (according to Crenshaw) that it is a fanciful image, not accurate information. My point is not about whether the story is literal, but about a conceptual connection present in that context; the lamb is like a daughter. The same is true with the story of Jonah. I am not interested in whether this is 'history' in some eighteenth-century sense. Again there is a conceptual connection; the animals are clothed in sackcloth. If the household is destroyed, so are the animals; they are saved or destroyed together. Job's friends offer sacrifices, says Crenshaw, that were not part of their household. But the text is silent about the source of the seven bullocks and seven rams. On my view, animals are conceived as becoming part of the household by acquisition, even if they were not before. Crenshaw says that when Solomon sacrificed a thousand burnt offerings at Gibeon, this would equal the number of his wives, and so 'fiction has here replaced fact'. But again, my point is not about historicity, but about a conceptual connection. Solomon's extraordinary expense exactly shows the extraordinary extent of his household.

Crenshaw does not think that the prophetic images of the end time imply vegetarianism. He says that the focus is not on animals except to stress the taming of wild beasts to ensure the safety of people. But the text not only says that a little child shall lead them, but puts together the wolf and the lamb, the leopard and the kid, the calf and the lion, the cow and the bear, and says the

---

[1] Thanks to Gary Anderson for this point.

lion shall eat straw like the ox. They, all of them, shall not hurt or destroy in all my holy mountain. I cannot see the emphasis where Crenshaw locates it.

Domestication, he says, does not alter genetic makeup. But it does. The animals we breed are different biologically from their wild ancestors.

On the second point, Crenshaw says that the moral gap functions to exonerate the deity by shifting blame to humans from God. But it could only do so under two conditions: either we do not do evil (and so do not deserve this 'shift') or we are not responsible for the evil we do. I don't think either of these claims is true.

Crenshaw thinks there is 'canonical witness' to God having sex with Eve, and this is reinforced from non-scriptural sources. His evidence from scripture, which he concedes is debatable, is the word *qana* in Genesis 4: 1, where Eve says 'I have begotten a man from the Lord.' Note that the verse starts, 'Now Adam knew Eve his wife, and she conceived and bore Cain.' (NKJV) Also, Proverbs 8 uses 'erotically charged' language for the relationship between God and wisdom, but I feel like using Crenshaw's own remarks about not taking the texts too literally.

On the third point, Crenshaw thinks it strange to believe that our deaths are in God's hands as well as our lives ('It is a strange providence indeed that kills' (142)). But it is a perfectly familiar point within the life of faith that 'there is a time to die', and that we are dependent creatures and should take our lives and their span as a gift. This is, however, a long argument, and Crenshaw has devoted much of his life to the problems of theodicy. We cannot solve these problems here.

Crenshaw thinks that the divine presence was 'problematic to many in Israel'. But on my reading of scripture, they *did* want the presence, but they also wanted holiness, the two things together and not disastrously apart. Crenshaw asks, 'Did anyone other than priests, who had much to gain, really think so highly of sacrifices? Clearly, opinions were divided, as [Hare] acknowledges.' (142) But I do not acknowledge this. The prophetic critique of sacrifice, I suggested, is directed at renewal and reform not at replacement.

Finally, Crenshaw thinks a good God could not command animal sacrifice, but he does not comment on my point from Maimonides, which is important to the chapter, and which I should probably have emphasized more than I did. I did not try to argue that animal sacrifice is *now* commanded by God. Maimonides took the same position. If we ask, why did God command it *then*, the suggestion is that God was again making a concession. The context was a people who were used to sacrificing to idols. God required them to make the sacrifices only to God but did not (in the divine mercy) stop them sacrificing completely, because they needed still to worship in some way familiar to them. We might add that God replaced human sacrifice by animal sacrifice, as in the story of the binding of Isaac. This view is not the evolutionist view I condemned, that thinks of sacred history as having a primitive stage of magic and an advanced stage of ethics. But it does hold that God's commands, like those of human parents to their children, are given in relation to our development.

Crenshaw holds that applying the adjective 'good' to the deity portrayed in the Hebrew scriptures requires a redefinition of the word 'good'. I agree that the goodness of God is not exactly like the goodness of human beings. But we can see analogies, and in the present case the analogy is that God is like a good parent giving his or her children a way to live by the standards God also reveals to them.

REFERENCES

Anderson, Gary A. 1987. *Sacrifices and Offerings in Ancient Israel*. Atlanta: Scholars Press.

——1992. 'Sacrifice and Sacrificial Offerings', in *The Anchor Bible Dictionary*. New York: Doubleday, 878–9.

Balentine, Samuel E. 2006. *Job*. Macon: Smyth & Helwys.

Ben Zvi, Ehud (ed.). 2006. *Utopia and Dystopia in Prophetic Texts*. Helsinki: Finnish Exegetical Society; Goettingen: Vandenhoek & Ruprecht.

Cohen, Jeremy. 1989. *'Be Fertile and Increase, Fill the Earth and Master It': The Ancient and Medieval Career of a Biblical Text*. Ithaca, NY: Cornell University Press.

Cohn-Sherbok, Dan. 2006. 'Hope for the Animal Kingdom: A Jewish Vision', in *A Communion of Subjects: Animals in Religion, Science, and Ethics*. New York: Columbia University Press, 81–90.

Crenshaw, James L. 1992. 'Theodicy', in *Anchor Bible Dictionary*, vi. New York: Doubleday, 444–7.

——2001. 'The Reification of Divine Evil', *Perspectives in Religious Studies*, 28: 327–32.

——2005. *Defending God: Biblical Responses to the Problem of Evil*. New York: Oxford University Press.

——2008. *A Whirlpool of Torment: Israelite Traditions of God as an Oppressive Presence*. Atlanta: Society of Biblical Literature. 1st edn. 1984.

Davidson, Donald. 1984. 'Truth and Meaning', in *Inquiries into Truth and Interpretation*. Oxford: Oxford University Press.

Douglas, Mary. 1966. *Purity and Danger: An Analysis of the Concepts of Pollution and Taboo*. London: Routledge and Kegan Paul.

Fishbane, Michael. 2003. *Biblical Myth and Rabbinic Mythmaking*. Oxford: Oxford University Press.

Gerstenberger, Erhard S. 1996. *Leviticus: A Commentary*. Old Testament Library. Louisville, Ky.: Westminster John Knox Press.

Girard, René. 1977. *Violence and the Sacred*, trans. Patrick Gregory. Baltimore: Johns Hopkins University Press.

——1987. 'Generative Scapegoating', in Robert Hammerton-Kelly (ed.), *Violent Origins*. Stanford, Calif.: Stanford University Press.

Gunton, Colin. 1989. *The Actuality of Atonement*. Edinburgh: T. & T. Clark.

Hamerton-Kelly, Robert. 1994. *The Gospel and the Sacred: Poetics of Violence in Mark*. Minneapolis: Fortress Press.

Hare, John E. 1996. *The Moral Gap: Kantian Ethics, Human Limits, and God's Assistance*. Oxford: Clarendon Press, 248–56.

Hubert, Henri, and Mauss, Marcel. 1964. *Sacrifice: Its Nature and Functions*, trans. W. D. Halls. Chicago: University of Chicago Press.

Kant, Immanuel. 1798/1996. *Conflict of the Faculties*, trans. by Allen Wood and George D. Giovanni. Cambridge: Cambridge University Press.

Keel, Othmar. 2007. *L'Éternel féminine: une face caché du Dieu biblique*. Geneva: Labor et Fides.

Klawans, Jonathan. 2001. 'Pure Violence: Sacrifice and Defilement in Ancient Israel', *Harvard Theological Review*, 94/2: 151.

——2002. 'Interpreting the Last Supper: Sacrifice, Spiritualization, and Anti-Sacrifice', *New Testament Studies*, 48: 1–17.

——2006a. 'Sacrifice in Ancient Israel: Pure Bodies, Domesticated Animals, and the Divine Shepherd', in *A Communion of Subjects: Animals in Religion, Science, and Ethics*. New York: Columbia University Press.

——2006b. *Purity, Sacrifice, and the Temple*. Oxford: Oxford University Press.

Laato, Antti, and de Moor, Johannes C. (eds.). 2003. *Theodicy in the World of the Bible*. Leiden/Boston: Brill.

Leach, Edmund. 1976. *Culture and Communication: The Logic by which Symbols are Connected*. Cambridge: Cambridge University Press.

Levenson, Jon D. 1988. *Creation and the Persistence of Evil: The Jewish Drama of Divine Omnipotence*. Princeton: Princeton University Press.

——1993. *The Death and Resurrection of the Beloved Son: The Transformation of Child Sacrifice in Judaism and Christianity*. New Haven: Yale University Press.

Levine, B. A. 1989. *Leviticus*. Philadelphia: Jewish Publication Society.

Lucas, Ernest C. 1995. 'Sacrifice in the Prophets', in Roger Beckwith and Martin Selman (eds.), *Sacrifice in the Bible*. Grand Rapids, Mich.: Baker Book House.

McCarter, P. Kyle, Jr. 1984. *II Samuel*. New York: Doubleday.

Maimonides. 1956. *The Guide for the Perplexed*, trans. M. Friedländer. New York: Dover.

Mason, Jim. 1993. *An Unnatural Order*. New York: Simon and Schuster.

Miles, Jack. 1995. *God: A Biography*. New York: Vintage Books.

Milgrom, Jacob. 1991. *Leviticus 1–16*. The Anchor Bible. New York: Doubleday.

Newsom, Carol A. 1996. *The Book of Job*. The New Interpreter's Bible IV. Nashville: Abingdon Press.

Patton, Kimberley. 2006. 'Animal Sacrifice', in *A Communion of Subjects: Animals in Religion, Science, and Ethics*. New York: Columbia University Press.

Penchansky, David, and Redditt, Paul L. (eds.). 2000. *Shall Not the Judge of All the Earth Do What Is Right? Studies on the Nature of God in Tribute to James L. Crenshaw*. Winona Lake, Ind.: Eisenbrauns.

Robertson Smith, William. 1927. *Lectures on the Religion of the Semites: The Fundamental Institutions*, 3rd edn., ed. Stanley A. Cook. New York: Macmillan.

Robins, Jill. 1998. 'Sacrifice', in Mark Taylor (ed.), *Critical Terms for Religious Studies*. Chicago: University of Chicago Press.

Sasson, Jack M. 1990. *Jonah*. New York: Doubleday.

Schwartz, Baruch J. 1991. 'Priesthood and Cult in Ancient Israel', *Journal for the Study of the Old Testament*, Supp. 125, Sheffield, 34–66.

——1995a. 'The Bearing of Sin in the Priestly Literature', in D. P. Wright et al. (eds.), *Pomegranates and Golden Bells*. Winona Lake, Ind.: Eisenbrauns, 3–21.

——1995b. *Leviticus*, in *The Jewish Study Bible*. Oxford: Oxford University Press.

——1996. '"Profane" Slaughter and the Integrity of the Priestly Code', *Hebrew Union College Annual*, 67: 15–42.

Scully, Matthew. 2002. *Dominion: The Power of Man, the Suffering of Animals, and the Call to Mercy.* New York: St Martin's Griffin.

Simon, Uriel. 1967. 'The Poor Man's Ewe-Lamb: An Example of a Juridical Parable', *Biblica*, 48: 207–42.

Skinner, J. 1922. *Prophecy and Religion.* Cambridge: Cambridge University Press.

Terrien, Samuel. 1985. *Till the Heart Sings.* Philadelphia: Fortress Press.

Tiemeyer, Lena-Sofia. 2006. *Priestly Rites and Prophetic Rage: Post-Exilic Prophetic Critique of the Priesthood.* Forschungen zum Alten Testament. Tübingen: Mohr Siebeck.

Tylor, E. B. 1873. *Primitive Culture*, 3rd edn. New York: H. Holt.

Webb, Stephen. 1998. *God and Dogs: A Christian Theology of Compassion for Animals.* Oxford: Oxford University Press.

Weinfeld, Moshe. 1972. *Deuteronomy and the Deuteronomic School.* Oxford: Oxford University Press.

Wenham, Gordon J. 1995. 'The Theology of Old Testament Sacrifice', in Roger Beckwith and Martin Selman (eds.), *Sacrifice in the Bible.* Grand Rapids, Mich.: Baker Book House, 79–80.

Wright, David P. 1987. *The Disposal of Impurity.* Atlanta: Scholars Press.

5

God Beyond Justice

Mark C. Murphy

> Unless we want to deny to the concept of morality all truth and all
> reference to a possible object, we cannot but admit that the moral law
> is of such widespread significance that it must hold not merely for all
> men but for all rational beings generally.
>
> (Kant, *Groundwork* 2, 408)

> 6. Ethics is 'autonomous' and is to be derived, if from anything, from
> rationality. Ethical considerations will be the same for any rational being.
>
> (Anscombe, 'Twenty Opinions Common Among
> Anglo-American Philosophers')

I

There are many divine actions recorded in scripture that might be used to
focus one's mind on the question of God's goodness. Consider but one, the
massacre of the Jerichoites by the army of the Lord.

[The angel of the Lord told Joshua:] 'The Lord has given you the city and everything
in it. It is under the Lord's ban. Only the harlot Rahab and all who are in her house are
to be spared, because she hid the messengers we sent....'
   As the horns blew, the people began to shout.... The wall collapsed, and the people
stormed the city in a frontal assault and took it. They observed the ban by putting to
the sword all living creatures in the city: men and women, young and old, as well as
oxen, sheep, and asses.[1]

This is, to put things mildly, a disquieting text. There are various hermeneutical
maneuvers that one could employ with respect to it that would make its
presence less disquieting, but I am not interested here in the plausibility of
these maneuvers, either generally or in respect of this particular text. I will

   Thanks for comments and discussion to Mike Bergmann, Mike Rea, Wes Morriston, Robert
Gressis, Clint Hall, Kelly Heuer, Paddy McShane, and Alex Pruss.
   [1] Josh. 6: 16–17, 20–1 (*New American Bible*).

suppose that this text makes a set of assertions, to be construed literally, regarding what God commanded the army of the Lord to do, and what they subsequently successfully did. And I want to know whether this story, if literally true, would morally discredit the being who ordered the bloodbath. I say, 'No': God's ordering the destruction of Jericho does not morally discredit God.

Answering 'No' to this question may generate a second worry. If we answer 'No', do we not then lose any grip that we had on the notion that God is a lover of justice, and that in his dealings with us God is perfectly just? Again I say 'No': it casts no doubt either on the view that God is a lover of justice or on the conviction that all of God's dealings with us conform to the norms of justice.

II

How is God's ordering the destruction of Jericho supposed to morally discredit God? God is supposed to be perfectly good, and any sort of moral error would discredit God. But it is plain that this ordering of the destruction of this city—the adults and the children alike—constitutes a moral error, whoever performs it. So God, with respect to Jericho, got things wrong, and so God is morally discredited.

I argue that we have nothing like an adequate basis for holding that God's ordering the destruction of Jericho counts as moral error. I take it that any evidence that God morally erred would appeal to God's treatment of the Jerichoites. It may also be true that God morally erred with respect to the Israelites, in the same way that an army captain morally errs with respect to those under his or her command if he or she commands them to target non-combatants. But that the captain acts wrongly with respect to those under his or her command depends on the captain's acting wrongly with respect to the non-combatants—treating them as appropriate targets. Similarly, if God acts wrongly with respect to the Israelites in ordering them to destroy Jericho, this error is parasitic on the error of treating the Jerichoites as appropriate objects of destruction.[2] So our attention will be wholly focused on God's treatment of the Jerichoites.

---

[2] It is true that even if God were not as such morally unjustified in realizing the destruction of Jericho, it could be the case that what the Israelites were being called upon to do was so horrifying that taking part in it is either objectively marring of their lives or so subjectively psychologically damaging that God would be wronging them in directing them to do it. But we are given no evidence from the text of psychological damage; this seems a contingent matter, which those who wish to portray God as unjustified here would be ill advised to rely upon. It may be that what they are being asked to do here is objectively marring—that the Israelites' lives

Consider the following two claims concerning God's treatment of the Jerichoites:

1. God *acted wrongly with respect to* the Jerichoites in the destruction of Jericho
2. God *wronged* the Jerichoites in the destruction of Jericho

There is more than a verbal difference here—to judge that one *acted wrongly* with respect to someone is a different normative assessment than to judge that one *wronged* someone. The former concerns what Michael Thompson has usefully labeled 'monadic' normativity, the latter 'bipolar' normativity.[3] *Acting wrongly in φ-ing* is a *monadic* property of an agent; even if the act of φ-ing takes some direct object x, x features, as Thompson remarks, as 'raw material' for the wrong action—even if the value of x is an agent, that place could equally well have been occupied by rare birds or old buildings (Thompson 2004: 344). *Wronging in φ-ing* is, by contrast, a *bipolar* matter, for which one needs both an agent and a patient; the agent is, as in the case of monadic normativity, a *wrongdoer*, but there is also a *victim*, who is wronged by the action.

Initially the clearest way to see the difference between the two notions is to note that while there is a limited class of objects that can be wronged, potential victims of wrongdoing, one can act wrongly with respect to anything that has any sort of value. One can think that to destroy a rainforest without further reason is itself to act wrongly with respect to the rainforest. All this requires is that the rainforest have value that should not be disregarded or devalued in one's deliberation and action. This value could be merely instrumental, but it is also possible that it be intrinsic value. The rainforest might be an intrinsically valuable entity such that it would be wrong to destroy it, or *the rainforest's existing* could be an intrinsically valuable state of affairs, such that it would be wrong, *pro tanto*, to act so that this state of affairs no longer obtains. This might be true of art objects as well: they might be valuable, instrumentally or even intrinsically, such that one would act wrongly with respect to them in destroying or defacing them. But the Amazon rainforest and Picasso's *Guernica* are not possibly *victims* of

---

may be in some way ruined by engaging in this slaughter, and this independently of whether the acts that they are being called upon to perform are morally justified. (For discussion of this notion of 'marring', see Rosalind Hursthouse's discussion of tragic dilemmas (Hursthouse 1999: 71–87). This would require further discussion of the notion of marring, I think. But it does not seem at all obvious to me that it is necessarily wrong to order another agent to do something that is objectively marring of that agent's life, any more than it is necessarily wrong to order another agent to do something that will result in that agent's death. So even if we conclude that this divinely commanded action would mar the lives of the Israelites, it would not follow without additional contested premises that God's giving this command morally discredits God.

[3] See Thompson 2004: 333–84.

wrongdoing. They are not *parties* who can be wronged. Indeed, on most plausible conceptions of wronging, it is obvious that one can act wrongly with respect to someone who is not thereby wronged by one's action: this is the category of self-regarding immorality. Justice, on the classical conception, is always toward another.[4] So one cannot wrong oneself, though one can act wrongly *with respect to* oneself, by eating too much, drinking too much, goofing off too much, reading too much philosophy, etc.

One might think that this initial way of distinguishing *acting wrongly with respect to* from *wronging* suggests that to wrong someone just is to act wrongly with respect to something that falls into a particular privileged class—say, agents, or humans, or fellow citizens, or whatever. But that is also false: I cannot wrong myself, though I belong to the privileged class of beings that can be wronged. Even if we qualify matters so that to wrong is to act wrongly with respect to some member of the privileged class who is not the agent, the analysis still fails. For the sake of argument, take the privileged class to be *all humans*. Suppose that out of self-respect I ought to act in ways that will enable me to advance my worthy projects in the future. I thus should show myself to be a trustworthy cooperator, because those who show themselves to be trustworthy cooperators are better able to advance their worthwhile projects. I therefore should keep my promises to you, in order to show myself to be a trustworthy cooperator. If all this were true, and I think it is true, I would be acting wrongly with respect to you by breaking promises that I make to you. But these considerations would not make it the case that I would be wronging you by breaking my promise to you. *As far as these considerations go*, I do not *owe* you promise-keeping; you are not a *victim* of my promise-breaking; you have no *title to insist* that I do as I promised. *As far as these considerations go*, you are simply 'raw material' for wrongdoing; the considerations raised do not show you to be a victim if I fail to keep promises to you. But that shows that wronging cannot be analyzed as acting wrongly with respect to some member of a privileged class. It is a different sort of relationship, not the same relationship restricted to a certain group of parties.

I have suggested that the truth of (1) (that God acted wrongly with respect to the Jerichoites) does not entail the truth of (2) (that God wronged the Jerichoites). But, while there are respectable and powerful arguments to the contrary, I will take the truth of (2) to non-trivially entail (1).[5] By 'non-trivially' I mean that it is not just that we will not count as a case of wronging x any case in which one does not act wrongly with respect to x. (This was

---

[4] Aquinas, *Summa Theologiae*, IIaIIae 58, 2.

[5] Allowing this entailment does not make my task easier; it makes it harder. For if this entailment does not hold, then one might be able to concede that God wronged the Jerichoites while denying that God acted wrongly.

Mill's view: he writes that in those cases in which we find it so important to utility to override the normal rights that we ascribe to folk, we save at least the verbal forms of the inviolability of justice by denying that justice really requires such action.[6]) I will take it that *x wrongs y* is a *verdictive* on x's action—that it condemns that action as defective.[7] Again, as Thompson puts it, hedging a bit, 'The consideration operates pairwise'—between potential wrongdoer and potential victim—'and the rest of the world is, at least to a certain extent, closed out' (Thompson 2004: 334). So while (1) does not entail (2), (2) does—I will grant—entail (1).

Having made the relevant initial distinctions between wronging someone and acting wrongly with respect to him or her, I can now set out my central theses regarding God's treatment of the Jerichoites. If one wishes to say that these divine actions morally discredit God, then one must affirm (1) that God acted wrongly with respect to the Jerichoites. But I say that there is no defensible argumentative path to (1) that does not require establishing (2): that God wronged the Jerichoites. While I grant that establishing (2) would suffice to prove (1), (2) is itself implausible. Thus we have no adequate basis for holding that God morally erred in his treatment of the Jerichoites.

III

The only really plausible argument for the claim that God acted wrongly with respect to the Jerichoites takes the claim that God wronged the Jerichoites as a premise. Note that I am claiming not only that this is the most obvious way to argue the claim but also that it is the only really plausible way. Why?

The only alternative to such an argument that I can see would be framed in terms of intrinsic value and how it is fitting to respond to it. It is plain, after all, that we could not appeal to merely instrumental irrationality in showing that God acted wrongly—to do so we would need to know more about God's ends, and the effectiveness of the giving of the order and its results in light of those ends, to make that sort of claim; and we have no independent knowledge that would enable us to criticize God's action on such grounds. We would have to argue, that is, from normative premises about what sort of ends God could or must have in order to argue that God's action was instrumentally irrational; but

---

[6] Mill, *Utilitarianism*, ch. V: 'By this useful accommodation of language, the character of indefeasibility attributed to justice is kept up, and we are saved from the necessity of maintaining that there can be laudable injustice.'

[7] See Foot 2001: 78.

if that is the argument, then it is the conviction that there is no end that God could have had that would necessitate the destruction of the Jerichoites that is carrying all of the weight.

We should then appeal directly to the intrinsic value of the Jerichoites. Obviously these are valuable beings. We might want to say that it was (to put it crudely) wasteful, heedless of their value, to treat them in the way that God treated them. But I think that even granting the notion of intrinsic value at stake here—goodness from the point of view of the universe, intrinsically to-be-promoted or to-be-respected—the claim that God's actions involved a failure adequately to respond to that value is shown to be unjustified by appeal to the sorts of considerations that skeptical theists have brought forward in responding to the problem of evil. Put briefly, the skeptical theists have argued against the claim that the existence of these worldly evils calls into question the existence of a perfectly good God by denying that we have adequate reason to believe that we are well positioned to assess whether there are goods that justify the permission of those evils.[8] Now suppose that this is the charge of the critic who holds that the destruction of Jericho involves God in moral error: that there is such a thing as fully intrinsic value, not simply value *for* or *of* humans, but simply good; that the Jerichoites are themselves intrinsically valuable beings; and that God acted in disregard of that value in ordering their destruction. If this is the charge, then we should, following the skeptical theists, challenge the critic's warrant for affirming the third of these claims. For there is no reason to suppose that the human being's grasp of intrinsic value and the means of realizing it is sufficient to give us justified confidence that God inadequately responded to the intrinsic value of the Jerichoites. To take the most obvious point, the destruction of the Jerichoites is, so far as we know, part of or the best means to an organic unity that has greater (or not lesser) intrinsic value than would be available by leaving Jericho more intact.

We can frame this reply as a dilemma. Suppose that we say that the value of the Jerichoites at stake in the argument is some anthropocentric[9] conception of value, whether objectively or subjectively characterized. It would be bizarre to claim that some instance of divine agency is *ipso facto* defective because it is a failure to act optimally with respect to anthropocentric goodness, just as it would be bizarre to claim that some instance of human agency is defective because it is a failure to act optimally with respect to goldfish-centric goodness, Kudzu-vine-centric goodness, or amoeba-centric goodness. On the other hand, suppose that we say that the value of the Jerichoites at stake in the

---

[8] See, for example, Michael Bergmann's work on skeptical theism, some of which is summarized in Bergmann 2009: 374–99.

[9] For the notion of anthropocentric value, see Wiggins 1987: 87–138.

argument is a non-anthropocentric conception of value—say, Moorean intrinsic value.[10] While there may be plausible arguments that what makes for anthropocentric goodness must be in principle knowable by human beings, there is no plausible argument that what makes for some sort of intrinsic, non-anthropocentric goodness must be in principle knowable by human beings.[11]

One might reply here[12] that an appeal to skepticism regarding the sorts of goods and evils in light of which God is acting in ordering the destruction of Jericho flies in the face of the fact that we are given via divine revelation an account of the precise reasons for this destruction—that the Jerichoites, through their wickedness, have defiled the land, and (of course, relatedly) that the Israelites are not to get mixed up with these people.[13] Once we are given these reasons, we can see that the means employed—the total destruction of the Jerichoites—are obviously disproportionate to these objectives, and so we gain no purchase in our defense of God's order to destroy Jericho. But I am not moved from my skepticism by the citing of these reasons. No doubt that in making intelligible God's command we should advert to the wickedness of the Jerichoite community, and should view God's command as in some way a response to that wickedness. But that is perfectly compatible with our having only the dimmest sense of the goods that may be involved with God's directing the army of the Lord as he did and the evils that may be involved with God's taking alternative courses of action.[14]

---

[10] See G. E. Moore, *Principia Ethica*, §§ 50, 55.

[11] As Robert Gressis pointed out to me at the conference at which this chapter was presented, I should allow that we humans can have some grip on some varieties of non-anthropocentric goodness—I do think that we can grasp what is good and bad for a fern, say, or an earthworm. What I want to deny is that non-anthropocentric goodness that is 'above' us—think God and angels—is something that we must have a natural capacity to grasp. I also want to say that intrinsic goodness is something that we should have *no* confident assessment about our ability to grasp.

[12] As Wes Morriston replied to an earlier draft of this chapter; his searching comments and his own published work on the subject have been extremely useful in keeping properly in focus the difficulty of the problems faced by those who want to offer moral rather than interpretive or historical replies to the question of divine action in the Hebrew scriptures. See Morriston 2009: 9.

[13] Deut. 7: 1–10.

[14] I am preparing dinner for an old college friend whom I haven't seen in twenty years and with whom friendly relations uneasily fell apart for stupid reasons; my 3-year-old child wants to play. He is tugging at my pants leg. 'Why can't you play?' 'I'm making dinner for a friend.' What I say is true. But given a philosopher to represent his interests, my son could argue that this reason could be satisfied in two minutes by putting frozen chicken nuggets and french fries into the oven, leaving ample time for play. But what more should I say, or what should I have said instead? Should I try to explain in detail why I am spending the time that I am spending—not just throwing frozen food into the oven, but painstakingly working on a meal that will evoke memories of our earlier years and better times shared, perhaps to help repair the break but at least to ease any resentment that might remain over the falling out—to a 3-year-old? Is he going to get it? No. But 'I'm making dinner for a friend' is true and puts him on the right track.

There have been some replies to the skeptical theist reflections on the problem of evil that retort that the truth of these reflections would undercut ordinary human agency.[15] These replies have merit only to the extent that our ordinary human agency is appropriately regulated by estimates of the non-anthropocentric value to be realized in and through action.[16] As far as I can see, there is no reason to think that such value makes a difference to what I owe my fellow humans as a matter of justice; and other virtues—temperance, courage, benevolence, and so forth—seem to be oriented by ordinary anthropocentric value. I think that it is true that, to the extent that ordinary human agency is to be regulated by non-anthropocentric value, the skeptical theists' view would undermine that agency. But there is little reason to suppose that this is an objection either to the skeptical theists' position on the problem of evil or to my position on the normative assessment of divine action.

IV

Our question reduces, then, to that of whether God *wronged* the Jerichoites in ordering their destruction. I say God did not wrong them, as there are certain preconditions that must hold for one party to wrong another, and those preconditions do not hold by nature in the case of God and human beings.[17]

My argument here consists in a set of considerations concerning two recent attempts to elucidate the nature of wronging, both with respect to the plausibility of these recent attempts and their bearing on the case at issue. I will first consider an attempt to give an account of wronging that would support the claim that God and the Jerichoites are situated such that a wronging relationship naturally can hold between them, that offered recently by Darwall in *The Second-Person Standpoint* (2006). Darwall's view entails that I am in error in holding that God and the Jerichoites are not situated so that they can stand in a wronging relationship one to the other; I thus argue that his view is implausible as an account of the nature of wronging and at any rate fails to supply an argument for any thesis strong enough to support the claim that God is capable of wronging the Jerichoites. I will then turn to Michael Thompson's recent treatment of the subject, arguing that while it points to a more promising account of wronging, it renders implausible the

---

[15] Cf. Almeida and Oppy 2003: 496–516.

[16] Which seems to be the basic point of Trakakis and Nagasawa's appeal (2004) to a distinction between 'God-justifying' and 'us-justifying' reasons.

[17] I say 'by nature'; I'll comment on the importance of this qualification later in the chapter.

view that God and the Jerichoites are related so as to make possible God's
wronging them.

Darwall's view is that wronging is a second-personal phenomenon, not
reducible to (say) improperly responding to impersonal value (2006: 13). To
wrong someone is to violate an obligation to him or her, and what makes it true
that one has an obligation to another is that that other has the authority to
demand some line of conduct from one (2006: 14). Being the bearer of such
authority makes others accountable to one, and makes it possible for one to be
wronged by them. To employ Darwall's favorite example—drawn from Hume—
what makes it the case that you are wronging me by standing on my gouty toes
(2006: 5) is not merely that there is impersonal disvalue to the pain caused to me,
nor even that I am valuable from some suitably impartial point of view, and thus
my foot is a sort of 'sacred ground' (2006: 9) on which others have strong reason
not to tread. What makes this a case of wronging is you have an obligation
to me not to step on my gouty toes, and you have this obligation just because
I have the authority to demand that you not stand on my gouty toes.[18]

Put as starkly as I have put it, the view is very puzzling. Darwall is clear that
obligations are second-personal reasons for action; that you are obligated not
to step on my toes is a reason for your not doing so, and it is essential to
Darwall's view that it be such a reason—charges that one violated an obligation
presuppose, Darwall thinks, that the party so charged had sufficient reason
to perform the obligatory act (2006: 28). But the presence of my authority to
demand that you not ϕ does not, all by itself, establish any such reason for
you not to ϕ. That's not the way that authority works. Authority is a *power*,
a power to generate new reasons for action by performing the relevant speech
acts.[19] The mere fact that I have the authority to demand that you not step on
my gouty toes does not give you any reason not to step on my gouty toes, any
more than the mere fact that the state has the authority to require you not to
drive more than 50 miles per hour on the highway gives you a reason not
to drive more than 50 miles per hour on the highway. It is not until the state
uses this authority by promulgating a new traffic law that you have the relevant
reason, and on Darwall's view as stated you would not have the relevant reason
not to step on my gouty toes until and unless I demand that you not do so.
Which would be an absurd view.

Darwall's attempt to explain how x can be wronged in terms of x's authority
to demand a certain sort of treatment is doomed to founder on the plain fact
that agents can be wronged even without issuing any demands that they be

---

[18] Darwall 2006: 101: 'Moral obligations are the demands . . . agents have standing to address
to one another.'

[19] Cf. Raz 1984: 24; see also Murphy 2002: 10–12.

treated in certain ways.[20] It does seem right that when A's ϕ-ing wrongs B, B characteristically has the authority to *insist* that A refrain from ϕ-ing. But *insisting* differs from *demanding* in that insisting presupposes the existence of a *prior* norm of action, one that will presumably both account for why certain acts would be instances of wronging and why the potential victim is entitled to insist that those acts not be performed. So, in the case with which we are concerned, we would have to ask whether it is plausible that there are such prior norms in place which both entail that God's ordering their destruction counts as wronging the Jerichoites and gives the Jerichoites authority to insist that God not perform such an action.

In a moment I will turn more directly to the question of whether it is plausible to hold that such prior norms are in place. But suppose that for now we waive this worry about authority, obligation, and wronging to ask whether Darwall's view, were it sustainable, would provide a basis for the claim that God could wrong the Jerichoites.

Call the authority to demand that others act in a certain way toward one 'second-personal authority'. Call the capacity to act on such demands 'second-personal competence'. Darwall argues that the class of parties who have second-personal authority are all and only those who have second-personal competence (2006: 269–74). But if God naturally has second-personal authority with respect to the Jerichoites, as most theists would affirm, then the Jerichoites have second-personal competence with respect to divine commands, and so the Jerichoites have some sort of second-personal authority with respect to God. If that is right, then the Jerichoites are, at the very least, beings of the sort who naturally can be wronged by God. My suggestion—that the Jerichoites are not naturally beings of that sort—would have to be mistaken.

The key thesis to be defended is the claim that those who possess second-personal authority are all and only those who possess second-personal competence—in particular, the entailment from second-personal competence to second-personal authority.

Here is the argument. Darwall argues that when one gives second-personal reasons—e.g. by commanding—one presupposes that the addressee can freely and rationally determine him- or herself by those reasons. In making a (non-defective) authoritative demand, then, the party addressed must not only be able to act on the demand, but be able to do so rationally—being able (in

---

[20] Darwall suggests that we might understand the relevant demands as those made by 'the moral community' 'implicitly' (2006: 290 n. 22). I have no idea what this moral community is such that it is able to perform speech acts, and indeed has done so, albeit implicitly. A move from implicit actual demands to hypothetical demands would gut Darwall's view; hypothetical demands are not demands.

some sense of 'able') rationally to take there to be reasons of the right sort to do what is demanded. All that seems fine; it is, Darwall reckons, the difference between guidance by coercion, manipulation, or conditioning and guidance by authority. But Darwall thinks that from this it follows that the party with this second-personal competence must have a certain sort of authority:

Relating to someone in a demanding way . . . requires warrant by the requisite second-personal reasons, that is, that simply demanding conduct or attempting to coerce it from someone is illegitimate, a violation of the other's authority as second-personally competent. *It follows that one demand that anyone has the authority to make is that he not be subject to demanding (coercive) conduct that cannot be justified by second-personal reasons.* (2006: 272, italics in original)

If from the fact that one in demanding presupposes that the party addressed can freely and rationally determine his or her own conduct by the demand it were to follow that the party addressed has the authority to demand that he or she only be given demands that fall within these parameters, then Darwall's view, if otherwise sound, could provide a foothold for the view that God wronged the Jerichoites. If we know that God has the authority to make demands on them, and such authority must (according to this argument) always be reciprocal, we know that the Jerichoites are, shall we say, potential victims at God's hands—beings that it necessarily makes conceptual sense to cast as the wronged in light of some divine action.

But even granting Darwall the soundness of the background view of wronging, the argument is unsuccessful. Suppose we grant that *something has gone wrong* if the party purporting to exercise authority gives a demand that the party to whom the demand is addressed cannot rationally act on. The putatively authoritative demand is a misfire of some kind, the act gone wrong. But we have already distinguished between an act *going wrong with respect to* someone and an act *wronging* someone. The fact that an authority would be acting wrongly with respect to those whom he or she commands does not entail that those with respect to whom he or she is acting wrongly have authority to make any sort of demands to stop that wrongful treatment. All it shows is that the putative authority is making an error of some sort, not that others are entitled to demand that he or she stop making that mistake. And without that entitlement, we do not have the foothold that would render plausible the claim that the Jerichoites naturally stand to God as beings who are entitled to demand certain treatment from him.[21]

---

[21] Of course, my criticism of Darwall does require the concession that it makes conceptual sense to ask what would count as God's acting wrongly with respect to the Jerichoites. It is no part of my argument to deny the sense of that; my claim is just that we are in no position to assess what actions in particular would count as God's acting wrongly with respect to them.

I have claimed that Darwall's analysis of wronging is defective and at any rate fails to sustain the view that the Jerichoites are naturally possible victims of divine action, beings who would be wronged by God's acting in a certain way with respect to them. I have suggested that the characteristic authority to insist on a certain line of conduct can make sense only as part of an account of wronging if there are prior norms that explain that authority. We would do well, then, to ask what would have to be in place for there to be this sort of prior norm to hold, and whether these conditions are plausibly satisfied in the case of God and the Jerichoites.

Without claiming to offer anything like a full theory of wronging, Thompson has offered in his rich discussion of the topic a couple of very plausible necessary conditions of wronging the implications of which I want to draw out here. For one party to wrong another, these two must belong to the same 'dikaiological order'. But it is not sufficient for two to belong to this common normative order that the rules by which they are bound have a common *content*; they must also have a common *source*. Consider how plausible this is with respect to one sort of minor dikaiological order—that found in games. What is necessary for me to cheat you in a game is, among other things, of course, that we are playing the same game. But to be the same game is not merely a matter of the qualitative character of the norms being followed, but also something about its origin, the community of players the norm-acceptance of which makes for that game, and so forth. Suppose that on one side of a mountain range we play marbles, and on the other side of the mountain range you and your friends play schmarbles (but you call it 'marbles'), and there is no common history, no interaction of any sort between the communities.[22] I of the marbles and you of the schmarbles meet on the mountaintop, admire each other's sets of marbles/schmarbles, and commence flicking our small spheres of glass inside a circle marked in the dirt. The problem is that we are not playing a game. I am trying to play marbles with you; you are trying to play schmarbles with me. I cannot cheat you at marbles; you're not playing marbles. I cannot cheat you at schmarbles; I am not playing schmarbles. So there is no game at which I am cheating you—we are not under a common order, tied together by a set of rules. Any objection to my conduct in terms of wronging can stick only by moving outside the order of marbles/schmarbles, to some order that we do share—say, that of our common humanity—in which my attempts to, say, deceive or manipulate you are themselves marked as wrongs. So the first constraint that an account of wronging must meet is

---

[22] This is a more trivial example along the lines of Thompson's Lombards/Schlombards case; see Thompson 2004: 373.

that if one party can wrong another, the norms by which they are bound must have a common source.

The second of these is that sharing a dikaiological order involves—and this does seem to be a key point on which Darwall and Thompson agree—mutuality, as folks under such an order are linked together normatively. Thompson thinks that this entails that those parties who are linked by relations of right have to—in the normal cases—be capable of grasping and acting on the concepts of right of that order. There is no dikaiological order, Thompson argues, unless inability to grasp that order becomes *extraordinary* rather than *ordinary*. We cannot make sense of a class of persons being *subject* to a dikaiological order without the general capacity of those subject to it to act on it. Those under the rules of chess are *characteristically* able to grasp its rules; those under the law of the United States are *characteristically* able to follow its norms; etc. This is what gives plausibility to the view that adequate promulgation is essential to legal orders; it also gives plausibility to publicity constraints that some writers impose on accounts of justice. It of course does not follow that everyone under a normative order grasps the rules that link him or her to others within that order; a novice can be fully bound by the rules of chess and a child fully bound by the rules of justice. But it cannot be the ordinary run of things that the standard member of the group under a dikaiological order cannot grasp its norms.

Suppose that we allow that these are genuine constraints on dikaiological orders. The question is whether it is plausible that there is a dikaiological order naturally shared by God and human beings that would make possible God's wronging the Jerichoites. But it seems to me that, even without a full theory of wronging, the concession that these are necessary conditions of the presence of such an order renders implausible the view that God and the Jerichoites naturally share a dikaiological order.

God and humans share a dikaiological order only if they are linked by a set of norms that have a common source. But it is unclear how this is to be. Thompson notes that it is very implausible that the form of rational agency is itself such a source; abstractly considered, the form of rational agency is exhibited by corporations and teams, not beings to whom we take ourselves to be bound by ties of justice (2004: 379–80). Indeed, any attempt to argue that there is naturally a set of norms to which both God and humans are subject, and thus which can tie us to God as a matter of justice, is open to the following difficulty. The justice under which we act is essentially constraining. It binds us, setting limits to our action. Even if there were a will that naturally and necessarily cleaves to what is just, a Kantian holy will informed by a grace that ensures compliance with the norms of justice, what we are describing is a will that acts within the constraints set by justice. But I take it that what we may call *God's justice* is *not* something that is essentially constraining—that it is neither true that God experiences the norms of justice as constraints on God's willing nor that God's will is simply necessarily such that it never goes contrary to these constraints. Our dikaiological order is something that those under it are subjected to. God is not naturally subjected to anything. So I cannot see that we and God are both under a common form of justice.

So there is one worry arising from the 'common source' constraint. But there is also a worry arising from the conceptual grasp constraint. This constraint is that for those who are under a dikaiological order, inability to grasp the contours of that order must be extraordinary. Think about what this would entail. It would entail that any norms of justice in which God is naturally linked to created rational beings would be limited in their complexity to what the dimmest kind of rational being can characteristically grasp. What affirming the possibility of wronging in these cases would mean is that God is, ex ante, constrained by a form of justice that binds those of the meagerest intelligence and agency along with any more exalted. It seems perverse that this would be true—that the form of justice to which a perfect God would be subject would be constrained by the limits on the agency of the most meager kind of created rational being.

I have been arguing that God and humans do not, by nature, share a dikaiological order, and it is only in sharing such an order that the possibility of wronging arises. It follows from this that God did not wrong the Jerichoites in ordering the destruction of their city. As I argued in Section III, the claim that God wronged the Jerichoites is the only plausible route to the conclusion that God acted wrongly with respect to them. So I say that we lack a rational basis to hold that God acted wrongly with respect to the Jerichoites.

V

One might think that the view that I have described is too strong, for it has implications about God and wronging that we have reason to reject, even apart from concerns about God's relation to the Jerichoites.

For one thing, the claim that God and humans do not naturally share a dikaiological order does not entail only that God cannot naturally wrong humans; it also entails that humans cannot naturally wrong God. But I think this is the correct result. Suppose that God, having made us, had chosen not to cooperate with any human beings, or in any way to relate to us second-personally. (The point of these qualifications may be unclear, but I will make clear their relevance in a moment.) God might nevertheless communicate with us, not linguistically through speech acts subject to linguistic norms, but merely causally, by implanting in us certain beliefs, including beliefs about God's existence and the sort of greatness that God has. God might also in nature reveal himself not by speaking but by showing.[23] If such were the case, it would still be true that we are acting wrongly with respect to God by blaspheming God, by withholding honor, etc. But we would not be, I say, wronging God. We do not wrong the beautiful painting or the perfectly thrown pass or the well-crafted argument by failing to acknowledge and respond to it, though we act wrongly with respect to these things by not responding to them as they are. They do not share a dikaiological order with us. If God shared no such order with us, we could act wrongly with respect to God, but could not wrong God.

One might also claim that this view proves too much with respect to God's relationship to human justice. For one might claim that the view I have defended rules out not only the bare logical possibility of God's having wronged the Jerichoites in the destruction of Jericho; it also rules out God's ever wronging *anyone*, not on substantive moral grounds (say, God's being a perfectly good being), but on the grounds of the logic of wronging. But we want to say, don't we, that God is a lover of justice? And we want to say, don't we, that God is just, perfectly so, and that (e.g.) if God had told the Israelites that the walls of Jericho would come down if they followed his bidding, and the walls did not come down, then God would have wronged the Israelites?

Yes, we do want to say this, and I do not think that we are barred from saying these things truly. God *is* a lover of justice, of humans not wronging each other, of humans honoring each other's rights. Justice is good for humans in community, and as a human's good is fixed in part by what is good for humans in community, doing justice is good for humans individually as well. God's loving justice is thus, if nothing else, a matter of God's loving human beings. If one thinks that this love of human beings is a necessary feature of God, then God's love of human justice will be necessary; if contingent, contingent. (I hope that no one who claims that God's love of humans is only contingent will complain that on my view God's love of the justice that binds us humans would be contingent as well.)

But God's being a lover of human justice does not explain how it is possible for God's action ever to be properly assessed in terms of human justice, any more than my being a lover of the order that is exhibited by life in a bee colony would explain how I could be wronging the bees when I traipse over to the colony and, free-riding on bee justice, take their artisan honey.

---

[23] For a noting of the importance of the distinction between God's speaking and God's revelation more generally, see Wolterstorff 1995: 9–11.

Consider, though, the following analogy. God can cause thoughts to form in human minds as God wishes. God can cause us to have true beliefs or false beliefs, correct or incorrect judgments, appropriate or inappropriate desires. But if God wants to guide our thoughts and desires *by speech*, then God is going to have to subject himself to linguistic norms, those of language generally and of a particular language, in order to do so. By subjecting himself to linguistic norms, by entering into our linguistic practices to communicate with us, we can characterize what it would be for one of God's speech acts to be defective. If God were intentionally to make false assertions, or to direct us to do what we lack reason to do, then God's speech acts could not be described other than as defective.

Linguistic norms are typically norms of bipolar normativity, norms that connect speaker and hearer. God can avoid being subject to these norms by refraining from engaging in our linguistic practices in communicating with us. Justice norms are all norms of bipolar normativity. God can avoid being subject to these norms by refraining from engaging in our cooperative practices in dealing with us. But if God chooses to deal with us not simply causally but also cooperatively, then God enters into the human form of justice. If God chooses to deal with humans cooperatively, or more broadly, *second-personally*—as he did with the Israelites—then God has to subject himself to justice norms in order to do so.

The moral is: of them with whom God cooperates, we can speak coherently of what it would be for God to wrong them, and so make sense of the praise given to God that God would never do such a thing, because God is perfectly faithful. To those with whom God is not cooperating, we cannot speak coherently of what it would be for God to wrong them, for God neither shares nor enters into the form of justice with them. *The slightest breach of promise or smallest lie to the Israelites by God would have been a divine injustice, and would have morally discredited God; the total destruction of the Jerichoites was not, and did not.*

VI

It is reasonable to ask *how far* God's entering into a relationship of cooperation with some human beings places God under the norms of justice with respect to those human beings. Does God's placing himself under those norms last just as long as the cooperative project, say? Or does it outlast it? Does God's placing himself under those norms place God under all norms of justice? Or only under those norms that are, roughly speaking, relevant to the common task?[24] I have no settled view on these issues, except that they have now been made simply academic. For God became a human being, and in so doing entered our dikaiological order once and for all.

VII

My central concern has been to show that God's ordering of the destruction of Jericho is not morally discrediting, in that God acted in some way that the moral order precluded God from acting. But one might say that even if this mission were to succeed, it would leave a distinct task undone, and indeed might very well make that distinct task harder to perform. For one might claim that God's actions with respect to the Jerichoites were discrediting in a different way: God's doing that either showed or made God a being of the sort that it would be wrong for humans to give their allegiance to. Perhaps God didn't do anything wrong—there were, so far as we know, no relevant standards of normative assessment by which God could be properly faulted for God's actions—but *we* would be doing something wrong, perhaps even wronging some of our fellow humans (the Jerichoites, perhaps?), by allying ourselves with that being. This is not an unfamiliar phenomenon. If our longstanding family business is going under due to some perfectly fair but hardnosed competition from a rival, we may rightly think both that our rival is not doing anything wrong with respect to us but nevertheless I ought not to ally myself with this rival. Doing so exhibits a sort of wrongful disloyalty, a lack of solidarity with my family; the same might be said by the critic of the view I have defended, holding that even if God cannot be properly faulted for God's treatment of the Jerichoites, nevertheless good old anthropocentric value requires unity with our fellow humans over and against this alarming being who is so awesome but seems nevertheless so, well, uncivilized.

---

[24] In correspondence Morriston has properly pressed on me the question of how I read the Noachic covenant (Genesis 9). No doubt that reading it in a sufficiently strong way could commit me to the view that God was in the sort of cooperative enterprise with the Jerichoites that would place them in a common dikaiological order. I will note that everyone has the job of making intelligible the claim that God there makes a covenant not only with some rational being or beings but with 'all mortal creatures' (Gen. 9: 17); once we make explicit what could possibly be involved with God's making a covenant not only with Noah and Noah's descendants but also with any living woodchucks and those woodchucks' descendants, it is far from clear that what we are dealing with is anything like God's entering into an ongoing cooperative relationship that would be mediated by the human dikaiological order.

I have less to say on this subject. The key point is the disanalogy between the business competition case and the case we are here concerned with. For God loves us, all of us, and that makes all the difference here. This generates the easy retort 'Some love!' I confess that I do not know exactly what to say about God's love and the destruction of the Jerichoites. But here are initial remarks in the direction that strikes me as most promising.

As I am sure is true with respect to all parent–child relationships, I do an awful lot of things that are such that my children, especially the younger ones, do not understand how they are compatible with my love for them.[25] My children see how I deal with them, in ways that must look very arbitrary, very severe in some cases, very lax in others. Without saying that I really know what I am doing I am very confident that they lack a justified belief that I am faulty in the specific ways that and to the degree that they must think that I am faulty. And they of course have counterevidence, in favor of the view that I love them, from my treatment of them. But there is one piece of evidence of my love for them that is distinct from their assessment of the ways that they are benefited and burdened by my actions, and it is a piece of evidence that they are at least slightly better suited to evaluate. It is, to put it plainly, that I enter into their condition. I crawl on the floor, I play their games, and so forth. Much (not all) of this is joy, but it is only joy on account of the fact that I love them.

We likely understand little about God's aims and purposes save the little of which God has assured us in his speaking to us. But, as in the case of my children and me, there is another bit of evidence, and that is not what God does to and for us, but what God does with respect to his own status in dealing with us: he bothers to speak to us, to enter into our condition, to hear and respond to our entreaties, and finally even to become one of us.

---

[25] Just two days before writing these words I was provided with a clear example. My 6-year-old son Cormac had a loose tooth. I inspected it and said to my wife, 'Will you get me the needlenose pliers so that I can pluck out this tooth?' My three-year-old son Finnian, in earshot of this exchange, went ballistic. 'Not to my brother!' he yelled, then curled up in a ball behind my desk chair, crying. He was not to be consoled. When the pliers arrived and I took up my stance to remove the tooth, Finn extricated himself bravely, yelled at me (calling me a 'meanie-foo'), and punched me, surprisingly hard and relentlessly, in the left kidney. He was of course comically misguided. But I could not help but admire his pluck, love of justice, and desire to defend his usually-but-not-always-kind older brother.

Comments on 'God Beyond Justice'

Wes Morriston

The walls of Jericho have fallen. The army of the lord busies itself with the task at hand—killing every living creature within the city. An Israelite captain wrests a small child from the arms of its terrified mother and decapitates it. A moment later, he thrusts his sword into her heart. It's a big job, but by sundown all the inhabitants of Jericho are dead. The ground is soaked in their blood.

What does the fact (if it is a fact) that God commanded the ancient Israelites to do this tell us about his moral character? Is he, to put it in a sanitized way, guilty of 'moral error'? Professor Murphy can find no ground for such a judgment. In order to show that this command 'morally discredits' God, one must show that God *acted wrongly with respect to the Jerichoites*, and the only way to do that, he thinks, is to show that God *wronged them*. But God was not related to the Jerichoites in a way that made it possible for him to wrong them. So he is not 'morally discredited'.

Murphy begins by considering the suggestion that God acted wrongly with respect to the Jerichoites merely by disregarding their intrinsic value. His response is that we are in no position to make such a judgment. God knows vastly more than we about the consequences of the extermination program. For all we know, he may have had wonderfully good plans and purposes that are best served by commanding the systematic slaughter of these particular men, women, children, and animals. The fact that we don't see how all this killing serves a sufficiently worthwhile goal has no tendency whatever to show that it does not do so.

I am unmoved by the appeal to 'skeptical theism' in this context. What we are concerned with, after all, is the moral character of *the God the Hebrew Bible*, and *its* authors do not leave us in the dark about the reasons for genocide.[1] It is

---

[1] Murphy explicitly acknowledges this point, and says this about it. 'I am not moved from my skepticism by the citing of these reasons. No doubt that in making intelligible God's command we should advert to the wickedness of the Jerichoite community, and should view God's command as in some way a response to that wickedness. But that is perfectly compatible with our having only the dimmest sense of the goods that may be involved with God's directing the

said to be a way of preventing the Israelites from marrying Canaanites and joining them in the worship of their gods (Deut. 7: 1–6). *This* reason is not beyond our ken. If anything, it is only too humanly comprehensible, and it is not difficult to evaluate. We can think of any number of other ways in which an omnipotent being might have inoculated the Israelites against apostasy without commanding them to engage in indiscriminate slaughter. Moreover, the biblical record makes it abundantly clear that the chosen method did not get the job done. God's supposed plan simply did not pan out.

This is not a 'no-seeum' inference of the sort typically targeted by skeptical theists. The argument is based on what we *do* see. We *see* that the stated reasons for genocide are very bad. Granted that the goal of setting the Israelites apart as a people devoted to the service of Yahweh is a worthy one, the means employed to achieve this end are both vile and inefficacious. It is highly unlikely that a God who is worthy of our worship would be so incompetent or so uncaring.

We also see that using the Israelites to do this ugly job would be exceedingly bad for *their* moral and spiritual development. Murphy brushes off this charge, denying that there is any evidence of 'psychological damage' to the Israelites in the texts. That may be so. But when I say that commanding the Israelites to slaughter the inhabitants of Jericho was bad *for them*, I do not necessarily mean that it made them worse than they already were. What I do mean is that divinely mandated genocide would have made it more difficult for them to learn that all persons are worthy of respect and consideration.

It is obvious that the genocide texts were written by people who saw nothing wrong with killing non-combatants in warfare, since there is no moral tension in the stories they tell. If the battle of Jericho really did take place as described, the victorious army was no doubt already quite used to killing women and children. That in itself is troubling. After receiving the Law, and after decades of special training in the wilderness, the people of God should not be operating on such a low moral level—unless, of course, the Law and the training left out vitally important information about how persons should be treated.

I turn next to the question whether God *wronged* the Jerichoites. Murphy argues that he could not have, since he and they were not subject to a

army of the Lord as he did and the evils that may be involved with God's taking alternative courses of action.' (156) What Murphy stresses is that God may have been motivated by *other* goods and evils of which we have 'only the dimmest grasp'. To this last point, I am inclined to reply: 'Perhaps so, but since the reasons given in the text are clearly bad, and since what is at issue here is the moral character of God *as he is presented in this text*, my point stands.' I suspect that Murphy does not share my conviction that the reasons for genocide given by Deuteronomy are very bad reasons, but I am not sure why.

common set of moral requirements. Here is a capsule summary of Murphy's argument.

In order for persons to share a 'dikaiological order', two things must be true. First, they must be subject to normative rules having a *common source*. Second, it must be possible for nearly everyone in the moral community to *understand* the norms by which they are all bound. Except in special circumstances, neither condition is satisfied by God in relation to human beings. The first is not satisfied because God is sovereign, and cannot be subject to any external 'source' of moral obligation. The second is not satisfied because 'any norms of justice in which God is naturally linked to created rational beings would be limited in their complexity to what the dimmest kind of rational being can characteristically grasp', (163) and because it is 'perverse' to suppose that God's justice could be subject to such limits. Only if God chooses to 'cooperate' with us can it be possible for him to wrong any of us. When the walls of Jericho fell, God had entered into a covenant with the Israelites, and was actively cooperating with them, but God had entered into no such covenant with the Jerichoites and was not cooperating with them. Under the circumstances that obtained at that time, it was therefore possible for God to wrong the Israelites, but impossible for him to wrong the Jerichoites.

Does this mean that if—today—God commanded the faithful, with whom he is 'cooperating', to slaughter men, women, and children with whom he is not 'cooperating' he would not be 'wronging' the latter? Apparently not. Murphy tells us that when God became a human being, he entered our dikaiological order 'once and for all'. In this way, the slaughter of the Jerichoites is tucked safely into the pre-Christian past, and sets no dangerous precedents for us.

Let's pause for a moment to note how difficult it is to square these claims with the biblical record. Isn't God supposed to have been cooperating with human beings long before there were any Israelites? We are all in some sense—however figurative—the sons and daughters of Adam and Eve, and God entered into important relationships with them and all their children. He cared for Adam and Eve and held them responsible for their disobedience in the garden. He found Abel's sacrifice acceptable, and held Cain responsible for killing his brother. He put a mark on his forehead to warn others not to kill him. He made an important promise to Noah after the great flood. He walked and talked with Abraham—who, it must not be forgotten, had *two* sons, one of whose descendants were *not* Israelites. God spoke to the mother of that other son and promised that her son too would be the father of a great nation. All of this long pre-dates the Jerichoites. Interaction and cooperation and promise-giving are present in these stories. Why—on Murphy's account—is this not sufficient to bring God into the human dikaiological order? What more is required?

Here is another small point. Murphy seems to accept the biblical claim that the Jerichoites were extremely wicked, and that this goes some way toward explaining why God would want them dead. Wickedness in this context must surely involve rebellion against God. But if the Jerichoites had no relationship to God (other than a distant causal one), it is hard to see how *they* could have been in rebellion against him. If, on the other hand, they did have some important relationship to God, how can we be sure that this relationship did not make it possible for God to wrong the Jerichoites? Murphy's account is not sufficiently detailed to answer these questions—questions which, from the point of view of the Jerichoites, at any rate, are far from being merely 'academic'.

Let's return to Murphy's argument for saying that God is not *by nature* so positioned as to be capable of wronging the Jerichoites. One of his principal reasons for taking this line is that God does not by nature satisfy the 'source constraint' for participation in our dikaiological order. Why not? Murphy's answer seems to hinge on the requirements of divine sovereignty. God would not be God if he were subject to an external standard of justice.

To this I reply: God would not be God if he were not supremely just in all his dealings with creatures made in his image. But that can be so only if there are moral standards that he fully and completely satisfies. You may fold these standards into God's nature if you don't think they should be external to God. But the fact remains that if God creates a living, breathing, self-conscious, free agent, he creates something possessing a certain dignity—some*one* who deserves respect, and who is therefore capable of being wronged by him. If God has children, created in his own image, he does not have to 'cooperate' with them in order to make it wrong for him to abuse them. *Failure to cooperate would itself be a form of abuse.* (We might call it *abandonment*.) Does this compromise God's sovereignty in some way that should trouble theists? No more, I think, than the fact that God does not get to decide whether two and two make four.

What of Murphy's claim that if God were subject to our norms of justice, he would be subject to norms that are 'limited in their complexity to what the dimmest kind of rational being can characteristically grasp'? I do not feel the force of this consideration. God knows more than we about everything. No doubt that goes for the nature of justice as much as for anything else. But it doesn't follow that we know nothing about justice, or that none of what we do know is applicable to God. Indeed, I would say that the most fundamental principles of justice set *minimum* conditions that God must satisfy in order to be a just ruler.

To appreciate this point, it may help to do a small thought experiment. Imagine a distant planet on which God has created two species of non-humans who are free, self-conscious, and rational. Call them the Alphas and the Betas. God chooses the Alphas as his own and at one point in their history he becomes incarnate as an Alpha. But God cooperates with the Betas in no way. Occasionally, however, he orders the Alphas to wage an extermination campaign against a city inhabited by Betas. He tells the Alphas that he does this to provide *Lebensraum* for them. The Alphas are duly grateful.

I do not have an analysis of 'wronging' that I am prepared to defend, but it does seem to me that whatever view we adopt, it must accommodate our bedrock moral intuitions. Mine tell me that in this little story the Betas are *victims* of gross *injustice*. As far as I can see, Murphy is unable to accommodate this intuition.

I turn next to Murphy's suggestion about the way in which God can and does bind himself to us by entering our dikaiological order. When, as was the case with ancient Israel, God cooperates with a people, Murphy says that he 'subjects himself' to 'justice norms'. In this case, and only in this case, can we speak coherently of God's wronging anyone. But as Murphy himself notes, many questions remain unanswered. What, exactly, is involved in such 'cooperation'? *Which* norms of justice does God place himself under when he cooperates with us? Could God cease cooperating and thereby 'escape' from our dikaiological order? Murphy says he has no settled view about these matters, but that such questions 'have now been made simply academic' by the incarnation. (166)

This is much too quick for me. Even today, there are isolated tribes that know nothing of the Christian gospel. God has not, to borrow an analogy from Murphy, gotten down on the floor and 'played with them'! So, then, would God be wronging them if he commanded us to exterminate them and take their land? In one sense, this question is purely 'academic'. No Christian would take seriously the possibility of such a divine command. But we need to know *why* we should not take this possibility seriously. Without answers to the above-mentioned questions about the nature of divine cooperation and its relation to justice norms, I do not see how Murphy can say whether God would be wronging those tribes if he issued such a command. The same goes for the Jerichoites. The details really do matter.

But suppose, for the sake of argument, that God cannot be faulted for *wronging* the Jerichoites. At this point, Murphy imagines his critic asking: *Don't our standards of justice require solidarity with them 'over and against this alarming being who is so awesome but seems nevertheless so . . . uncivilized'?* (166) Good question. Murphy responds by asserting that 'God loves us, all of us', and that this 'makes all the difference'. (167) God may sometimes do strange and terrible things that we cannot understand. But that is a familiar enough phenomenon. Our children don't always understand what we're up to. Even so, they should trust us, because they have plenty of evidence of our love.

I fail to see how this speaks to the condition of the Jerichoites. They are God's children too, created in his image and after his likeness. They have acquired a lot of false beliefs and odious religious practices. They know nothing of Yahweh save that he is the god of a fierce tribe that wants to kill them and take their land. What evidence of Yahweh's love do *they* have? What evidence, for that matter, do *we* have that God cared for them? If there is a story in which God shows his love for the Jerichoites, it is not to be found in the Hebrew Bible. How, then, can *our* hearts not go out to them in sympathy? How can we not side with them against this 'alarming' and 'uncivilized' god?

Reply to Morriston

Mark C. Murphy

Wes Morriston's comments on my chapter are very searching and thus very welcome. In responding I will focus on two issues of disagreement between us: first, on the appeal to skeptical theism in my defense of the view that God did not act wrongly with respect to the Jerichoites; and second, on the use to which I put the idea that God does not naturally share a dikaiological order with us. I will conclude with a clarification of my views on the appropriate stance for us to take with respect to the destruction of the Jerichoites.

1. ON SKEPTICAL THEISM

In order to get us focused on the question whether God can naturally wrong human beings, I wanted to put to the side the possibility that God could have acted wrongly with respect to the Jerichoites without wronging them. I justify setting aside the claim that God could have acted wrongly with respect to the Jerichoites without wronging them on the basis that we are in no position to assess the reasons God had for ordering their destruction. Morriston responds that scripture tells us in fact what God's ends were and how far they were achieved by God's giving that command, and what we learn is that the ends were on their face insufficient to justify the command and that those ends were in any case not realized. We must therefore judge that God acted wrongly with respect to the Jerichoites (Morriston, pp. 168–9, above).

We should distinguish between the sorts of ordinary reasons that we give one another in justifying our conduct and what Joseph Raz calls 'complete reasons' (1975: 22–5), where a complete reason is a fact that includes everything that is necessary to entail the choice-worthiness of the action for which it is a reason. We do not trade in complete reasons when we are justifying our conduct to one another, for obvious reasons of time, redundancy, and so forth. Nor do we typically try to give all of the reasons that we have. But if we are trying to make explicit the justifications of our actions, an accounting of our complete reasons is what does the job.

So of course I allow that scripture reports God's reasons for giving the order, and that these involve the general wickedness of the Jerichoites and the tendency for the Israelites to get mixed up in this wickedness. But what should interest us are God's complete reasons, what makes the order choice-worthy. And my point is that we haven't much of a clue what those complete reasons will look like.[1] (Any line of reasoning that explicitly or implicitly makes use of the counterfactual 'If I were to command the destruction of the Jerichoites, what would my reasons be?' is a very bad way of figuring out God's reasons.)

As to the insufficiency of the order to bring about the end sought: Morriston assumes—I don't understand the criticism otherwise—that God's end in giving the command was the non-existence of Jerichoites. It does not follow from God's giving the command 'Exterminate the Jerichoites' that God's end was that there be no Jerichoites.[2] Even if the total elimination of the Jerichoites were the favored outcome, that it was not fully realized would show nothing toward the failure of justification of the command without a further argument that for this end to be justified it would have to be fully realized. And, what's more, this assumes that all of God's reasons for giving the command involve end-states to be brought about by the Israelites' attempt to obey the command; but a little reflection makes clear that there are justifying reasons for the mundane commands we give that go beyond end-states to be realized through obedience.[3]

2. ON GOD AND OUR DIKAIOLOGICAL ORDER

Morriston rightly notes that I should say more, and say it more plausibly, about the way that divine action can be subject to assessment within the human dikaiological order. There are numerous criticisms here, some of

---

[1] Anyone who assumes that he or she understands well the various ways that the Jerichoites' wickedness can enter into God's reasons for actions is assuming badly. Think of something as commonplace as *taking nutrition*, and how differently it enters as a good into the lives of: an amoeba, a red oak, an earthworm, a German shepherd, a 1-year-old human, a 6-year-old human, and a 40-year-old human. My 6-year-old barely grasps the various ways in which eating can enter into the human good. Why should I think that I have any but the faintest grip on the way that a people's wickedness can make a difference to God's reasons with respect to them?

[2] A sergeant may order a private under her command to scrub the latrine so well that it sparkles. In so doing the sergeant must, if commanding non-defectively, take it to be possible to scrub the latrine so well that it sparkles, and must intend the private to take that objective as his guide to conduct. But that is compatible with the sergeant's having as her objective only the reasonable cleanliness of the latrine, or even with the sergeant's having as her objective the failure to clean in accordance with the standard she has set, thus justifying the infliction of discipline.

[3] This point is emphasized in Eleonore Stump's contribution; see pp. 186–93, below.

which are invited by my own failure to express my view plainly,[4] so let me try to re-sketch my overall view in a way that makes clear how I would address them. The history of relationship between God and human beings is one in which God entered sporadically and for his own good purposes into cooperative endeavors with individual humans and groups of humans; and I want to say that *within* those transactions it is coherent to assess God's action in terms of our dikaiological order. I do think, though, that we are *now* tied to God in our normative order for a different reason, and one that extends to all human beings: that God has become incarnate as a human, and as it is a sufficient condition to be part of the human dikaiological order to bear a human nature, God is now fully bound to us by ties of justice. (This is, I would say, one more way in which God humbled himself to share in our humanity.)

So there are two ways for God to enter into the human dikaiological order: in a limited way through cooperative activity, and in an unlimited way through coming to share our human nature. Some of Morriston's objections suggest that God's cooperation with *some* humans must place God into a common dikaiological order with *all* humans; I don't at all see why that would be, since my point is that the human dikaiological order functions in that context just as those terms of interaction that make cooperation between God and those humans possible, and it is unclear why God's being under the human dikaiological order would extend beyond those cooperative endeavors. Some of Morriston's objections ask why God is now bound by ties of justice even to those with whom there is not divine cooperation;[5] my reply is that I do not appeal to expansive divine cooperation to explain God's now being bound to all of us by ties of justice but rather to the fact that we now share with God a common nature.

---

[4] Here is one of my clearly unclear passages: 'Of them with whom God cooperates, we can speak coherently of what it would be for God to wrong them, and so make sense of the praise given to God that God would never do such a thing, because God is perfectly faithful. To those with whom God is not cooperating, we cannot speak coherently of what it would be for God to wrong them, for God neither shares nor enters into the form of justice with them' (p. 165, above). This makes it look like the only way to be in a dikaiological order with anyone else is to be in a relationship of cooperation; and so the relevance of the incarnation would be only that God has initiated a more thoroughgoing cooperative relationship with human beings. This is not my view. Humans, even those who are not cooperating with each other, share a dikaiological order simply through bearing a common human nature. My point in this unclear passage is that until God comes to bear our human nature in incarnation, the only way to enter the human dikaiological order is through cooperative enterprises with humans.

[5] I do not concede that there are any such persons. But universal divine cooperation with human beings is not the basis on which I claim that God is now and will forever be part of our human dikaiological order.

3. ON SYMPATHY AND SOLIDARITY

I want to conclude by addressing Morriston's final questions regarding the Jerichoites: 'How, then, can *our* hearts not go out to them in sympathy? How can we not side with them against this "alarming" and "uncivilized" God?' (Morriston, p. 173, above).

I think that our hearts *should* go out in sympathy with the Jerichoites. I fully agree with Morriston on this. I do not think, though, that anything I say involves siding with God against the Jerichoites. I do of course hope to side with God. But I do not aim to side against the Jerichoites.

In Question 19, Article 10 of the Prima Secundae of the *Summa Theologiae*, Aquinas asks whether we are bound to conform our wills to the divine will. Aquinas, unsurprisingly, distinguishes. We must will *formally* what God wills; for God wills what is good, absolutely speaking. But we need not will in particular, *materially*, what God wills—God may will that we aim at particular things that God nevertheless does not aim to realize. His example is illuminating: even if the order of justice requires a man's execution for a crime, so that the judge must will the man's execution, the man's spouse is *not* required to will his execution; indeed, her vocation makes salient the particular good of his life, not the official care for the common good. In the case at hand: I do not think that we are bound to will the destruction of the Jerichoites. It was not given to us to destroy them, and we are not commanded to hate them or have any sort of contempt for them. Indeed, we ourselves are, like the Jerichoites, sinners, living, like the Jerichoites, in sinful communities, and we should have solidarity with them, and should feel about them just what Morriston demands that we feel about them. It would be inhuman, and I would even call it unjust, not to. I part ways with Morriston not when he asks us to gaze sorrowfully toward the Jerichoites but only when he asks us to look accusingly at God.

REFERENCES

Almeida, Michael, and Oppy, Graham. 2003. 'Sceptical Theism and Evidential Arguments from Evil', *Australasian Journal of Philosophy*, 81: 496–516.

Bergmann, Michael. 2009. 'Skeptical Theism and the Problem of Evil', in Thomas P. Flint and Michael C. Rea (eds.), *The Oxford Handbook of Philosophical Theology*. Oxford: Oxford University Press, 374–99.

Darwall, Stephen. 2006. *The Second-Person Standpoint*. Cambridge, Mass.: Harvard University Press.

Foot, Philippa. 2001. *Natural Goodness*. Oxford: Oxford University Press.

Hursthouse, Rosalind. 1999. *On Virtue Ethics*. Oxford: Oxford University Press.

Morriston, Wes. 2009. 'Did God Command Genocide? A Challenge to the Biblical Inerrantist', *Philosophia Christi*, 11: 7–26.

Murphy, Mark C. 2002. *An Essay on Divine Authority*. Ithaca, NY: Cornell University Press.

Raz, Joseph. 1975. *Practical Reason and Norms*. Oxford: Oxford University Press.

Raz, Joseph 1984. *The Morality of Freedom*. Oxford: Oxford University Press.

Thompson, Michael. 2004. 'What is it to Wrong Someone? A Puzzle about Justice', in R. Jay Wallace et al. (eds.), *Reason and Value: Themes from the Moral Philosophy of Joseph Raz*. Oxford: Oxford University Press, 333–84.

Trakakis, Nick, and Nagasawa, Yujin. 2004. 'Skeptical Theism and Moral Skepticism: A Reply to Almeida and Oppy', *Ars Disputandi*, 4.

Wiggins, David. 1987. 'Truth, Invention, and the Meaning of Life', in *Needs, Value, and Truth*. Oxford: Oxford University Press.

Wolterstorff, Nicholas. 1995. *Divine Discourse: Philosophical Reflections on the Claim that God Speaks*. Cambridge: Cambridge University Press.

6

The Problem of Evil and the History of Peoples: Think Amalek

Eleonore Stump

1. INTRODUCTION

Writing about Benjamin Netanyahu in the *New York Times* (2009), Jeffrey Goldberg says,

> I recently asked one of his advisers to gauge for me the depth of Mr. Netanyahu's anxiety about Iran. His answer: 'Think Amalek.' 'Amalek', in essence, is Hebrew for existential threat.

It is amazing that, so many centuries after the battles between the Amalekites and the Israelites, the biblical stories of the Amalekites should still have a political role to play. But if the biography of any one human being is a complicated affair, the histories of peoples are very much more tangled. In this case, although the Amalekites and the Israelites are ancestral enemies, in fact, in the biblical stories, both peoples are part of the same family. The progenitor of the Amalekites was born to one of the sons of Esau, the twin brother of Jacob, who was one of the ancestors of the whole Israelite people. So, in the stories, the Amalekite people and the Israelite people are cousins, of a sort, at least in their origins. In this chapter, I want to look at one episode in the enduring narrative history of these two related peoples, namely, the story told in 1 Samuel of Samuel and the Amalekites. This story raises the problem of evil in a powerful way, and it is more difficult to deal with than the usual examples illustrating the problem of evil at least partly because the protagonists in the story include whole peoples.

The story is too long to reproduce in its entirety, but here are what I take to be the most salient bits of the story, in the contemporary translation by Robert Alter (1999: 89–91).

Samuel said to Saul, '...Thus says the Lord of Hosts, "I have made reckoning of what Amalek did to Israel, that he set against him on the way as he was coming up from Egypt. Now, go and strike down Amalek, and put under the ban everything that he has, you shall not spare him, and you shall put to death man and woman, infant and suckling, ox and sheep, camel and donkey". And Saul summoned the troops and assembled them at Telaim...And Saul struck down Amalek from Havilah till you come to Shur. And he caught Agag king of Amalek alive, and all the people he put under with the edge of the sword. And Saul, and the troops with him, spared Agag and the best of the sheep and the cattle, the fat ones and the young ones, everything good, and they did not want to put them under the ban. But all the vile and worthless possessions, these they put under the ban....And Samuel came to Saul, and Saul said to him, 'Blessed be you to the Lord! I have fulfilled the word of the Lord.' And Samuel said, 'And what is this sound of sheep in my ears, and the sound of cattle that I hear?' And Saul said, 'From the Amalekites they have brought them, for the troops spared the best of the sheep and the cattle in order to sacrifice to the Lord your God, and the rest we put under the ban.' And Samuel said...'the Lord sent you on a mission and said to you, "You shall put under the ban the offenders, Amalek, and do battle against them till you destroy them all." And why did you not listen to the voice of the Lord, for you pounced on the booty and did evil in the eyes of the Lord?' And Saul said to Samuel, 'But I listened to the voice of the Lord and went on the way the Lord sent me, and I brought back Agag king of Amalek, but Amalek I put under the ban. And the troops took from the booty sheep and cattle, the pick of the banned things, to sacrifice to the Lord your God at Gilgal.' And Samuel said, 'Does the Lord take delight in burnt offerings and sacrifices as in listening to the voice of the Lord?...Since you have cast off the word of the Lord, he has cast you aside as king.' (1 Sam. 15: 1–23)

And the story, which goes on for a bit more, finally finishes with Samuel's killing Agag, the king of the Amalekites.

2. REACTION TO THE STORY

This story is a good example of narratives in the Hebrew Bible that prompt outrage in many contemporary readers. It is important to me to say at the outset that while I reject the views of those who react in this way, I share their sensibilities. Whatever I may *think* about issues involving violence against other human beings—pacifism or capital punishment, for example—my sensibilities are ungovernably against the killing of human beings. I don't think that I myself could intentionally kill another human being, even in extreme circumstances. I would rather kill myself than kill a child. Cruelty to animals makes me sick. As far as that goes, I can't bring myself to eat meat;

I am a lifelong vegetarian. But I do accept this story as part of divine revelation, and this story presents God—a God who is supposed to be good—as commanding the Israelites to kill every human being among the Amalekites, including the children, and to slaughter all the animals. Why shouldn't we—why shouldn't I—reject this story as non-veridical and morally repellent?

One way to reject the story would be to claim that it is not true and not in any way, direct or indirect, part of a divine revelation. But, in religious terms, the cost for this reaction to the story would be high. It would require not only the rejection of the traditional Jewish and Christian view that the entire Hebrew Bible has to be taken as divinely revealed; it would in effect require the rejection of the entire idea of divine revelation in these texts. If one text purporting to be part of a divine revelation is to be rejected because it strikes us as incompatible with our moral intuitions, then other texts alleged to be divinely revealed will also need to be examined to see if they should be rejected for similar reasons. And now our moral intuitions are the standard by which the texts are judged. In that case, the texts do not function as divine revelation is meant to function, as a standard by which human beings can measure and correct human understanding, human behavior, and human standards.

Another way to reject the story would be to reinterpret it in some radical way, for example, as an allegory (as patristic commentators often read biblical texts), so that the reinterpreted text says something very different from its obvious literal meaning. But the cost of this sort of move is not much different from rejecting the story outright as not true, and it has the same effect. Human standards and understanding judge the texts; they decide which texts can be taken literally and which have to be taken allegorically. Consequently, the texts do not supply a standard by which human affairs and human views can be corrected.

I realize, of course, that some people take this story and others like it as a good reason for rejecting any idea that these texts constitute a revelation on the part of a good God. But letting one set of contemporary interpretations of some biblical stories serve as the basis for jettisoning the many centuries of tradition of more than one religion strikes me as hasty and rash. I do not mean to say that we should rethink our moral standards and be prepared to take genocide and the wholesale slaughter of animals as morally acceptable for the sake of preserving traditional Jewish and Christian views about revelation. On the contrary, it seems to me that there is something loathsome about a willingness to endorse anything at all as long as it lends support to religious practices or beliefs. What I am suggesting instead is that there is some reason for diffidence about *interpretations* of the stories in the biblical texts if those interpretations require the rejection of a central view on the part of more than one of the major monotheisms.

3. A THOUGHT EXPERIMENT

At this point, I would ask, 'So, what then *are* we to make of this story about Samuel and the Amalekites?', except that this is not a question that would be worth trying to answer in this context. That is because the 'we' in question hold such varying beliefs, relevant to the story, that a coherent answer to the question 'What are we to make of this story?' would be hard to come by. In these circumstances, I want to approach the story in a different way. I want to consider a putatively possible world which is very similar to the actual world and which includes the existence of evil, but in which the central claims of Christianity are true. (I say 'putatively possible' because I recognize that, in virtue of the problem of evil, some people think there is no such possible world.) With this putatively possible world briefly and only partially described, I want to ask, as a thought experiment, whether the story of Samuel and the Amalekites could be literally true in a world of that sort.

Here is a partial description of the putatively possible world of the thought experiment.

In this world, there is an omniscient, omnipotent, perfectly good God who created the world and governs it. Human beings are also created by God, and they are everlasting; they do not cease to exist at bodily death. God loves everything that he has made, and he desires all human beings to be united to him in love forever. But because human beings have free will in some libertarian sense, even God cannot unilaterally bring about union between himself and a human person. For there to be such union, a human person has to be willing to be united to God; his will has to be in accord with the will of a perfectly good God. Everything that happens in the world happens in accordance with God's will, at least in the sense that God permits it, even if he permits it only in light of what human beings themselves will. Finally, there is an objective moral standard for human beings. That standard is in accordance with God's will, and God communicates it to human beings by one means or another. Among other things, this divinely willed and communicated moral standard forbids murder as incompatible with God's will; it also mandates a certain standard of care for animals.

Can the story of Samuel and the Amalekites be true in a world of this sort?

4. THE PROBLEM WITH THE STORY:
THE FIRST HYPOTHESES

To some people, it will seem abundantly clear that, in a world of the sort I have described, this story could not be true. But what exactly is the matter with this story if we try to read it as literally true in the world of the thought experiment?

Here is a first, obvious thought. Someone might suppose that the God of the putatively possible world in the thought experiment could not will the death of a child or of any human being at any age. But, clearly, this is not right. In the world as I have described it, every human being who dies, without exception dies because that death is in accordance with God's will, either God's active will or God's permissive will.

Without doubt, the death of human beings in general, the death of children in particular, raises the problem of evil. Certainly it does. Of course it does. But the problem of evil cannot be addressed adequately in passing in one short chapter whose main focus is something other than the problem of evil in general.[1] And I want the questions for the thought experiment at issue in this chapter to focus not on the problem of evil in general, but on what is particular to the story of Samuel and the Amalekites. The death of human beings is not something particular to the story about the Amalekites.

So, for the sake of focusing the thought experiment, I am now adding to the description of the putatively possible world of the thought experiment the stipulation that God has some morally sufficient reason for allowing the suffering of human beings and animals, and that the morally sufficient reason includes benefits that defeat their suffering. On this stipulation, each sufferer is the protagonist of his own life story, and in that story his suffering is defeated by benefits that accrue to him from his suffering. In making this stipulation, I am granting at the outset that nothing in this chapter provides any help with the problem of evil in general. For purposes of this chapter I want to examine the problems particular to the story about the Amalekites and not the problem of evil as a whole.

Nonetheless, there is one thing more worth noting here before I move on: nothing in the story about the Amalekites requires the interpretation that the Amalekite children suffered in dying, as the objection above assumes they did. We ourselves know how to protect children from suffering during the depredations of serious medical procedures; if we can do it, then an omnipotent

---

[1] I address the problem of evil in general in Stump 2010.

God could do it too. And nothing in the story rules out the possibility that God protected all the Amalekites, children and everyone else, in this way in the process of death. I am not claiming that the story mandates the supposition that God did so. I am just pointing out that it doesn't mandate the supposition that God didn't do so either.

If the problem of evil is bracketed, however, what is the matter with this story?

Here is a second suggestion. Apart from the suffering of the Amalekites, someone might suppose that the real problem with the story is that, in the story, God wills not the death of various individual persons but the destruction of a people, the Amalekite people. The God of the possible world I described loves everything he has made. It seems that such a God could not want the annihilation of a whole people.

But why should we think so?

To begin with, why suppose that God's goodness requires him to keep in existence perpetually any group of people that happens to have come into existence as a group? Many families, clans, tribes, peoples, and nations come into existence. Why think that God's goodness requires that they stay in existence? In the ongoing history of human civilization, nations and peoples arise and perish continually. Is it likely that this process by itself could be the foundation of an argument for the non-existence of an omnipotent, omniscient, perfectly good God? I don't think such an argument would be easy to make.

But in this story God *wills* this people to go out of existence; and, in the story, God says, by way of explanation, that he remembers what the Amalekites did to the Israelites generations earlier when the Israelites were coming out of Egypt. So, someone might suppose that the real problem with the story lies in the story's implication about God's motive in willing the eradication of the Amalekite people. Some people understand the story to imply that the God of the story intended genocide as retributive punishment on the Amalekite people for wrongs committed by their distant ancestors. On this reading, the real problem with the story is not that God wills the end of the Amalekite people but that he wants the end of the Amalekites as unjust retributive punishment on the current generation of Amalekites.

But here, too, it is worth noting that the story does not have to be read in this way. Nothing about the story requires that we read into it God's willing the end of the existence of the Amalekites as punishment that is both retributive and unjust. Here is another possible interpretation. I am not endorsing this interpretation; but I am offering it only to show that multiple interpretations are possible here. Suppose that the Amalekites, who in generations past attacked the rearguard of the wandering Israelites, have since then gotten progressively worse and worse. Seeing their trajectory, God is seeking to end now the people that they are, before this people becomes truly monstrous. God remembers where they began and sees where they are going, and so he judges it better *for the Amalekites* to cease existing as a people. The story does not force this reading but it does not rule it out either. And this reading is compatible, in my view, with the God of the thought experiment. If we consider the case of a moral monster such as Himmler, it is not hard to suppose that it would have been better for him if he had died before he lived to perpetrate the atrocities he committed. It seems to me that the same thought could at least in principle apply to a people as well.[2] In that case, the eradication is not any kind of punishment for the Amalekites.

So since the story does not have to be read as attributing to God a will for unjust retributive punishment, I do not think that the reading that does make this attribution has identified a real problem with the story.

5. THE PROBLEM WITH THE STORY: A HARDER CASE

No doubt, there is a lot more that needs to be said about worries raised by the sufferings of the Amalekites and God's willing of that suffering; but I want to leave all of it to one side in the interest of highlighting what seems to me a more difficult kind of worry that is raised by things specific to the story.

Someone might suppose that the real problem with the story is not that it is God's active or permissive will that a particular people cease to exist through a terrible mode of death but rather that in this story God brings about the end of their existence by commanding another group of people to kill them. If in the world of my thought experiment it is true that God forbids people, the Israelite people included, to murder, then, on this supposition, it could not also be true that God commands the Israelite people to murder the Amalekites, as he seems to do in this story.

This objection seems to me more on target but still not quite right. For one person Cain to murder another person Abel, many more things need to be

---

[2] And there are other interpretations as well. For example, it is possible that a people or a nation be engaged in acts or practices that are morally wrong without its being the case that the human agents who do such things be worthy of punishment for them. Think, for example, of the practice of footbinding in China. If the people or nation are mired in very many such practices, one might think it better that the people cease to exist without judging that the human beings who currently constitute the nation or people are worthy of punishment for the practices of the group.

true than the simple fact that Cain kills Abel. For that killing to count as murder, it also needs to be the case that Cain desires to end Abel's life and decides on his own authority to do so. But this is not what we find in the story about the Amalekites. In the story, the Israelite people do not decide on their own authority to end the lives of the Amalekites. God tells them to do so. The authority authorizing these deaths at this time is God. Because the Israelite people act on God's authority in killing, the killing lacks one of the conditions of murder. Even those opposed to capital punishment will grant that the officially sanctioned state authority responsible for executing those condemned to capital punishment is not committing murder in the fulfillment of his duties, although he is killing someone. In the same way, the Israelite people is officially sanctioned by the highest authority, and so the Israelites are not committing murder when they kill the Amalekites. For this reason, God's command to the Israelite people is not a command to murder, and it doesn't violate the prohibition against murder in the divinely sanctioned and promulgated moral code of the world of the thought experiment.

Nonetheless, even if in the story what God commands the Israelite people does not count as murder on their part, it does seem that there is still something morally deplorable in God's commanding them to do this killing. Even if the Israelites are not committing murder in killing the Amalekites, it seems that there is something morally corrupting for the Israelite people in its engaging in the wholesale killing of human beings and animals. And it is not compatible with God's goodness to will the moral corruption of a people. So, even if the death of all the Amalekites and the death of their animals were compatible with the existence of a good God, as I have stipulated that it is in the possible world of the thought experiment, it seems that God's actively engaging the Israelite people in killing the Amalekites and their animals couldn't be.

6. THE NATURE OF GOD'S AIMS: A FIRST PUZZLE

But this objection ought to precipitate a question that the story about the Amalekites should have raised in any case. If in the story God's purpose is that the Amalekite people cease to exist as a people, then why doesn't God himself bring about that end? In the putatively possible world of my thought experiment, God is omnipotent and omniscient. So God could bring about the end of the Amalekite people simply by willing that it not exist any longer. Even in the world of the biblical stories, the God of the stories can bring about by himself the end of the existence of a large group of people. Think, for example, of the destruction of the cities of Sodom and Gomorrah. As far as that goes, think of the story of Noah's flood. In the story of Noah's flood, God in effect makes a new beginning to human history by the cultural analogue of an autologous bone marrow transplant. From the disordered culture of post-Fall human beings, God selects one small group that seems as free of post-Fall evil as human beings ever get. God destroys the other, evil peoples with a flood and multiplies the morally healthy group when it has been reintroduced into the environment. So, in the world of these biblical stories, it is possible for God to use the forces of nature to end the existence of whole groups of people. In the world of my thought experiment, God does not even need to use the forces of nature; an omnipotent God can bring about the end of the existence of a people just by willing it.

Furthermore, as the story of Samuel and the Amalekites makes clear, if eradicating the Amalekites is the end God is trying to achieve, then causing the Amalekites to cease to exist by means of commanding the Israelite people to kill them is not a good way to bring about the end God wants. It is part of the story that Saul willfully fails to do what he was commanded to do to bring about the eradication of the Amalekites. In fact, although the story seems to suggest that in the end none of the Amalekites survive, in the ongoing biblical narrative the Amalekites are again a fighting force worth worrying about only a few years later. Saul's successor, David, returns to his home of Ziklag to find that the Amalekites have burned the entire town and kidnapped all the women and children in it (1 Sam. 30: 1–3). If ending the existence of the Amalekite people was God's purpose, then God could have achieved his purpose better and more reliably by bringing it about himself rather than by commanding Saul and the Israelite people to do it for him.

Here it is worth stopping to reflect more generally on the things that God consigns to human agency, in the biblical stories and in the putatively possible world of my thought experiment. Consider, for example, the entire biblical system of law and punishments. On this law, which in the world of the biblical stories is the law God gave the Israelite people, if one person steals a sheep from another person, the community in which the thief lives or the appropriate officials of that community have to see to it that the thief gives back four sheep to the person from whom he stole (Exod. 22: 1). If one person murders another, the community or its officials have to put the murderer to death (Exod. 21: 12). And now a problem analogous to the one I just posed for the story of Samuel and the Amalekites should occur to us. If God wants theft and murder to be punished, why doesn't he do the punishing himself? Think just about the requirement of capital punishment for cases of murder. God could easily make it the case that anyone who committed murder inevitably died himself very soon afterwards. In the world of the thought experiment, as in the world of the biblical stories, God does not need human beings to carry out such punishments for him.

Furthermore, here, too, it is clear that if the end God wants is punishment for violators of the law, this end is much less reliably and successfully achieved by God's using human beings as agents to bring about this end.

And, clearly, this is only the beginning. If God does not like theft and murder and seeks to suppress them in human society, achieving this aim by means of punishments seems a particularly poor means to the end. The process has the very bad consequence that some human beings, the victims of theft and murder, suffer before the means meant to suppress theft and murder are used. The process is also highly unreliable, since it requires human beings to care about theft and murder, to be willing to do what it takes to find thieves or murderers, and to be committed to imposing the divinely mandated punishments just on the guilty. It also requires that human beings be successful in their efforts to do these things. Moreover, just as in the case of Samuel and the Amalekites, there is also a worry about the effects on the people enforcing the law and imposing the punishments. It is possible that human beings who impose punishments will be corrupted by imposing them. People who oppose capital punishment worry about the effects on a society that finds capital punishment acceptable. Pacifists think that any willingness to engage in war corrupts the people who accept participating in such violence.

Obviously, if God's aim is to suppress theft and murder in human society, there is a much better way for him to accomplish this aim than by means of a system of laws and punishments. Because God is omnipotent, by himself without any human help God could make it impossible for one human being to murder another or steal from another. There are myriad ways, limited only by our imagination to conceive them, by which God might do so. For example, he might simply make it a rule of the universe that human beings cannot do such things. If God can make a rule of the universe which has the result that elementary particles are entangled, then God could make a rule of the universe which limits human behavior in this way. And, contrary to what is sometimes claimed, God could do so without violating or abrogating human free will. A person could still freely *will* to steal or freely *will* to murder, even if he couldn't carry out successfully what he willed. Coveting and hating helplessly are not uncommon even in our world where theft and murder are possible.

So if we understand God's aims as the punishment of violators of the law, the suppression of moral wrongdoing, or the destruction of the Amalekite people, what we would have to say is that God has picked highly inefficacious ways to bring about his aims. But, on the thought experiment I am doing, this conclusion is a *reductio* of the hypothesis that these are God's aims. That is because in the putatively possible world of the thought experiment God is omniscient, omnipotent, and perfectly good; and so choosing very poor means to achieve his aims is not possible for God. This conclusion could be seen as an argument for rejecting the story; but it could also be seen as an argument for rejecting this interpretation of the story.

7. ANOTHER HYPOTHESIS

So, for the sake of keeping the thought experiment going, suppose we consider whether there isn't an interpretation of the story of Samuel and the Amalekites that makes God's main aim something other than the eradication or punishment of the Amalekites.

I propose to begin looking for such an interpretation by asking what it is about human agency that makes God value it even at the costs it brings with it. Why would God want war on the part of the Israelite people to be the means of ending the existence of the Amalekite people? For that matter, why would God want his laws about theft and murder to be enforced by human agency? Why would God even issue laws about human behavior? Why not just do everything himself?

Put that way, of course, the question suggests its answer. In the world of my thought experiment, what God wants ultimately, as regards human beings, is union with them. For a union of wills between a perfectly good God and a human person, however, the human person needs to have a perfectly good will, too. And, clearly, a will in this condition is not so easy to come by for human beings. It won't be easy to come by for omnipotent God either. That is because if God unilaterally determines a human will to be perfectly good, then the will in that human being is God's will, not the human person's. And in that case union is precluded, not achieved. For union, *two* persons, with two wills and two minds, are required. So one reason for God's valuing human agency is that it is necessary for union between God and human beings.

Thinking about God's attitude towards human agency in this way suggests another explanation of God's practice of issuing laws for human behavior and of leaving it to human beings to enforce those laws. For a people to adopt a law requires it to accept a certain standard of behavior, and for it to enforce that law requires it to have a commitment to the standard it accepts and to the person on whose authority the standard rests. On this view, one point of God's giving human beings laws and leaving the enforcement of those laws to human beings is not the effect of the system on the violators of the law but the effect of the system on the people entrusted with enforcing the law.

At the point in the biblical story at which God commands the destruction of the Amalekite people, the Israelite people is early in its history of formation as a people with a law. And so we might bring to bear on the story of the Amalekites considerations analogous to those about the divinely given law and the enforcement of that law. Just as, in the world of the biblical stories and in the world of my thought experiment, there is a point to making human beings responsible for a law God gives them, so it is not implausible to suppose that making the Israelite people responsible for God's eradication of the Amalekite people brings home to the Israelite people the moral and religious importance of God's judgments and the importance of their commitment to God. Saul is the first king of the Israelite people, who are at that point in transition from being a loosely knit aggregate of tribes to being one people bound together into a nation. Their short history between their coming out of Egypt and their coming together as a nation under a king is marked by reiterated episodes of alienation from God and disregard of the moral and spiritual practices God enjoined on them during the Exodus. Here, at the beginning of their existence as a nation, it may be that God commands them to be the agents of the destruction of the Amalekite people to bring home to them in this drastic way the importance of their relationship to God and the importance of God's judgments, including the divinely ordained practices that distinguish the Israelite people from the surrounding peoples.

Thinking about the story in this way helps to explain why God requires the Israelites to kill all the animals of the Amalekites. Animals represent wealth in this culture. If the Israelite people take the Amalekite animals for their own use, any use, even for use as sacrifices, then they begin to blur the distinction between acting as officially sanctioned executioners, as it were, and acting as brigands. On this way of interpreting the story, God commands the killing of all of the Amalekite animals so that the Israelites do not make a profit from victory over the Amalekites. Pillage and plunder are the rule for fighting in this day, as other stories, including other biblical stories, attest; and the desire to plunder others is one of the reasons people in this period go to war, even at the cost of the suffering and death that typically accrue even to the plundering victors. For the Israelite people to refrain from pillaging their defeated enemies is for them to be committed, in a way they will feel, to acting for God's purposes and not their own.[3]

---

[3] It is also notable in this connection that Saul saves alive the king of the Amalekites. In other stories, conquering kings take the rulers of the peoples they have defeated as living trophies of their victories. That this may be Saul's motive, at the beginning of his reign, is suggested by a

From the point of view of the Israelite people, God's command to destroy the Amalekites imposes on the Israelites the risk of serious bodily injury or death. Even victorious armies suffer casualties, and each person in the army knows that he could be one of the casualties. At the time God issues his command to the Israelites, the Amalekites are not attacking the Israelites. So the Israelites do not have self-defense as a motive for running the risks of combat. Because God has commanded the slaughter of all the animals, the Israelites do not have the motive of wealth either. In issuing his command, then, God is requiring the Israelites to be willing to risk themselves in war only for the sake of being committed to God and enforcing God's judgments. A person who risks his life for God and God's judgments commits himself to the acceptance of God and God's judgments in a very serious way.

This interpretation of the story also helps with another puzzle raised by different but related stories, the stories having to do with the Israelite people and the land. In these stories, God repeatedly promises Abraham or his descendants a gift of land flowing with milk and honey. But, as it turns out, not only is this land already possessed by somebody else—at a time in the world when it is very easy to find good uninhabited and unclaimed land—but in order to get this gift of land the Israelite people has to fight its current possessors for it. Why would the very powerful God of the stories give the Israelite people this land on this system? Even if there were some reason why the gifted land had to be this very land, already occupied by others, in the world of the stories it is abundantly clear that God could have destroyed the inhabitants of that land by himself, before he gave the land as a gift to the Israelite people. Why make the Israelite people fight for what is supposed to be God's gift to them? If God's aim is just getting land for the nomadic people of Israel, this system does not make much sense, in the world of the stories, or in the world of my thought experiment. But if God's purpose is to build a people for union with himself, and if getting the Israelite people to act as divinely ordained enforcers of God's judgments and the practices God enjoins on them by fighting against other peoples who reject those judgments and practices, then this way of giving the gift of land becomes more intelligible.

But what about the issue of moral corruption? Moral corruption is a matter of making someone morally worse than he otherwise would be. And, in principle, one people can certainly be corrupted by going to war to destroy another people it takes to be its enemy. But a lot depends on the condition of

different line in the story which describes Saul as building a monument celebrating his victory. But if making a profit is ruled out in the eradication of the Amalekite people, so is self-glorification on the part of the Israelites or their king, and for similar reasons. It blurs a distinction critical in the case.

the people engaged in the fighting and their reasons for warfare. The Israelite people go to war because of God's command. And in the world of the stories, as evidenced by biblical texts, and in the ancient Western world in general, as attested by such sources as we have in history and poetry, unending tribal warfare marked by savage practices is the rule in the time when God gives the Israelite people the command to destroy the Amalekites.

To take an example of such practices from the early history of the world of Genesis, before there was an Israelite people, there is a story in which the kings of four peoples and their armies make war with the kings of five peoples and their armies, and the story includes descriptions of widespread slaughter, enslavement of peoples, and pillaging of whole communities. After this, but still generations before Saul, when the Israelites take Jericho, they kill all the people in the city, including the women and children. The same is true of David, the successor to Saul, and his army when they invade the territory of the Geshurites, the Gezerites, and the Amalekites. In the period immediately before the story about Samuel and the Amalekites, the Israelites attack the Amalekites on their own authority, not God's; in this same period, they also fight with the Moabites, the Ammonites, the Edomites, and the Philistines, all of whom at some point also aggress against the Israelites. Furthermore, in the world of the stories, in the time of Saul's reign, the peoples around the Israelites are part of this same culture of fierce warfare. When the Ammonites initiate an attack against one Israelite community, the Israelite people of that community offer to surrender without fighting and to serve the Ammonites as the Ammonites wish; but the Ammonites are willing to accept this offer only if the Ammonites are first allowed to gouge out the right eye of every Israelite human being in that community (1 Sam. 11: 8).

So it is less clear than it might have seemed initially that, in the world of these stories, God's command to destroy the Amalekites risks the moral corruption of the Israelite people. At any rate, it is notable that God's command to destroy the Amalekites comes at this period in human history when internecine tribal warfare is common.

Another way of reading the story about Samuel and the Amalekites, then, is to see God's primary aim as focused on the effects of the fighting on the Israelite people, rather than the Amalekite people. The saga of the formation of the Israelite people begins in Genesis and continues through many books of the Hebrew Bible. The story of Samuel and the Amalekites is one episode in this saga of God's growing these descendants of Abraham into a particular kind of people in relationship with God. (I say '*these* descendants' because the Amalekites are descendants of Abraham, too.) I do not mean to say that in the world of the biblical stories, any more than in the world of my thought experiment, God cares only about the Israelite people. I mean only that the books of the Hebrew Bible have the Israelite people and their growth in relationship to God as the main concern of the story being told. It isn't possible to tell everything in one story. I also do not mean, and it is not part of my interpretation of the story of Samuel and the Amalekites, that in the story God uses the suffering of the Amalekites only for the sake of bringing any kind of benefit to the Israelites. In the world of my thought experiment, God loves all human persons, and he doesn't use the suffering of any human beings solely as a means to some good for others. In the world of my thought experiment, in some story we do not have, another one of the Abrahamic peoples, the Amalekites and not the Israelites, are the main protagonists; and the point of their suffering is the provision of benefits for them.

Someone might suppose that it isn't possible for the God of the thought experiment to provide benefits for both the Amalekites and the Israelites in this story just because the two peoples are at war. It can't be the case, for example, that both peoples win the war. But in the world of the thought experiment God's ultimate aim for all human beings is to bring them into union with himself. And this benefit is certainly something God can offer human beings even if they are at war among themselves.

8. THE NATURE OF GOD'S AIMS: THE SECOND PUZZLE

On the interpretation of the story I have just given, however, another perplexity arises, analogous to the one I raised for interpretations of the story in which the point of God's command is primarily the effect on the Amalekite people. If God's purpose in the story of Samuel and the Amalekites has to do with the formation of the Israelites as a people growing in their ability to be united to him, it seems that his plan is as unreliable and unsuccessful as I said that plan would be if its aim were the destruction of the Amalekite people. That is because very shortly after the events of this story the Israelite people is itself immersed in all the practices God has condemned on the part of the Amalekite people and all the surrounding peoples with whom God also commands the Israelite people to fight. So it seems as if, on the interpretation I have given of the story of Samuel and the Amalekites, God's plan is no more efficacious or successful in achieving God's ends than it was on the interpretation of the story I was trying to put aside.

Here it is worth thinking again of the other cases I mentioned in which God requires human agency, God's giving of the law prohibiting theft and murder, for example, and his requiring human enforcement of that law. Murder and theft were certainly not extinguished among the Israelite people by this means. Or think again about the story of Noah and the flood, which I said was the moral and spiritual equivalent of an autologous bone marrow transplant. In that case, the procedure seems a definite failure. The old moral disease returned almost immediately; the remission purchased by the flood was very short-lived. If God was hoping for a morally better world by means of killing off the evil peoples of the antediluvian world, he was sadly mistaken.

And now, in the world of my thought experiment, we have reached another *reductio*. The God of my thought experiment could not be sadly mistaken. He is omniscient, and as omniscient he will know that bringing a flood and eradicating all but a small group of a few good people will not solve the moral problem with the human species. *Mutatis mutandis*, the same point applies with regard to the God of the biblical stories. In the world of the biblical stories, God can predict things hundreds of years in advance, as when he tells Abraham that his descendants will be slaves for 400 years. So presumably the God of the biblical stories can also know what will happen in the life of a people a few generations hence. Even in the world of the biblical stories, God can know that his plans will fail.

So why would God bring a flood? Why would God give the Law? Why would he ask the Israelite people to enforce it? Why would he command the Israelite people to destroy the Amalekite people? In each of these cases, what looks like a plan to grow a people into a moral and spiritual condition that will enable them to be united with God turns out to be a failure. But this failure is one that could not be a surprise to the omniscient God of my thought experiment or to the God of the biblical stories either.

It could, however, be a surprise to us. That is, for each of the things God does—start over with a new people after the flood, set out laws governing the life of the Israelite people, get the Israelite people to be the enforcers of that law, command the Israelite people to act as officially sanctioned executioners against the Amalekite people—*we* might have thought that one or more of these plans would be an efficacious way to cure the moral disorder that seems to afflict all human beings everywhere.

Here, then, is a different way of understanding what God is doing in the stories in the Hebrew Bible. He is forming a people by showing them what will *not* work to cure them of what needs to be healed in them. This way of thinking about God's plans yields still another interpretation of the story about Samuel and the Amalekites.

On this interpretation, the story is one episode in a chronicle of the birth and ongoing formation of the Israelite people in which God's primary aim is to form this people for union with himself. (In the world of the thought experiment, there is also a story, only one which we do not have, whose main subject is the formation of the Amalekite people; and, in this story, the suffering of the Amalekites at the hands of the Israelites has a role to play in the relationship of this people to God, during the time of their existence as a people.) In the chronicle of God's formation of the Israelite people, God recurrently puts in place plans that might be thought to provide a cure of the moral disorder that makes union with a good God impossible.

Each of these plans is produced, shown to fail, and then abandoned. Noah's flood is followed by a different kind of attempt at the reproduction of a good human people. God develops a close relationship with Abraham and then builds Abraham's offspring into a particular people covenanted with God. By the time of Abraham's great-grandchildren, this strategy already looks very unsuccessful. Next, God lets the burgeoning Israelite people become enslaved in Egypt, and then he frees them in a floridly dramatic rescue, which includes giving them laws about how to live and punishments for violating those laws. But the people are hardly out of Egypt before this strategy begins to look highly unsuccessful, too. At this point, as the people is turning into a nation, God commands the killing of the Amalekite people, in a radical effort to impact the Israelite people, a more shrill and strenuous attempt to accomplish what requiring the Israelite people to enforce the law was meant to achieve. But the immediate aftermath of the attack on the Amalekite people is marked only by civil war among the Israelite people and lamentable evil on the part of its rulers. After this, under Solomon there is a period of peace and prosperity for the Israelite people, but prosperity is no more a cure for the human tendency to evil than any of the other divine plans were.

And so on and on. The chronicle continues in the production of new plans for the establishment of a good, just, loving people that can be united with a perfectly good God. As each plan is seen to fail, it is abandoned and succeeded by another one. There is no second recurrence of a flood. There is no new and better law given to the people. There is no second set of divine commands to the Israelites for the eradication of some other people. There is no second Solomon. Each of those plans for the formation of a people close to God and able to be united with him is shown to be unsuccessful and for that reason is also not attempted again. In the end, all these plans fail, in the sense that none of them constitutes the cure for the human tendency to evil; none of them results in the formation of a people cured of that tendency.

Taken together, however, these plans do succeed in another way. God's global plan in the overarching chronicle of the formation of the Israelite people involves the production of many short-lived plans doomed to failure; but the global plan does contribute to forming a people who can be united with God. That is because learning what won't work is sometimes an essential preliminary in the process of the discovery of what will work and of the willingness to accept it. We are familiar with this sort of phenomenon on a much smaller scale, in the lives of individual human beings, where the stakes and the suffering are correspondingly smaller. Sometimes a person is not willing to accept what is necessary for the regeneration of his life until everything else has been tried and found to fail. In the overarching chronicle, it is God's global plan, consisting of a series of localized failures, that is meant to be successful.

9. CONCLUSION

In this chapter, I have done nothing to address the problem of evil in general or the problem of evil as it is raised by the suffering of the Amalekites and their animals in the story. For the sake of the thought experiment, I have just stipulated that in the putatively possible world of the thought experiment there is some morally sufficient reason for God to allow the suffering of human beings and animals. If in the actual world there is no such reason, then, of course, we do not need to worry about the story of Samuel and the Amalekites. There are weightier and more pressing reasons for rejecting theism than this story. If it can be shown on grounds of the problem of evil that theism has to be rejected, then this story and others like it lose much of their interest. So in order to consider what there is about the story that is interesting and that raises the problem of evil in a way peculiar to the story, it helps to bracket the problem of evil in its general form, as I have done in the thought experiment.

On first reflection, it seems as if there are only two options as regards the story of Samuel and the Amalekites. Either reject the story, in one way or another, as making false claims about commands by God; or else accept those claims as true but at the cost of giving up deeply entrenched moral intuitions. But the thought experiment shows that these are not the only options for dealing with the story. On the reading of the story in the thought experiment, the story is part of a much larger narrative having to do with the raising of a people. Because we are a child-centered culture, we think a lot about the raising of human beings, one human being at a time. But we are not much accustomed to thinking about what it would be to form a people, or even the whole human species, over many centuries. That process is much harder to understand, but it shares some features with child-raising. We take one important goal for child-raising to be enabling children to desire of their own accord what is good—as regards nutrition, the life of the mind, interpersonal relations, social justice, and many other things as well. We understand that it is not easy to raise a child to turn out this way. It can't be accomplished just with lectures and lessons. It requires the exercise of agency on the part of the children and their own experience of what makes failure in life. Plainly, forming a people, or the whole human species, with an analogous goal is even more difficult and complicated.

The stories of the Hebrew Bible form one larger narrative about a process of formation of this sort for one people. When the story of Samuel and the Amalekites is seen within the context of the larger narrative, then its troubling features look different too. So interpreted, in my view, the story can be woven into the putatively possible world of my thought experiment. In the larger narrative that is the context for the story about the Amalekites, God values human agency not because, or not only because, the human agents bring about something in the world that God wants to have accomplished. Rather, God values it at least in part because of its effects on the agents. In the miserable process of formation through experience, one of the things a people can learn is what will not work to enable a people to become just, good, and loving.

If the story of Samuel and the Amalekites is not to be rejected, then I think that this is a more promising way to read it. At any rate, it seems to me that this way of thinking about the story would be helpful for Benjamin Netanyahu.

Comments on 'The Problem of Evil and the History of Peoples'

Paul Draper

Eleonore Stump's approach to the issue of the character of the biblical God is as nuanced as it is thought-provoking. She refuses to ask how *we* should interpret the story of Samuel and the Amalekites, because she recognizes that the plausibility of an interpretation is relative to the beliefs of the interpreter. For example, for Christians who believe the Bible to be, not revelation itself, but just a fallible human report of revelation, it would be foolish to take seriously the idea that a morally perfect God literally commanded the Israelites to slaughter the Amalekites. This is why Stump conducts a thought experiment. She asks a question, not about the actual world, but about a putatively possible world in which the central claims of her particular version of orthodox Christianity, which I will call 'Eleonorean Christianity', are true. In this way, she hopes to enable us to see the story of the Amalekites through her eyes and thus to appreciate why her interpretation of the story is plausible for someone with beliefs like hers. Second, Stump wisely refuses to discuss problems of evil that are not uniquely biblical (such as the problem of why God allows horrific suffering) even if those problems are raised by the story. Instead, she limits her attention to problems like why God commands one people to destroy another, problems that Eleonorean Christians face only because they believe that the Bible is divinely revealed.

Taking these nuances into account, we can describe Stump's project as follows. She wants to offer an interpretation of the story of Samuel and the Amalekites, and she wants to make at least three claims about that interpretation. First, she wants to claim that her interpretation takes the story to be literally true in its entirety. We can call this the 'literality claim'. Second, she

I am grateful to Michael Bergmann for helpful comments on a preliminary draft of this paper. I am also grateful to Daniel Frank and David Sislen for sharing their expertise on issues of translation and interpretation.

wants to claim that accepting her interpretation does not require Eleonorean Christians to reject any deeply entrenched moral beliefs. Let's refer to this as the 'morality claim'. And third, she wants to claim that her interpretation of the story is plausible *for Eleonorean Christians*. Let's call this the 'plausibility claim'. After briefly summarizing Stump's interpretation, I will challenge all three of these claims about it. In so doing, I will also implicitly challenge a fourth claim that she wants to make about her interpretation, namely, that it solves all of the uniquely biblical problems of evil raised by the story.

A key component of Stump's interpretation is that the purpose of God's command to exterminate Amalek is *not* to punish Amalek for what it did to Israel when Israel came out of Egypt. For that would involve punishing innocent Amalekites, not to mention their animals, and so would be unjust. Instead, God's purpose, or at least one of God's purposes, is to form Israel (the people or nation, interestingly, not the individual Israelites) for union with herself. The obvious objection is that, if this was God's purpose, then God failed miserably; for the Bible reports that Israel turned away from God shortly after the destruction of Amalek. How could an Eleonorean God, a God who is both omnipotent and omniscient, be so inept? Stump responds that this and many other apparent failures reported in the Bible might themselves be required for successfully forming Israel for union with God. The Israelite people might need to learn by first-hand experience what doesn't work in order to be willing to freely accept what does.

Stump's first claim about this interpretation is that it takes the story of Samuel and the Amalekites to be literally true in every detail. Part of what she means by this is that, on her interpretation, the entire story, including its *theological* elements, is a historical narrative and a perfectly accurate one at that. I agree that, on her interpretation, this is so; but I still want to challenge the literality claim. To begin to appreciate why, consider what, according to Samuel, are God's own words: 'I have made reckoning of what Amalek did to Israel, that he set against him on the way as he was coming up from Egypt. Now, go and strike down Amalek, and put under the ban everything that he has, you shall not spare him, and you shall put to death man and woman, infant and suckling, ox and sheep, camel and donkey' (Alter 1999: 87–8). In this passage, God states a rationale for her command to exterminate Amalek that is very different from the rationale Stump attributes to God. Of course, the passage doesn't explicitly say that what Amalek did to Israel a few generations before Samuel was born explains what God now wants Israel to do to Amalek. But an Eleonorean God would realize that such an interpretation of her words as reported by Samuel is very natural (to say the least), and not just for unsophisticated readers like me. The experts I have consulted about translation issues concerning this passage claim that the Hebrew word translated here as 'have made reckoning of' and in other English translations as 'have remembered' supports my point. To make a long story short, if a people (like Amalek) did something wicked and God remembers or makes a reckoning of that wickedness, then bad things are going to happen to that people, and they are going to happen because of what that people did. The suggestion of punishment is very strong, and the suggestion of an explanatory connection between the wicked act that God remembers and the bad things that happen is irresistible.

Of course, it is compatible with taking the story literally to claim that God did not tell Samuel all of her reasons for her command. But it is not compatible with a literal reading to imply, as Stump's interpretation does, that God's own explanation for her actions is woefully and needlessly incomplete and seriously misleading. If the reasons for God's command that God wants to reveal to us in the story of Samuel and the Amalekites have nothing to do with punishment, have more to do with Israel than with Amalek, and have more to do with Amalek's present or even potential future transgressions than with Amalek's *past* transgressions, then the God of the story did an extraordinarily poor job of explaining her command. I conclude that Stump's interpretation does not really take the story *literally*, especially given the Eleonorean Christian view that the Bible is God's revelation, and so presumably successfully reveals something (especially when it quotes God!).

Stump might respond that, to take the story in its entirety to be literally true, one need only accept as true every sentence in the story and every sentence that one knows to be logically or semantically entailed by those sentences. If this is her position, then that would explain why she feels free to suggest in one place (although this isn't part of her official interpretation) that perhaps the Amalekite children didn't suffer when they and their families were slaughtered. After all, she points out, the story doesn't explicitly say that they did suffer and an omnipotent God could certainly prevent their suffering. One wonders, though, why such an interesting and important part of the history of the event would be omitted. It's not as if the authors or Author of the Bible was generally reticent to report miracles. Further, exegesis of this sort appears to lead to absurdity. For example, why stop with the children? Why not say that perhaps none of the Amalekites and none of their animals suffered? Indeed, perhaps the whole experience for both the Israelite soldiers and the Amalekites was one of pure joy. An omnipotent God could certainly make this so and nothing in the Bible explicitly denies that this was so. Add to that a happy afterlife for all involved and one might conclude: problem solved. What is wrong with this, of course, is that such an interpretation is utterly implausible, even for an Eleonorean Christian, and part of the reason that it is implausible is that it takes the story literally only in a very impoverished sense of the word 'literally'. This is not to reject all interpretations that do not take the story literally, nor is it to assume that Bible stories wear their meanings on their sleeves; but it is to reject inter-pretations that are only *pseudo*-literal.

Allow me to make one final point about Stump's literality claim. It is important, I think, for anyone who makes such a claim to make every effort to imagine what the events described in the story would really be like. Stump does talk, at least in general terms, about the suffering of the Amalekites, about the possible moral corruption of the Israelite soldiers, and about the willingness of those soldiers to risk injury and death (and notice she talks about these things even though none of them is mentioned explicitly in the story and none is logically or semantically entailed by anything mentioned explicitly in the story). She neglects to mention, however, the horrible fear that many of the Israelite soldiers would have felt, not of dying or of being injured, but of killing—up close—of hacking into human tissue, of crushing another person's skull while looking into that person's eyes, of slaughtering defenseless children when one's instinct is to protect them. Much modern warfare is less horrifying than this and yet is horrifying enough to cause severe psychological damage to a significant percentage of soldiers. Stump empha-sizes that savagery was the rule at the time of Saul and Samuel, but it would be a mistake to think that ancient warfare was for that reason significantly less damaging psychologically. A few thousand years of human evolution, whether biological or cultural, has not changed us that much. Notice, too, that Stump can't respond to this aspect of the story by saying that the problem of why God allows psychological harm to come to soldiers is not uniquely biblical and so is beyond the scope of her chapter. For in the story the Israelites are obeying a command from God. In the story God *commands* the Israelite soldiers to perform acts that, whether or not they are morally permissible, are so horrific and so contrary to natural virtue that their performance risks severe psychological damage. And that does create a uniquely biblical prob-lem of evil. Of course, an Eleonorean God could have miraculously prevented such damage; but no one who asserts that God actually did that can correctly claim to be taking the story *literally*.

The second of Stump's three claims is that accepting the interpretation does not require one to reject any deeply entrenched moral beliefs. Stump says that, when we interpret Bible stories like the story of the Amalekites, we should not rethink our moral standards. For example, we should not, 'for the sake of preserving traditional Jewish and Christian views about revelation...be prepared to take genocide and the wholesale slaughter of animals as morally acceptable'. She continues, 'there is something *loathsome* about a willingness to endorse anything at all as long as it lends support to religious practices or beliefs' (my italics). So, for example, if some Bible story involved an apparent rape, then Stump would not be interested in trying to reconcile the literal truth of that story with Eleonorean Christianity by saying that rape is sometimes morally permissible, such as when God commands it. For her, if a Bible story implies that God commanded rape, then the story must be rejected, and the reason that it must be rejected is that we must not let our commitment to religious tradition or orthodoxy undermine our deeply entrenched moral belief that rape is wrong.

I agree with Stump's standard here, but I am convinced that her interpretation fails to meet that standard; for instead of rape, let us now consider genocide. Although the word 'genocide' did not appear until the 1940s, the belief that genocide, when performed by human beings, is in all actual cases wrong, like the belief that rape is always wrong, is very deeply entrenched, no doubt partly because of the Holocaust.[1] This explains why genocide, like rape, is a serious crime regardless of the circumstances, while the criminality of acts like homicide depends on the circumstances. This also helps to explain why it would generally be considered seriously morally wrong even to defend genocide, let alone to commit it.

As indicated above, Stump seems to agree with all this. She explicitly says that we should never be prepared to take genocide as morally acceptable. She seems to think, however, though she doesn't say this explicitly, that the Israelites in the story do not commit genocide because they do not decide on their own authority to kill the Amalekites and so their killing of the Amalekites is not *murder*. Genocide, however, is the attempt to destroy a people by any means. It is not true by definition that genocide involves murder. It could, for example, involve forced sterilization or killing because a legitimate political authority orders one to kill. Also, while genocide requires that one act with the intention to destroy a people, it does not require that the motive for one's action be to destroy a people. One's motive might be, for example, to obey what one believes to be a command from God. Thus, in the story of Samuel and the Amalekites, there is no question that God commands the Israelites to commit genocide.

This implies that the morality claim is false. For it is among the central claims of Eleonorean Christianity that God is omniscient, that God is morally perfect, and that there is an objective moral standard for human beings that is in accordance with God's will. It follows from these claims that *God would never command human beings to do something that is morally wrong for them to*

---

[1] I assume here that no *actual* act of genocide, including Israel's destruction of Amalek (if that event actually occurred), can be successfully justified by an appeal to self-defense or to the defense of other innocents.

do. Hence, Eleonorean Christians are committed to the claim that God would not command the Israelites to do something morally wrong. On Stump's interpretation of the story, however, God commands the Israelites to intentionally destroy a people—i.e., to commit genocide. Thus, accepting Stump's interpretation requires Eleonorean Christians to accept that some human acts of genocide are not morally wrong. Therefore, since it is a deeply entrenched moral view that all (actual) acts of genocide, when committed by human beings, are wrong, it follows that accepting Stump's interpretation requires Eleonorean Christians to give up a deeply entrenched moral view.

This brings me to the plausibility claim, the claim that, while Stump's interpretation may not be plausible for me or for the Dalai Lama or for God, it is plausible relative to the belief system of an Eleonorean Christian. My challenges to the literality and morality claims already implicitly challenge the plausibility claim. Indeed, if Stump were to respond to the first of those challenges by saying that the literality claim is true *given what she means by the word 'literal'*, then I would simply restate that challenge so that it explicitly challenges the plausibility claim. I also reject the plausibility claim, however, for other reasons. One such reason, which is all I have the space for here, is that an Eleonorean God is omnipotent and omniscient. Thus, the resources at God's disposal for influencing the Israelite people to turn to God are virtually unlimited. I conclude that, even if, because of free will, it is logically possible that an omnipotent and omniscient God has no better way to achieve her goal of forming Israel for union with her than to command Israel to slaughter all of the Amalekite people and all of their animals, no one, including Eleonorean Christians, should find this plausible. It might be possible, but the chance of it being true is exceedingly remote!

Reply to Draper

Eleonore Stump

I am grateful to Paul Draper for his thoughtful comments. It is impossible to do them justice in short space, but here is my best shot at doing what I can.

Imagine an intelligent being Max from a far-distant world in which all sentient beings live only in one very large edifice, outside of which there is nothing at all. None of these beings is ever seriously sick, and none of them ever dies. And now suppose that Max, who has seen nothing else of earth life, is somehow enabled to see a video of events inside a large city hospital on earth, where the Chief of Staff is a surgeon.

After seeing the video, Max is filled with moral indignation at the doctors and especially the Chief of Staff. Any suggestion that the doctors are benevolent towards their patients will be met by Max with incredulity. How can you say that the Chief of Staff is benevolent, Max will say, when he commands doctors obedient to him to plunge sharp objects into human beings first to render them helpless and then to slice them open with sharp knives?

But, Max, we will tell him, the doctors do these things only because the people are sick.

Because they are sick! Max will expostulate. Are you going to tell me that just because a person is sick, this sort of suffering is an acceptable punishment for him?

No, no, Max, we will say, the things done to the people aren't *punishments* for them.

But, Max will answer, didn't you just say that the doctors were doing these things to the people *because* they are sick?

Oh, Max, we will say, the doctors do these things to the people because the people are sick and the doctors are trying to heal them.

Heal them? Max will say with disbelief. How could slicing a human body open with a knife heal that body? On the contrary, human beings not only

I am grateful to John Foley and John Kavanaugh for helpful comments on an earlier draft of these remarks.

suffer dreadfully from what is done to them in the hospital but in fact they also get very much sicker. The video makes that clear.

There is some truth in that, Max, we will say. Sometimes people do get sicker in hospitals. But they are in the hospital in the first place only because they are seriously sick, and many of them would die without the care of the doctors. In the hospital, a lot of the people are healed; and they leave the hospital to live for a long time more.

Leave the hospital? Max will say with scorn. Are you trying to tell me that your interpretation of the hospital video requires you to believe in life outside the building? Why don't you go on to say that people leave the hospital with joy at being outside the building? Surely even you have to grant that this is a really implausible interpretation of the video. But here is what you can't get past. These doctors are engaging in torture. One of your own reference books in the hospital library, the *Oxford English Dictionary*, defines torture as the infliction of serious physical or psychological suffering. You can't deny that this is exactly what the doctors are doing. Torture is a terrible moral evil on any acceptable moral theory, and any person who commands it or engages in it is guilty of doing a terrible moral evil. And here's what else you can't deny. In commanding other doctors to torture people, the Chief of Staff is commanding what must constitute moral corruption or psychic trauma for these doctors. If nothing else will show you the point, consider just the children. How could anyone hold down a screaming child and do appallingly painful things to it without becoming morally corrupt or deeply traumatized? If a doctor weren't traumatized by what he was doing, he would be a sadistic bastard.

So here are your options, Max will say. You can deny that the video of the hospital tells a literally true story about the Chief of Staff. Or you can acknowledge that the Chief of Staff is evil. But you can't both take the hospital story as literally true and also accept the Chief of Staff as morally good. It just isn't possible.

But, of course, it is possible, as we know. The problematic disagreement between us and Max does not stem from a difference in moral theories. It stems from an enormous difference in world-views. Add Max's world-view to a story that is part of our world, and the result of this unhappy combination is a deeply distorted interpretation of the story.

Max doesn't really comprehend serious sickness. On the world-view Max brings to his interpretation of the video, what goes on in the hospital is all there is to life for human beings, and human beings would do beautifully, would live good and happy lives, if only the doctors would leave them alone. But we, who understand sickness as Max does not, have a powerful sense of the goodness of medical care. We recognize medicine as a means of giving sick people a chance at life—life outside the hospital—or a quality of life that they otherwise might not have. And we prize medicine for this reason. We think that even with all the suffering medicine inflicts on human beings, it is not only a good worth the price but in fact a good precious enough to be grateful for. We feel sorry for those who do not have access to modern medicine. Furthermore, because the idea of death doesn't really register with Max, Max also doesn't share our sense of the urgency and importance of medicine. Max doesn't feel it as we do when we say, for example, that without a bone marrow transplant this person will die. For us, the more we care about a person who is seriously sick, the more we are inclined to demand medical treatment for him. We want whatever medicine can do for our beloved sick person, and we want it now. We are so far from accepting Max's horror of medicine that, in fact, we are willing to fight to get for those we care about what horrifies Max to contemplate.

Furthermore, because in Max's world intelligent beings don't get sick and don't die and don't live outside the building, Max doesn't understand love as we do either. Max is supposing that no one who loved a person could subject that person to grievous suffering, the sort of suffering caused by serious medical treatments. But love wants what is good for the beloved, and it wants union with the beloved. When a person is seriously sick, then—as we grasp in a way Max does not—the worst may happen to that person. Without medical treatment, he may die. And if he does, he is lost to us, absent from us, with a finality love finds hard to bear. So, from our point of view, contrary to what Max supposes, the person who does not seek life-saving medical treatment for a seriously sick person in his care is the unloving person.[1] We feel only moral outrage at a parent who refuses life-saving medical treatment for her child on the grounds that it would hurt her to see the child suffer. The more we love, the more we are willing to endure the suffering of those we love in order to heal them and keep them from dying.

Finally, consider Max's view that inflicting painful medical treatments on people is torture. It is obviously perilous to take philosophical definitions of complicated concepts from reference works: Max and the *OED* are wrong in this definition of torture. The deliberate infliction of serious physical or psychological suffering is only the genus of torture, not its species. Many things that are morally good and worthy of prizing fall within that same genus. Prolonged exposure therapy as a cure for post-traumatic stress disorder is one example; medical treatments are another. To get a definition of

---

[1] The qualification 'life-saving' is meant to obviate the need for fine distinctions impossible to produce in this short space. I recognize, of course, that there are circumstances in which it is good to refuse medical treatments.

torture, what has to be added to the *OED* description is some additional information about the motivation and intentions of the person inflicting the suffering. When these have to do only with love, or at least with an overriding desire for the well-being of the sufferer, there is no torture. And that is also why those engaged in providing medical treatments do not become corrupted by what they do. To be willing to inflict suffering out of care for the sufferer is ennobling, not corrupting.

In the putatively possible world of my thought experiment, human beings are meant to live in everlasting joyful union with their Creator, who loves them. But it is possible for a human being instead to become seriously spiritually sick. If that sickness is bad enough, it is possible for a person to become one of the living dead, still functioning in some sense but spiritually dead, lost to love and union forever. To ward off this worst thing for human beings, a loving God will go to great lengths. He will endure even appalling suffering on the part of the human beings he loves if that suffering has a hope of healing them. This motivation behind God's allowing suffering makes a difference to the moral categorization of it. Genocide, like torture, is not properly defined without reference to some intention or motivation. Where the primary aim is healing, rescue from death, there is neither torture nor genocide. And just as it is possible to recognize what looks like torture as instead done in the interest of healing, however counter-intuitive such a recognition may seem to Max, it is also possible to recognize God's ending of the existence of civilizations, nations, and peoples as motivated by providential care. The willingness to endure even the infliction of great suffering on a person, or on a people, if only it has a chance of saving the sufferer does not make God a sadistic bastard. It makes him loving.

And that is why it is possible to take literally the story about Samuel and the Amalekites and also accept God as morally good.

In my view, this is the shortest way to explain the difference in interpretation between Draper and me.

REFERENCES

Alter, Robert. 1999. *The David Story: A Translation with Commentary of 1 and 2 Samuel.* New York: W. W. Norton.

Goldberg, Jeffrey. 2009. 'Israel's Fears, Amalek's Arsenal', *New York Times*, May 17.

Stump, Eleonore. 2010. *Wandering in Darkness: Narrative and the Problem of Suffering.* Oxford: Oxford University Press.

7

What Does the Old Testament Mean?

Richard Swinburne

I

Before we investigate whether the picture of God in the Old Testament is that of a loving God, we need to take a view about what various passages of the Old Testament mean—a matter which has been the subject of many disputes over many centuries. We can only resolve these disputes by a philosophical analysis of the rules for interpreting texts; and the first part of this chapter will seek to provide a very brief such analysis.

The meaning (in the wide sense of 'the truth conditions') of a token written sentence depends on the conventions of the language in which it is written and on the context of inscription. By the 'conventions of the language' I mean the conventions which determine how the meaning of the sentence is a function of the meanings of the individual words and the way in which they are put together. The conventions which determine the meanings of the words are ones of a kind to be found in a dictionary; the conventions which determine how the way the words are put together gives a meaning to the sentence are those to be found in books setting out the grammar and syntax of the language, as for example the conventions determining which sentences predicate a property of an object, which sentences are existential or universal, or hypothetical etc.

The context of inscription includes literary, social, and cultural contexts. The literary context is the literary work of which the sentence forms a part. The social context is the context of its production—who wrote it, when, and for which audience. The cultural context is that of the common beliefs of the society in which and for which the literary work was written. The literary and social contexts show us (among other things) who is being referred to by indexical expressions and proper names (e.g. which year is the one described

This chapter is based on material contained in Swinburne 2007, especially in part I and in chapter 10, some of which is also to be found in Swinburne 2009b: ch. 11.

as 'last year', or who is the 'John' mentioned in the sentence). The cultural context shows us (among other things) which literary genres were available to the author. Literary genres include historical works (each sentence of which purports to describe what happened by means of words used in literal senses), 'historical fables' (which purport to describe what happened only in its general outlines, with many passages filling these out in a way which does not purport to be accurate), works of fiction, allegories, metaphysical fables (which purport to convey some metaphysical truth by means of a fictional story), and moral fables (which purport to convey some moral truth by means of a fictional story). When we know the literary work to which a sentence belongs, and the genres available to the author, we can often recognize the genre of the work. When we know that, we will be on the way to knowing what it is for that sentence to be true; or, since for works of many genres (e.g. allegories or metaphysical fables) individual sentences do not have a truth-value on their own, what it is for some larger unit of the literary work which contains that sentence to be true. So when we read a sentence reporting what some politician said, when we know whether the sentence belongs to a historical work or to a historical fable, we will know whether it is claiming that the politician said exactly those words or whether it is merely claiming that it (together with other sentences ascribed to the politician) is the sort of thing the politician was apt to say in his speeches. Different genres use metaphor to different degrees. The literary and social contexts are also crucial for distinguishing when words are being used in unusual and especially metaphorical senses. If an author writes something which taken literally is quite irrelevant to the surrounding sentences and/or he clearly doesn't believe and/or doesn't believe that his readers believe it, it must be understood in an unusual sense.

So take a single sentence, 'Larry is an elephant.' Before we can understand it we need to know not merely what the dictionary meanings of the words are and how they are put together, but also the contexts. Knowledge of the cultural context tells us which genres are available. When we know the literary context, that is the literary work to which the sentence belongs, we can recognize which of these genres is that of that literary work, e.g. a zoo guide, a work of children's fiction which may be also a moral or metaphysical fable, or a letter. If the sentence is a sentence of a zoo guide, we still need to know the social context, for which zoo it was written and when, before we know what the sentence is telling us. If it was written for the London Zoo of 1950, it is telling us that Larry, an animal in that zoo, is an elephant. The truth conditions of the sentence are then clear. If there was an animal called 'Larry' in London Zoo in 1950, who was an elephant, the sentence is true; if there was such an animal but he wasn't an elephant, the sentence is false. (Whether the sentence is false or neither-true-or-false if there was no animal called 'Larry' is still a matter of philosophical dispute!) If we recognize the literary work to which the sentence belongs as a work of children's fiction, then the sentence is surely neither true nor false. If the whole work to which the sentence belongs has a clear moral or metaphysical message and so is a metaphysical or moral fable, the same applies. But we may say that the whole work is true insofar as that message is true, and false insofar as it is not. If the sentence occurs in an ordinary letter from a human mother writing about her son, then it clearly cannot be understood literally; it must be taken metaphorically. It must be ascribing to the son some feature possessed or believed to be possessed by elephants—e.g. being large and strong, with a good memory; and then it will be true or false insofar as the context makes it clear which feature is being ascribed and—if it is clear—insofar as the son has that feature.

II

The Bible is a big book, composed of many smaller books, most of them woven together out of yet smaller strands of writing, themselves being formed of smaller units, each with a different literary context (belonging to a different literary work), a different social context (a different author or compiler), and a different cultural context (different presuppositions and different kinds of available genres) at each stage of its inscription. Many sentences will therefore have several different meanings, arising from the fact that the sentence belongs to several different units, the smallest unit being a part of a larger unit which belongs to a yet larger unit and so on. Such a sentence will therefore have one meaning as a sentence of a small unit, a different meaning as a member of a larger unit, and a further different meaning as a sentence of a yet larger unit. (I shall for the present make the assumption that the 'author' or compiler of each unit is the human author or compiler who would be picked out as such by ordinary historical investigation.)

So let us begin by going back to the smallest units, the bits of poetry and story and oracle from various sources from which the books of the Bible were put together, the units which do not contain any smaller units which had any life of their own in speech or writing; and consider a biblical sentence as belonging to such a literary context. To determine what the unit (and so the individual sentence) means, the biblical scholar must locate the original social and cultural contexts of its production. Detection of the relevant contexts is not an easy task, and some of the conclusions of biblical scholars about context are speculative. But discovering the contexts is in principle a soluble task and, insofar as they can solve it, biblical scholars can tells us the meaning of the sentence as originally written (or spoken). For example, Isaiah 7: 14 (in the Hebrew) says 'A young woman is with child and shall bear a son, and shall name him Immanuel.' ('Immanuel' means 'God with us'.) The original literary context is clearly that of Isaiah 7: 7–17. The social context seems to be that of a speech of Isaiah to King Ahaz, which the cultural context shows to be a prophecy. So the sentence says that the queen (or perhaps Isaiah's wife) will bear a son who will be regarded as symbolizing God's presence with his oppressed people. So understood the sentence may well be true. In Daniel 12: 1–2 an angel predicts an end to the world after the death of a king whose anti-Jewish activities are described in the second half of chapter 11. Historical scholarship shows fairly convincingly that this chapter was written by an unknown writer in the second century BCE and that 'the king' described in chapter 11 was the writer's contemporary the Seleucid King Antiochus IV. Knowledge of this cultural context shows this verse also to be a prophecy. So in this case the sentence is false. There are however many units of the Old Testament for which we do not know nearly enough about the cultural context to know to which genre the unit belongs. A crucial example is Genesis 1–2: 4a. Was this intended as literal history—'days' meaning days? In my amateur view probably not; it is what I call a metaphysical fable describing in a poetic way the dependence of all things on God.

The units were put together by compilers with the aid of connecting verses into larger units such as the J, E, D, and P sources of the Pentateuch, and these were put together into the 'Books' of the Hebrew Bible. And then the Hebrew Bible was translated into Greek as the Septuagint; and this (or similar translations) were used by many Jews as their Bible. And finally the Hebrew Bible was incorporated into the Christian Bible as its 'Old Testament'. Sewing units together gives them a new literary context, and also a new social and cultural context—that of the compiler; and so—sometimes—a very different meaning.

The most familiar modern secular example of this is where one author puts a number of his previously published papers together into one volume, and adds a preface explaining that while he republishes the papers in the form in which they were originally published, he now wishes some of them to be understood with certain qualifications; or, more radically, that he does not now agree with the argument of some of the earlier papers but republishes them in order to show what is wrong with them. In such a context the author is not expressing the views contained in the papers, but rather quoting them; and the meaning of the whole is what the author says it is in the preface, with the qualifications which he makes there—even if that was not the meaning of the papers as originally published. For an example of a preface by someone other than the original author which changed the meaning of the book, consider Osiander's preface to Copernicus' *De Revolutionibus*, saying that this detailed work, which seemed to claim that the earth revolved annually around the sun, was meant by the author to mean only that the assumption that the earth revolves around the sun is useful for making detailed calculations of astronomical phenomena. The meaning of the work with the preface was now very different from its meaning without it. On a smaller scale the addition of a footnote may correct something in the text, saying that it is to be understood in some unusual way.

A biblical example where the addition of certain verses changes the whole message of the book is Ecclesiastes, where the addition of verses at the end (12: 13–14), purporting to summarize its message, really gives it a radically new message. A skeptical book becomes a God-centered book. Footnotes are not a device known to ancient writers. Their substitute for a correcting or amplifying footnote is a verse correcting the previous verse, or a connecting verse saying that the next paragraph fills out the previous one. Daniel 12: 12 seems to be a verse correcting the previous verse in respect to the number of days until the 'end'. Genesis 2: 4a has the function, according to Childs (1983: 150), of explaining that the narrative of Genesis 2, which in various ways contradicts that of Genesis 1 (one example is that plants seem to be created before man in Genesis 1, but after man in Genesis 2—see Genesis 2: 5, 7, and 9), is to be read as a detailed filling out of Genesis 1 in some respects.

III

So what is the context in terms of which Christians should understand a sentence of the Bible? Christians see the Bible as having unique authority because they hold that the biblical books were 'inspired' by God the Holy Spirit, inspired in the sense that God breathed into the human author or authors what they should write. God was therefore the 'ultimate author' of the Bible. Christians have never wished to deny that these books were written by human authors, as is evident by the fact that so often there are references to 'I' who did certain things, which can only be construed as a reference to such an author, and by the discrepancies of style of different books. But the Church taught that the main message of the text came from God and was true, and contained 'revelation without error'[1] about God's nature, actions, and

---

[1] A phase used in the chapter on revelation of the decrees of the First Vatican Council. See Tanner 1990: 806. Vatican I's claim clearly follows from the doctrines of divine inspiration (in

intentions, and human obligations towards him. That was the genre of the Bible and it is that status which made it 'the deposit of faith' (or at least the main part of it[2]) from which Christian doctrine may be derived. I cannot see that the content of those books by itself provides adequate justification for that view. Certainly the Bible contains many deep truths, but so do many other great religious and secular works. This high view of the Bible can only be adequately justified on the grounds that the Church founded by Jesus, whose divine authority was authenticated by his life, death, and Resurrection, recognized it as having such a unique authority. The Church determined which books formed the Bible, and it only reached a more or less final view about this after four centuries of debate about it.

So, the Church was claiming, the social context was of books ultimately authored by God (working through the idiosyncrasies of style and culturally conditioned beliefs of its human authors), and—since the revelation was intended (the Church taught) for all humans—all humanity was their intended audience. 'Holy Scripture', wrote Gregory the Great, 'is a letter of God Almighty to his creature.'[3] Hence all the books together formed the literary context for the interpretation of a given sentence. The cultural context in which these books came to have their final form was that of the Church of many centuries, and in particular of the first five centuries during which in determining which books formed part of the Bible it developed a view which followed from its understanding of the social and literary contexts of biblical books about how they should be interpreted. My inquiry for the rest of this chapter into the meaning of the Old Testament will be an inquiry into what is its meaning if it has the contexts which the Church declared it to have in ascribing to it its unique authority. Under any other understanding of the contexts of biblical books, although they have much historical interest, they have no authority for Christians. It is because the Church's view about the contexts of the first part of the Christian Bible depends on its view that it is the first part of a two-part literary work that I have entitled my chapter 'What Does the Old Testament Mean?' rather than 'What Does the Hebrew Bible Mean?'

---

the stated sense) and authorship, and would have been accepted by all the Fathers. The Council of Ephesus (CE 431) referred to the Bible ('scripture') as 'inspired by God', as did many subsequent documents recognized as authoritative by both Catholic and Orthodox Churches. Although God is not described as the 'author' of scripture by any Council before the Council of Florence (CE 1442), God's authorship of them was the unquestioned view from early times. (See for example Origen's *Philocalia* 2.4.)

[2] Some Orthodox and Catholic councils and theologians have taught that the 'deposit' from which doctrine may be derived includes also 'unwritten traditions'. See Swinburne 2007: 188–9.

[3] *Epistolae* 4.31.

As with all texts, biblical passages should be understood in their most natural literal sense if that is possible given its contexts. But it follows however from the social context of the biblical books (as we are now understanding this) that we cannot understand the sentence in such a sense if doing so would involve ascribing to God a belief which on other grounds we believe that he does not have. Biblical sentences should be understood in the light of God's beliefs, as revealed in other biblical sentences (which form the literary context) and the central beliefs of the Church about what Christ had taught which it held before most of the New Testament had been given its canonical status.

God has true beliefs about Christian doctrine. So, when a sentence understood literally contradicts what we know from other sources about Christian doctrine it must be understood in some other sense. The early Christian theologians, the Fathers as they are called, were well aware that there are many biblical passages which when understood in their most natural literal sense are ambiguous or inconsistent with what they believed to be established Christian doctrine, or simply irrelevant to it. It was for that reason that in the late second century CE Marcion, a priest in Rome, advocated that the Old Testament should not be regarded as Christian scripture. The orthodox reassertion of the canonical status of the Old Testament was led by Irenaeus, but he stressed the temporary and metaphorical nature of certain parts of it. The key to understanding scripture was to understand it in a way consistent with Christian doctrine. 'Every word' of scripture 'shall seem consistent' to someone, wrote Irenaeus, 'if he for his part diligently read the Scriptures, in company with those who are presbyters in the Church, among whom is the apostolic doctrine'.[4] That view was the more or less unanimous view of the Fathers. The famous rule of Vincent of Lerins that the faith was what was believed 'always, everywhere and by everyone'[5] was given by him in answer to the question how scripture should be interpreted. So diverse were the interpretations of scripture that his rule was meant as a guide as to which interpretation should be adopted. Scripture consists of what is approved as such by the universal Church, he wrote elsewhere, and it should be interpreted in accordance with 'Catholic Teaching'.[6]

This led to some radical interpretation of passages of the Old Testament which, taken on their own, seem inconsistent with a Christian view of the nature of God, as shown for example in the teaching of the Sermon on the Mount. Some passages seem to endorse a view of God as vindictive, or to pronounce curses on innocent people. One small example is Psalm 137: 9,

---

[4] Irenaeus, *Against Heresies* 4.32.1.   [5] *Commonitorium* 1.2.   [6] Ibid. 1.27.

which pronounces a blessing on those who smash against a rock the children of Babylonians (who had taken Jewish leaders as captives to Babylon). Other passages represent God as too much like an ordinary embodied human being of limited power and knowledge. At the beginning of the third century the highly influential theologian Origen commented on one such passage (the Genesis 2–3 story of the garden of Eden):

Who is so silly as to believe that God, after the manner of a farmer 'planted a paradise eastward in Eden', and set in it a visible and palpable 'tree of life' of such a sort that anyone who tasted its fruit with his bodily teeth would gain life?[7]

God also has true beliefs about science. Yet some biblical passages seemed to state or presuppose scientific views incompatible with what the more educated Fathers believed that learned Greeks had established. Thus Greek science held that the 'natural places' of the four 'elements' were in the form of (roughly) concentric spheres—a spherical earth in the middle of the universe covered by a sphere of water, water by air, air by fire; outside the sphere of fire lay sun, moon, and planets, and finally a solid sphere in which the stars were embedded. The 'firmament' referred to in Genesis 1: 6–8 is then naturally assumed to be this solid sphere. But the Old Testament compares it to a stretched 'skin' (Ps. 104: 2) or to a 'vault', the curved roof of a building (Isa. 40: 22 in a Latin version); and so to a curved covering to a flat earth, not a sphere. Greek science did not allow there to be water above the 'firmament', as claimed by Genesis 1: 7. And a literal interpretation of the 'days' of creation described in Genesis 1 involved there being 'light' on the first day before the sun, the source of light, was created on the fourth day! The Fathers disagreed about whether the biblical passages understood in their most natural sense or the works of learned Greeks provided the best guide to science and so to what God believed about science.[8] But it was generally regarded as permissible to take well-agreed Greek science as the best guide to God's beliefs.

Interpretation often involved choosing one rather than another possible literal meaning (although perhaps a less natural one) of the passage. But sometimes, and to varying degrees, all the Fathers dealt with incompatibilities

---

[7] *On First Principles* 4.3.

[8] Among the Fathers who denied that the earth is a sphere was Justin Martyr (*Questions and Reponses to the Orthodox* 130) who cites Isaiah 40: 22 as evidence for the earth's flatness, in addition to the apparent absurdity of there being plants and people in the Antipodes who are upside down. Augustine (1982: bk. 2, ch. 9) argued that if it is proved (that is, by normal secular reasoning) that the earth is spherical (as he seems to think it is) then we should interpret the biblical passage accordingly. For Augustine's own positive view on the possible meanings of Psalm 104: 2 see later in this chapter. For a list of Fathers who took opposite positions on the flat earth controversy see the editor's note in *Patrologia Latina* 6.427.

with Christian doctrine by adopting a radical metaphorical interpretation of the text. The passage which I quoted from Origen continues:

And when God is said to 'walk in the paradise in the cool of the day' and Adam to hide himself behind a tree, I do not think that anyone will doubt that these are metaphorical expressions which indicate certain mysteries by means of a story which does not correspond to actual events.

Among biblical passages which some of the Fathers interpreted in this way were accounts of savage or other immoral conduct by Israelites, and prophecies (for example, in the Books of Isaiah or Ezekiel) that God would avenge the mistreatment of Israel by various foreign nations (Tyre, Sidon, Egypt, etc.) whose citizens might not seem to deserve such vengeance.

The Fathers had available to them a whole set of objects or properties commonly associated with the people, places, and actions referred to in the Old Testament, which provided symbolic meanings for the words which normally designated the latter. The key to understanding the Old Testament, claimed Origen, is the New Testament teaching of the Kingdom of God as the New Jerusalem (roughly, Heaven), the Church as the New Israel, and Jesus as the new Moses or Joshua, who leads the people of the New Israel to the New Jerusalem in the way that Moses and Joshua led the people of the Old Israel to the 'promised land' of Canaan. Then all Old Testament talk about 'Jerusalem', even if sometimes it can be understood literally as referring to the earthly city of Jerusalem, must be held to have a spiritual reference to the heavenly Jerusalem. So, Origen continues, the prophecies prophesying that God would give different fates to different foreign enemies of Israel are to be understood as prophecies that God would award different fates in the afterlife to different kinds of sinners who really do have the vices ascribed by the prophecy to the inhabitants of Tyre or Egypt. And although few of the Fathers would interpret the Old Testament in quite such a radical metaphorical way as Origen, many of them gave a metaphorical interpretation to Psalm 137: 9 ('Happy shall they be who take your little ones [the children of Babylon] and dash them against the rock'). Since the Jews became enslaved in Babylon, 'Babylon' comes to represent evil generally; and Jesus had compared relying on him (Jesus) to building one's house on a rock.[9] Psalm 137: 9 was then interpreted as a blessing on those who take the offspring of evil which are our evil inclinations, and destroy them through the power of Jesus Christ.

Origen's way of treating the Bible was adopted by Gregory of Nyssa in the next century, and also (rather more cautiously) by Augustine at the beginning

---

[9] Matt. 7: 24.

of the fifth century; and it became one standard approach to the Bible. Gregory points out that there is much immoral conduct apparently commended in the Old Testament: 'What benefit to virtuous living can we obtain from the prophet Hosea, or from Isaiah having intercourse with a prophetess unless something else lies beyond the mere letter?' But the 'mere letter' is only 'the apparent reprehensible sense'; a metaphorical interpretation turns it into 'something having a divine meaning'.[10] Augustine's basic rule was the same as that of Origen and Gregory: 'we must show the way to find out whether a phrase is literal or figurative. And the way is certainly as follows: whatever there is in the word of God that cannot, when taken literally, be referred either to purity of life or soundness of doctrine, you may set down as metaphorical.'[11]

Among the Fathers who thought that the Bible should be understood in the light of any well-established Greek science was Augustine.[12] Much of his commentary *The Literal Interpretation of Genesis* was designed to show that the sentences of Genesis could be understood in literal senses compatible with Greek science, even if not perhaps the most natural literal senses. For example, he argued that perhaps in speaking of the shape of the 'firmament' as a 'vault' the Psalmist (104: 4) 'wished to describe that part which is over our head', which looks like a vault to us. Or he suggested maybe the 'firmament' means simply the sky, not the solid sphere postulated by Greek science, but a region of air above which water vapor is as light as air (and so forms the region of 'water above the sky'). But he also felt the need to interpret passages apparently concerned with scientific matters in metaphorical ways. He interpreted the light created on the first day as 'spiritual light', the light which gives to creatures true spiritual understanding. Even so there was the problem of how there could be days before there was a sun, created according to Genesis on the fourth day. So, like several others of the Fathers, Augustine held that all the things described in Genesis 1 were created simultaneously (as Genesis 2: 4 seems to suggest); and he developed a very idiosyncratic view that talk about the six 'days' of creation is to be interpreted as talk about stages in the knowledge of creation possessed by the angels.

The highly metaphorical way in which Origen, Gregory, and Augustine read some of the Old Testament seems quite unnatural to us. But they lived in a cultural atmosphere where large-scale allegory seemed very natural; it was a very familiar genre in terms of which it was natural to interpret any passage

---

[10] *Commentary on the Song of Songs*, Prologue.

[11] *On Christian Doctrine* 9.10.14.

[12] Augustine writes with regard to such disputes about the 'literal interpretation' of Genesis that 'it is a disgraceful and dangerous thing for an infidel to hear a Christian, presumably giving the meaning of Holy Scripture, talking nonsense' about scientific matters (1982: bk. 1, ch. 19).

which you did not think could be understood literally. The Jewish philoso-pher Philo in the first century BCE had already given a highly allegorical interpretation of Genesis and other Old Testament books. Several commen-tators of classical and later Greece even interpreted the narrative poems of Homer, the *Iliad* and the *Odyssey*, which told the story of the Trojan war and of Odysseus' return to Ithaca, allegorically. Metrodorus of Lampsacus inter-preted the heroes and heroines of the Iliad as items of astronomy and physics—Agamemnon as the aether, Achilles as the sun, Helen as the earth, etc.—and so interpreted the *Iliad* as a scientific treatise.

Origen and Augustine and many others thought that much of the Old Testament had metaphorical meaning in addition to literal meaning, but what I have been pointing out is that sometimes for good reason they denied that it had a literal meaning in cases where we, thinking of biblical passages as having only human authors, would think that they did have literal meaning. And if they needed biblical authority for their method of interpretation, they needed to look no further than St Paul who explicitly denied that the Old Testament command 'You shall not muzzle an ox while it is treading out the grain' should be interpreted literally. Its meaning was, he said, that congregations should provide adequate remuneration for church leaders.[13]

Origen, Gregory, and Augustine lived during the period in which the Church was deciding which books (including all the books of the Old Testament) belonged to the Bible and which did not; and it is doubtful whether we would have today's Bible without that Church's general recogni-tion of the necessity of understanding it in the light of Christian doctrine and the permissibility of understanding it in the light of established science. Origen was the most influential Christian theologian subsequent to St Paul; and although after his death suspected of heresy for reasons having nothing to do with the way in which he interpreted scripture, his influence in this latter respect was profound. Gregory of Nyssa was one of the leading bishops of the Council of Constantinople which approved the Nicene Creed including its claim that the Holy Spirit 'spoke by the prophets', and Augustine was the theologian who influenced the development of theology in the West far more than any other early theologian. This tradition of interpretation was common to much subsequent biblical interpretation both in the East and the West. A discussion of the rules of biblical interpretation widely influential in the West was the twelfth-century Hugh of St Victor's *Didascalion*. 'Sacred Scripture', Hugh wrote, 'has three ways of conveying meaning—namely history, allegory, and tropology.' By 'allegory' in the narrow sense in which he uses the term in

---

[13] 1 Cor. 9: 9–10.

this paragraph, Hugh understands a metaphorical interpretation conveying Christian doctrine; by 'tropology' he understands a metaphorical interpretation conveying moral instruction. 'To be sure', he continues, 'all things in the divine utterance must not be wrenched to an interpretation such that each of them is held to contain history, allegory, and tropology all at once', as some had taught. There are, he asserts firmly, certain places in the divine page which cannot be read literally.[14] When the Church recognized the authority of the Bible, it gave us at the same time a method for interpreting it: the 'patristic method' which I have now set out. There is no justification for taking the one without the other. No other method of interpretation makes it plausible to suppose that the Bible contains 'revelation without any error'. Many conservative Protestants, especially 'evangelicals' of recent centuries, largely rejected the patristic method, claiming instead that sincere Christians can understand the Bible simply by reading it, and derive all Christian doctrine from it without any prior assumptions about the content of doctrine. But notoriously so many apparently sincere Christians have reached very different views about the meaning of so many biblical passages. More liberal Protestants have sought to interpret the Bible in the way that 'the biblical authors' intended it. But, as I illustrated in the earlier part of this chapter, there is no one human biblical author of any biblical sentence—there is a different author at each stage when a sentence is incorporated into a new context; and anyway many of these contexts are simply not discoverable.

The patristic way of interpreting a biblical sentence in the light of the rest of the Bible and of God as its ultimate author does have the consequence that a sentence may not have been understood by its first or any of its human authors. The Fathers assumed that the human author of a biblical sentence (and for each sentence they usually assumed there was only one such author) normally understood its meaning; but they allowed that that might not always be the case. How could they not allow this, since the purported author of the book of Daniel claimed not to understand his own prophecies—'I heard, but I understood not'?[15] And Augustine taught that the spirit often inspires people to utter a message which they do not understand.[16] So the Fathers would not have been disconcerted to discover that the real author of Daniel 11 thought that he was recording a prophecy about the reign of Antiochus. They would have said that he simply didn't understand his own prophecy.

The Fathers of the Church who accepted the achievements of Greek science were not committed to the view that there was no more science to be discovered. Indeed Augustine claimed that how we should interpret a certain

---

[14] *Didascalion* 5.2 and 6.4.   [15] Dan. 12: 8.   [16] *On Divine Questions* 2.11 14.

passage depended on what might be established in future.[17] So, if we are to interpret the Bible by the method of the Fathers, and if we accept (as we surely should) the view of the more enlightened of them that many of the human authors of the Bible expressed false scientific views, we must interpret it in a way compatible with modern science as well as with established Christian doctrine. And what goes for science, clearly goes for history and geography also—see for example that (to us) evidently false historical passage, Genesis 5, about long-lived patriarchs. Catholic, Orthodox, and (as far as I know) mainstream Protestant bodies have never laid down which passages are to be understood literally and which metaphorically, except in the case of those passages which incorporate Christian doctrines contained in creeds or other doctrinal definitions. For other passages we must use the patristic method.

So, for example, since Matthew 1: 23 claims that the birth of Jesus from a virgin mother is a fulfillment of Isaiah 7: 14, we too must take Isaiah 7: 14 as being a prophecy of this event (whether or not it is also to be understood in a literal sense). The Hebrew word meaning 'young woman' was translated by the Septuagint as 'virgin'; and it is this translation which Matthew uses in his statement of the prophecy. That is a reason for taking the Septuagint as of equal inspiration with the Hebrew text, which is how the Orthodox Church regards it. And since Daniel 12: 1–2 would be false in its timing of the end of the world if we take Daniel 11: 21–45 in its original sense we must understand chapter 11 in a more metaphorical sense than did the original writer of this chapter. (And of course no Christian body (before perhaps CE 1600) ever understood the latter passage in what we now know to be its original sense.)

The view which I have been putting forward seems to entail the view that God inspired some passages of scripture which would have been understood at the time of their first inscription not merely in some sense which we recognize as clearly false, but as endorsing a view of God and human conduct which we recognize as clearly immoral. Would God really have inspired not merely passages which contained (as then understood) false science or history or geography, but a view of God as savage and vindictive—for example Psalm 137: 9, or the affirmation attributed to God that he will punish children and grandchildren for the sins of their parents,[18] or the command to the Israelites when they entered Palestine to annihilate all its Canaanite inhabitants?[19] Even

---

[17] In considering whether there could have been days before the creation of the sun on the fourth day, Augustine wrote that 'there will be nothing in such a supposition contrary to the faith until unerring truth gives a lie to it. And if that should happen, this teaching never was in Holy Scripture but was an opinion proposed by man in his ignorance' (1982: 1.19). So how we ought to interpret scripture depends on what science *will* discover.

[18] Exod. 20: 6.   [19] Deut. 7: 2.

if a later generation could get a deeply religious message from all this, would this justify the apparent deception involved in such 'inspiration'?

In response I have three separate points to make. The first is that since there is no one human author of any passage, the doctrine of divine inspiration is not committed to any view about which authors of any passage were inspired—those who wrote down the original pericope, or those who incorporated it into some larger unit which would give it a different sense. The smallest unit may not have been inspired at all; the inspiration came to the compiler of some larger unit to use it in a context which would give it a different meaning from its original meaning. The Fathers who claimed that the Bible was inspired tended to believe that the first five books of the Old Testament (the Pentateuch) were written by Moses, all the Psalms were written by David, and all the Wisdom literature was written by Solomon. In this belief of course they were mistaken; but my point is that they saw quite large chunks of the Bible as 'inspired'. Hence they wouldn't have understood Psalm 137: 9 as 'inspired' apart from the context of the whole book of Psalms with its message that God forgives sins (Ps. 103: 3) and that he will be acknowledged by Gentiles and Jews alike (Ps. 138: 4). And at the very same time as Psalm 137 must actually have been written, Jeremiah wrote his letter to the Jewish exiles in Babylon (part of a book believed to be equally inspired), telling them in God's name to 'seek the welfare of the city where I have sent you into exile, and pray to the Lord on its behalf, for in its welfare you will find your welfare'.[20] The Jewish exiles would not have been justified in taking Psalm 137: 9 as having the simple message that it would seem to have as an isolated text.

My second point is that, as some of the Fathers recognized, there is a 'principle of accommodation'. Novatian wrote with respect to attribution to God of bodily emotion: 'The prophet was speaking about God at that point in symbolic language, fitted to that state of belief, not as God was but as the people were able to understand.'[21] And this principle may be applied to moral

---

[20] Jer. 29: 7.

[21] *De Trinitate* 6. This principle can be found in Philo, and was advocated by Clement of Alexandria. Clement wrote that when God is spoken of in the Bible as though he experienced human passions, we must not think of him as having feelings like ours, since 'In as far as it was possible for us to hear, burdened as we were with flesh, so did the prophets speak to us, as the Lord accommodated himself to human weakness for our salvation' (*Paedagogus* 1.9.88, PG 8.356). It was developed and used frequently by Origen who compares God talking to us to a parent using baby-talk to talk to a two-year-old child. See Hanson 1959: 224–31. For later Fathers see Hanson 1970. Aquinas invokes this principle on seven separate occasions in *Summa Theologiae* 1a 65–74 when discussing the description of creation in Genesis 1. He puts the point in terms of 'Moses was speaking to an ignorant people', meaning a people ignorant of the discoveries of Greek science.

instruction as well. There are certain moral truths which a primitive people are too primitive to grasp, or at any rate to continue to hold. One of these truths may be that, while individuals may well suffer in consequence of the sins of their parents (since God gives to parents responsibility for their children, and wrongdoing by parents often has bad consequences for the children), the children have no guilt for the sins of their parents. Maybe this subtle distinction was beyond the capacities of the first recipients of Exodus chapter 20, with its attribution to God of the intention to 'punish' children for the sins of their parents and grandparents. But later parts of the Old Testament emphasized very firmly that children are not guilty for the sins of their parents.[22] Jesus too recognized that Moses, speaking on God's behalf, was limited in how strong a message he could give to ancient Israel. Jesus prohibited all divorce (with one possible exception), whereas—the Pharisees pointed out—'Moses allowed a man to write a certificate of dismissal and to divorce [his wife].' Jesus responded that Moses only wrote this commandment because of their 'hardness of heart'.[23] And that the Jewish Law was a temporary law issued by God because of human inability to keep a greater law was a major theme of St Paul in the letter to the Galatians,[24] and developed by Irenaeus.[25]

But, if primitive people could not learn many moral truths, why did God make primitive people? It is good that students should have the opportunity to work out the answers to questions for themselves. That involves them having the choice between struggling to work out the answer and not bothering to think about it; and it involves some students having the opportunity to help others to find the answer, even if in the end they still need and get quite a bit of help from their teacher. Analogously, it is good for whole peoples to have the opportunity to work things out for themselves, even if they need and get quite a bit of help from God in due course. So while the inspiration would have been only very limited, and we cannot ascribe the status of 'revelation without error' to the way the text was originally understood, I find it plausible to suppose that God inspired the writing of biblical books some parts of which, as originally understood, have an inadequate morality, which were capable of being understood as time progressed in a far deeper way.

My third point is to suggest that while quite a lot of the things God is said in the Old Testament to have done would have been very wrong for anyone

---

[22] Jer. 31: 29 and Ezek. 18: 2.

[23] Mark 10: 2–9. Matt. 5: 31–2 claims that Jesus permitted divorce on grounds of *porneia*, often translated 'unchastity'. Mark mentions no such exception.

[24] Chapter 4 passim.

[25] Irenaeus calls the Old Testament laws 'the laws of bondage' which were cancelled by Christ's 'new covenant of liberty'. See his *Adversus Haereses* 4.16.5.

other than God to do, and many of the things which God is said to have commanded would have been very wrong for anyone else to do unless commanded by God, many of these are ones which God has the right to do and command and which he has good reason to do and command. I will be very brief in making this point, because whether God has the right and good reason to do and command various actions is a major concern of a number of other chapters in this volume. I will concern myself only with God's right to command actions; and I will illustrate my view by considering the contention of various Old Testament books that God had commanded the Israelites, when they entered Canaan, to kill all the Canaanites. While there are surely necessary truths independent of the will of God (such as the obligation not to lie and the obligation to keep promises, except perhaps under exceptional circumstances), one of these necessary truths is that people have a duty (within limits) to please their benefactors. God is our supreme benefactor. Pleasing a benefactor involves obeying his commands.[26] If God is our creator, our life comes as a temporary gift from him; and he can take it back when he chooses. If A has the right to take something back from B, A has the right to allow someone else to take it back for him. And if A is God, he has the right to command someone else on his behalf to end a life. God therefore has the right to order the Israelites to kill the Canaanites. God's reason for issuing this command, according to the Old Testament, was to preserve the young monotheistic religion of Israel from lethal spiritual infection by the polytheism of the Canaanites,[27] a religion which included child sacrifice[28] and cultic prostitution.[29] Such spiritual infection was without doubt a very real danger. When monotheism had become more deeply rooted in Israel, such an extreme measure was not, according to the Old Testament, required again. It was a defensive measure necessary to preserve the identity of the people of Israel. While the Israelites would not have had the right to take this extreme measure without the explicit command of God, he had the right to issue that command. God surely also had a reason for using the Israelites, rather than natural processes such as disease, to kill the Canaanites, which was to bring

---

[26] For a fuller-length defense of the claims of the last three sentences see, for example, Swinburne 2009a.

[27] Deut. 20: 17–18. It may be urged that this reason for killing the Canaanites was not the actual reason why the original Israelite invaders killed the Canaanites. Perhaps not, but they would have thought that they had God's authority for their actions. In any case my concern in this chapter is not with their reasons, but with the morality of the claim in Deuteronomy and elsewhere in the Old Testament that God commanded the killing. And I am arguing that God had the right to command this, and that his reason for commanding this, as reported in Deuteronomy, is a moral one.

[28] Deut. 12: 31.   [29] 1 Kgs. 14: 24.

home to the Israelites the enormous importance of worshiping and teaching their children to worship the God who had revealed himself to them, and no other god. Even today and without a divine command many people would think it justified to kill people who had an infectious lethal disease and refused to be kept isolated from the rest of the population. Those who think that an infection which leads to spiritual death is as bad an evil as one which leads to natural death will think that there are reasons (though not of course adequate reasons) for the Israelites to kill the Canaanites even without a divine command. I give this as an illustration that deeper reflection on God's right to command actions, and the reasons he might have for doing so, may lead us to recognize more inspiration by God of the early Israelites than we are at first sight inclined to recognize.

Bearing these three points in mind, I revert to my main contention, that to determine what the Bible and so the Old Testament means when it is regarded as God's revelation to all humanity involves interpreting it in the light of a prior understanding of Christian doctrine and true scientific (historical and geographical) theories. And that may give it a sense a long way away from its sense if interpreted as the work of some human author or authors, and makes it plausible to hold that it is a divinely authored and inspired text.

Comments on 'What Does the Old Testament Mean?'

Wes Morriston

We are indebted to Professor Swinburne for a sophisticated account of the composition of scripture and of the hermeneutical possibilities for dealing with problematic biblical texts. Here I shall concentrate exclusively on what he has to say about *morally* problematic passages.

I once heard a lay reader breeze straight through Psalm 137, not stopping at the appointed place, so that the congregation was treated to the final two verses:

> O Daughter of Babylon, doomed to destruction,
> Happy the one who pays you back
> For what you have done to us!
> Happy shall he be who takes your little ones,
> And dashes them against the rock! (Book of Common Prayer 1979: 792)

I remember only one thing about the homily that morning. The preacher began by saying, 'We were not fortunate in the choice of Scripture for today.' I left church thinking that if any part of the Bible could be discarded, surely we could let this bit go. It seemed obvious that these words were written by someone whose heart was filled with resentment and hatred, who craved revenge, and who had no problem with killing innocent children to get it.

However, Professor Swinburne thinks it is a mistake to emphasize what the *human* author of the text had on his mind. A text may be interpreted in different contexts and may have multiple meanings. In the case of the Bible, the most important of these is *God's* intended meaning. When we interpret texts like this one, we must take into account God's beliefs—insofar as these are known to us through settled Christian doctrine or through careful reading of other biblical texts (especially, perhaps, New Testament ones). When we do this in just the right way, even morally offensive passages may turn out to have a divinely intended and entirely wholesome meaning.

It is at this point that Professor Swinburne appeals to the hermeneutical methods of the Church Fathers. Many of them felt free to read problematic texts in a metaphorical or allegorical way. Read that way, Psalm 137: 9 can be interpreted as a blessing on those who destroy their evil inclinations through the power of Christ (Swinburne, p. 217, above).

Several worries come to mind right away. First, it's hard to see Psalm 137: 9 as an effective way of communicating this message. It's only because we have other, less misleading words and deeds and metaphors and traditions of interpretation to work with that we can strain to find a benign meaning in this text. Why, then, would God inspire the inclusion of such potentially misleading and dangerous words in a work addressed to all human beings, very few of whom could be expected to understand them in their intended sense?

Second, we've at best taken care of only part of the moral problem posed by Psalm 137. The verse about bashing 'little ones' on a rock is immediately preceded by another that speaks of 'paying you back for what you did to us'. Bitter resentment and revenge are unhealthy and morally subpar, to say nothing of the fact that they are wholly incompatible with the ideals embodied in the life and teachings of Jesus. There is nothing metaphorical about verse 8, and *it* is surely the proper context for interpreting verse 9.

Third, it's not easy to see how divine inspiration is supposed to work in such a case. Does God inspire someone to write hate-filled words, intending that hundreds or thousands of years later others will interpret them metaphorically? Professor Swinburne explains:

... [T]he doctrine of divine inspiration is not committed to any view about which authors of any passage were inspired—those who wrote down the original pericope, or those who incorporated it into some larger unit which would give it a different sense.[1]

Inspiration, it seems, can operate at different levels. Some of the smallest units may not have been inspired at all, and inspiration may have arrived only when someone included them in a whole capable of giving them the meaning God wanted them to have.

But what about the Jewish exiles who were the first to encounter Psalm 137? Wouldn't they have been justified in hearing verse 9 in the naive, natural way? Professor Swinburne says not. At that very time, he points out, Jeremiah was writing a letter to the exiles in which he tells them in God's name to 'seek the welfare of the city where I have sent you into exile, and pray to the lord on its

---

[1] Swinburne, p. 222, above. The reference is to Jer. 29: 7.

behalf, for in its welfare you will find your welfare' (Swinburne, p. 222, above).

Let's try to put ourselves in the shoes of the Israelite exiles. We obviously haven't read the New Testament and can't take the rock featured in Psalm 137: 9 as a metaphor for the power of Christ, but we are strongly under the impression that Jeremiah speaks for God. We've just read his letter, and we're about to sing Psalm 137. Naturally enough, we experience a certain cognitive dissonance. How to resolve it? Only one thing comes to my mind. God, through Jeremiah, must be saying, 'Don't sing psalms like that. It was *I* who sent you into exile. The Babylonians were merely my chosen instrument. There is no blessing for those who take revenge on them.' If that would have been a reasonable interpretation for the exiles in Babylon, why not for us today? Which takes us right back to my original position. *Discard the obnoxious verses of that psalm. They don't speak for God.*

Now Psalm 137: 8–9 is far from the only morally problematic passage in the Bible. Interestingly, Professor Swinburne does not give a metaphorical interpretation when he discusses other disturbing texts. For example, the claim in Exodus 20 that God visits 'the iniquity of the fathers upon the children to the third and the fourth generation'[2] is directly contradicted by Ezekiel 18, but no attempt is made to restore consistency by finding a metaphor in the Exodus passage. Nor does Professor Swinburne provide a metaphorical or allegorical interpretation of the numerous passages in which God is represented as commanding the extermination of various peoples. His explanations in these cases are quite different.

The threat to punish later generations for the sins of their ancestors is explained as follows. What's true is only that later generations may suffer as a consequence of the sins of earlier ones. But in the period in which this part of Exodus was written the ancient Israelites were a primitive people, incapable of understanding the 'subtle' distinction between this true claim and the untrue claim that God would *punish* later generations for the sins of the fathers. So why did God create primitive people? Well, it's good for primitive people to have an opportunity to 'work things out for themselves, even if they need and get quite a bit of help from God in due course' (Swinburne, p. 223, above).

I see no reason why the generation in question could not have understood the relevant distinction if it had been given to them. But suppose they could not have. What bearing does this have on the correct interpretation of Exodus? Is the suggestion that *we*, who can make the relevant distinction, should read Exodus 20: 5 as saying merely that evil befalling later generations

---

[2] Exod. 20: 5.

is a natural consequence of the sins of earlier ones? That this is what God is telling *us* in this text? If so, then it seems to me that it would be much simpler just to say that Exodus got this particular thing wrong, and that Ezekiel made the appropriate correction. But then I am not committed to the view that there are no falsehoods anywhere in the Bible. For those who do have that commitment, perhaps the best they can do is to suggest that at the *deepest* level of interpretation Exodus 20: 5 doesn't mean what it plainly says.

What, finally, of the divinely mandated genocides? What about the war against the Canaanites? Some of the Church Fathers interpreted this as an allegory, with the Canaanites representing evils that must be conquered if we are to 'occupy the promised land of the Kingdom of heaven'. What has to be 'exterminated' is our 'evil inclinations' (Swinburne 2007: 271). In this chapter, however, Professor Swinburne makes no use of this interpretation. He appears to read the relevant passages as straightforward historical narratives. God really did command the extermination of these nations. He had a right to do so, he had good reasons for doing so, and the Israelites had an obligation to obey. As the creator of life, God has a right to take it. And if God commands someone else to do the job for him, that is his prerogative. In this case, God needed to preserve Israel from a 'lethal spiritual infection by the polytheism of the Canaanites, a religion which included child sacrifice and cultic prostitution' (Swinburne, p. 224, above). No doubt God could have accomplished the same thing by sending a plague to kill off the Canaanites, but he had a good reason for using the Israelites to do the job. Exterminating vast numbers of Canaanites, we are told, 'would bring home to the Israelites the enormous importance of worshiping and teaching their children to worship the God who had revealed himself to them, and no other god' (Swinburne, p. 225, above).

Professor Swinburne tries to weaken resistance to the idea that God commanded the ancient Israelites to practice genocide by drawing an analogy between physical and spiritual disease.

Even today and *without a divine command* many people would think it justified to kill people who had an infectious lethal disease and refused to be kept isolated from the rest of the population. Those who think that an infection which leads to spiritual death is as bad an evil as one which leads to natural death will think that there are reasons (though not of course *adequate* reasons) for the Israelites to kill the Canaanites even without a divine command. (Swinburne, p. 225, above; my italics)

I take it that all that's needed to turn these 'inadequate' reasons into *adequate* ones is a divine command.

There is no way to cram into this short response everything that needs to be said. I'll be able to gesture in the direction of just a few of the most important points. First, I am not one of those who would think it right simply to *kill* people with a deadly infectious disease who won't voluntarily isolate themselves. I would have to be convinced that no less drastic measures were available—a condition that hardly applies to an omnipotent being.

Second, there is plenty of what Professor Swinburne would surely count as 'infection which leads to spiritual death' around today, and as far as I can see the people suffering from it do little to isolate themselves from the rest of the population. So, then, should we be open to the possibility of a divine command to exterminate, say, pimps and prostitutes? Or perhaps 'evangelical atheists' of the Richard Dawkins type? I should think not. We would rightly treat anyone who said God had commanded him to kill Richard Dawkins as a madman. But then I see little reason to be open to the possibility that God commanded the ancient Israelites to exterminate men, women, children (and animals!) because their alien religious practices were an 'infection' that might lead to 'spiritual death' for the Israelites. That some anonymous ancient author, possessing a conception of God's character very different from our own, thought that God had commanded such atrocities provides little reason to believe that he did.

Third, the problem is not so much about what God has a 'right' to do as about what a perfectly good and loving God would do with and to the Israelites and the Canaanites. Does God not love them both?

Fourth, there is quite a lot to be said against the proposed rationale for commanding the Israelites to slaughter men, women, and innocent children. For one thing, exclusive devotion to God is not the only thing the Israelites would have learned from being the instruments of death and destruction. Killing men, women, and children—even when it's all part of a so-called *herem*—can only be bad for the moral and spiritual development of a person or a people. It makes life seem cheap, expendable, not worth saving. If I thought that such deeds had been commanded by a god whose primary reason for commanding them was to prevent us from worshiping other gods, I would be terrified. But I hope I would not submit to so vile a command. The ancient Israelites mightn't have been capable of such discrimination. But precisely because we have a purer conception of deity, we must refuse to believe that God commanded them to do such things.

Fifth, God's supposed plan to isolate the Israelites didn't work out very well. According to the biblical narrative, there were always plenty of foreigners around. The Israelites frequently succumbed to precisely the temptation that was supposed to have been prevented by the genocides. Indeed, the very passage in 1 Kings that Professor Swinburne cites to show that the Canaanites practiced cult prostitution *also* says that Judah 'did according to all the abominations of the nations which the lord drove out before the people of

Israel'.[3] The story of a divided kingdom, of ten lost tribes, of exile and diaspora, makes it clear that at least this part of God's supposed plan was a failure.

Finally, something must be said on behalf of the much maligned Canaanites. The children, at least, were innocent. But what about the adults? What evidence—really—do we have for thinking that they were in willful rebellion against God? No doubt they viewed the Israelites as enemies. But that doesn't imply that they knew that temple prostitution and child sacrifice were wrong, or that they knowingly disobeyed the one true God! The Canaanites undoubtedly had many false beliefs and harmful practices. But was *genocide* the appropriate response to their ignorance and error? Would it not have been both fairer and more loving to *show* them the error of their ways? Or did God simply not care for Canaanites?[4]

What, then, shall we conclude? Given the extreme difficulty of twisting these morally problematic texts into something digestible, and the moral peril of worshiping God as they represent him, it would be better simply to say, 'No, God did not do these things; no, these parts of the Bible are mistaken.'

---

[3] 1 Kgs. 14: 24.

[4] Many scholars think that the Israelites were not all that different from the Canaanites. For example, it is far from clear that the Israelites did not, at this early period in their history, sacrifice some of their children *to Yahweh*. For evidence of this practice, see Exod. 22: 29–30, Exod. 34: 20, and Judg. 11: 30–40.

Reply to Morriston

Richard Swinburne

I claimed that if the Bible (including the Old Testament) is to be understood as 'revelation [from God] without error', it should be the Bible interpreted in the way that some of the Fathers taught us; that is in the light of Christian doctrine (including Christian moral teaching) and scientific knowledge. God's 'inspiration' of the Bible might involve God's inspiration not of the first author of short passages but of compilers of these into larger units. So there is no need to hold (and I don't hold) that God had any role in inspiring the first human author of Psalm 137: 9. But what I refuse to say is what Professor Morriston seems to want to say of that verse and other passages which he regards as morally inadequate, that they are simply false: 'They don't speak for God.' And why I refuse to say this is because I think that these passages have different meanings according to the context in which they are inscribed. And when regarded as part of the Christian Bible, and interpreted in the way that that demands, they certainly do 'speak for God'.

But then isn't it misleading for God to inspire a revelation so easily capable of being misunderstood? The Bible is not merely a collection of true sentences; it's also a record of a progressive understanding of those sentences by the Israelites working things out for themselves—with God's help. Most of its sentences which require reinterpreting in the total Christian context have therefore a limited degree of important truth in a narrower context. That includes Exodus 20: 5; part of its original meaning—that children of bad parents will suffer—is surely true. It also includes Psalm 137: 8. 'Happy shall they be who pay you back for what you have done to us.' Wrongdoers deserve punishments, that is, those wronged by them have a right to exact punishment from them, even if it is often better that they should not exact punishment, but instead show mercy. The Babylonians had wronged the Israelites; and so deserved punishment; and the verse is right in giving approval to the exaction of punishment, even if there might be (although there isn't always) a better action than exacting punishment. The lesser truth is worth enunciating.

Professor Morriston writes that I do not give a metaphorical interpretation when I discuss other disturbing texts. The Church Fathers thought that many passages had three or four different true divinely inspired meanings, but that for only some of these was there no literal meaning. There was no agreed view about which passages did and which did not have a literal meaning. (All the Fathers however agreed that one whole book could not be understood in a literal sense—the Song of Songs. As Gregory of Nyssa put it (1987: 36–7), 'What is described there is a marriage; but what is understood is the union of the human soul with God.') Having shown their method by one example, my point was that if there is good (moral, historical, or other) reason to suppose that some passage is not true in a literal sense, it should be interpreted in a metaphorical sense. There was no reason for me to discuss in detail just which passages these were. If the atheist establishes her point that a certain passage taken literally depicts God as evil, then we should interpret it metaphorically—because the Church gave us the Old Testament with this as a permissible way of interpreting it. But the Fathers did understand most of the apparently historical passages of the Old Testament as at least 'historical fables' in the sense described in my main chapter; and I see no reason to depart from this understanding.

In particular, the Fathers usually claimed that although the command to exterminate the Canaanites had a deeper meaning, it also had its historical meaning. I follow them in this because I do not think there is any need to reject the historical interpretation on moral grounds. Most of Professor Morriston's objections to the idea that God might command such extermination are also objections to God causing suffering and death to the innocent at all; which takes us into the problem of evil which there is no space to discuss adequately here.[1] But the only good answer to the problem of evil must include the claim that there are things more important than a long life or the absence of suffering; and a good God may well provide them for humans with all their logically necessary cost. For example, of course God loves the Canaanites; but it is good for them, as for all of us, to have the opportunity of forming our characters by means of heroic choices—which only become available to us in the face of suffering and death. And I re-emphasize that God does not wrong the Canaanites (including their children) if he makes the gift of life shorter for some of them than for some other humans. If there is a God, he has made it abundantly clear that the 'gift' of life is a temporary one which he makes as long or short as he chooses. To use an analogy, I may lend

---

[1] For my full-length discussion of the problem of evil, see Swinburne 1998.

you a book, saying, 'you can have this until I want it back'. I don't wrong you if I let other people use a book for a longer period than I let you use a book.

One thing desperately important for a human character is to reverence the right things and that includes worshiping the necessary being, who is omnipotent, omniscient, perfectly free and good, and the source of the existence of all other things including us. The command to exterminate was a unique command issued to bring home this truth to its hearers and thereby preserve the identity of what turned out to be a unique religion, and—in my view—the source for all later human communities of that unique religion developed in a further unique way. Of course the command to the Israelites was not obeyed fully—humans have free will; they don't always obey commands. But most of them got the message.

REFERENCES

Augustine. 1982. *On the Literal Interpretation of Genesis*, trans. J. H. Taylor. New York: Newman Press.

Book of Common Prayer. 1979. *The Book of Common Prayer.* New York: The Seabury Press.

Childs, B. S. 1983. *Introduction to the Old Testament as Scripture*, 2nd edn. Chester: SCM Press.

Gregory of Nyssa. 1987. *Commentary on the Song of Songs*, trans. C. McCambley. Brookline, Mass.: Hellenic College Press.

Hanson, R. P. C. 1959. *Allegory and Event.* Chester: SCM Press.

Hanson, R. P. C. 1970. 'The Bible in the Early Church', in P. R. Ackroyd and C. F. Evans (eds.), *The Cambridge History of the Bible*, vol. i. Cambridge: Cambridge University Press.

Swinburne, Richard. 1998. *Providence and the Problem of Evil.* Oxford: Clarendon Press.

Swinburne, Richard. 2007. *Revelation: From Metaphor to Analogy*, 2nd edn. Oxford: Oxford University Press.

Swinburne, Richard. 2009a. 'What Difference Does God Make to Morality?', in R. K. Garcia and N. King (eds.), *Is Goodness Without God Good Enough?* Lanham, Md.: Rowman and Littlefield.

Swinburne, Richard. 2009b. *Was Jesus God?* Oxford: Oxford University Press.

Tanner, N. P. (ed.). 1990. *Decrees of the Ecumenical Councils.* Lanham, Md.: Sheed and Ward.

8

Reading Joshua

Nicholas Wolterstorff

'Yahweh, Mighty King, lover of justice,' declaims the Psalmist (Ps. 99: 4).[1] And Abraham asks rhetorically, 'Shall not [you, Yahweh], the Judge of all the earth, do what is just?' (Gen. 18: 25). How then can Yahweh authorize Joshua and his army to slaughter everybody in the city of Hazor (Josh. 11: 5–11)? 'The Lord is just and upright, all his ways are just,' sings Moses (Deut. 32: 4). How then can that same Moses speaking on behalf of that same God enjoin Israel to 'utterly destroy' the seven nations living in the land of Canaan (Deut. 7: 1–2)? 'Love your enemies,' said Jesus, 'so that you may be children of [God], your Father in heaven' (Matt. 5: 44). Can this possibly be the same God who enjoins Israel to show no mercy to the seven nations (Deut. 7: 2)? I understate when I say that for those of us who are Jewish readers of Hebrew scripture or Christian readers of Christian scripture, there is a serious problem here.

The problem is not that we have absorbed modern enlightened views about ethical and theological matters and are, as such, morally offended by the picture of genocidal slaughter in Israel's conquest of the land as reported in the book of Joshua, and religiously offended by the picture in Deuteronomy of God as enjoining such slaughter. Our problem is rather that we have been formed in our understanding of God by the biblical acclamations of God as just and loving and shaped in our ethical thinking by God's command to do justice and love mercy. But the picture of God that we get in Deuteronomy and Joshua seems in flagrant conflict with those acclamations and with that command. Yet Joshua is part of our canon; we cannot simply ignore it, denounce it, or toss it out.

In my book *Justice: Rights and Wrongs* (2008), I spent some time articulating how justice is understood in the Hebrew and Christian Bibles. I highlighted, among other things, the intimate connection repetitively drawn

I thank John Mulholland for significant bibliographical assistance in research for this chapter; and Howard Wettstein, Michael Rea, and Michael Bergmann, for comments on an earlier draft.

[1] All biblical references are from the *New Revised Standard Version*.

between the presence of justice in society and the fate of the socially vulnerable—widows, orphans, aliens, and the impoverished. I did not take the next step of asking how we are to understand the fact that some of God's actions as presented in scripture seem patently unjust on scripture's own understanding of justice. That's what I propose doing in this chapter. I will not have time to consider all the problematic cases. I will focus on what everyone agrees are the most egregious purported examples of divine injustice—the genocidal slaughter that God is apparently presented in the book of Joshua as having enjoined Israel to perpetrate in its conquest of 'the promised land'.

I

To prepare the ground for my own address to the problem, I propose looking first at a contemporary interpretation of Joshua, that of the Old Testament scholar Walter Brueggemann in his recent book *Divine Presence and Violence: Contextualizing the Book of Joshua* (2009), and then at a traditional interpretation, that of John Calvin in his commentary on Joshua.

Brueggemann confines himself to discussing chapter 11 of the book of Joshua. But chapter 11 contains the story of the slaughter of everybody in Hazor; so the fact that Brueggemann does not discuss the entire book is not, for our purposes, a significant limitation. What is reported as befalling Hazor at the hands of Joshua and his army was typical of what is reported as befalling other cities at their hands.

Brueggemann describes his interpretive strategy as blending a literary approach to the text with a sociological approach. His literary approach leads him to focus on the world of the text itself, rather than treating the text as a more or less accurate report on the world 'out there' (2009: 6). His sociological approach leads him to discuss the social situation of the Israelites, as that comes to expression in the text. To these two approaches he adds a theological inquiry: how did the participants in the world of the text 'appropriate its revelatory claim' (2009: 5) and how should we, who 'stand outside the narrative, [but who] take it as canonical, and heed it as revelatory' (2009: 43), appropriate its revelatory claim? He does not discuss the formation of the text, nor does he discuss how the original readers of the text would have appropriated its revelatory claim.

Brueggemann says little about how Israel came to be in the land of Canaan or about how the book of Joshua presents them as coming to be there. He does, however, refer approvingly to the two influential books of Norman K.

Gottwald in which Gottwald deals with exactly those questions, *The Tribes of Yahweh* (1979), and *The Hebrew Bible* (1985).

Gottwald takes note of three models that have been used for understanding how Israel came to be in 'the promised land': *the conquest model, the immigration model,* and *the social revolution model* (1985: 261–76); he prefers the last of these. He also takes note of three models that have been used for understanding Israel's social organization: *the pastoral nomadic model, the religious league model* (*amphictyony*), and *the socioreligious retribalization model* (1985: 276–88); he prefers the last of these as well.

There would be no point in describing these models in any detail; the titles Gottwald uses are sufficiently indicative for our purposes here. Though the conquest model undeniably governs the first several chapters of the book of Joshua, by the time we get to chapter 11, Israel has already been in the land for some time; what Brueggemann highlights are the indications he finds in Joshua 11 and elsewhere of the social revolution model. From things he says along the way, however, it's clear that he follows Gottwald in holding that the social revolution and socio-religious retribalization models are not only to be found in various Old Testament texts but fit what did in fact happen.[2] Here is Brueggemann's description of Israel's social structure and situation:

In Joshua 11, of course, we have no Israelite monarchy. But we do have monarchies, which in this narrative are antagonistic to Israel. Following the model of Gottwald, I regard 'Israel' as an antimonarchic, peasant movement hostile to every concentration, surplus, and monopoly. Conversely it follows then that every such city-state as those listed in vv. 1–5 would regard Israel as a threat, for Israel practiced a social alternative that had to be destroyed. Thus we can read the mobilization of the Hazor king with sociological realism as a conflict between competing social systems. (2009: 20)

The textual clue, for Brueggemann, to the fact that Israel is up against a league of oppressive monopolistic monarchies is the reference in the text to *horses and chariots*: 'They came out, with all their troops, a great army . . . with very many horses and chariots' (11: 4). He explains the import of the phrase 'horses and chariots' as follows: 'Following the general analysis of Gottwald, the city-states are to be understood as monopolies of socioeconomic, political power that are managed in hierarchical and oppressive ways. . . . "Horses and chariots" reflect the strength and monopoly of arms that are necessary and available for the maintenance of the economic and political monopoly' (2009: 15). Israel, being an egalitarian peasant movement, has no horses and chariots.

---

[2] Gottwald summarizes what he thinks happened thus: 'a socially and politically insurgent people had carved out a living space in a broad movement of insurgency against the Canaanite city-states' (1985: 248).

In v. 6 of Joshua 11 we read that 'the Lord said to Joshua, "Do not be afraid of [Hazor and its allies], for tomorrow at this time I will hand over all of them, slain, to Israel; you shall hamstring their horses, and burn their chariots with fire".' What we have here, says Brueggemann, is

The disclosure that Yahweh gave permission for Joshua and Israel to act for their justice and liberation against an oppressive adversary. This revelatory word of Yahweh, given directly without conduit or process, is only authorization for a liberating movement—which is sure to be violent, but only violent against weapons. . . . What is revealed is that Yahweh is allied with the marginalized, oppressed peasants against the monopoly of the city-state. It is not a summons to violence (though its practice might be construed so) but only a permit that Joshua's community is entitled to dream, hope, and imagine freedom and is entitled to act upon that dream, hope, and imagination. (2009: 23–4)

But what, then, are we to make of vv. 7–9, where we read that 'Joshua came suddenly upon them with all his fighting force. . . . And the Lord handed them over to Israel. . . . They struck them down, until they had left no one remaining. And Joshua did to them as the Lord commanded him; he hamstrung their horses, and burned their chariots with fire.' After a couple of intervening verses the carnage is described a second time: Joshua and his army 'put to the sword all who were in [Hazor], utterly destroying them; there was no one left who breathed. And all the towns of those kings, and all their kings, Joshua took, and struck them with the edge of the sword. . . . As the Lord had commanded his servant Moses, so Moses commanded Joshua, and so Joshua did; he left nothing undone of all that the lord had commanded Moses' (vv. 11–15).

Brueggemann's suggestion is that, in their perpetration of violence against the inhabitants of Hazor and its allies, Joshua and his troops went far beyond Yahweh's mandate. He observes that Yahweh's only direct speech in Joshua 11 occurs in v. 6. Accordingly that speech is 'the normative revelation within the text. It mandates destruction of a quite specific kind in order to give liberated Israel room to exist. It sanctions neither more nor less than this. . . . One may imagine that Israel took that limited, disciplined warrant of Yahweh and went well beyond its intent or substance in its action, out of rage and oppression' (2009: 37–9). Yahweh does indeed mandate violence, but only of 'a specific kind: tightly circumscribed' (2009: 39).

And that is what you and I, outside the narrative, should appropriate millennia later as its revelatory claim (2009: 61–5). The book of Joshua, rather than offending the understanding of justice that we have gleaned from scripture, presents a vivid application of that understanding. 'The God of the tradition is passionately against domination and is passionately for an egalitarian community' (2009: 39).

II

If this interpretation of Joshua 11 is plausible, and if it can plausibly be employed as the hermeneutic key to the other stories of conquest in the book, it would solve most of our moral and theological concerns.[3] The book of Joshua would be a story of liberation theology in action, along with reports of some all-too-human excesses engendered by rage at oppression. I think it is not plausible, however. I find Brueggemann's interpretation problematic on two fundamental points.

First, I find problematic his suggestion that, in the world of the text, Yahweh mandated Israel to do no more than hamstring the horses of its opponents and burn their chariots. Many readers of the book of Joshua seem to come away with the impression that Yahweh repeatedly issued a direct mandate to Joshua to exterminate the population of some city. It has to be conceded to Brueggemann that this impression is mistaken. Apart from the episode reported in Joshua 11, there is only one example of Yahweh directly mandating Joshua as to how he is to treat the inhabitants of the conquered cities. Joshua 8: 1–2 reads as follows: 'Then the Lord said to Joshua, "Do not fear or be dismayed; take all the fighting men with you, and go up now to Ai. See, I have handed over to you the king of Ai with his people, his city, and his land. You shall do to Ai and its king as you did to Jericho and its king."' Joshua is earlier reported (6: 21) as having exterminated the entire population of Jericho along with all its animals. Thus in chapter 8, Yahweh is represented as having directly mandated the extermination of the population of Ai.

But back now to chapter 11. Recall Yahweh's 'revelatory speech', as Brueggemann calls it: 'I will hand over all [the inhabitants of Hazor and its allies] to Israel; you shall hamstring their horses and burn their chariots with fire.' It's true that the only *mandate* here is the mandate to hamstring the horses and burn the chariots. But in saying that he will 'hand over' all the inhabitants, surely Yahweh is implying that he is *authorizing* Israel to 'take' them; and the distinction between authorizing extermination and mandating extermination seems to me morally and theologically insignificant.

Brueggemann might concede the point and go on to observe that, in his speech to Joshua, Yahweh does not say what he is authorizing Israel to do with the inhabitants of Hazor and its allies. We go beyond the text when we conclude that Yahweh authorized Israel to slaughter all the inhabitants; Israel

---

[3] Perhaps not all of them; a point made to me by Michael Rea is that hamstringing their horses seems unnecessarily brutal.

could instead have taken them as prisoners of war. Point taken. But to see why it does not yield the conclusion Brueggemann wants, let us now question why he attaches the significance he does to the fact that, in chapter 11, there is no direct revelation from Yahweh to Joshua mandating extermination, only a direct revelation mandating the hamstringing of horses and the burning of chariots.

Recall v. 15 of the chapter: 'As the Lord had commanded his servant Moses, so Moses commanded Joshua, and so Joshua did; he left nothing undone of all that the Lord had commanded Moses.' What Moses, speaking on behalf of God, commanded Joshua to do, was by no means privy to Joshua; the entire people knew of God's command. In chapter 8 we read that Joshua 'read all the words of the law, blessings and curses, according to all that is written in the book of the law. There was not a word of all that Moses commanded that Joshua did not read before all the assembly of Israel' (vv. 34–5). Surely the participants in the world of the text of Joshua 11 would have treated, as a revelation from God, not only what was directly revealed to Joshua but also what was revealed to Moses and handed down to Joshua and the people. And in the course of reading to the people what Moses had commanded, Joshua would have read to them something like the following passage: 'When the Lord your God brings you into the land that you are about to enter and occupy, and he clears away many nations before you . . . and when the Lord your God gives them over to you and you defeat them, then you must utterly destroy them. Make no covenant with them and show them no mercy' (Deut. 7: 1–2).

So I am baffled as to why Brueggemann thinks that, in the world of the text of chapter 11, Israel thought that the only normative revelation from Yahweh was Yahweh's direct mandate to Joshua to hamstring the horses and burn the chariots. Israel remembered Yahweh's mandate, revealed to Moses for his successor, that the surrounding nations be exterminated; they understood Joshua and his forces as doing exactly that. It's simply not possible to interpret the text in such a way that Yahweh neither mandates nor authorizes anything more than the destruction of horses and chariots and the 'taking', in some manner or other, of the inhabitants.

The second component in Brueggemann's interpretation that I find problematic is his suggestion that Yahweh's overall intent was to authorize Israel to defend its egalitarian peasant social structure against attack from the monarchs of the oppressive city-states in the region. I do not doubt that Brueggemann is right in what he says about the significance of the phrase 'horses and chariots'. It is indeed plausible to flesh out the world of the text with the idea that the monarchs in the region were confiscatory and oppressive, and would not have wanted their subjects to know about an egalitarian alternative to their own hierarchical social structure. (Though it's worth noting that the phrase 'horses and chariots' occurs nowhere else in the book than in chapter 11.) But when we interpret the book of Joshua, including chapter 11, in the light of the conviction of the participants in the world of the text that they were enacting a mandate from Yahweh revealed to Moses, then it becomes clear that it is thoroughly implausible to make this social-revolutionary interpretation dominant, let alone exclusive.

One gets the impression from Brueggemann that Yahweh was indifferent as to whether or not Israel worshipped Yahweh; Yahweh's only concern was that Israel be enabled to live its egalitarian peasant life free from oppression. But when the revelation given to Moses, as reported in Deuteronomy, is brought into the picture, the point of Yahweh's mandate is starkly clear and very different from what Brueggemann suggests.

Yahweh is a jealous God[4] who wants Israel to worship Yahweh and Yahweh alone. But Israel finds the idolatry of pagan religion almost irresistibly alluring. Yahweh is presented as mandating extermination to remove the temptation of idolatry. The passage from the opening of Deuteronomy 7 that I quoted a few paragraphs above continues as follows:

Do not intermarry with them, giving your daughters to their sons or taking their daughters for your sons, for that would turn away your children from following me, to serve other gods. . . . But this is how you must deal with them: break down their altars, smash their pillars, hew down their sacred poles, and burn their idols with fire. For you are a people holy to the Lord your God. . . . You shall devour all the peoples that the Lord your God is giving over to you, showing them no pity; you shall not serve their gods, for that would be a snare to you. (7: 3–6, 16)[5]

Why not just smash the idols? Why exterminate the idolators? No doubt because smashing idols is far from sufficient for eliminating paganism; the pagans carry their paganism within them. But the texts hint at another reason as well, a mysterious one that no commentator that I have consulted explains to my satisfaction. In Deuteronomy 7: 25–6 we read, 'Do not covet the silver or the gold that is on [the idols] and take it for yourself . . . for it is abhorrent to the Lord your God. Do not bring an abhorrent thing into your house, or you will be set apart for destruction like it. You must utterly detest and abhor it, for it is set apart for destruction.'[6] The Hebrew term translated as 'set apart for destruction' is *herem*. The idea is picked up in the book of Joshua. Speaking of Jericho, Yahweh says to Joshua, 'the city and all that is in it

---

[4] Among the many OT passages declaring the jealousy of Yahweh is Josh. 24: 19: Yahweh 'is a holy God. He is a jealous God.'
[5] See also Deut. 20: 16–18.
[6] See also Deut. 13: 17 and Lev. 27: 28–9.

shall be devoted to the Lord for destruction.... Keep away from the things devoted to destruction, so as not to covet and take any of the devoted things and make the camp of Israel an object for destruction.... [So] they devoted to destruction all in the city, both men and women, young and old, oxen, sheep, and donkeys' (6: 17–21). The population of Jericho was exterminated because it was 'devoted to destruction' by Yahweh; the population of at least some of the other cities was understood in the same way. One surmises that people, animals, and objects were devoted to destruction by Yahweh because they were intimately connected to the local pagan cult. But what, more precisely, was understood by *herem*, I do not know.[7]

III

Let us now turn to an example of a traditional theological interpretation of Joshua, that of John Calvin.[8] Unlike Brueggemann, who concentrates on explicating the world of the text while making no explicit commitments as to the extent to which the world of the text fits the real world, Calvin takes for granted that the text tells us what actually happened. Of course, to find out from the text what actually happened we must interpret it correctly. In the course of his commentary, Calvin does not shrink from declaring that the text is sometimes hyperbolic,[9] that on some points it doesn't matter whether it is fully accurate,[10] and that on some points we are left with what seem to be incompatible claims.[11] But Calvin never so much as considers the possibility that the text does not claim that Yahweh commanded Joshua and his troops to

---

[7] Why was the livestock of Jericho devoted to destruction (*herem*) whereas that of Ai was not? Israel was allowed to take the livestock of Ai as booty. In his commentary on Joshua, K. Lawson Younger, Jr. says that the kind of warfare represented by *herem* 'does not originate in a theology of "holy war" peculiar to OT theology but is a political ideology that Israel shared with other nations in the ancient Near East. In that contest, all wars waged by a nation were 'holy "wars," dedicated to the glorification of its deity and the extension of the deity's land and reign.' I do not find this of much help in understanding the idea.

[8] I will be using the translation of Calvin's commentary on Joshua made in the nineteenth century by Henry Beveridge (1949).

[9] About Josh. 11: 23, which in Calvin's Latin text says that 'Joshua received the whole land entirely,' Calvin says that 'it was far from being true that Joshua had actually acquired the whole land...' (1949: 175–6).

[10] About Josh. 10: 13, which reads, 'the sun stopped in midheaven, and did not hurry to set for about a whole day', Calvin says, 'I do not give myself any great anxiety as to the number of the hours...' (1949: 154).

[11] For example, 'How are we to reconcile the two things—that the people did not obtain the full and complete inheritance promised to them [by God], and that yet God was true?'

exterminate the seven nations; thus the way of dealing with our question that Brueggemann pursued is not open to him.

It was because the 'iniquity' of the nations had 'reached its height', says Calvin, that God 'determined to destroy them. This was the origin of the command given to Moses' (1949: 174).[12] By using Israel as his agent, Yahweh could thus at one and the same time fulfill his promise to give Israel a land of its own and 'purge the land of Canaan of the foul and loathsome defilements by which it had long been polluted' (1949: 97). Since Yahweh, 'in whose hands are life and death, has justly doomed those nations to destruction, this puts an end to all discussion [about the justice of God's commands]. We may add, that they had been borne with for four hundred years, until their iniquity was complete. Who will now presume to complain of excessive rigour, after God had so long delayed to execute judgment' (1949: 97)? And if it be protested that the 'children, at least, were still free from fault' (1949: 97), the answer is that they too 'perished justly, as the [human] race was accursed and reprobated' (1949: 97).[13]

In saying that the rationale for the extermination command was God's desire to punish the Canaanite nations for their wickedness, Calvin is going beyond what the texts of Deuteronomy and Joshua say. The book of Joshua gives no rationale for the command; the rationale given in Deuteronomy is that God desires to free the land from idolatry and thus to remove temptation from Israel. We do read in Deuteronomy 9: 5 that 'because of the wickedness of these nations the Lord your God is dispossessing them before you'; but nothing is said about extermination of the population on account of their wickedness.

Calvin realizes that the fact that Yahweh chose not to exterminate the nations present in the land by some 'act of God' but instead by employing Israel as his agent raised some problems, potential or actual. It was and is God's will that nations act justly in their prosecution of warfare; and one condition of the justice of a nation's war is that it go to war only in self-defense. Likewise it was and is God's will that individuals and nations temper retributive justice with mercy. If these were God's will for the conduct of warfare, how can God command Israel to act as his agent of extermination?

Calvin thinks the first of these potential problems proved not to be actual; in each case, Israel was attacked. 'The kings beyond the Jordan [i.e., those in league with Hazor], as they had been the first to take up arms, justly suffered

---

[12] Calvin does not explain what he means by his cryptic phraseology 'their iniquity had reached its height', nor what he means by his alternative phraseology 'their iniquity was complete'.

[13] Calvin repeats this point in his comment on 10: 40, 1949: 164.

the punishment of their temerity. For the Israelites did not assail them with hostile arms until they had been provoked. In the same way, also, the citizens of Jericho, by having shut their gates, were the first to declare war. The case is the same with the others, who, by their obstinacy, furnished the Israelites with a ground for prosecuting the war' (1949: 174).

Here too Calvin is going beyond the text. It's true that the kings of the north who had joined in league with Hazor (ch. 11), and the five kings of the south who were threatening to attack Israel's protectorate, Gibeon (ch. 10), acted aggressively toward Israel. But there is no indication whatsoever that the city of Ai initiated hostilities. And the fact that Jericho locked its gates against the Israelites seems to me more plausibly interpreted as a defensive measure on its part than as an act of aggression.

Though Calvin held that Israel's engaging in battle did not raise a theological or moral problem—its battles were just because it was responding to aggression—there was a closely related issue that he found more difficult to deal with. Joshua 11: 19 reads, 'There was not a town that made peace with the Israelites, except the Hivites, the inhabitants of Gibeon.' The clear implication is that the reason Israel attacked and devastated the towns is that they refused to make peace; had some town offered peace conditions, then both justice and the rules of warfare of the time required that Israel accept the offer and refrain from battle. But Israel was under orders from God, issued by Moses, not to make peace with any of the nations but to clear the land of wickedness.[14] So what good would it have done them had the inhabitants of one of the cities offered peace? Calvin puts the issue pointedly:

This sentence [11: 19] appears, at first sight, contradictory to what is everywhere said in the books of Moses, that the Israelites were not to enter into any league with those nations, or make any terms of peace with them, but, on the contrary, to destroy them utterly, and wipe out their race and name. Seeing the nations were thus excluded from the means of making any paction, and would in vain have made any proposals for peace, it seems absurd to ascribe the destruction . . . to their obstinacy.

For, let us suppose that they had sent ambassadors before them with olive branches in their hands, and had been intent on pacific measures, Joshua would at once have answered that he could not lawfully enter into any negotiations, as the Lord had forbidden it. Wherefore, had they made a hundred attempts to avoid war, they must, nevertheless, have perished. Why, then, are they blamed for not having sought peace . . . (1949: 173)

---

[14] In Deut. 20: 10–18, Moses says that Israel is to offer peace terms 'to all the towns that are very far from you', but is to exterminate the towns of the region 'so that they may not teach you to do all the abhorrent things that they do for their gods and you thus sin against the Lord your God'.

What is Calvin's solution to the problem he identified? God hardened their hearts (Joshua 11: 20), says Calvin, so that none of the towns ever did in fact offer peace.[15] The Israelites, 'forbidden to show them any mercy, were met in a hostile manner, in order that the war might be just. And it was wonderfully arranged by the secret providence of God, that, being doomed to destruction, they should voluntarily offer themselves to it, and by provoking the Israelites, be the cause of their own ruin' (1949: 174). Had the Israelites not been the target of aggression in each case, they would have found their 'minds unsettled' by the predicament of being forbidden by God 'from entering into any covenant' while at the same time knowing that it was unjust to 'take hostile measures without being provoked'. God's command to Israel, meant to implement his intent to punish the nations for their iniquity, 'would have failed of its effect had not the chosen people been armed to execute the divine judgment by the perverseness and obstinacy of those who were to be destroyed' (1949: 174).

In short, since Israel acted only defensively, Calvin thinks it was just for Israel to engage in battle with the Canaanite peoples. But what about Israel's manner of conducting its battles? In particular, what about its practice of extermination? How can that be considered just?

Had Joshua 'proceeded of his own accord to commit an indiscriminate massacre of women and children, no excuse could have exculpated him from the guilt of detestable cruelty, cruelty surpassing anything of which we read as having been perpetrated by savage tribes' (1949: 163). But Joshua did not act on his own. He was following God's orders. 'When any one hears it said that Joshua slew all who came in his way without distinction, although they threw down their arms and suppliantly begged for mercy, the calmest minds are aroused by the bare and simple statement, but when it is added, that so God had commanded, there is no more ground for obloquy against him, than there is against those who pronounce sentence on criminals. Though, in our judgment at least, the children and many of the women also were without blame, let us remember that the judgment-seat of heaven is not subject to our laws' (1949: 163).

Theologians and philosophers have offered three quite different reasons for holding that 'the judgment-seat of heaven is not subject to our laws'. Some have held that God is beyond all moral categories; the category of justice, for

---

[15] The one exception was the Gibeonites, who, pretending to live a good distance away, offered peace, which Israel then accepted and swore to honor. The story is to be found in Joshua 9. Calvin does not find it easy to explain why Israel is not judged for this failure to implement the extermination decree.

example, simply does not apply to God. Others have held that to say that something is just is simply to say that God wills it, so that to ask whether or not God's doing so-and-so is just is not to pose a serious question. Yet others have held that though God is just in all his ways, sometimes it is impossible for us to see the justice in what God has done.

Only the last of these is compatible with the fact that God is praised in scripture as always just. Obviously such praise is not compatible with the first position. But a bit of reflection shows that it is also not compatible with the second. If 'just' simply means *willed by God*, then to say that God acted justly in doing so-and-so is not to praise God but simply to declare that God willed to do what God did do. Calvin's position is the third. 'The infants and children who then perished by the sword we bewail as unworthily slain, as they had no apparent fault; but if we consider how much more deeply divine knowledge penetrates than human intellect can possibly do, we will... acquiesce in his decree' (1949: 117). God has 'hidden reasons into which, though it may perhaps be lawful to inquire soberly, it is not lawful to search with prying curiosity' (1949: 111). Rather than engaging in curious prying we must 'keep our minds in suspense until the books are opened, when the divine judgments which are now obscured by our darkness will be made perfectly clear' (11949: 04).

These comments of Calvin strike me as not fitting together very well. The first suggests that there is wickedness in human beings that is evident to God but not to us. Whereas the infants of the seven nations look morally innocent to us, God discerns that they are not; and it is their wickedness that makes it not unjust for God to order their extermination. But given Calvin's doctrine of universally shared original sin, to which he explicitly appeals a couple of times in his commentary, we know why those infants do not have a right against God to life; we don't have to await the opening of the divine books to find out. The second passage seems to be making a different point. By 'hidden reasons' for the destruction of the infants I would guess he means that we do not understand why God was not merciful to these infants when he is merciful to others, given that all are tainted by original sin.

Not only do the comments not fit together very well. A part of Calvin's thought that gets expressed in other places and is relevant here goes without mention. Calvin assumes here that the only relevant consideration is a person's moral worth or unworth. But in his comment on Genesis 9: 6 ('Whoever sheds the blood of a human, by a human shall that person's blood be shed; for in his own image God made humankind'),[16] he makes the following quite remarkable statement:

---

[16] Translated and edited in the nineteenth century by John King. I am using the 1948 reprint.

Men are indeed unworthy of God's care, if respect be had only to themselves; but since they bear the image of God engraven on them, He deems himself violated in their person. Thus, although they have nothing of their own by which they obtain the favour of God, he looks upon his own gifts in them, and is thereby excited to love and to care for them. This doctrine, however, is to be carefully observed, that no one can be injurious to his brother without wounding God himself. Were this doctrine deeply fixed in our minds, we should be much more reluctant than we are to inflict injuries. (1948: 295)

The fact that we all possess 'no small dignity' (1948: 296) on account of bearing 'the image of God engraven' on us, and the fact that God is 'excited to love and care for' us upon beholding this reflection of himself in us, plays no role in Calvin's discussion of the justice of God's ordering the destruction of the seven nations, infants and children included. At the end of his comment on Joshua 10 Calvin asks rhetorically, why 'should not the Lord perceive just ground for [the death of an] infant which has only passed from its mother's womb? In vain shall we murmur or make noisy complaint, that he has doomed the whole offspring of an accursed race to the same destruction; the potter will nevertheless have absolute power over his own vessels, or rather over his own clay' (1949: 164). The divine potter does indeed have absolute power over the vessels he has made. But what if those vessels bear engraven on them the image of the divine potter? Does not the potter take that into account?

IV

If one believes that the text of Joshua claims that God commanded Joshua and his army to exterminate the population of all the cities in the promised land, if one believes that the text in this respect fits what actually happened, and if one also believes that God is just, then Calvin's line of interpretation, the third of the three I mentioned above, seems to me the only theological interpretation possible—problematic though Calvin's own version of that line is. And if we take seriously what Calvin says in his comment on Genesis 9: 6, that we human beings have two sorts of worth, ineradicable worth as bearers of the image of God and variable worth as moral creatures, then we will have even more reason than Calvin cited to conclude that we'll have to wait until the divine books are opened to understand how God's extermination decree could be just.

There are, in principle, two strategies that one could employ to avoid adopting that third line of interpretation. One could argue that the text doesn't actually claim that God ordered the extermination of the local population; or one could concede that the text does claim this, but go on to argue that, in this respect at least, the text does not fit what actually happened. One might have textual-critical reasons for holding that the text does not fit the facts; some critics have argued, for example, that the text is riven with ideology. One might have archeological reasons: there seems to be no evidence of widespread devastation of Canaanites cities at the time Israel would have entered the promised land.[17] Or one might have theological reasons: one might argue that it's clear from God's revelation in Jesus Christ that God wouldn't do that sort of thing. I propose following the first strategy. I think the text does not claim that God ordered extermination.[18] That puts me in league with Brueggemann. But for the reasons that I indicated earlier, I do not think that Brueggemann was successful in arguing the point.

Just as theological considerations might lead a person who believes that the text claims that God ordered extermination to conclude that, in this respect at least, the text does not fit the facts, so too theological considerations might lead a person to offer an alternative interpretation of the text, an allegorical interpretation, perhaps.[19] Nonetheless, in my interpretation of Joshua I will not appeal to any such considerations. I will argue that a careful reading of the text in its literary context makes it implausible to interpret it as claiming that Yahweh ordered extermination.

I take it to be a near-consensus among Old Testament scholars that the text of Joshua as we have it today was intended as a component in the larger sequence consisting of Deuteronomy, Joshua, Judges, 1 and 2 Samuel, and 1 and 2 Kings. The sequence as a whole, after telling the story of Moses' instructions to Israel in general and to his successor Joshua in particular, goes on to narrate the story of Israel's coming into the promised land, of its conquests, of the emergence of the monarchy, of the monarchy's decline after a brief period of glory, and of Israel's being carried off into exile. It is also a near-consensus that this sequence of writings received its near-final form during the reign of King Josiah and reflects the religious reforms that he initiated; and that it received its final form during the Exile in Babylon. In the final paragraph of 2 Kings we read that in the thirty-seventh year of his exile, King Jehoiachin of Judah was released from prison by the king of Babylon. I propose that we interpret the book of Joshua as a component within this larger sequence—in particular, that we interpret it as preceded by Deuteronomy and succeeded by Judges.

The story in Joshua 11 of Israel's conquest of Hazor and its allies concludes thus: 'So Joshua took the whole land, according to all that the Lord had

---

[17] On the archeological evidence, see the summary in Gottwald 1985: 260–9.

[18] In Wolterstorff 1995 I argue that, strictly speaking, texts don't say anything; it's those who authorize a text, be that the author, the editor, or whoever, who say things by means of the text. But to simplify the discussion above, I will speak as if texts do say things.

[19] See Wolterstorff 1995: chs. 12 and 13.

spoken to Moses; and Joshua gave it for an inheritance to Israel according to their tribal allotments. And the land had rest from war.' Now consider the opening of Judges:

After the death of Joshua, the Israelites inquired of the Lord, 'Who shall go up first for us against the Canaanites, to fight against them?' The Lord said, 'Judah shall go up. I hereby give the land into his hand.' Judah said to his brother Simeon, 'Come up with me into the territory allotted to me, that we may fight against the Canaanites; then I too will go with you into the territory allotted to you.' So Simeon went with him. Then Judah went up and the Lord gave the Canaanites and the Perizzites into their hand; and they defeated ten thousand of them at Bezek. (1: 1–4)

So whereas the book of Joshua says that Joshua and his troops took the whole land, the book of Judges opens by narrating some of the battles Israel fought after Joshua's death.

What are we to make of this? Well, we could follow Calvin and hold that the sentence 'Joshua took the whole land' is hyperbolic, the literal truth being that some of the land remained to be conquered by Israel after Joshua's death. Or we could take that sentence as literal and hold that the battles of which we have been told in the preceding chapters of Joshua are just a sample of the battles Joshua fought in taking the whole land. Moses had already said that 'the Lord your God will clear away these nations before you little by little; you will not be able to make a quick end of them'—the reason being that 'otherwise the wild animals will become too numerous for you' (7: 22).

The second of these proposed solutions faces the problem that just one chapter after being told that Joshua took the whole land, we read, 'Joshua was old and advanced in years; and the Lord said to him, "You are old and advanced in years, and very much of the land still remains to be possessed"' (13: 1). What then follows is a rather long list of areas that had not yet been conquered, along with instructions to Joshua to allot land to the twelve tribes, including land that had not yet been conquered.

Both of the proposed solutions face the problem that the narration in Judges reports that Judah and Benjamin, after Joshua's death, attacked, among other cities, Hebron (1: 10) and Debir (1: 11), whereas Joshua and his forces were already described in Joshua 10 as having attacked Hebron (36–7) and Debir (38–9) and striking down 'by the edge of the sword' every person in them. So after Joshua's death, Judah and Benjamin are said to conquer cities whose populations Joshua was said to have exterminated. Neither of the solutions proposed can deal with this problem.

It should also be noted that it is explicitly stated, both in Joshua and Judges, that the population of some of the conquered cities was not exterminated.

Joshua 13: 13 tells us that 'the Israelites did not drive out the Geshurites or the Maacathites; but Geshur and Maacath lives within Israel to this day.' And the opening chapter of Judges mentions a rather long list of other cities whose inhabitants Israel did not exterminate. 'The Benjamites did not drive out the Jebusites who lived in Jerusalem; so the Jebusites have lived in Jerusalem among the Benjamites to this day' (1: 21). 'Manassah did not drive out the inhabitants' of its area—five cities are named—'but the Canaanites continued to live in that land. When Israel grew strong, they put the Canaanites to forced labor, but did not in fact drive them out' (1: 27–8). And so on, for five more examples of the same point. The litany concludes with a message from the angel of the Lord: 'I brought you up from Egypt and brought you into the land that I had promised to your ancestors. I said, "I will never break my covenant with you. For your part, do not make a covenant with the inhabitants of this land; tear down their altars. But you have not obeyed my command. See what you have done. So now I say, I will not drive them out before you; but they shall become adversaries to you, and their gods will be a snare to you"' (12: 1–30). Be it noted that the angel does not say that Israel had been commanded to exterminate all the inhabitants. Israel was commanded to tear down the altars.

Those whose occupation it is to try to determine the origins of these writings will suggest that the editors had contradictory records, oral traditions, and so forth to work with. No doubt this is correct. But those who edited the final version of these writings into one sequence were not mindless; they could see, as well as you and I can see, the tensions and contradictions—surface or real—that I have pointed to. So what is going on?

Anyone who reads the book of Joshua in one sitting cannot fail to be struck by the prominent employment of formulaic phrasings. One of these, not all that important for our purposes, is the occasional formulaic listing of the seven nations that is to be found already in Deuteronomy: 'the Hittites, the Girgashites, the Amorites, the Canaanites, the Perizzites, the Hivites, and the Jebusites.' Far more important is the formulaic clause 'struck down all the inhabitants with the edge of the sword'.

The first time one reads that Joshua struck down all the inhabitants of a city with the edge of the sword, namely, in the story of the conquest of Jericho (6: 21), one makes nothing of it. But the phrasing—or close variants thereon—gets repeated, seven times in close succession in chapter 10, two more times in chapter 11, and several times in other chapters. The repetition makes it unmistakable that we are dealing here with a formulaic literary convention. And the fact that it is a formulaic convention, coupled with the fact that Judges hammers home the point that Israel did not by any means wipe out the population of all the cities that it did battle with, argues for its being a mistake to interpret the clause as meaning, literally, that Joshua and his troops struck

down with the edge of the sword all the inhabitants of all the cities they did
battle with. The author/editor of the book of Joshua was not claiming,
speaking literally, that Israel conquered all the cities in the land, nor was he
claiming that Israel slaughtered all the inhabitants of all the conquered cities
with the edge of the sword.[20]

On the assumption that Deuteronomy and Joshua are parts of the same
sequence of books, this interpretation of Joshua forces a back-interpretation
of Deuteronomy. If 'struck down all the inhabitants with the edge of the
sword' is a literary convention when used to describe Joshua's exploits, then it
is likewise a literary convention when similar words are used by Moses in his
instructions to Israel in general and to Joshua in particular. There is no
indication that, in its conquest of Jericho, Israel did not fully obey Yahweh's
instructions. So if we do not take it as literally true that Israel slew all the
inhabitants of Jericho with the edge of the sword, then we also cannot take it
as literally true that Yahweh ordered them to do so.

All readers of the book of Joshua, not just those who read it in one sitting,
will also be struck by the highly ritualized character of some of the major
events described. The book is framed by its opening narration of the ritualized
crossing of the Jordan and by its closing narration of the equally ritualized
ceremony of blessing and cursing that took place at Shechem; and the
conquest narrative begins with the ritualized destruction of Jericho. In addition to these ritualized events there is, as we noted earlier, the mysterious
sacral category of *being devoted to destruction*.

V

So what are we to make of it all? My suggestion is that the book of Joshua
has to be read as a theologically oriented narration, stylized and hyperbolic
at important points, of Israel's early skirmishes in the promised land, with
the story of these battles being framed by descriptions of two great ritualized events. The story as a whole celebrates Joshua as the great leader of his
people, faithful to Yahweh, worthy successor of Moses. If we strip the word

---

[20] Younger 1990: ch. 5 compares the conquest narratives of Joshua 9–12 with conquest
narratives from other ancient literature. Though he does not quote any phraseology directly
similar to 'and he struck down all the inhabitants with the edge of the sword', he does quote
other literature in which the conqueror is said to have killed all the inhabitants of the conquered
city. Younger concludes that the 'syntagms' in Joshua declaring complete annihilation 'are to be
understood as hyperbole. Just like other ancient Near Eastern conquest accounts, the biblical
narrative utilizes hyperbolic, stereotyped syntagms to built up the account' (1990: 228).

'hagiography' of its negative connotations, we can call it a hagiographic account of Joshua's exploits. The book is not to be read as claiming that Joshua conquered the entire promised land, nor is it to be read as claiming that Joshua exterminated with the edge of the sword the entire population of all the cities on the command of Yahweh to do so.[21] The candor of the opening chapter of Judges, and of Yahweh's declaration to Joshua in his old age that 'very much of the land still remains to be possessed', are closer to a literal statement of how things actually went.

The editors of the final texts of Joshua and Judges—assuming they were not completely mindless—evidently had no problem with placing next to each other, in their multi-volume series, these two ways of narrating Israel's acquisition of the land: the stylized, hyperbolic, and hagiographic style of the book of Joshua, and the down-to-earth style of the opening of the Book of Judges. Nor did they have a problem with preserving a passage in Deuteronomy which declares that the conquest will take a long time, and another which declares that intermarriage among captive populations is allowed (Deut. 21: 10–14). They did not even have a problem with inserting into the Book of Joshua itself an element of the down-to-earth style of Judges with their report of Yahweh's declaration to the aged Joshua that much of the land remained to be possessed.

What are we to make of such dissonance? What would be the point of prefacing a multi-volume story of Israel's life in the promised land and its exile therefrom with a stylized, hyperbolic, and hagiographic story of how Israel came to be in the land that it inhabited, framed by reports of two great ritualized occasions? Shall we reach for the deconstructionist line, and say that what we have here is an almost paradigmatic example of an ideological history bearing its own deconstruction within it?

Gottwald suggests something along these lines. The Deuteronomistic historian of Joshua through 2 Kings appears, he says, as 'an astute author-compiler who deliberately mixed a profusion of data and interpretations about partial and total conquests in order to show the ambiguous success of Israel in the land as a combination of mixed peoples, many of whom did not fit the profile of later nationalistic orthodoxy. Indeed, the inclusion of the "scandalous" annals and story of Judges 1 and 17–21 may well be a supreme instance of the [Deuteronomistic historian's] ideology of suspicion toward too-neat historical interpretations.'[22]

---

[21] Robert G. Boling, the author of the notes to Joshua in the HarperCollins Study Bible, says (p. 342) that 'It appears that the emergence of Israel, out of prolonged struggle for better life in Canaan, has been stylized as occurring all under Joshua's exemplary leadership.'

[22] Gottwald 1985: 260. In 1979: 147–9, Gottwald develops this line of thought more fully.

This is possible, I suppose. The presence of what I have called the 'down-to-earth' style in Judges is to be understood, Gottwald suggests, as the editor's way of saying to the reader, don't believe all that stylized nationalistic hagiography that you read in the preceding book. Believe me instead. Things were much messier than as described there; and our blood is not as pure as we would like to think it is.

Possible; but in my judgment, not very likely. For the skeptical editor's intent to be successful, not only would his own story have to be more believable than the story he wanted to undermine; the ordinary reader would have to discern that it was the intent of the skeptical editor to undermine the stylized nationalistic story. But if the average readers saw that that was what the skeptical editor was up to, what would be the point of preserving the stylized nationalistic story? Why not just toss it out? Someone might be tempted to reply that the nationalists were in a position of power and saw to it that their version was not discarded. But if they had such power, why didn't they suppress this obvious attempt at undermining their story?

Let me suggest an alternative resolution of the puzzle. Start with the following question: can a people employ and hand on two quite different narratives about roughly the same events in its history, one stylized, hyperbolic, and hagiographic, the other down-to-earth? Can we, present-day Americans, employ and hand on two such narratives about roughly the same events? Or do the down-to-earth narratives told by our academic scholars force the disappearance of the stylized narratives?

Is it still possible for us to tell uplifting stories, stories meant to teach a moral lesson, about the noble Puritans and Washington's heroic crossing of the Delaware, or have our academic historians stopped our mouths from telling such stories? My own impression is that, though the fate of stylized uplifting stories about our past designed to teach a lesson is more precarious among us than it was among our predecessors, their fate has not yet been sealed. We still think that they are good at least for children and young people. And let's not overlook the fact that a good many academic writers of history draw a moral lesson for present-day readers from the story they tell—about the fate of an empire when it over-extends itself, for example.

Over and over the story-teller in Joshua declaims, as if it were a litany, 'And they slew all the inhabitants with the edge of the sword.' Someone responds, 'but the descendants of some of those inhabitants are living next door'. To which the story-teller replies, 'Don't be so literal minded!' When I ask the high school kid living next door how his basketball team fared the night before and he says, 'We slaughtered 'em,' I don't infer that there were at least five dead young men on the basketball floor.

What might have been the function for Israel of having the story of its origins told as we find it in Joshua? I think its function for Israel in the time of religious reform under King Josiah would have been slightly different from its function for Israel when in captivity. Its function for Israel when still living in the land would have been prophetic, with an emphasis on admonition. It's no accident that Joshua comes first among the books of the prophets in the Hebrew Bible. Yahweh gifted Israel with a land flowing with milk and honey in which it could live in fidelity to Yahweh. The book reaches its climax when, at the great ceremony at Shechem, the aged Joshua commands, 'Choose this day whom you will serve, whether the [pagan] gods your ancestors served in the region beyond the River or the gods of the Amorites in whose land you are [now] living.' 'As for me and my household', he declares, 'we will serve the Lord.' To which the people respond, 'Far be it from us that we should forsake the Lord to serve other gods; for it is the Lord our God who brought us and our ancestors up from the land of Egypt.... Therefore we also will serve the Lord, for he is our God' (24: 15–18). If Israel fails to serve Yahweh alone, it has only itself to blame; it cannot blame Yahweh. And if it resists idolatry and worships only Yahweh, it will find that it is blessed by Yahweh.

The function of the story for Israel in exile would likewise have been prophetic, but with a different emphasis; consolation rather than admonition would be prominent. No matter how dark its present situation may be, Israel can trust that if it once again worships and obeys Yahweh and Yahweh alone, Yahweh will somehow once again deliver it.

I anticipate that many of my fellow Christians will reject this reading of Joshua simply on the ground that it is not literal. The considerations that I cited as forcing a non-literal reading will be treated by them as a challenge to imagine harmonizing scenarios. There must have been two cities named 'Hebron' and two named 'Debir', one of each being conquered by Joshua and one of each being conquered after his death by forces from the tribes of Judah and Benjamin. Something like that.

But why must all biblical narrations be interpreted as literally true in all their details? We all tell stories about what happened that are not literally true in all their details; they serve other functions than putting facts into people's heads. Why would not the same be true for some of the narratives in scripture? Nobody thinks that the parabolic narratives that Jesus told are literally true. And as to the doctrines of biblical inerrancy and infallibility, they are only relevant after we have determined what the writers or editors of the biblical materials were claiming; they are irrelevant to the determination of what they were claiming.

VI

The book of Joshua is dangerous literature. Those suffering under oppression who read the book scarcely notice the reports of extermination; certainly they do not dwell on them. What looms to the fore for them is God's promise of a new day coming. That's how the Jews in the ghettos of Europe would have read it; that's how the African-American slaves were reading it when they sang, 'Joshua fought the battle of Jericho'; that's how the so-called blacks and coloreds in South Africa read it.

The book becomes dangerous when it falls into the hands of those in power, especially those engaged in colonizing. Colonists are strongly tempted to read it as authorizing violent conquest in the name of God. That's how some of the American colonists read it, that's how some of the Afrikaner colonists read it, that's how some Israelis today read it, as they attempt to dispossess the Palestinians. Having discovered that our theological problems with the book of Joshua rest on misinterpretation, we are left with the fact that it is politically dangerous literature.

Comments on 'Reading Joshua'

Louise Antony

Professor Wolterstorff has set himself the task of explaining 'how we are to understand the fact that some of God's actions as presented in Scripture seem patently unjust on Scripture's own understanding of justice'. I quote his words, because I am not sure I understand exactly what this project is. It's clearly not just a matter of explaining why the Bible contains apparently contradictory messages and claims. That would be easy, at least in principle. We know that the Bible had many different authors and redactors, working at different times and with different purposes, so it's unsurprising that the work as a whole harbors inconsistencies. Many contemporary Jews and Christians[1] recognize this, and find it consistent with their piety to treat the biblical narratives as literary products of their times, rather than as accurate chronicles of God's deeds.

But Wolterstorff thinks that this is an inadequate response—or perhaps, an incomplete response—to the tensions that trouble him. Although he is not at all hostile to the scholarship that leads many to reject the historical accuracy of narratives like Joshua 11, he feels that to simply 'toss . . . out' the offending portions of scripture would be somehow to ignore or deny the canonical status of the texts. Again, I am not sure exactly what attitude Wolterstorff is recommending, but he seems to have something like this in mind: if these stories are part of the corpus that authority and tradition take to embody the revealed word of God, then it must be presumed that they make some contribution to God's revealed message, whatever shortcomings they might have as literal chronicles, and however disturbing they may seem on the surface.

In that case, the exegetical project would be to uncover each of these contributions, to find what Wolterstorff (following Brueggemann), calls the 'revelatory claim', hidden within each problematic story. Wolterstorff is

---

[1] And Muslims as well, for all I know.

willing to leave open the possibility that a given story harbors more than one such message, and indeed, that the message may be different for different readers at different times. But he believes that there must be some such point for every reader at every time. His specific project, then, in this chapter, is to identify a revelatory claim contained within the discomfiting saga of Joshua's conquest of the promised land, one that might still speak to us, now.

Wolterstorff is not prepared to deny the enormity of genocide (whether by appeal to the moral worthlessness of humanity or by appeal to our ignorance of the divine plan, stratagems both employed by Calvin), but neither is he willing to violate the text. Fortunately, he argues, there is a third way: 'one could argue that the text doesn't actually claim that God ordered the extermination' (p. 248, above). Wolterstorff says that he is going to pursue this line: he 'will argue that a close reading of the text in its literary context makes it implausible to interpret it as claiming that Yahweh ordered extermination'. Citing largely internal, literary evidence, Wolterstorff argues that the phrase 'strike down all the inhabitants with the edge of a sword' should not be taken literally, but rather as a poetic trope, a quasi-ritualistic phrase that means something like 'score a decisive victory'. As such it is part of a 'stylized, hyperbolic, and hagiographic' nationalist narrative, one that coexists with a more prosaic, 'down-to-earth' account of actual events. Such narratives, Wolterstorff says, have their place. Even though they would be false if taken literally, they can still serve to 'teach a moral lesson', in the way that stories about 'the noble Puritans and Washington's heroic crossing of the Delaware' function in American society to inspire our citizenry.

In the course of developing this reading of Joshua, Professor Wolterstorff raises a number of fascinating questions about interpretation, both literary and biblical. Since I am not qualified to discuss any of them, I hope he'll forgive me for focusing on the end product of his substantial efforts, and registering my objections to his very original response to the problem that motivated the convening of this conference.

I have three problems: first, I am not persuaded by Wolterstorff's brief remarks that 'hagiographic hyperbole' ever has a morally valuable function to serve. Second, I do not find the particular 'revelatory' content Wolterstorff identifies in the Joshua hagiography to be morally benign, much less inspiring or uplifting. Third, and finally, I do not understand how the strategy Wolterstorff adopts can possibly cope with the scores of passages throughout the Hebrew Bible in which God endorses, commands, or performs immoral acts. For the sake of brevity, and because the relevant passages are well known to all readers, I will not say anything more about this third issue.

1. As I explained above, Wolterstorff contrasts 'down-to-earth' narratives, told by 'academic historians', with 'stylized, hyperbolic, and hagiographic' narratives. About the latter he asks,

Is it still possible for us to tell uplifting stories, stories meant to teach a moral lesson, about the noble Puritans and Washington's heroic crossing of the Delaware, or have our academic historians stopped our mouths from telling such stories?

This is a rhetorical question. Professor Wolterstorff provides the answer, which he seems to presume we'll all agree with: 'We still think that they are good at least for children and young people.'

To which I reply: Whaddya mean 'we', white man? It's not at all clear to me that any good is accomplished by telling children things we know to be false, but which we pretend are true. Fictionalized history, it seems to me, is simply pernicious. It impedes true understanding. I have no problem with falsehood, *per se*; it's the pretending that disturbs me. Falsehood *per se* is called 'fiction', and its forms include the novel, the drama, the fable, and the parable, all of which can be and have been put to excellent pedagogical use. (Jesus appears to have been a master of the last, as Wolterstorff observes.) But how could it be important to *pretend* that the British settlement of Massachusetts had something to do with the value of religious freedom? Either the *falsity* is essential to the edifying effect or it's not. If it is not essential, then we needn't continue to pretend. If it is essential, however, then whatever 'edification' is achieved is illusory, for it depends upon a falsehood, and must evaporate if the falsehood is exposed.

Wolterstorff's allusion to historians' having 'stopped our mouths' worries me a little as well. It has tinges of those fatuous complaints about the galling strictures of 'political correctness', registered, typically, either before or after the complainant has produced an exemplary token of the allegedly proscribed type. The fact is that false history *hurts* people, often by obscuring, white-washing, or denying terrible crimes that have been committed against them or their ancestors, thereby delaying or preventing an honest reckoning of the costs they have suffered and the debt owed them by the privileged. In the United States, false history encourages in us a naive and simplistic nationalist self-conception that facilitates quietude in the face of unspeakably unjust and destructive policies, affecting everyone in the world.[2]

Professor Wolterstorff acknowledges that a hagiographic narrative like Joshua is 'dangerous when it falls into the hands of those in power'. I very much appreciate his condemnation of two particular uses to which the Joshua

---

[2] I urge you all to read, in this connection, Klein 2009.

narrative has been put in recent times. (And I applaud his courage, it being a feature of the genuine 'political correctness' that now governs public discourse that criticism of Israel must be instantly branded 'anti-Semitic'.) But I submit that fictionalized, hagiographic narratives are *typically* in 'the hands of those in power', and deployed in just such dangerous ways. History belongs to the victors, after all. The propagandistic value of false histories is a feature, not a bug.

I do not think this drawback is much mitigated by the consideration that liberatory (or otherwise morally salutary) messages can be drawn from hagiographic narratives. Enslaved Africans in North America were stripped of their own native cultures, languages, religions, and myths, and forced by circumstance to draw inspiration from whatever sources they could. The fact that such brutally oppressed people managed to find some succor in the sacred stories of their oppressors hardly redeems those tales. There is, in the end, a limit to the elasticity of symbols and stories. What value could Native American children possibly derive from the *Schoolhouse Rock* tune 'Elbow Room' that depicts in song the 'needs' driving European colonists to move west, without, of course, mentioning the slaughter and dispossession necessary to clear the way?[3] How can the descendants of enslaved Africans view the Confederate flag as a symbol of honor and courage?

2. Let us set such scruples aside, however, and suppose along with Professor Wolterstorff that it can be morally beneficial to a group to create, preserve, and promulgate 'hagiographic' narratives. Even with this granted, I fail to see how Professor Wolterstorff is going to fulfill his interpretive task. It's not enough to find a way of denying that God ordered genocide; we need still to ask about the rhetorical purpose served by canonizing a narrative according to which he did.

Founding myths and hagiographies typically highlight virtues and values the group hold dear, or at least claim to hold dear. Here, for example, is a story about the Puritan emigration taken from a history website for children:

About 1563 AD, some people in England decided that they wanted to follow a way of life that they thought would be more according to what God wanted. They called themselves 'the godly', but other people called them 'Puritans' . . . Like other people who had different religious ideas from their neighbors—for example the Quakers—the Puritans got into trouble in England. Some of them were killed. So some of the Puritans decided to leave England and start a new town in North America.[4]

---

[3] Here's a stanza: 'The way was opened up for folks with bravery | There were plenty of fights | To win land rights | But the West was meant to be | It was our Manifest Destiny!'

[4] http://www.historyforkids.org/learn/northamerica/after1500/religion/puritans.htm.

This is a foundation myth about religious freedom, or more broadly, freedom of conscience. The story encourages the belief that our nation's commitment to such freedom stretched back to its very beginnings. This is a fantasy, of course, but that's not the point here.[5] The point, rather, is that those who tell and retell this story do so as a way of expressing their own commitment to this value, and their pride in belonging to a nation of people who share it.

If we look at the problematic passages Wolterstorff is considering, what values do we see enshrined? Domination and ruthlessness. Moses tells the Israelites that when they face the seven nations, 'and when the Lord your God gives them over to you and you defeat them, then you must utterly destroy them. Make no covenant with them and show them no mercy.'

These are not the values that Wolterstorff has in mind; he imagines that, for Israelites living in Canaan, the meaning of the narrative was admonitory—do not betray your God. For the generations in exile in Babylon, the meaning shifts: the story now provides 'consolation': 'No matter how dark its present situation may be, Israel can trust that . . . Yahweh will once again deliver it' (p. 255, above). Any port in a storm, but . . . The first meaning has God threatening the Israelites: worship me, or you'll end up like the Hazorites. The second meaning makes the story of Joshua into a revenge fantasy: *you* Babylonians think you've enslaved *us*, but just wait till our God gets back— then you'll all be put to the sword, but good! Or maybe not—maybe instead, a wistful recollection of what God has done for them in the past, along with the hopeful thought that if they reform, God will once again favor them—by slaughtering their enemies.

I think it's also necessary to talk about chauvinism, or, rather, since we're being candid here, about *racism*. There seems to have been some kind of agreement reached among nice people that no one will be so rude as to mention in public the obvious fact that the notion of a 'Chosen People' is morally repugnant. I have reason to think that the consensus of silence on this point is achieved through a duet of equivocation: the Jews allow the Christians to think that they're chosen, too, and the Christians forbear from telling the Jews they've been superseded. Without this complementary patronizing, ecumenical prayer breakfasts would be impossible. But the filthy truth is that the God of the Hebrew Bible plays favorites. Not so bad if there are many gods, so that every people has one, and thus *some* fighting chance in a conflict with Yahweh's tribe. But if the God of the Hebrew Bible is supposed to be the *only* God, the universalist God of the philosophers, then his favoring the

---

[5] The inconvenient facts that are denied or glossed over: the Puritans were political, not religious refugees, and their new regime was at least as intolerant of religious disagreement as was the society they had left.

Israelites over other peoples is unforgivable. Why is it just for God to prefer the freedom of his people to the lives and well-being of innocent Egyptian children? Why is it OK for him to dispossess the members of the seven nations, and give their homelands to his people? I realize that various apologists have argued that the peoples destroyed by God or by Israel as his agent were morally corrupt and deserving of death. But this hardly distinguishes them from the Israelites themselves, about whom God is constantly fuming and whom he is constantly threatening to destroy.

But perhaps the notion of a 'Chosen people' is itself part of a hagiographic narrative, not to be taken at face value. In that case, we must ask, as we did before, what meaning the stylized narrative might have for the people who tell it, who treat it as their history and the foundation of their culture. I think the meaning is clear. Readers of these narratives can only be edified to the extent that they are able to identify with the 'Chosen' people, the people whom God has elected to defend and protect. And I do not see how that attitude can fail to warrant a kind of self-importance or self-centeredness, a feeling of superiority, and, even more dangerously, a feeling of unearned entitlement. I was raised a Catholic, and encouraged to believe that the New Covenant with Jesus transcended the Old, Abrahamic Covenant, and that anyone could 'choose to be chosen' by accepting Christ as Lord and Savior. I don't think we need to linger on the horrors wrought by 'overly zealous' missionaries and other grimly determined evangelists. 'Chosen-ness' is an invitation to cloak one's own opinions and values with divine authority. I think it's inherently dangerous.

In closing, let me return to my first theme, and consider the 'edifying' effect of believing that God is on your side. I can see the utility of such a belief—and I don't say this with disparagement. Many of my non-believing friends have told me that they experienced real grief when they lost their faith, grief over losing something that religion had provided them—a profound sense of purpose, or a feeling of connection to something fundamental and eternal—things for which there seemed to be no secular replacement. But to just that extent, the edification they had derived from the 'revelatory claim' to which they were responding depended on just those elements of the message that (by their later lights) turned out to be false. My theist friends all assure me that God, the one, true God, does not hold the attitudes evinced by Yahweh in the Hebrew Bible. My concluding question, then: what edifying message can we derive from the Hebrew Bible if we eliminate the assumption that God takes sides?

Reply to Antony

Nicholas Wolterstorff

Let me address, in sequence, the two main questions that Professor Antony raises concerning my chapter 'Reading Joshua'. Do hagiographic histories and biographies ever have a morally valuable function? And did such a history have, and does it continue to have, a morally valuable function in the case of the Book of Joshua?

About the first, she says that though she has no problem with falsehood *per se*—she cites fiction—she doubts that *pretending* that some falsehood about the past is true ever serves a good purpose. 'The fact' is, she says, 'that false history *hurts* people.' But my view is not that the stories of conquest in the Book of Joshua are false. My view is that the writer of Joshua was not asserting—speaking literally now—that Joshua slew with the edge of the sword all the inhabitants of all the Canaanite villages. Had the first readers of the book been inclined to overlook the superabundance of literary conventions and tropes and take it as literally true, the very next book in the Deuteronomistic series, Judges, would have told them that Joshua was not to be read as literally true history. Perhaps Judges is to be so read, but not Joshua.

So what was the writer asserting—assuming that he did not intend it as pure fiction, which I very much doubt? Not at all easy to tell. When a high school basketball player says that his team slaughtered the other team last night, what is he asserting? Not easy to tell. That they scored a decisive victory? Maybe. But suppose they just barely eked out a win. Was he then lying? Maybe not. Maybe he was speaking with a wink-of-the-eye hyperbole.

But these points about falsehood, pretense, and figurative speech are really only side issues. The main issue is whether hagiographic narratives, be they presented in literal or highly figurative language, are ever acceptable. Obviously lots of hagiographies are horrible. But are they all? Professor Antony apparently thinks so.

I have my doubts. My impression is that most biographies of Susan B. Anthony, of Mahatma Gandhi, of Martin Luther King, Jr., of Bishop Tutu—not to mention those of St Francis—have a hagiographical quality. They are not sober, disinterested scholarly histories—though let it be added that scholars sometimes also write hagiographies. They are celebrations of great women and men. Are they to be condemned on that account? I don't think so. I think that such narratives serve a variety of important functions, including important functions in liberation movements.

Are they false? No doubt there are falsehoods in them; but overall most of them are not false. They are selective, indeed. But all histories are selective; how could they not be? So the question is whether it is ever responsible to write a biography of someone that one regards as a great person with the aim of showing his or her greatness, playing down but not ignoring his or her flaws. Or is there something inherently wrong in that? Not so far as I can see.

But what about the Book of Joshua? Joshua is an unusually complicated example of the genus of hagiography. I would say that our problems lie not so much with its hagiographic character as with its use of ritualistic, and highly figurative militaristic, language about the emergence of Yahwism in Canaan; it's this that makes it dangerous literature. It's all too easy to take the language literally.

Suppose that Israel in exile did not take it literally. Did reading Joshua make any positive contribution to their religious, moral, and social existence? My guess is that it functioned for them as a blend of admonition and consolation. Though Israel was being punished for its infidelity, nonetheless God would somehow deliver them from oppression. But since Israel now had no swords with whose edges it could slay people, its deliverance would have to be by very different means from that depicted in the book of Joshua. It seems to me that those functions of admonition and consolation might well have been good things—though Professor Antony is right to observe that how we answer that question depends, to some extent, on what we make of Israel's chosenness.

Suppose that others in other times and places have read Joshua figuratively. Are there any situations in which, for those others, it made a positive contribution to their religious, moral, and social existence? Did it make a positive contribution to the longing for liberation of the African-American slaves in the US South when they sang, 'Joshua fit the battle of Jericho'? I think it did. But to substantiate that judgment would require a knowledge of the relevant history that I do not possess.

REFERENCES

Brueggemann, Walter. 2009. *Divine Presence and Violence: Contextualizing the Book of Joshua*. Eugene, Ore.: Cascade Books.

Calvin, John. 1948. *Commentary on Genesis*, trans. and ed. John King. Grand Rapids, Mich.: Wm. B. Eerdmans Publishing Co.

Calvin, John. 1949. *Commentary on Joshua*, trans. Henry Beveridge. Grand Rapids, Mich.: Wm. B. Eerdmans Publishing Company.

Gottwald, Norman K. 1979. *The Tribes of Yahweh: A Sociology of the Religion of Liberated Israel, 1250–1050 B.C.E.* Maryknoll, NY: Orbis Books.

————1985. *The Hebrew Bible: A Socio-literary Introduction*. Philadelphia: Fortress Press.

Klein, Naomi. 2009. 'Minority Death March: Jews, Blacks, and the "Post-Racial" Presidency', *Harper's Magazine*, September.

Wolterstorff, Nicholas. 1995. *Divine Discourse*. Cambridge: Cambridge University Press.

————2008. *Justice: Rights and Wrongs*. Princeton: Princeton University Press.

Younger, K. Lawson, Jr. 1990. *Ancient Conquest Accounts: A Study in Ancient Near Eastern and Biblical History Writing*. Sheffield: Sheffield Academic Press.

Part III

Theological Perspectives

9

What About the Canaanites?

Gary A. Anderson

In the 1980s the political scientist Michael Walzer wrote a book titled *Exodus and Revolution* (1985) that traced the history of effects of the story of Israel's exodus from Egypt. Of special interest was the way this biblical story inspired subsequent reform and revolutionary movements in Western political history. This book became the occasion for a tart response from the late literary and postcolonial theorist Edward Said.[1] In his review, Said argued that Walzer was much too generous to the biblical story. Rather than laying the groundwork for a vision of true liberation, the story of the Exodus cannot be separated from its conclusion: the despoiling of another nation's right to live on its land. However much one would laud a God who took the side of the oppressed Israelite slaves in Egypt, what was one to make of the same God who had no concern for the moral rights of the Canaanites who were about to be displaced? For Said, of course, this was no idle question. Being of Palestinian descent, he felt a close kinship to the Canaanites who had been robbed of their land by virtue of a decree of the God of the Jews. 'There is no Israel', Said declared, 'without the conquest of Canaan and the expulsion or inferior status of Canaanites—then as now.'

The subject of this debate was discussed more recently and at great length by the biblical scholar John J. Collins.[2] He seconds Said's concern about the way the biblical text authorizes a violent invasion and occupation of another people's land. As with Said, he argues that this moral horror was not limited to the age in which it was perpetrated. 'One of the most troubling aspects of this biblical story', Collins concludes, 'is the way it has been used, analogically, over the centuries as a legitimating paradigm of violent conquest—by the Puritans in Ireland and in New England, by the Boers in South Africa, and by right-wing Zionists and their conservative Christian supporters in modern Israel.' Though Collins agrees with Walzer that the Hebrew Bible is 'a great

---

[1] Said 1986: 86–106. See also Walzer and Said 1986.
[2] See Collins 2005.

repository of humanistic values, and arguably the strongest voice crying out for justice in the Western tradition', those very values are deeply compromised by 'the central biblical doctrine of the divine election of Israel, with its consequent authorization of the chosen people to take the land, and lives of others' (2005: 67). Reading the Bible through the eyes of the Canaanites, Collins argues, will go a long way toward correcting the egregious acts of barbarity that this foundational text has set in motion: the expropriation of the land of the Native Americans, black South Africans, and Australian Aborigines. If we listen carefully to the voices that have been silenced by the canonical text then the story of the Exodus will lose much of its moral voice as a witness to human liberation.

But I need not cite scholars such as these to set the framework for this chapter. When I teach the Bible to students at Notre Dame they see the problems themselves without any prompting from postcolonial theorists. Students who are appalled at the ethnic cleansing that has occurred in Darfur wonder how they could ever regard certain texts found in the book of Joshua as the word of God. Could the Bible they reverently listen to on Sunday underwrite such acts of egregious cruelty they so vigorously oppose during the rest of the week? Given that the conquest of Canaan is the logical denouement of the exodus from Egypt, perhaps even this powerful story of liberation from oppression is simply another cog in the wheel of a larger narrative frame that inscribes an endless cycle of oppression.

There can be no question that the story of the conquest presents contemporary readers of the Bible with a significant moral problem. I propose to address this question in an unconventional manner and so it might be a good idea to briefly outline my approach. I will begin (section 1) by reviewing the historical dimensions of the problem—that is, the archeological evidence for the conquest itself. From there I will turn to the conquest as the canonical biblical text presents it (sections 2–4). I will not address, however, the stories found in the book of Joshua *per se*. Instead I will begin with a consideration of ways in which various nations or peoples have understood their relationship to the land and how this contrasts with Israel (section 2). I will then articulate the nature of Israel's 'supernatural' tie to her land (section 3). Finally I will consider the literary and canonical context in which the promise of the land is made to Abraham and his posterity (section 4). Understanding these chapters is crucial because it provides the context in which God will deed the land of the Canaanites over to Abraham. I will contend that only by attending to this foundational story can we address the moral questions raised by the events of the conquest documented in Joshua. I should add that my focus will not be on the question of the *means* of expulsion (the command to slay all the Canaanites, even women and children) but the *problem* of the expulsion itself.

Though both issues provide a challenge for the religious reader, nothing one says about the means will make any sense without a justification of the end.[3]

1. HISTORICAL CRITICISM AND THE CONQUEST OF CANAAN

One answer that can be given to this moral problem comes from the results of a historical-critical reading of the Bible. Archeological work in the land of Israel has demonstrated that the conquest of Canaan as described in the book of Joshua simply did not happen.[4] Moreover, the Bible's claim that the Israelites were a people wholly unlike those who resided in the land of Canaan is also hard to reconcile with a number of historical facts.[5] First of all, the Hebrew language is, in fact, nothing other than a dialect of ancient Canaanite. The farther back we go in time the closer the linkages between ancient Hebrew and its related tongues. Moreover, the material culture of the sites that we know were inhabited by ancient Israelites do not show distinctive signs that would distinguish them from non-Israelite sites. Indeed archeologists find it difficult to distinguish Israelite and Canaanite settlements.[6] In other words, it seems most likely that the Israelite nation—in considerable contrast to what the biblical narrative reports—arose from the indigenous population. Most historians would argue that the earliest Israelites settled at first in the hill country of Judea and Samaria. There, in relative isolation from the great Canaanite city-states in the rich agricultural valleys, they were able to establish an independent tribal polity. Only gradually over a few centuries did the power of this tribal group expand to the point that they could lay claim to some of the surrounding urban centers. It was probably in the days of kings David and Solomon that the boundaries we see described in the latter chapters of the book of Joshua came to define the Israelite nation.

If this historical reconstruction is accurate, then the stories of a violent conquest and expulsion of the native population were written down long after the period they purport to document. In short, those stories are not historical

---

[3] Which is not to say that the end somehow justifies the means. The means, in my view, remain contested ground and would require a further essay. My point is that if the conquest is wrong under any terms, what is the purpose of discussing any particular set of circumstances?

[4] It is rare indeed for biblical scholars to agree on almost any question, but historical critical scholars are virtually unanimous on this one. For a balanced approach to the question see Stager 1998.

[5] On the close relationship between Hebraic and Canaanite culture see Cross 1973.

[6] On this problem, see Mazar 1990: 353–5.

records of what really happened, but after-the-fact literary fictions. Israel did not wipe out the Canaanites in a genocidal fashion. Yet erasing this problem from the historical record does not solve all our problems. For we are still left with a sacred text that tells us about a God who demanded such an expulsion. What is the religious reader to make of a God that would authorize the expulsion of an entire people from their land?

An answer to this requires that we know something about the literary and theological intentions of the author of these biblical narratives. Most modern scholars would interpret these stories against the background of the Deuteronomistic historian, the figure who was responsible for the corpus of stories with which we are presently concerned. For this writer, active during the period of Josiah's great reforms, these stories served to urge the Israelites to greater vigor in eliminating all signs of idolatry within their own nation. Given that the danger of the presence of indigenous Canaanites had long since passed, the Deuteronomistic historian understood this particular narrative of Israel's origins as a means of focusing the mind on the horrors of turning aside from the worship of the one true God. In other words, the elimination of the Canaanites was a metaphoric way of addressing the purity of heart that Israel was to strive for in her devotion to the one God. Just as Israel was commanded to wipe out any presence of idolatry at its founding, so in the present a similar vigilance was to be kept toward the veneration of the one true God.[7] Strikingly, this metaphoric or perhaps 'spiritual' reading accords with several Fathers of the Church who also denied that the stories in Joshua were to be understood in a literal-historical fashion. Origen, for example, wrote the following about the taking of Canaan (2002: 127):

Would that the Lord might thus cast out and extinguish all former evils from the souls who believe in him—even those he claims for his kingdom—and from my own soul, its own evils; so in me, nothing of wrath; so that no disposition of desire for any evil may be preserved in me, and no wicked word 'may remain to escape' from my mouth. For thus, purged from all former evils and under the leadership of [Joshua], I can be included among the cities of the sons of Israel, concerning which it is written, 'The cities of Judah will be raised up and they will dwell in them' (Amos 9: 14).

For Origen the elimination of the Canaanites from the land of Israel was not to be read as a historical fact; it was a means of inspiring Israel to moral and spiritual purity.[8]

---

[7] The best exposition of this perspective is to be found in MacDonald 2003: 97–123, but esp. 108–23.

[8] The discerning reader may note that there is much in common here with the way many modern Muslims have argued that the Koranic term 'jihad' should be understood.

2. NATIONAL IDENTITY AND THE LAND: 'WHERE ARE THE HITTITES?'

But let us return to the question of the text's simple sense and dispense for the moment with matters of historical reconstruction. For however we reconstruct the history behind the creation of the biblical text, we are still left with the portrait that the canonical text has left the Church. The Bible, as it stands, makes it crystal clear that Israel assumes possession of a land that originally had belonged to others and that by dint of considerable divine aid Israel succeeds in wresting control of this land for its own better benefit. Is there anything morally salvageable in a tale such as this?

A good place to begin is with the question of the relationship of various peoples of antiquity to the lands in which they resided. As has been long noted, the great civilizations of the ancient Near East have long since disappeared. The Indo-European peoples (known as the 'Hittites') that resided within the land mass of what is now Turkey were replaced in the Middle Ages by invading marauders from the plateaus of central Asia—a people whose defining marker for Western cartographers was the language they spoke (and still speak), Turkish. The Arab invaders of the seventh and eighth centuries eventually dispelled the native populations of Egypt and classical Mesopotamia and the indigenous languages that were spoken in these regions (Coptic and Aramaic) were slowly replaced by Arabic. Similar changes took place in Syria-Palestine and the lands that bordered it; they all succumbed to the Muslim invaders and soon became Arabic speakers as well. (It is worth recalling that at the beginning of the Crusades, much of the Middle East was predominantly Christian and ruled by a Muslim minority.) Similar shifts, of course, are in evidence in Europe as well.

A casual glance at an historical atlas will reveal that the ethnographic and linguistic configuration of Europe was quite different in late antiquity from what was to emerge in the Middle Ages and early modern period. Indeed, the ethnographic landscape of Europe changed remarkably within the framework of the twentieth century (bounded by the two great wars) and was not settled in the area of Yugoslavia until the last few decades.

Of course grand shifts in population also took place in the ancient Near East and the results were not lost on the ancients.[9] They were well aware that population shifts of rather dramatic proportions took place over the scope of

---

[9] The incursion of the Philistines into Syria-Palestine is a good case in point. On the migration of these 'Sea Peoples', see Stager 1998.

human history. The prophet Amos seems to be aware of just this sort of transformation when he writes: 'Did I not bring Israel up from the land of Egypt, and the Philistines from Caphtor and the Arameans from Kir?' (9: 7–8).[10]

What is striking about the people of Israel is that according to the Bible they assume their identity *prior* to the occupation of any particular piece of land (so the story told of the patriarchs in Genesis through the exodus from Egypt and wandering in the wilderness toward the promised land) and their identity endures *after* that land is taken away from them in 587 BCE when the Babylonians invaded, destroyed the capital city of Jerusalem and its temple, and carried away its leading citizens as exiles to Babylonia. Though the people were to return a couple of generations later, their occupation of the land of Israel would again be interrupted by the Roman invasion in CE 70 when the temple was once again reduced to rubble and the peoples dispersed to the various corners of the empire. It was not until the late nineteenth century under the inspiration of the budding Zionist movement that Jews in great numbers began to return to the promised land. (Though it is worth stating that there has been a continuous Jewish presence in the Holy Land from the early period to the modern day. Modern Zionism simply increased the number of Jewish residents.)

The relationship of the Jews to their land is by all accounts a remarkable matter in the annals of world history. This was already noticed in the book of Esther when Haman tells King Ahasuerus, 'There is a certain people scattered and separated among the peoples in all the provinces of your kingdom; their laws are different from those of every other people, and they do not keep the king's laws, so that it is not appropriate for the king to tolerate them' (3: 8). Other exiled peoples, Haman implies, were easily assimilated into the culture of the Persian empire. The Jews, however, due to their tenacious obedience to their native laws, stand apart from all others and as a result, Haman argues, constitute a threat to the integrity of the king's dominion. St Augustine several centuries later also noticed this peculiar feature of the Jewish people. But he, being a Christian, did not count this feature as an odd ethnographic detail but a sign of divine providence. That the Jews still survive in spite of their role in having God's messiah crucified is proof that God acts in accord with the teaching of the gospels and continues, Augustine argued, 'to love His enemies'. Though this position is considerably better than that of Haman, one still winces at the description of the Jews as 'God's enemies'.[11] Yet what is important for our purposes is Augustine's historical observation that Jewish

---

[10] All Bible references are taken from the *New Revised Standard Version*.

[11] On the remarkable role of the Jewish people in Augustine's thought and its decisive influence in later Christian thought and practice, see Fredricksen 2009.

identity has survived in spite of the Diaspora and in contrast to conventional historical patterns. This fact, Augustine argued, demanded a theological explanation.[12]

The Catholic novelist and occasional philosopher Walker Percy provides a theological explanation for the perseverance of the Jews that is likely to find a more positive resonance among Christians informed by texts such as Nostra Aetate from Vatican II.[13] He argues that the Jewish people, as a people, point toward the reality of the God who has tied his identity to them:

Where are the Hittites? Why does no one find it remarkable that in most world cities today there are Jews but not one single Hittite even though the Hittites had a great flourishing civilization while the Jews nearby were a weak and obscure people? When one meets a Jew in New York or New Orleans or Paris or Melbourne, it is remarkable that no one considers the event remarkable. What are they doing here? But it is even more remarkable to wonder, if there are Jews here, why are there not Hittites here? Where are the Hittites? Show me one Hittite in New York City. (Percy 1075)

The Hittites, of course, had a connection to their land that they and their neighbors would have understood as enduring. Yet history has defied these expectations. Enter rapacious invaders and whatever was left of a venerable Indo-European culture went into rapid decline. The Jews, on the other hand, have been without land longer than they have possessed it yet the miraculous preservation of their identity is difficult to explain save for the gracious protection of God.

3. NATURAL AND PROVIDENTIAL CLAIMS TO THE LAND

So what are we to make of the perseverance of Jewish identity and its peculiar relationship to the promised land? No understanding of the conquest story can avoid the larger question of the unique way in which Israel's relationship to the land is laid out in the Bible and subsequent Jewish history. The person who has done the best job on this problem is the Israeli biblical scholar Uriel Simon. In an important book on the relationship between biblical thought and contemporary Israeli politics he takes up the question of Israel's claim to its land.[14] He begins by making a distinction between a natural and a providential tie to a land. A natural

---

[12] See now the brilliant new book by Paula Fredricksen (2009). There she traces the implications of Augustine's thinking on the treatment of Jews in the Middle Ages.

[13] See Haynes 1991.

[14] Simon 2002. See my discussion of this book and its relationship to the modern Zionist movement in Anderson 2005.

tie, he writes, 'means that a people dwells on its land and the very fact of its dwelling there gives it a right of ownership over it. And so the nations of the world see their claims to their lands. Their attachment to the land is thought to be a "natural right," that is, the fruit of significant historical events such as: place of one's birth, site of lawful immigration, conquest, lengthy period of ownership, development of a unique culture and so forth. This natural tie is held by the consciousness of the nation as a foundational fact. The people are expected to defend their land and independence but they do not, for the most part, fear being uprooted from it.' In contrast to this, a providential tie to the land is guaranteed by 'a divine promise that precedes (both temporally and logically) the actual possession of the land and is not conditioned by it'.

To both types of ownership there are advantages and disadvantages. Those who possess a natural tie to their land enjoy a continuous link to their land. When uprooted from their land—as the Hittites eventually were—their identity as a people comes to an abrupt end. Israel, however, never enjoyed a sense of a continuous link to her land. Built into the very fabric of her covenant was the threat that if she disobeyed God's law in the way in which the Canaanites did, she too would lose her land. In Moses' last address to the Israelites prior to their entry into the land he writes:

When you have had children and children's children, and become complacent in the land, if you act corruptly by making an idol in the form of anything, thus doing what is evil in the sight of the Lord your God, and provoking him to anger, I call heaven and earth to witness against you today that you will soon utterly perish from the land that you are crossing the Jordan to occupy; you will not live long on it, but will be utterly destroyed. The Lord will scatter you among the peoples; only a few of you will be left among the nations where the Lord will lead you. (Deut. 4: 25–7)

Israel stands under the very same danger that was once visited upon the Canaanites. Yet for Israel all will not be lost; should Israel repent of her sins there is always the possibility that God will restore her to the land. And so the text continues: 'From there you will seek the Lord your God, and you will find him if you search after him with all your heart and soul. . . . Because the Lord your God is a merciful God, he will neither abandon you nor destroy you; he will not forget the covenant with your ancestors that he swore to them' (4: 29–31). Though Israel occupies a land that carries with it a threat to whomever would deign to settle there, her entitlement to that land is based on a divine covenant and no human power can stand in the way of its promises.

Let me be certain to stress one point here. I have learned after several attempts at laying out Simon's perspective that many readers are not sufficiently patient in their attention to detail. When Simon says that Israel's tie to the land is supernatural, some understand this to mean that Israel's right to the land trumps all moral responsibility. The worries of Edward Said return with a vengeance. Yet for Simon, these worries are ill founded. It is people who feel a natural tie to their land who believe that their right to ownership endures in spite of any moral obligation. Do Swedes, Poles, the British, or any other modern people believe that their right to their land is grounded in the keeping of specific commandments? Not even the atrocities of the Nazis in the Second World War led to the deportation of the German people. The land of Germany is still the patrimony of the German people. Will Germany remain the land for German-speaking peoples a hundred, five hundred, or even a thousand years from now? Maybe or maybe not; there is no way of knowing. But it is highly unlikely that should the German nation disappear the consciousness of the German people will endure. They would go the way of other extinct peoples before them such as the Hittites.

Israel, on the other hand, remains unique. Even without a land her identity is rock-solid and eternal. Her link to her land is supernatural—that is it is guaranteed by God—but that does not mean that at any given period of time she will be in possession of it. The word supernatural is used here in its etymological sense; Israel's relationship to her land does not conform to normal historical patterns—in that sense, it exceeds the natural. According to the Bible, Israel's possession of that land is conditioned on the grace of God and the moral stature of the people. To enjoy a supernatural link to the land is, paradoxically, to stand under a conditional promise. Unlike the Swedes, the Poles, or the Germans there is no sense that the land of Israel is Israel's permanent possession in the sense that she will enjoy continuous ownership over it. God is free to drive the Jews from the land just as he drove out the Canaanites before them. But unlike the Canaanites, even without a land, Israel's national identity will endure. As St Paul reminds us—the promises to Israel were and are irrevocable (11: 28–9).

4. THE PROMISE MADE TO ABRAHAM

Our current despisers of biblical religion may still carry within their hearts some significant reservations regarding the arguments of Simon. Okay, it might be conceded, Israel's attachment to the land is conditioned on clear moral principles. In this sense, Israel's claim to the land stands in a more precarious position than that of other peoples' claims to their own lands. But this does not address in any way the problem of Israel's founding story. When she enters the land of Canaan, the land is not devoid of inhabitants. Her gain is another's loss. The eviction of the Canaanites is still at base an immoral act.

The God of the Bible in his election of Israel does not seem to be accountable to the principles of justice.

To address this concern we need to return to the Bible and the way in which it tells the story of how the promise of the land is first made. The opening chapters of the book of Genesis depict the gradual decline of the human race. Beginning with the disobedience of Adam and Eve in the garden, the murder of Abel by his brother Cain, the despicable violence set in motion by Cain's descendants, and concluding with the building of the urban center of Babel, the story of the origins of human civilization is depicted in very dark terms. Given that the story of the flood is both a sign of the end of God's patience with respect to the world he has created and a determination to start afresh—this time picking as the ancestor of the human race a man who was renowned for his righteousness—it is particularly tragic that immediately after the flood human rebellion returns, this time expressed in the building of a large city-with-a-tower in the vicinity of Babylon (Gen. 11: 1–9). The overt purpose of this venture is to provide the peoples who descend from the loins of Noah a means of 'making a name for themselves' (11: 4). In the world of ancient Near East leaving a name behind was tantamount to living forever and thus there was a lot of interest in such a venture. The most common ways of establishing a name were through one's offspring or public monuments.

God was clearly unhappy with the builders of this tower because they believed that their eternal renown could somehow be achieved by their own human efforts. In response to this hubris, God descended from heaven, confused the languages of the builders and then scattered them across the face of the earth. No longer would human beings be able to unite their efforts in common cause. Given that God had created human beings with free will he could not force them to do his bidding. But by dispersing them over the globe he could lessen the potential of these creatures to carry out the evil they intended.[15]

The story of Babel is important to get right because it sets up the famous lines of the twelfth chapter of Genesis: 'Now the Lord said to Abra[ha]m, "Go from your country and your kindred and your father's house to the land that I will show you. I will make of you a great nation, and I will bless you, and make your name great, so that you will be a blessing. I will bless those who bless you, and the one who curses you I will curse; and in you all the families of the earth shall be blessed"' (12: 1–3). Several points are made in this text. But for our purposes, the most important is the promise that God will *make Abraham's name great*. Unlike the story of Babel, the emphasis is placed on divine as opposed to human action. This is embedded more deeply in the text

---

[15] On this point see the insightful treatment of Leon Kass in Kass 2003.

than one might gather at first glance. God has told Abraham that he will make a great nation of him yet the reader has already, a few verses earlier, been alerted to the surprising fact that Abraham's wife Sarah is barren (11: 30). How will that work? As the story unfolds things get even worse, Sarah is not only barren but post-menopausal (18: 12). Pregnancy within the course of natural causes simply will not happen. The only way Abraham will be the beneficiary of children will be through divine intervention. By allowing Sarah to give birth to Isaac, God makes clear that it is he who will grant Abraham a great name.

When Abraham sets off for the land of Canaan (Gen. 12: 4ff.), he departs with a very different set of expectations from those of other immigrants. Rather than expecting to improve his lot in life as is the expectation of most immigrants, Abraham sets off to a land that he knows *nothing* about solely on the grounds of a divine command ('Go . . . to the land that I will show you'). Whatever doubts he might have had about the probability of realizing what was promised were pushed aside. Abraham obeyed the voice without hesitation and set forth toward an unknown destination.

But things did not unfold in quite the way that Abraham might have hoped. Though he gave up everything to follow his God, the possibility of becoming a great nation seems to decrease as the years he marks in Canaan grow in number and the chances of fathering a child grow less and less. In his distress he asks the Lord whether his servant might be the one who will be his heir (15: 1–3). God quickly waves off that possibility and assures Abraham that however bleak things may appear his offspring will eventually be as numerous as the stars of the sky (vv. 4–5). To confirm the terms of this promise God makes a covenant with Abraham. But during this ceremony as the day grows old and a deep darkness descends, God tells Abraham:

Know this for certain, that your offspring shall be aliens in a land that is not theirs, and shall be slaves there, and they shall be oppressed for four hundred years; but I will bring judgment on the nation that they serve, and afterward they shall come out with great possessions. As for yourself, you shall go to your ancestors in peace; you shall be buried in a good old age. And they shall come back here in the fourth generation; for the iniquity of the Amorites is not yet complete. (15: 13–16)

The offspring will come, God assures, as will the possession of the land. But prior to the attainment of the latter, Abraham's children will descend to a land and be enslaved there. After 400 years of miserable oppression they shall be led out to assume ownership of what is rightfully theirs. Shocking words, these. Four hundred years in antiquity (as in modernity!) is nearly an eternity. What kind of hope is this?

There can be no surprise that this piece of information was withheld from Abraham back in Genesis 12—who would set out for any land with this future in view? The children of Abraham would have to bide their time as sojourners in a land where their claim to title was not recognized. And to make matters worse, they would mark much of this time as slaves in Egypt suffering the contempt of a Pharaoh whose primary intention was that of eliminating this budding nation once and for all. Israel's undeserved suffering is a necessary component in the way God's justice will be served.[16] And here is the point whose significance must be underscored: *Even if the land of Canaan will become part of the eternal patrimony of the descendants of Abraham it is not a land that God can simply hand over at will. The rights of the citizens who presently reside upon it must be respected.* God will not evict them until their immoral ways justify such a punishment. This holds true even if God's chosen people must endure the grimmest sort of trial that can be imagined. Election may have its privileges, but it also has a cost.

But we can say even more than this. In Genesis 12, as we have noted, God tells Abraham to set forth for a land that God will show to him. There he will become a great nation, be invested with a great name, and through his progeny all the nations of the earth shall receive blessing. As the chapter proceeds the promise seems to be put at great risk when a famine strikes and Abraham and Sarah are forced to migrate to Egypt (12: 10–20). Yet miraculously God oversees their momentary exile and, instead of losing everything while abroad, Abraham returns to Canaan with great worldly wealth (12: 20 and 13: 2). As chapter 13 opens, we learn that Abraham has become so well to do that the land of Canaan does not seem to be sufficiently capacious for the large flocks and herds that he and his nephew Lot now control (13: 5–7). One might have thought that Abraham, who holds legal title to this land, would have reminded his nephew of what divine providence has wrought and ordered him to emigrate to another land. What value is a legal promise if it has no teeth?

Yet Abraham does not pull out his contract and dress down his nephew. Rather than taking advantage of the favorable terms God had bestowed, he displays a remarkably generous spirit toward Lot: 'Let there be no strife between you and me, and between your herders and my herders; for we are kindred. Is not the whole land before you? Separate yourself from me. If you take the left hand, then I will go to the right; or if you take the right hand, then I will go to the left' (vv. 8–9). Lot recognized the advantage that Abraham had

---

[16] For the discerning Christian reader the Christological parallels are striking. Just as Israel, God's beloved nation, must suffer in order to realize the vocation and promise she has been given, so will Jesus, God's beloved son.

given him and wasted no time in taking advantage of it: 'Lot lifted his eyes and saw that the plain of Jordan was well watered everywhere like the garden of the Lord, like the land of Egypt . . . So Lot chose for himself all the plain of the Jordan and Lot journeyed eastward; thus they separated from each other' (vv. 10–11). (Unknown to Lot is the nature of his future neighbors. His choice will prove tragic though he could have had no inkling of that when he made his choice.)

God rewards Abraham's generosity by deeding the remainder of the land of Canaan to him. He declares: 'Lift your eyes and look from the place where you are, northward and southward and eastward and westward; for all the land that you see I will give to you and to your offspring forever. I will make your offspring like the dust of the earth; so that if one can count the dust of the earth, your offspring also can be counted. Rise up, walk through the length and breadth of the land, for I will give it to you' (vv. 14–17). What is striking is the intertextual allusion to the behavior of Lot. Whereas Lot lifted up his own eyes, saw the best piece of land, and then took it for himself, it is God who, in response to Abraham's graciousness, enjoins his servant to lift his eyes and see the land that has been given to him (the diction of the original Hebrew is exactly the same). Just as the builders of the tower wanted to make a name for themselves rather than be granted a name by the grace of God, so Lot desires to construct his own earthly kingdom rather than receive his patrimony as a gift. The land that Abraham receives as an *eternal* possession comes in the wake of his *generosity* toward it.[17] If we combine a reading of this text with our earlier text that will require Abraham and his descendants to wait 400 years before taking title to the land promised them we can see that it is a great oversimplification to read the promise of the land to Israelites as unilateral land grab that negates the just claims to the land of the previous inhabitants. The acquisition of the land is not only grounded in justice (the sins of the Canaanites must come to full term prior to their eviction) but in grace as well (Abraham's receipt of the land as an eternal patrimony is grounded in his act of generosity toward his nephew).

We might add that when Abraham purchases his first plot of land in the land of Canaan near the end of his life (Gen. 23), he takes extraordinary measures to be fair in his financial dealings. Ephron, the Hittite, initially offered to deed the land over as a gift. Abraham, however, vigorously insisted

---

[17] One cannot help but think of the Christological pattern witnessed in Philippians 2— Christ only inherits the name that was due him from all eternity once he has shown a willingness to forgo its legal claims. So Abraham only receives the land of Canaan as an *eternal* patrimony after he has shown himself willing to part with its most valuable acreage. The making of a great name is predicated on an act of generosity rather than legal entitlement.

on paying the first price that Ephron names—a rare and somewhat foolish thing to do. This is not the sort of behavior one would expect in any sort of business dealing, let alone someone who believes that the promise he has received from God would allow him special privileges with respect to the land. Abraham strives to be scrupulously fair to the original owners of the land.

In summary, we can say that Said's reading of the Bible is deeply flawed. The text does not award a land to Israel in a manner that immorally voids all previous claims. Quite the opposite, the gift of the land to Israel can only take place when the sins of the Canaanites will be of sufficient number and magnitude so as to justify their expulsion. In the Bible's understanding, the land that Israel will inhabit has a certain sanctity that makes it different from all the other lands of the earth. It cannot bear oppressive or licentious behavior (see Lev. 18: 24–30). God, due to his abundant mercy, will be patient with such activity up to a point. In Abraham's day, the Canaanites were granted some 400 years to amend their ways; the Israelites would, in turn, be granted a similar amount of time prior to their exile at the hand of the Babylonians. The way in which the Canaanites and the Israelites differ is that Israel is the beneficiary of an eternal promise. Her attachment to the land is not natural as it was for the Canaanites but supernatural. Though Israel would be driven from the land, her eviction would not be eternal. Unlike the Canaanite peoples who once lived in the land, the people-hood of Israel would not disappear once she had lost her land. Just as God sustained their identity in the Diaspora, so God would be free to bring them back whenever he wished but—and this point must be emphasized—*always in accordance with the character he established in the foundation narratives of Israel's origins.* If Abraham was generous toward Lot (Gen. 13) and punctilious in his relations with the Hittites (Gen. 23) then we should expect the same sort of behavior from his offspring in the future. In this respect, the biblical story in its full canonical witness does not provide a charter for the stealing of another people's land.

Comments on 'What About the Canaanites?'

Nicholas Wolterstorff

Professor Anderson in his chapter 'What about the Canaanites?' and I in my essay 'Reading Joshua' both focus our attention on Israel's conquest of the land of Canaan as depicted centrally in the book of Joshua. But whereas I focus on the justice of the mode of conquest, specifically, its apparently brutal and genocidal character, Professor Anderson focuses on the justice of the mere fact of conquest.

Anderson observes that archeological and historical evidence provides us with an answer to one question concerning the morality of the actions Israel is depicted as having performed. There is near-universal agreement among the relevant specialists that there is no archeological or historical evidence of a foreign people occupying the land of Canaan at the time in question, let alone having done so in destructive, genocidal fashion. Israel's stories of the conquest, says Anderson, 'are not historical records of what really happened, but after-the-fact literary fictions'.

If there never was a conquest, then of course there never was a genocidal conquest. One problem solved. I assume that by calling the stories 'fictions' Anderson means that they were made up; I assume he also means that they are presented in the fictive rather than the assertoric mood. If they were made up but asserted as true, then the writers would have been lying; and I feel sure that Anderson does not want to say that.

Anderson goes on to observe that to conclude that the conquest never happened and that the stories of conquest are fictions is by no means to solve all the problems of those of us who regard the Hebrew Bible/Old Testament as a sacred text. Even if the expulsion never happened, what are we to do 'with a sacred text that tells us about a God' who demanded and authorized 'the expulsion of an entire people from their land'?

I infer from Anderson's discussion as a whole that though he believes the stories of conquest were made up, the stories about God's mandating conquest were not made up; and that these latter stories are presented in the assertoric rather than the fictive mood.[1] But this is a puzzling blend. What sense would it make for the Deuteronomic writers to combine, into one narrative, made-up stories about the conquest told in the fictive mood with non-made-up stories about God's mandating the conquest told in the assertoric mood?

If there never was a foreign people invading the land of Canaan and taking it by conquest, then there was also no such thing as God mandating a foreign people to do so—unless, of course, one holds the odd view that God mandated some people to invade and conquer the land but that none ever did. If the stories of conquest were made up, then the stories of God's mandating conquest must also have been made up. And if the writers were telling the made-up stories of conquest in the fictive mood, then they must also have been telling the made-up stories about God's mandating conquest in the fictive mood. If they had told them in the assertoric mood, they would have been lying.

As for myself, I neither believe that the stories of conquest were made up and told in the fictive mood, nor that the stories about God's mandating such conquest were made up and told in the fictive mood. My view is that the book of Joshua was never meant to be read literally. If we read it in conjunction with the book of Judges, and if we pay due attention to the highly figurative character of its language, we see that it is not a story, be it fictional or non-fictional, about a brutal genocidal conquest of an entire land. And if that is true, then I think we must infer that it is also not a story, be it fictional or non-fictional, about God's commanding such conquest.

Over and over in the book of Joshua we find the line 'and they slew all the inhabitants with the edge of the sword'. Suppose one asked some present-day high school basketball player how his team fared in the game they played the night before, and suppose he says, 'We slaughtered 'em, wiped 'em out, just like coach told us to.' What can one conclude from that comment about how his team treated their opponents and how their coach wanted them to treat their opponents? Very little. That their coach fired them up to win the game and that they did. That's about it.

I trust that the distinctions I have been using between what's made up and what's not made up, between what's presented in the fictive mood and what's presented in the assertoric mood, and between words used literally and words used figuratively, do not give problems. Let me use the concept of the world of the work. I hold that the contents of the world of the work of Joshua were not

---

[1] Anderson appears to assume that if the stories about Israel's conquest were made up and presented in the fictive mood, then their presence in our sacred text poses no problem. That seems to me not correct.

(for the most part) made up by the writers, and that the writers presented that world in the assertoric rather than the fictive mood. But I also hold that in presenting the world of the work, they were in good measure not using language literally. It proves to be no easy task to figure out what is in fact the world of the work—what is in fact the world that the writers projected and presented in assertoric mood to their readers with their highly figurative use of language.

Back to Anderson's chapter. On his view, we are to take literally what the stories say about God's mandate of conquest. Though he is quite clearly of the view that this aspect of the stories is presented in the assertoric mode, it's not central to his purposes on this occasion to argue that point, nor is it central to his purposes on this occasion to decide whether this aspect of the stories is true. He wants to get at what he calls the 'simple sense' of the texts with respect to what they present God as doing in the story; and they have that sense whether or not they are presented in the fictive or assertoric mood, and whether or not they are true.

The first part of his way of dealing with the question of the justice or injustice of what God is presented as doing is to highlight a theme that is sounded over and over in the texts, namely, that God promised this land to Abraham and his descendants, it being assumed that the members of Israel are Abraham's descendants. (Anderson adds that God's gift of the land to Abraham and his descendants was 'grounded' in the generosity Abraham displayed when he allowed his nephew Lot to take the better land. Not only do I not find it said in the text that God's generosity was grounded in Abraham's generosity; the suggestion that it was so grounded seems to me to strike a false note. God did not choose Abraham as the initial patriarch in the story of redemption because he was especially good.)

In the normal case, the right of a people to a certain territory is based on natural phenomena of one sort or another. Israel was unique. The land of Canaan belonged to Israel because God promised it to them. It did not belong to the Hittites, the Perizzites, and all the rest of them. Had God not promised the land to Israel, those other peoples would have had a right to it by virtue of the natural phenomena that normally give a people title to a certain piece of land. But God promised it to Israel, and so it belonged to Israel. Israel's God-given right trumps the prima facie natural right of the resident peoples.

Anderson follows the Israeli biblical scholar Uriel Simon in calling Israel's right to the land a *providential* right, in contrast to a natural right; and he mentions some interesting and important things that Simon says about providential rights to land in general, and about Israel's providential right in particular. To a degree unique among the nations of the world, Israel's identity has not depended, and does not depend, on its occupation of land.

Israel's dwelling in the land at any particular time is thus an act of special providence on God's part, not a condition of Israel's existence. And it is open to God to establish, as a condition for Israel's abiding in the land, that Israel remain faithful to Yahweh. Yahweh's expulsion of Israel from the land, should Israel become faithless, would not be sentencing Israel to extinction.

Anderson points out that from the fact that Israel had a God-given right to the land, it does not follow that Israel had a right to *take* the land when and as it wished. Even though the land belongs to 'the eternal patrimony of the descendants of Abraham, it is not a land that God can simply hand over at will. The rights of the citizens who presently reside upon it must be respected.' Anderson postpones for another day the question of what this implies for legitimate and illegitimate *ways* of taking the land, and concentrates on the conditions that must be satisfied for Israel to have the right to take its land in some way or other from the present inhabitants. He interprets the texts as saying that if and only if the inhabiting nations deserve the divine punishment for their misdeeds of being conquered, does Israel have the right to take by conquest the land that belongs to it.

Let's pull things together: Israel has a right to this land on account of God having promised it to them as Abraham's descendants; and it has the right to *take* the land now because its present inhabitants deserve being punished by God for their misdeeds by having the land taken from them. So Israel is in the clear; it acts justly in taking the land. And God is in the clear; God authorized Israel to take its promised land only if the inhabitants at the time were so wicked as to deserve being punished by God for their misdeeds by having their land taken from them.

Let me make three critical comments about this 'solution' to the problem. First, Anderson's argument gives the wrong impression as to the rationale for Yahweh's mandate and for Israel's taking. Over and over what is cited as justification for Israel's taking the land is simply that God promised it to Israel; nothing is added about its being right for Israel to take it only if the inhabitants are exceedingly wicked. And over and over what is cited as justification for extermination of the inhabitants is that Israel is so susceptible to the lure of idolatry that the practitioners and paraphernalia of pagan worship must be eliminated if there is to be a people of Yahweh. It's true that in Deuteronomy 9: 5 we read that 'because of the wickedness of these nations the Lord your God is dispossessing them before you'. But this is by no means the dominant rationale.

But suppose the rationale Anderson cites for God's mandating the conquest were in fact the dominant rationale for God's mandate—and that the inhabitants were in fact exceedingly wicked. Are God and Israel then in the clear with respect to the occupation of the land—the mode of occupation being another matter? It's not obvious that they are.

If God justly promised the land to Israel, then the land belongs to Israel; no problem there so far as I can see. But suppose that some 400 years intervene between the time God made the promise and the time Israel arrives at the borders of the land to occupy it. And suppose that, in the meanwhile, a sizeable number of thriving city-states have developed in the land. Does this not cast doubt on the justice of the original open-ended promise? Should God not have attached a qualifier? Should God not have said: I give you the land provided that, when you are in a position to take it, it is virtually empty? No such qualification is even hinted at in the texts. Suppose that the UN promises to some people a piece of land that is heavily occupied by one or more other nationalities. Such an action is not unknown in our times. Is such a promise just? I think not.

Suppose that the divine promise is indeed qualified, but not as I have just now suggested but as Anderson suggests: I give you the land provided that, when you are in a position to take it, the inhabitants are exceedingly wicked. Would that promise be a just promise? Anderson seems to take it as obvious that it would be. I'm not sure.

But third: even if we answer that last question in the affirmative, so that both God and Israel are, so far forth, in the clear, we have made no significant advance in determining what those of us who regard these texts as sacred are to do with them. For even if there is some way for Israel to take the land that leaves both God and Israel in the clear, there remains the stubborn fact that the texts present God, on a literal reading, as mandating genocide across the entire land, and they present Israel, on a literal reading, as obeying that mandate.

Anderson takes literally what the texts say about God and God's relation to Israel. He abstracts from the details of the story by asking whether Israel would have been morally justified in taking the land *in some way or other*, and by asking whether there was *some way or other* of taking that God could justly mandate Israel to employ. But affirmative answers to those abstract questions help not at all in dealing with what the texts say concerning the specific way in which Israel did in fact conduct its conquest, and concerning the specific mandates for conquest that God did in fact issue. If we take literally what the texts say about Yahweh's injunctions concerning Israel's mode of conquest, then we are up against the fact that the texts present Yahweh as mandating extermination of the resident population.

I see no other solution to the problem than a wholly different line of interpretation. These texts are highly stylized, metaphorical, hyperbolic, and the like in how they present Israel's conquest of the land, in how they present

Joshua's role in that conquest, and in how they present Yahweh's mandate for conquest. They are not allegories; I do not propose adopting Origen's solution. But in good measure they are not literal. The world they project for us is not a world in which God literally mandates Israel to conquer the entire land with genocidal brutality and in which Israel literally does exactly that. These texts are not for the literal minded.

Reply to Wolterstorff

Gary A. Anderson

Let me address three points. First, Professor Wolterstorff does not believe that the gift of land to Abraham is grounded in the generosity of Abraham toward his nephew Lot. He argues instead that God 'did not choose Abraham as the initial patriarch in the story of redemption because he was especially good'. Though this is true with respect to the call Abraham hears in Genesis 12, it is not as true for the remainder of the tale. In Genesis 22: 15–18, for example, the call of Abraham that was first mentioned in Genesis 12 is paradoxically given a new and completely different explanation—because Abraham was obedient to God's command to sacrifice his son, he has now fully merited the terms of the promise. The reader of the Bible must pay careful attention to how the promise functions in each story in which it occurs. There is not a single, monochrome picture of this founding event.

At the conclusion of the story of Abraham's separation from Lot, we learn several new details about the promise that go beyond what was stated in Genesis 12: 1–3. First, that it will be eternal (13: 15); second, specific details about the territory it will comprise (13: 14–17); and thirdly, that Abraham is to walk back and forth through 'the length and breadth of the land'. The action of walking across a piece of territory in such a fashion has often been understood as the legal custom of formally taking possession. Read this way, the formal boundaries of the land are deeded to Abraham on the grounds of his gracious behavior toward Lot. I see no other reason why our biblical author would have attached these details to the narrative of Abraham and Lot's separation.

Secondly, the function of Genesis 15: 12–16, the text that declares that Abraham's descendants must wait some 400 years (as slaves in Egypt!) in order for the Canaanites to act sufficiently wickedly that God can justly drive them from the land. Wolterstorff thinks that I am 'extrapolating' from what scripture says by making this claim. 'Over and over,' he writes, 'what is cited as justification for Israel's taking the land is simply that God promised it to Israel; nothing is added about its being right for Israel to take it only if the inhabitants are exceedingly wicked.' In this instance, Wolterstorff shows the same inability to understand my point that he showed in his own chapter on the exegesis of Calvin.

In section III of his chapter, while expounding the exegesis of John Calvin, he writes: 'It was because the "iniquity" of the nations had "reached its height", says Calvin, that God "determined to destroy them. This was the origin of the command given to Moses."' In a footnote to this citation, Wolterstorff says, 'Calvin does not explain what he means by his cryptic phraseology "their iniquity had reached its height", nor what he means by his alternative phraseology "their iniquity was complete".' As a result Wolterstorff cannot accept Calvin's exegesis of the book of Joshua because this rationale goes 'beyond what the texts of Deuteronomy and Joshua say'.

What Wolterstorff has missed is that Calvin's 'cryptic phraseology' is nothing other than a recycling of the language of Genesis 15. Calvin reads the stories of the conquest in terms of how the land was deeded to Israel in the first place. Genesis 15 is the lens through which he reads the story of the conquest in the book of Joshua. I fail to see why this is an 'extrapolation' and has no relationship to scripture. It has everything to do with Israel's canonical witness and the way in which Calvin and I have read it.

Finally, Wolterstorff makes a strange allusion to the United Nations near the conclusion of his remarks. Could we imagine, he asks, the UN deeding a piece of land to a particular people that is already occupied by another nation. But what, I would wish to ask, does this have to do with the Bible? Divine authority is incommensurate with that of the UN. God, according to the Bible, is the ultimate owner of all land and ruler of every kingdom. He is free to remove kings from their thrones (see the book of Daniel) and nations from their lands (including Israel). The mandate of the UN gives it no such power. The theological question, it seems to me, is does God act justly in the biblical story when he exercises his royal prerogatives? One must begin with the presuppositions of that story in order to evaluate its moral claims. I have argued in my chapter that the God of the Bible lives up to his reputation as a just and equitable ruler of the universe.

REFERENCES

Anderson, Gary A. 2005. 'How to Think about Zionism', *First Things* (April).

Collins, John J. 2005. 'Exodus and Liberation in Postcolonial Perspective', in John J. Collins, *The Bible after Babel: Historical Criticism in a Postmodern Age*. Grand Rapids, Mich.: Eerdmans, 53–74.

Cross, Frank M. 1973. *Canaanite Myth and Hebrew Epic*. Cambridge, Mass.: Harvard University Press.

Fredricksen, Paula. 2009. *Augustine and the Jews: A Christian Defense of Jews and Judaism*. New York: Doubleday.

Haynes, Steven. 1991. 'Theology as Fiction and Fiction as Theology: Karl Barth and Walker Percy on the "Jews"', *Journal of Literature and Theology*, 5: 388–407.

Kass, Leon. 2003. *The Beginning of Wisdom: Reading Genesis*. New York: Free Press.

MacDonald, Nathan. 2003. *Deuteronomy and the Meaning of 'Monotheism'*. Tübingen: Mohr-Siebeck.

Mazar, A. 1990. *Archaeology of the Land of the Bible*. New York: Doubleday.

Origen. 2002. *Homilies on Joshua*, trans. B. Bruce. Fathers of the Church 105. Washington, DC: Catholic University of America Press.

Percy, Walker. 1975. *The Message in the Bottle*. New York: Picador.

Said, Edward. 1986. 'Michael Walzer's "Exodus and Revolution:" A Canaanite Reading', *Grand Street*, 5 (Winter): 86–106.

Simon, Uriel. 2002. *Seek Peace and Pursue it* (in Hebrew). Tel Aviv: Yediot Aharonot.

Stager, Lawrence E. 1998. 'Forging an Identity: The Emergence of Ancient Israel', in M. Coogan (ed.), *The Oxford History of the Biblical World*. New York: Oxford University Press, 123–76.

Walzer, Michael. 1985. *Exodus and Revolution*. New York: Basic Books.

——and Said, E. 1986. 'An Exchange', *Grand Street*, 5 (Summer): 246–59.

10

Canon and Conquest: The Character of the God of the Hebrew Bible

Christopher Seitz

PREFACE

A confession at the outset. I am not persuaded it is possible to *justify* the ways of God, though *speaking of God rightly*, to use the language of God to Job (42: 7), is something both desirable and possible. At issue is whether the Bible is competent to do that in its canonical shape and intention. It will be my larger point to say that God is most truly grasped *as God* when in address to humanity one begins neither with noetic assent nor moral approval. One is more likely confronted at a threshold disorienting and overwhelming, before it becomes transforming, merciful, and life-giving. When this has transpired, the New Testament speaks of being ready to give a defense—not of God—but of the faith that is in us. This volume is premised on the notion of philosophical defense of God, and yet my invited role is as a biblical theologian. So in order to give that angle due credit, some distinction between *justification* and *proper speaking* is in order.

This entails a precedent theological conviction, namely, that God does not exist in sublime mystery behind the language used about him, but is reliably and truthfully revealed in the totality of what two testaments of scripture say about him. These testaments do not give us human projection from below, but statements from inside a privileged revelation of God to Israel and in Christ, to the Church and world. The truthfulness of these statements is conveyed *by their totality*, by charting a range or dialectic within which God makes himself known. This is different than searching for a *discrimens*—a moral Geiger counter—by which to accept or reject discrete statements about him—in this sense I am somewhat sympathetic to the atheist rejection of God

I acknowledge with gratitude the research assistance of Mr. Robert Kashow.

whatever is said about him, as against the theist who may believe God is *behind* biblical language in a mode of hoped for discoverability and justification.

In the words of Paul, to the degree that God can be grasped in his mystery as God at all, it will be in his severity and mercy equally. As with Paul, this grasping of God, or being grasped by God, takes place inside a struggle to understand the totality of his dealings with humanity—the long story—for which Paul in Romans 11 supplies the conclusion: 'behold the mercy and the severity of God' (11: 22). Mercy and severity both, for only as related, inseparable, can they convey the truth of the mystery of God's imperative manifestations with us—what the classical tradition called God's economic life revealed through the totality of scripture.

In the present chapter, these theological bearings are brought, through the lens of what the early Church called the Rule of Faith, to a reading of the Conquest—because that is held to be a heinous, unjustifiable episode in God's dealings with the world. The Rule of Faith prevented the reading of scripture such that 'one portion be repugnant to another', or in the lovely pictorial image of Irenaeus, creating from the mosaic of scriptures' parts the portrait of a fox instead of a king. For the challenge was always what to make of the totality of scriptures' statements, a mystery finally grounded in the Trinity itself. I take some heart then in the conference title, 'My Ways Are Not Your Ways'. The name the OT gives to a God whose ways are like mine is an idol.

It should be clear then that my intention is to understand what the Bible means when it speaks of God, rather than to explore strategies for moving out of that mode into apologetic defense, independently conceived. I would rather have the Bible to speak for itself and that is a subset of believing that the *canonical character* of Christian scripture is adequate to the task on its own terms, once that character is acknowledged to be (1) a genuinely critical reality and (2) a necessary condition for properly hearing God's address from scripture. As with Arius, attenuated hearing of scripture (and so of grasping rightly God's character) is usually a subset of not knowing how scripture's parts cohere and inform one another. This happens when individual sentences are abstracted from their context and read as discrete statements, and so are not heard in relationship to a larger vista of two testaments in one scriptural witness. The *character of God* is inextricably connected with the *character of Christian scripture as a twofold witness*. An apologetics that only deals with assertions about individual statements has a steep climb and will fail to grasp how critical is an appreciation of the Bible in its canonical form.

1. 'THE HEBREW BIBLE', TANAK, AND A TWO-TESTAMENT CHRISTIAN CANON

The following introductory remarks are intended to indicate the theological and hermeneutical parameters of an essentially biblical-exegetical starting point, around which this volume is taking its bearings, 'The God of the Hebrew Bible'. What is a 'Hebrew Bible' and who are 'the Hebrews' and how is the God of this Bible truly God? Presumably a 'Hebrew Bible' is a Bible that contains the Old Testament of the Christian Bible in some sense, and so that indicates the literary-exegetical locus for our discussion (Seitz 1996, 1997). Thus far the literary-exegetical context, but the theological and hermeneutical dimensions are there for clarification. That the so-called Hebrew Bible 'in some sense' points to the first testament of Christian scripture implies both that the Old Testament is part of the Christian Bible, but also that its ability to speak Christianly is in question, requires clarification, needs a moral palliative, and so forth. Hence recourse to the neutral language ('Hebrew Bible') is not entirely at home in either traditional Jewish or Christian contexts.[1]

For the secular world, I suspect the issue is not all that sophisticated, for the second part of the Christian Bible speaks of God preparing eternal damnation, of the Law's being more stringent by moving inward to desires and motivations, of fates of judgment more severe than Sodom and Gomorrah, and so forth. It includes more final, universal examples of the divine routing of evil forces in the world (in the exorcisms by Jesus, in Paul's understanding of the Cross, or in Revelation's gory scenes of final judgment) than the Conquest's more episodic account of *herem*, if one is assuming a late modern, Western universe in which punishments by God are themselves morally questionable in the nature of the case.

The character of God as assumed by the New Testament's frame of reference is itself a challenging question, for to speak of Jesus Christ as God, or Son of God, is of course to speak the language of accordance (Childs 1970; Seitz 1998). To whom is Jesus Christ referring when he speaks of identity with the Father? Or when he says, 'before Abraham was, I am'? Or when he or Paul

---

[1] 'Hebrew Bible' is sometimes used in the modern period to avoid the language 'Old Testament' and this for a variety of different reasons. Jews do not have a 'Hebrew Bible' any more than Christians do; the term is a neologism. See Seitz 1996, 1997. Professor Anderson made the point nicely in his response when he spoke of the term 'Hebrew Bible' appearing in an Israeli newspaper and of having to transliterate it because it was not the customary term used by Jews to refer to Tanak.

speaks of the Eternal Name being given to him? Christian theology has answered that in two ways. To call the God of the OT the Father of Jesus Christ is one somewhat under-determined way to do that; to call the God of the scriptures preceding the NT the triune God is the dogmatically determined way to do that.[2] But both are non-negotiable options for early Christian reflection. The NT assumes both aspects to be true and to be related inextricably; this is the way it speaks of God in its literal sense. The Rule of Faith in its most clear ante-Nicene expression is an exegetically generated confession that 'the God of the Hebrew Bible'—to use the language of this volume—is one with the Son who came in the flesh and now dwells with the Father at the right hand, from whence he came.[3] That is, the Church read the scriptures of Israel through the lens of a rule, or canon of truth, in which the character of God was understood as that with which the work of Christ was to be correlated, as a work only finally comprehensible 'in accordance with the scriptures'. How the scriptures would declare this accordance was manifold, and the NT would in time give a relatively comprehensive account of that, in terms of prediction, typological anticipation, figural action inside Israel, moral order in Christ, salvation history, and so forth.[4]

The earliest Church Fathers stressed this character of God in the Old Testament for three decisive reasons. The first was simply that they were following the example of Christ himself, who accepted an authoritative scriptural legacy which adumbrated him and his life in the Godhead, promised his appearing, showed him the character of his Father in the widest public sense, and so forth. Related to this, intimately, was his own example in Luke, whereby Christ opened the first disciples' eyes to himself 'in Moses and all the

---

[2] See the penetrating discussion of this in the translational-theological reflections of Martin Luther in Helmer 2002. See also Soulen 1999; Yeago 1993; Rowe 2002.

[3] The OT is the locus of the Rule of Faith's application in the early Church. 'We must remember that by "Scripture" the Fathers, up to Irenaeus, Hippolytus, and Theophilus of Antioch, usually meant the Old Testament. At first this was the only approved and recommended collection of writings. But the *paradosis* of the Church, faithful to that of the apostles, was precisely this transmission of the Christ-event, as based documentarily on the Old Testament writings and, at the same time, explaining the meaning of these writings' (Congar 1966: 31).

[4] Irenaeus provides innumerable examples of this ontological identification, as he sees it, illumining the scriptures of Israel. Speaking of Christ as Logos, 'This is He who, in the bush, spoke with Moses and said, "I have surely seen the afflictions of my people who are in Egypt, and I have come down to deliver them." This is He who ascended and descended for the salvation of the afflicted, delivering us from the dominion of the Egyptians, that is, from all idolatry and ungodliness, and saving us from the Red Sea, that is, from the deadly turbulence of the heathen and from the bitter current of their blasphemy . . . and [also] gave [us] twelve springs, that is, the teaching of the twelve apostles; and killing the unbelievers in the desert, while leading those who believed in Him and were infants in malice into the inheritance of the patriarchs, which, not Moses, but Jesus ⟨gave us an inheritance⟩, who saves us from Amalek by stretching out His hands and leading us into the Father's Kingdom' (*Demonstration*, 46).

prophets'. Well into the second century Papias will recall the aged Polycarp speaking of Christ based upon the live testimony to him he received from John the Elder, and yet even this speaking Papias says was done 'in accordance with the scriptures' (Seitz 2008).

The second factor was the awareness that the authority of the New Testament as a scriptural testimony to Christ gathered its convicting force on the basis of the existence of a prior scriptural witness in Israel, which served as its template and warrant, and also as a statement of the fulfillment and accordance of this scripture in Christ. The Church heard Christ proclaimed by the scriptures it inherited, and formed a New Testament scripture by a process of analogy, and by an exegetical confession and elaboration that the New Testament was speaking of Christ in ways consistent with, and informed by, what the Old Testament said of God (von Campenhausen 1962).

The final factor, decisive for the early Church, is one that can be obscured now by virtue of (1) the present form of the canon and (2) the tragedy of the separation of the Church from its location in the context of Jewish Christian life. On this account, the Old Testament will threaten to become an older or former thing only, dangerously close to a 'history of religion' prior to 'the religion of Jesus'. Because the Church Fathers not only understood this potential, but also witnessed it in various specific challenges in the early Church, the Rule of Faith emerged to articulate and guide the theological speech of the Church in its widest sense. The Rule of Faith in the earliest period stipulates that the God of Israel is the Father of Jesus Christ and the triune God of Christian confession. Who God was and how he acted and was witnessed to within Israel (in his operations within a specific historical context, or what is called, in theological reflection, God's 'economy') is a faithful reflection both of who he is in his eternity (God's 'ontology') and also who he has revealed himself to be in the incarnate Son, God's word (logos).

In the present context, then, we face a different challenge than the early Church. For them, the ontological claims were paramount.[5] For us, the historically differentiated potential of a two-testament witness to One God means the economic challenge will dominate—even within the context of creedal Christian faith and apologetics. In this context, several matters have become virtually axiomatic. The focus on the human author comes with the correlate of historical differentiation, in the light of a very sophisticated account of what is now meant by a biblical 'author'. But even in the more

---

[5] Bray 2003. The Greek word 'economy' refers to God's revealed activity through time, in Israel and in the period of Christ's earthly life, and also in his life in the Church and world. This economic life is held to be a faithful reflection of who God is in his own ontology, his life as Father, Son, and Holy Spirit, from all eternity. See essays in n. 2.

traditional model, human authorship in the unsophisticated form of 'Moses wrote' or 'Isaiah said' operated against a backdrop of concern that one God was inspiring the speech of these diverse authors, and so the limits of economic difference were set by convictions that one and the same God was speaking consistently.

To speak of a 'Hebrew Bible' is to pay attention to the canonical reality that one God is spoken of in two economic dispensations, and this is the grander, final Christian exegetical landscape against which any and every sense of temporal distinction—within the testaments individually and also across them—plays itself out.[6] The distinction Old and New, or even Hebrew Bible and Christian Bible, points to the potential for seeing economic difference in the work of God, and even seeing this as requiring an inquiry into God's own 'moral life and development', as 'the divine protagonist' in a long narrative story with differentiated parts. The question is not the existence of distinctions in God's temporal work, but the potential for so differentiating this that God's character—YHWH for Jews or named as the Christian God, Father, Son, and Holy Spirit—is rendered problematical. To raise the question of the morality of God is not simply to interrogate one economic moment judged to be heinous (can YHWH command *herem*?) It is to raise the question of how a witness to God's economic life is a true statement of his character across the totality of that life, and so about his character as God: YHWH in Tanak, or Father, Son, and Holy Spirit in Christian scripture.

It will be our task to show that moral problems were not typically so ordered theologically in traditional Christian reflection because to do so would have been to separate the economic from the immanent accounts of the triune God (and the testaments one from another). The instinct was to assume a truthful immanent account of God, reflecting God in his eternity, and so then to ask how this might be a truthful account of our present life in him. The episodes of God's historical activity were taken to be truthful accounts, the total sum of which revealed God in his triune eternity. So Augustine would read the bashing of babies on the rock in Psalm 137 as having to do with the Rock, Jesus Christ, and our sins. He was not 'spiritualizing' a 'problematical' account of God in his economy with Israel. He was not approaching a 'Hebrew Bible' that belonged to someone else, or that referred imperfectly to the true God in its literal sense, and that required an

---

[6] This is also what makes the analogy between OT and NT broken with Jewish scripture (Tanak) and Talmud. The second testament claims to comprehend the literal sense of the OT as speaking of God's final action in Christ, prophetically and typologically both. This finality is uninaugurated for Jews, or belongs in the context of promise and fulfillment and obedience to God's law.

adjudication of God's character on the basis of an eternal criterion. The economic account (what the literal sense of the psalm conveyed in respect of Israel, the Edomites, Babylonian exile) was transparent to the immanent and eternal Godhead, thus obliging Augustine to ask in an immediate way what this might have to do with the Church's present life in Christ. Augustine did not believe he was working with a Bible which presented him with problems, revealed to be such by virtue of some external criterion. This first prophetic witness had an immediate applicability conveyed spiritually, in Christ, the Rock. The spiritual sense for Augustine was the literal sense.

In the context of the Conquest, Augustine will deal with sophisticated questions of free will and predestination. In this manner, God's will to destroy evil extends to his hardening the hearts of the opponents of Israel—a 'hardening' of the moral problem that appears to go beyond the literal sense of the broad account of the Conquest, so concerned is Augustine to defend the sovereignty of God ('The wills of men are so much in power of God, that He can turn them whithersoever it pleases him . . . by a counsel most secret to Himself').[7] Therefore, in reference to Joshua 11: 20 he comments, 'It was of the Lord to harden their hearts, that they should come against Israel in battle, that they might be exterminated.'[8] With reference to Joshua 16, as if anticipating the theme of this volume, Augustine concludes in a way customary for him.

One should not at all think it a horrible cruelty that Joshua did not leave anyone alive in those cities that fell to him, for God himself had ordered this. However, whoever for this reason thinks that God himself must be cruel and does not wish to believe then that the true God was the author of the Old Testament judges as perversely about the works of God as he does about the sins of human beings. Such people do not know what each person ought to suffer. Consequently, they think it a great evil when that which is about to fall is thrown down and when mortals die.[9]

Augustine, Jerome, Cyprian, Origen, and others reflexively conclude that God's righteousness is such that these Conquest stories are immediately about us and about our own moral state of affairs.[10] Equally, they see the 'God of the Hebrew Bible' as the One God with whom they have to do (Heb. 4: 11) and insist that this is so as a first-order affair: Jesus is himself active in

---

[7] Augustine, 'On Grace and Free Will' in the Anti-Pelagius Writings, ch. 41 (NPNF, 5: 461).

[8] Ibid.

[9] Augustine, Questions on Joshua 16.

[10] Cyprian, *The Treaties of Cyprian* Treatise XI, 'On the Exhortation to Martyrdom' I: 5 (ANF 5: 499); Origen, *Against Celsus*, book 7, ch. XIX (ANF 4: 618); Augustine, *Moral Treaties of St. Augustine, 'To Consentius: Against Lying'*, ch. 41 (NPNF 1, 5: 461); Jerome, Letters, Letter LXXXVI, 'To Abigaus' (on Josh. 6: 20).

Joshua's army. Jerome speaks of those 'opposed to the Gospel Army' and Jericho as 'a type of the overthrow of the world by preaching the Gospel'. Who is at work in this overthrow if not Jesus himself, Jerome concludes without lengthy explanation or defense. Concerning the five kings 'who previously reigned in the land of promise', Jerome will conclude without hesitation or need for argument: 'Jesus entered the body itself and slew them, that the source of their power might be the instrument of their death.'[11]

Examples like this could be multiplied, but the point is the reflexive collation of the ontological and the economic: there is no detachable 'God of the Hebrew Bible'. We now turn to the interpretation of the Conquest from a time closer to our own. Thus far it has been important to show that the 'moral challenge' (if that is the way to state it) was dealt with in a very different way. The ontological character of God's work as YHWH meant that the economic example of the Conquest was both a specific matter within the history of Israel, belonging to specific events of that day, and at the same time it revealed something essential and truthful about God's holiness and his abhorrence of idolatry that served as a warning to contemporaries. If one believes idolatry to be death-dealing, as did the Church Fathers and others, then it would follow for them that God alone was in a position to take such forces on and bring their death-dealing to an end, even working with terribly flawed agents who failed (so Calvin's estimate of Israel). If on the other hand, one believes God's vengeance is a function of his eccentricity or is unrelated to anything so serious that it must be abolished for life to be given (so the tradition), one is likely to conclude that another way should have been found or that such depictions show God to be, as previously thought, a God unworthy of himself or a fiction imposed by a nation seeking their own welfare and justifying their actions by attributing them to God.

Thus far the theological and hermeneutical context within which a discussion of 'the God of the Hebrew Bible' is situated, so far as classical Jewish-Christian reflection is concerned. From a Biblical Theological perspective the danger of recourse to a 'God of a Hebrew Bible' is the forfeiture of the Bible's canonical form and the implications of that for proper interpretation. To read the Bible as a container of sentences and paragraphs, to be held up for approval or justification, is to raise questions of hermeneutics and the consideration of canonical form. It is also to read the Bible independently of those communities which recognized its canonical form (as Tanak or Christian scripture) as ingredient in the proper handling of its complex world of discourse. So from a Biblical Theological perspective, this volume raises the

---

[11] Jerome, *Against Jovinanus*, book 1, ch. 21 (NPNF 6: 362).

question of *what kind of Bible* is being presupposed for discussion: a canonical scripture whose form is essential to proper appreciation, or a neutral text with an assemblage of independent assertions about God made at this or that moment, as products of human imagination and self-assertion. How one answers that question will say everything about what one sees as the problem to be solved: God's character, or proper consideration of the relationship between the Bible's form and content, in the light of the communities who have read it in accordance with its canonical form.

2. CONQUEST AND HISTORY IN THE MODERN PERIOD

In the middle of the nineteenth century a monument to straightforward Biblical Theology was produced by Tübingen professor Gustav Oehler, translated immediately into English by George Day of Yale (Oehler 1883). The biblical-historical-theological portrayal matched seamlessly the canonical presentation of the Law and the Prophets: Mosaism followed by Prophetism followed by Scribalism. At almost the same time, the Strasbourg scholar Eduard Reuss was lecturing on the Pentateuch and was concluding in his lectures that the Law was later than the Prophets and the Psalms than them both—the single most destabilizing insight in the history of biblical interpretation.[12] It would be left to Julius Wellhausen (1957) to produce the grand consolidation and synthesis with which his name is now associated. Oehler and Wellhausen would stand as tributes to the opposing guard-rails governing the unruly traffic of the late nineteenth century.

Because Joshua was considered part of the source-critical reconstructive universe—one spoke of a Hexateuch—and because Deuteronomy was pivotal in anchoring the temporal scheme for the development and plotting of the sources, the Conquest would naturally be open to a fresh interpretation. If Deuteronomy was the book of the Law found in the period of Josiah, and if it was composed at that period, then its depiction of the Conquest was *long after the fact*. To be sure, the theory allowed for the existence of earlier sources. But typically these contained traditions which were more candid about the failure of the Conquest properly to be undertaken. That is, the more ideal—if also morally difficult—portrayal was separated out as *ingredient in the very notion*

---

[12] 'The prophets are older than the law and the psalms are later than both' is the way he would come to phrase it when he finally published his views in 1881 (1881: vii). In the preface, he refers to his lectures in the summer term of 1834 when this view came to him.

of sources. The diachronic reshuffling of the biblical account meant that we now saw things as they really were. The Conquest sputtered and failed, Israel did not do what God demanded, and indeed the difficult demands of God were introduced after the fact to indicate the moral failure, rhetorically enhancing that by showing what happens when one does not do as God had commanded. This became a virtual Deuteronomic leitmotif and a good way to know when one was running into the D source outside of Deuteronomy: an etiology of the difficulties Israel would endure through failure to obey God is the D theme par excellence. Judges emerged then as the reality check on the ways things really were. Achan became the paradigmatic example of Israel's life lived under judgment. What God had commanded for Israel's good—the execution of *herem*—Israel had failed, with significant exceptions, to complete, and so the unhappy consequences of disobedience played themselves inexorably out.[13]

Roughly speaking, this much-later-than-the-events 'ideal account' of the conquest is held by scholars like Mason (1997: 69–75), Mayes (1979: 183), Weinfeld (1993), and Stern (1991: 99–121). Why does one produce an ideal account? It could be a way to explain why things turned out as they did; God commanded, Israel disobeyed and paid the penalty. Still, the language may be counter-intuitive. When it is used to indicate that *herem* was not carried out in reality, but represented an ideal, it is objected by other scholars that *herem* was indeed a cultural reality at the time in question, practiced widely throughout the ANE. So others mean that characterizing conquest in utopian terms was intended to discourage imitation by indicating it was an ancient practice and so trapped in past time, as it were. When one moves the diachronic landmarks and adjusts the canonical presentation the problems do not go away, precisely because it is difficult to comprehend the motivation of later authors and editors. By one account, the ideal portrayal serves to underscore Israel's disobedience, and that seems persuasive enough. On another account, the point was to show such a utopian and idealistic portrayal that all would conclude it was from some bygone time, and inimitable. Nevertheless, because the present form of the canonical portrayal insists that the command is God's, the etiological reading only moves the moral problem into a realm of historical reconstruction, geared to a speculative single audience intention. God's character in such a retrospective understanding remains God's character all the same.

A subset of this reading has been proposed by Braulik (1997). Exilic additions are argued to exist in Deuteronomy 6: 17–19 and 11: 22–5 and

---

[13] Martin Noth's extremely influential description of the Deuteronomic History and its thrust has been modified, but also retained in some form on this basic theological point.

these do not mention destruction of the Canaanites. Returning exiles (his proposed audience) would see that chapters which look ahead to a time after punishment, that is, return from exile, also fail to mention destruction of the Canaanites, and indeed see the Gibeonites included in the covenant (29: 1–30: 10). This reading requires a very subtle understanding of the intended audience, and while it does underscore features we should not miss in the canonical portrayal, it ignores the fact that canonical literature in its very nature resists this kind of clear temporal fixation.

It is a point worth stressing that chapters of the present Deuteronomy— leaving aside any historical critical reconstruction—do look ahead to Israel's punishment: the Law killed, to use the language of 'second-use'. To the degree it did not kill the Canaanites, it killed Israel. The final form of Deuteronomy does not leave us with the impression that what Israel failed to do, it must try harder and do again, when it returns from exile. That is a point worth emphasizing. Because the canonical presentation of Deuteronomy seeks a wider temporal frame of reference, it also tells us that it is written for ensuing generations. These generations are anticipated in their own right, and the vocation laid upon them is to learn from the lessons of disobedience, not to return to the starting point and imitate the vocation laid upon a generation now past. That is, the canonical form of Deuteronomy *handles the question of subsequent audiences in its own right*, and not simply as grist for historical-critical reconstructions of this.

Note how differently Deuteronomy deals with the vocation set before ensuing generations when it comes to the Decalogue. The rhetorical point is almost overstated: the Law was given, not to the old fathers, but to you, you here today, all of you (the generation that will enter the promised land). That Law is as much theirs as the first generation's, and more so: for the first generation died in the wilderness because of disobedience. The generation addressed now is in a new spot, and obedience is possible, and can be done. When we move to the final chapters of Deuteronomy, we see that the new generation failed as well, so the point is reasserted again. The Law is not too hard, it can be done, and indeed, provision for obedience is a special gift God intends on the other side of punishment. God has set down a law demanding obedience, and he has also understood that it must raise up as well as kill, for kill it will. How can the righteous provision of the Law remain what it is, as well as the character of God as righteous, and yet Israel be forgiven and granted new life? Deuteronomy in its final canonical form is about answering this question, and the same question sits over vast swaths of the Old Testament in its canonical presentation, including how God can be this God with the nations outside the covenant, 'slow to anger and of great compassion, yet by no means clearing the guilty'. We will need to return to this point later.

Thus far we have been trying to understand the rhetorical presentation of Canon and Conquest in its canonical form. We would be remiss to leave out mention of a further modern option for interpretation. This option can be tied up with more conservative estimates of the historicality of the narratives in question, and so a refusal to assign them to later sources. That is, the canonical portrayal of Deuteronomy and Joshua was not an idealized but a real account of affairs. God drove out the Canaanites because of the danger they represented to Israel as they came out of Egypt. The canonical perspective would recall the Canaanites as the sons of Ham, whose sexualized humiliation of Noah was recorded in Genesis 15. The worship practices of these Canaanites and their colleagues was tied up with sexualized accounts of the nature of God and the consequence of this—if prophets like Hosea are to be so interpreted—was a manipulation of sexuality, the rhythms of nature, and a gross distortion of what it means for God to be God, creator of male and female and not ontologically enclosed within a cultic re-enactment of that, invoked to ensure fertility. The worship practices of the Canaanites not only paid tribute to this understanding of the gods, but involved worshipers in such rites via imitation. But however one understands the history of religion dimension, the canonical presentation does not hide from this fact as a major index for why the Canaanites are to be so treated. The Canaanites and their religion would be a snare. They are described as haters of God. Israel would be commanded to live into God's decision to drive them out, and much of the idealized character of the actual practice of *herem* surely is intended to underscore that God is working his righteous will, rather than that a well-equipped and superior army is defeating foes as this happens in ways familiar to us. The exceptions (Rahab, Gibeonites) are reminders that the Lord compassionate and merciful is the Lord of all the earth, and so refuses to turn the nations into stereotyped non-Israelites.

The benefit of the conservative historical account is that the canonical portrayal is not dismantled. As we have seen, even reconstructions that argue the *herem* project is retrojected from a later context of concern really only defer the moral question of God's character. The canonical approach argues that later editors defer to the narrative form in which their secondary elaborations are made. On this understanding, even a later editor does not seek to address only a single audience at a specific point in time, but uses the full canonical form in its present shape so as to speak meaningfully about *herem*, God's character, and other matters. A sophisticated canonical reading is able to comprehend a wider range of theological penetration, in which several things may well be true at once. So the seriousness of the problem of Canaanite religion and practice is not erased. But the idea that a later editor sought to focus on Israel's disobedience, in ways that are familiar from the perspective of Deuteronomic theology, and so paid particular attention to the problems that would result in time by a failure to deal with false religion is also plausible. The plausibility of this view can be seen by attending to the wider canonical perspective. That is, the so-called Deuteronomistic redaction is itself an effort to understand the implications of disobedience as the march of history plays itself out under God's providence. Israel was finally sent into exile, and previous generations were lost in a vortex of disobedience, and one central reason for that was their involvement in religious practices that eroded a sense of God's character, his revealed will, so that what he had intended as a blessing became a curse. The canonical portrayal does not focus on a God with a happy face for Israel and a stern face for everyone else, but insists that idolatry is a form of death and that God desires life.

It is attention to the larger canonical portrayal that governed the perspective of the early Church interpreters. Reflexively they reacted to *herem* as a subset of God's holiness. They assumed an account of final causes that permitted them to speak of counsels secret to God alone, within which his dispensations of blessing and curse unfolded. They understood the episodes of punishment as these unfolded in Deuteronomy and Joshua to constitute real events in past time, though their understanding of them did not move to the level of imitation or simple identification with the mind of God. Again the complexity of the canonical portrayal likely guarded them from this reflex. Israel had been condemned and killed by the Law meant to give life, when all was said and done. So the moral lesson to be drawn was not that Holy War was something one ought to go out and do better, but rather that it served to expose the darkness in the human heart, whether in the form of false religion and idolatry, or in the form of a failure to live as God commanded and desired, and so to be brought before his character as the one who kills and brings alive, the lord compassionate and merciful, slow to anger and abounding in steadfast love, but who will by no means clear the guilty. Precisely in God's judgment of his own people would the knowledge of him be communicated to the nations. It is these larger canonical notes that prevented the Church Fathers from thinking that *herem* was something belonging to a bygone age when gods delivered eccentric commands, precisely because the heart of the New Testament's message was in accordance with the deep mystery of God's justice and mercy as revealed in the Old Testament and brought to climax in the Cross and Empty Tomb. It remains now to look more closely at the canonical portrayal to see how Jerome could speak of a Gospel Army and a Jesus at work at its head, thus resisting by instinct any effort to sentimentalize Jesus or his own special moral teaching in the manner of eighteenth- and nineteenth-century liberal Protestantism.

3. CANON AND CONQUEST: BROADENING
THE CANONICAL LENS

The larger narrative context within which accounts of *herem* occur is what is usually called the Deuteronomistic History. This narrative is comprised of the book of Deuteronomy (from the Pentateuch) and the Former Prophets, consisting of Joshua, Judges, First and Second Samuel, and First and Second Kings. We leave Ruth to the side for a moment. Martin Noth's explanation for the composition, collation, and final editing of this History we have already touched upon from a different angle. The History tells why Israel was sent into exile. Despite the warning of prophets to obey the Law, and in spite of the exemplary conduct of a few individual kings, to whom God had given promises of longstanding trust and commitment, Israel's disobedience finally led to the destruction of Jerusalem and the exiling of its population. Others argued for more ameliorating notes in the overall thrust of the History, and views of redactional supplements and additions are not without their proponents. But the basic theory has held. The separation of Deuteronomy from the History, to serve now as the final book of the foundational Pentateuch, has also been viewed as significant. The Law given at Sinai is for the generations yet to come; Moses is the first and foremost of a succession of prophets, who are referred to in the History and in the Prophetic books proper; and finally Deuteronomy serves to reflect on the failure of the past generation, and the anticipated failure and punishment of the generations to come, with a promise that God will forgive and that the Law's good force will remain forever.

Seen in this light, Joshua describes the model successor to Moses, and gives indication of successful and also unsuccessful efforts to live into God's promises, which include the destruction of the Canaanites as a threat to these promises. The opening chapters of Judges focus on the piecemeal and incomplete settlement of the tribes of Israel, 'after the death of Joshua'. Here we read a candid account that states what was not accomplished: 'Manasseh did not drive out ... Ephraim did not drive out ... Zebulon did not drive out ... Asher did not drive out ... Naphtali did not drive out.' Chapter 2 serves as a moralizing introduction to all that follows in this book, picking up on the effects of leaving gods of various kinds round about them through the failure to do what God had commanded. Now there is defeat in battle, plundering from the nations, and abandonment by God into the power of their enemies; 'they were in sore straits' (2: 15). God will not drive out nations now. He will send Judges, whose positive effects will be shown to be temporary and tragic.

The nations are left, then, as a test, and for the most part, Israel will fail that test. The book of Judges ends with a somber announcement. 'Now every man did what was right in his own eyes; there was no King in the land.' The vortex of sin and punishment is inescapable, and Israel is locked in its grip. 1 Samuel opens with the same notes of despair and desuetude. The priesthood is corrupt, judges cannot resolve the situation, kingship requires a different model than Israel or the nations know. Hannah sees into a hopeful future of restabilization, though the reason for that and the character of the resolution are locked in the mysterious counsels of God.

The book of Ruth has two locations in the canon, and in my view was intended to be a book whose logic could operate in both. In the Writings, Ruth follows Proverbs and provides a narrative account of the ideal wife, as described in Proverbs' last chapter. Boaz describes Ruth in exactly these terms. But the Writings are also works which can and do migrate in many Christian lists, because the Writings are a diverse collection and their internal organization is not critical to their interpretation in the same way as books in the Law and the Prophets. Placed inside the Deuteronomistic History, following Judges, Ruth shows the faithfulness of the non-Israelite, whose trust in the God of Israel does not just save her mother's property, but provides her and her mother both with children. The genealogy with which the book closes locates the courageous action of Ruth within the salvation history of Israel, and that history is traced back to another heroic non-Israelite, namely, Tamar the Canaanite, who before the descent into Egypt had preserved the line of Judah. Now in the midst of a vortex of judgment almost as severe as the exterminating opening chapters of Exodus, Ruth preserves the line again. The sojourner in the midst of Israel becomes the preserver of Israel's future life and hope, as the son born to her (and Naomi) becomes the great-grandfather of the King who will reverse for a season the dark period of disobedience. Ruth is not a Canaanite, but a Moabite. She is not a nation to be driven out, but as Israel is driven out in famine and in loss, Ruth the Moabitess returns with her mother-in-law and so becomes a blessing, she to Israel and Israel to her, in fulfillment of the promises spoken long ago to Abraham.

Herem must be considered within a long account of how God shows himself to be faithful to his promises, both with Israel and through them to the nations. An account of Deuteronomy and Joshua which is divorced from Judges and Ruth will only give us isolated verses, isolated episodes, and it will not do sufficient justice to the personal character of God, which must be seen over the course of time, through punishment, death, new life, and promised future. Obviously the Church Fathers did not read *herem* in the context of Lockean democratic concerns, but rather they saw it as comprehensible only from the standpoint of the character of God. But in turn, that character could not be grasped apart from a full account of God's life with Israel and the nations, and not one addressed to one episode only. There is no access to an account of God as 'loving' absent an account of his justice and holiness, and vice versa. This dialectic is absolutely central to the account of God in OT and NT and it cannot be spliced into segments, the one more persuasive than the other and so more salutary and capable of commending trust. Trust comes from an encounter with the Living God, who tears down and brings life both. If it is true that the fear of God is the beginning of wisdom, then such wisdom is as much a function of being grasped by God's holiness as it is weighing accounts of his activity and deciding for or against him. Should God belong to this latter frame of reference only, he would not be the biblical God. The scriptures of Israel therefore make no distinction between mercy and justice when it comes to fearing God. It belongs to God's character as God that mystery lies at the heart of mercy and his justice. With thee is forgiveness, therefore you are to be feared (Ps. 130: 4).

Consistent with this, it should be borne in mind that the authority of the Old Testament for the early Fathers was conveyed precisely through those texts that spoke of things like *herem*. For them it is primarily the life and death character of God's work in Israel that indicates the character of him as God alone. The concern of the early Church and the tradition was not with God's life as morally upright and so worthy of our attention or respect, for it was not possible to understand morality apart from God's revealed character and will. The greater concern was with acknowledging his identity, as over against false gods, and seeking better to live within a life given anew by him. That life and death character is experienced, from Israel's standpoint, in the promise to deliver from a situation of extermination, such as we see at the beginning of Exodus with the Pharaoh's murder of the Hebrew boys. But it immediately manifests itself within Israel as a threat, as much as a promise: a hand leprous and then whole, a night encounter to kill Moses, death of a generation in the wilderness. In such a context what might it mean to speak of God as morally good or morally deficient? God's character is experienced in acts of promise and fulfillment, but always set against a backdrop of moral seriousness of the highest order. The revelation of the name of God is a personal encounter with him as he shows himself to be, the Lord, the Lord, gracious and merciful. Moses is reassured when God promises life and relationship in the midst of death and broken fellowship (Exod. 32–4).

Perhaps unsurprisingly, it is in the context of a somber reassurance of God's presence in holiness and awe that the author of Exodus speaks what we might refer to in this volume as 'the morality of God', of God making his *goodness* pass by before Moses. 'I will make all my goodness pass before you' (Exod. 33: 19). The implication of this collocation is that goodness has a logic understood in the context of acknowledgement, within a scene of death and threatened relationship. One discovers one is dealing with 'I will be as I will be' and the only language for that in the OT is the language of God's *name.* So the verse continues, 'and [I] will proclaim to you my name the lord; and I will be gracious to whom I will be gracious, and will show mercy on whom I will show mercy' (Exod. 33: 19). As Exodus clarifies it, there can be no external appeal to 'the good' by which God can be measured, for goodness is a derivative of the revelation of God's character, manifested by his holy presence and holy irreducibility. Paul understands this on his side of affairs when struck blind, Peter when shown to be a traitor, Aaron when building a calf of gold, David when confronted with his abrogation of all that bound him to God.

Goodness is understood from within the context of a life lived in relationship, and not by an external grid, when the OT reflects on how goodness might be measured. It is the audacious reality of God's personal life in relationship that gives the early Fathers warrant for saying that the Old Testament is a scriptural witness to the living God unlike any they know or have known, and that is a conviction they bring to these scriptures having experienced the same reality in the light of the Cross and Empty Tomb. Origen speaks of the commands of God through Moses as unlike anything ever commanded to humanity and as such instantly transformative and a witness to his character as the true and only God. As the early Fathers strain to square statements like the one to follow in Exod. 33: 20, 'you cannot see my face', with those which say God was seen, the conclusion they draw is that the old covenant fathers saw the Logos itself and so saw God but did not see the Father, due to God's mercy and forbearance. From within this relationship of sight and a yet greater sight, one can begin to understand goodness and its death-like absence. That is a claim the Old Testament/Tanak lodges and for the early Fathers it is a claim consistent with what they have come to know of God in Christ, leaving them as the only confession: that the God of the Old Testament is the triune God, a matter as much for doxology as for intellectual assent. The depiction of God in the Conquest did not threaten that confession; rather, in the character of its fearsome seriousness, at a pivotal moment in God's life with a hard-hearted people, it established it.

Comments on 'Canon and Conquest'

Evan Fales

Christopher Seitz provides an extended reflection on the history of Christian interpretation and appropriation of the Hebrew Bible—or Tanak—from the early days of Christianity to recent scholars in the so-called canonical tradition associated with Brevard Childs. It's not always clear where Professor Seitz simply reports on the views of these thinkers, and where he endorses them. But he clearly does mean to endorse the thesis that estimation of the character of Yahweh requires an assessment of the portrayal given by the canon taken as a whole, with individual passages or episodes not to be read in isolation from that larger context. And he seems to endorse, perhaps as a matter of faith, the position that the god of the Bible is the 'triune God'—just, merciful, patient, loving, and determined, over the ages, to show His people the way to the light. Therefore those Tanakic (and NT) passages that seem to portray a different sort of Lord must be understood in recognition of the controlling constraint of divine goodness.

I must issue here a disclaimer. Professor Seitz's fields of expertise, Bible scholarship and theology, aren't my own; as behooves a novice in those areas, I'll try to exercise caution. Nevertheless, I will suggest interpretive possibilities that diverge from the apologetic mainstream.

Clearly, the traditions of the Tanak were indispensable to the formation of NT theology. Jewish millenarianism, forged in the crucible of the Babylonian captivity and re-ignited during Seleucid and then Roman occupation, forms the background for the early Christian movement's quest to understand its destiny.[1] But the Jewish traditions proved a mixed blessing, and debate over their status

---

[1] The Gospels can be read on an ideological (as opposed to psychological) level as *Bildungsromanen* which, in the person of Jesus, transform the category of tribal king ('Son of David') into that of imperial sovereign ('King of Kings'), a theme already anticipated in Isaiah but theoretically much more elaborated in the NT. Such a story, by its very nature, required rooting in the soil of tribal (here, Jewish) history and tradition, while bearing fruit in the wider atmosphere of the Roman imperium. That such ideas could be taken quite seriously is shown by Eusebius' allegorical depiction of Constantine as the *parousia*, a claim repeated by Constantine in his keynote address to the bishops at the Council of Nicea (see Eusebius, *Life of Constantine*, bk. III, § 15).

was fierce. Ultimately, some of the detractors, like Marcion, were branded heretics. Nevertheless, Seitz is concerned to show how the two-testament canon
reflects an ultimately unified understanding of God and His providence.

That's not an easy case to make. Much can be said, on grounds of interpretive
charity, for understanding a work, penned by a single author or even assembled
from different sources by one or a few redactors, as aiming to convey a
coherent, unified message. Perhaps something can be said for such unity also
when an ideologically unified group of editors assembles selected works into a
canon. But the more diverse the works, in terms of genre, provenance, and
dates of composition, and the more complex the history of canonization itself,
the more problematic assertions of unity become. The tortured history of
formation of Christian canon and creed is hardly what one would expect
from an omnipotent God working wisely and effectively to convey authoritative revelation,[2] but thoroughly consonant with provisional settling of humanly contentious social/political disputes.[3] On that score alone, we should expect
in the Christian Bible some continuity of major themes but hardly anything
like the expression of a single, consistent theology.

The unity thesis implies that the difficult passages of the Tanak, such as the
genocidal commandments, are somehow to be read against the overarching
biblical understanding that God is merciful and just. But what underwrites
that conclusion? How is it determined that the biblical God is merciful and
just? Certainly there are passages that say so; but then there are the rebarbative
passages. The presumption needs argument; and so far as I can tell, Seitz
doesn't offer one. It may be that Seitz accepts something like these three
premises, from which such an argument might be constructed, by way of a
claim of unity of inspiration: (1) the God of theism exists; (2) the authors of
the biblical books worshipped and were guided by such a God; and (3) God
insured that scripture, taken as a whole and correctly understood, correctly
portrays his character. I would deny every one of these premises.[4]

---

[2] See, e.g., Ehrman 2005, 2007; Davis 1987; McDonald 2005: e.g. 233–9.
[3] Indeed, it should not be too surprising a discovery that what initially seem to be highly
metaphysical disputes about theological matters—e.g., the doctrines of the incarnation and the
Trinity—are inextricably, almost indistinguishably, bound up with such political questions as
royal authority. On the development of political doctrines out of the doctrine of the incarnation
(and its own political antecedents), see Kantorowicz 1957; also Beskow 1962. More generally on
the political dimensions of first-century Judaisms and Christianities, see e.g. Wright 1992 and
Horsley 1997.
[4] Concerning denial of the second, which will perhaps raise the greatest skepticism, see Fales
1976, 1977. Perhaps Seitz (p. 306, above) means to be suggesting a different argument that
ascribes to God the virtue of promise-keeping: '*Herem* must be considered within a long
account of how God shows himself to be faithful to his promises...' But is God faithful?
I know of no biblical prophecy that passes the evidential criteria for fulfillment, and of a number

Unlike Seitz, I do not start from what appears to be a position of faith on the nature of the biblical God, but insist upon evaluating any claims on the basis of the textual evidence in front of my nose. Since what's at stake is matters of right and wrong, life and death, such adherence to the evidence is, for me, a duty. And the evidence suggests, as does the title of my own essay, that the moral character of Yahweh is chaotic. But if unity be insisted on, it is perfectly possible to stand Seitz's position on its head: taking the biblical portrait of God fundamentally to depict Him as malicious, capricious, partisan, and cruel, one might argue, we must not 'sentimentalize' our reading of the passages that apparently claim the contrary, but somehow bring them into line with a general understanding of divine misanthropy.

How is insisting upon divine goodness actually to be justified? In the first place—and quite ominously—Seitz claims that the stringency of divine justice is, if anything, even more severe in the NT than in the Tanak.[5] So Jerome

could speak of a Gospel Army and a Jesus at work at its head, thus resisting by instinct any effort to sentimentalize Jesus or his own special moral teaching in the manner of . . . liberal Protestantism.[6]

One wonders what the 'unsentimentalized' moral teachings are. Should we reject the Sermon on the Mount on the 'sentimentalized' (straightforward) reading, which expresses truly revolutionary ideals worthy of an original religious prophet?[7]

Beyond this ill-inspired effort to minimize textual disharmony, the strategy of the Church Fathers appears to have contained three elements. First, they 'instinctively' read the stories of *herem* in the Tanak as providing moral instruction relevant for all ages and for their age in particular: most especially, that disobeying God brings terrible consequences. Second, they took Israel's

---

that history appears to have falsified; e.g. Isa. 13: 19–22, 62: 8–9; Ezek. 26: 1–14; Matt. 12: 39–40, 16: 27–8.

[5] As Seitz (and others) note, '. . . the Christian Bible speaks of God preparing eternal damnation . . . of fates of judgment more severe than Sodom and Gomorrah . . . It includes more final, universal examples of the divine routing of evil forces . . . than the Conquest's more episodic account of *herem*' (Seitz, p. 294, above).

[6] Seitz, p. 304, above. There's admittedly an unsentimental Jesus: the one who snubs his adoring mother at least thrice (Matt. 12: 46–50, Luke 2: 41–50; John 2: 3–4), tells an eager proselyte to neglect his father's burial, and condemns untold enemies (Matt. 12: 30; Matt. 18: 8) to eternal hellfire.

[7] At the same time, a sober reading of the Sermon within its social/historical context removes some of its luster. We are to love our enemies, but (elsewhere) hate kith and kin. The 'enemies' of the day being Roman occupiers, perhaps pacifism was a counsel of temporary expediency only. Still, among the less edifying efforts of Christian apologetes are attempts to tone down the challenging moral demands of the Sermon.

failure properly to execute the *herem* to justify the miseries subsequently visited upon it,[8] but not a latter-day crusade to complete the job. Third, they bit the bullet: *herem* was, after all, a just fate for the Canaanites.

These three strategies are not mutually reinforcing. The first strategy, which reads into the texts an allegorical morality lesson concerning the need to destroy evil inclinations within our hearts, cannot serve as an escape from the moral difficulties *herem* poses once it's admitted that this command really was given to Israelite armies poised on the borders of Canaan. Furthermore, even if the Church didn't understand later generations to be under mandate to finish the job left uncompleted by Israel, what was to stop them from understanding themselves to be justified in undertaking similar campaigns? Indeed, nothing *did* stop them, time and again, when opportunities to mount crusades against pagan or infidel provided motive to appeal to Joshua as precedent.

Thus the real weight of ancient apologetic rests on the third strategy. So Augustine:

> One should not think it a horrible cruelty that Joshua did not leave anyone alive . . . [One who does think this] judges as perversely about the works of God as he does about the sins of human beings. Such people do not know what each person ought to suffer.

In short, 'such people' are blind to what the Canaanites—men, women, children, and animals—truly deserve. That strategy had legs: it appealed, also, to Luther (who turned it ironically against the Jews) and Calvin, and it continues to have strong appeal today. It is an apologetic that condemns itself.[9]

Nor should we suppose that Augustine reflects a moral sensibility that applied only to judgments about long-ago episodes in sacred texts. Augustine railed against, and sometimes preached violence against, ideological opponents: Donatists, Jews, and pagans.[10] Luther wrote an incendiary anti-Semitic

---

[8] This apologetic implies that because Israel failed fully to obey the criminal commands of a cruel God, it was itself cruelly punished. Can one be forgiven for failing to commiserate with Israel's self-flagellation over failure to consummate evil, and a self-absorption that sees greater tragedy in its own downfall than in that of the nations it had so zealously terrorized?

[9] Christian apologetes regularly take at face value the accusations of gross immorality hurled by the Tanak against Canaan to justify genocide, ignoring the obvious point that mortal enemies regularly demonize their opponents. That is not acceptable historiography. The hard evidence of Canaanite sexual immorality is extremely sketchy, near as I can tell; see e.g. Dever 2005: esp. ch. VII; Budin 2008; and Marsman 2003: 727–9. See Day 2001 for demonization of names of gods. Moreover, sin was a matter of violating the covenant with Yahweh; but Canaan had no such covenant, even biblically, beyond the Noachic covenant.

[10] See, e.g., St Augustine, *A Treatise Concerning the Correction of the Donatists*, ch. 6, §§ 21 and 22, and Hinson 1995: 170–3. In fairness, be it said that Augustine sometimes argued for moderation of state penalties against those he opposed.

tract. Calvin burned a unitarian heretic. Contemporary evangelicals are more likely than non-evangelicals to approve the torture of Muslim 'terrorists.'[11]

What, finally, of the suggestion that Judges (and similar passages in Deuteronomy and 1 Samuel) are ahistorical 'ideal' reflections upon the holiness of God and the necessity of obedience, composed some centuries after the purported events?

A parable:[12] Earl and his wife Marthy adopt and raise nine orphan children, training them in the art of beating up and robbing the vulnerable, and, ultimately, in how to kidnap and sell into slavery smaller children. When they bungle a job or demur, retribution is swift and severe. The sons of Tricia, the youngest, discover this story in a diary kept by Joby, the oldest. *What does the diary teach about the character of Grandpa Earl?* Suppose it emerges that the story is essentially false, the product of Joby's fertile imagination. Can the diary still convey an important moral—perhaps the lesson that obedience to Earl is a paramount duty?

The parable makes clear what lesson the book of Joshua teaches: that *if the story of Joshua is false, then its authors have a morally corrupt imagination and an untrustworthy understanding of God; if the story is in its essentials true, then God is neither to be trusted nor worshipped—let alone obeyed.*

Coda: It is one thing to stand apart from the people of the Book and to condemn Yahweh, its hero. It must be another to live within the love of God, consumed by its radiance, and at the same time to suffer the heart-wounds of the Tanakic terror-tales; to be plunged into a sea in which peace and chaos, pride and shame, spin in blinding embrace like dervishes. Lest we be stricken like Miriam, we atheists ought not to heap scorn upon our worshipful brethren, but turn toward them in amazement. Mysterious the ways of Abraham's God? Mysteriouser the hope that dwells in the heart of the darkest nights of faith.

---

[11] Pew Research Center survey; see http://pewforum.org/docs/?DocID=156.

[12] With earnest apologies to the memory of the real Earl Ramsey who (with his wife Marthy until her untimely death) raised nine good foster children back in Sodom Laurel, a mountain cove in North Carolina. Earl and Marthy were wonderful people and devout Christians.

Reply to Fales

Christopher Seitz

The response from Evan Fales was difficult to assess. For the purpose of this response I will only indicate some areas of confusion and for further discussion.

1. Fales does not address historical-critical work on the Conquest and its limitations, which was a major theme of my chapter (how do diachronic methods create a plausible account of the date of the narratives in question, but avoid the moral question by breaking up the canonical presentation?). At one point he attributed to me a view I rejected: that speaking of ideal accounts from Deuteronomy did not resolve the moral problem. I nowhere called the account of Judges ideal and indeed classified it as the account historical criticism called frank and un-ideal. Fales lumps Deuteronomy and Judges together in ways that confused my account. I am not sure he understood the argument.

2. I accept that Fales does not have any rule of faith (or unfaith) that would correlate the character of God as triune with a canonical portrayal in which mercy and severity are aspects of a single, coherent divine will. But the alternative is not to reject the social political tensions modern historical studies valorize, and that was not my point. Historical criticism has done a superb job showing tensions between Paul and Peter, Works and Grace, sacrifice and a broken heart, J and P, Matthew and John, and so forth; no one doubts any of this. The question is whether such tensions are unresolved in the nature of the case, and so cannot point to a meaningful dialectic, grounded in God's character; it is as much a rule of faith to declare this cannot be so as it is to claim that it can. What is at issue is the relationship between the history of religion (with its messy competitions and politics) and the canonical text's appraisal of the finality of that. Here one must assess the march of time and the maturation reflected in the canonical text, which has not erased the difficulties but sees them from a specific angle of view. The literature on this is extensive.

3. I find curious the idea that the Sermon on the Mount contains revolution-ary ideals apparently commendable in some form, and yet this is the sermon which explicitly warns against the relaxation of a single matter in the law (Matt. 5: 17–20); there must be more to the sermon than meets the eye when it comes to new morality. Fales apparently wanted to find something salutary in the NT, as an atheist—the moral standards of the sermon as a kind of natural law—before he moves ahead in parenthesis to acknowledge an unsentimental Jesus after all. This selectivity in reading is precisely what happens when matters of literary form and context are not sufficiently factored into interpretation.

4. Crusades clichés are just that! Joshua is not needed if one wants to mount a campaign and justify it; one can consult the annals of horrors and find all sorts and conditions of justification, theistic and atheistic. The point of my chapter was that imitating any biblical episode is to invoke the judgment of God, which in pure form levels all playing fields and exposes the distance between human motivation and God's character, for our good. Humility before God's grace and mercy is not 'self-flagellation', which is one of many rhetorical excesses in Fales's account, but is the humility governing the life of a Mother Teresa or a St Francis—neither of whom understood Conquest apart from the Cross of Jesus Christ.

5. The main argument of my chapter is that failure to attend to the canonical shaping of the Bible will lead to selecting individual sentences or episodes and then trying to assess whether they stand up to something called moral scrutiny. That is, the Bible presents its account of God in accordance with formal constraints and a two-testament totality. It does not give us state-ments about God that are bits of discrete raw material, needing secondary refining in a moral smelting furnace where the dross is identified. By its very form, the canon assists in making sense of how serial statements about God's life in relationship to Israel are to cohere. It anticipates the questions of morality by providing a narrative form from which to assess them in accordance with that form. To read a part requires reading the whole. This is not an argument requiring a major apparatus from the history of religion to gain conviction, nor even a 'faith commitment'. That is, it does not derive from a thick account of how the canon came into being, what forces shaped it, what political concerns might have been at work. It is a low-flying observation, in this chapter grounded as much in general hermeneutics (how do texts deliver their larger intention) as in an account of the canon's formation (which is possible to construct, but which lies outside the assignment). See my recent book, *The Goodly Fellowship of the Prophets*, which speaks of the 'achievement of association' in the Old

Testament's early canonical development. That achievement can be grasped no matter what account of the political forces were that saw to its emergence, in time.

I do find his final statement moving and even profound in its own way, so it was worth moving through his response to get to that. My general sense of the chapters in this volume was that the ongoing discussion of the 'morality of God' was frequently happening without any clear picture of what was provoking the question to begin with, though for a volume in which many of the authors were philosophers, I was surprised at the level of emotion. Anyone can pick up a text of any kind and read it and register strong reaction. It does not take an 'expert' account of interpretation to insist that texts need careful attention to form and context, and also that they exist in relationship to a community whose habits must be formed by these same texts in order for their sense *to make sense*. There is very little evidence that Judaism was particularly slave-holding, child-sacrificing, genocidal, patriarchal, blood-thirsty, and violent, over against other nations. Somehow they read the Tanak, as did Christians the Old Testament, in such a way that God was not seen as either the human projection of such things, nor as commending them for successive generations, all the while drawing from them for an account of the spiritual life now to be lived under that same God. I have tried to explain in a short essay how this might be so.

REFERENCES

Beskow, Per. 1962. *Rex Gloriae: The Kingship of Christ in the Early Church*, trans. Eric Sharp. Stockholm: Almqvist & Wiksell.

Braulik, Georg. 1997. 'Die Völkervernichtung und die Rückkehr Israels ins Verheißungsland: Hermeneutische Bemerkungen zum Buch Deuteronomium', in M. Vervenne and J. Lust (eds.), *Deuteronomy and Deuteronomic Literature: Festschrift C. H. W. Brekelmans*. Leuven: Leuven University Press.

Bray, Gerald. 2003. 'The Church Fathers and Biblical Theology', in Craig G. Bartholomew (ed.), *Out of Egypt: Biblical Theology and Interpretation*. Grand Rapids, Mich.: Zondervan, 23–40.

Budin, Stephanie. 2008. *The Myth of Sacred Prostitution in Antiquity*. Cambridge: Cambridge University Press.

Campenhausen, Hans von. 1962. *The Formation of the Christian Bible*. Philadelphia: Westminster.

Childs, B. S. 1970. 'The God of Israel and the Church', in *Biblical Theology in Crisis*. Philadelphia: Westminster, 201–19.

Congar, Yves. 1966. *Tradition and Traditions*. London: Burns and Oates.

Davis, Leo Donald, SJ. 1987. *The First Seven Ecumenical Councils (325–787): Their History and Theology*. Wilmington, Del.: Michael Glazier.

Dever, William. 2005. *Did God Have a Wife?* Grand Rapids, Mich.: William B. Eerdmans.

Ehrman, Bart. 2005. *Lost Christianities: The Battles for Scriptures and Faiths We Never Knew*. New York: Oxford University Press.

—— 2007. *Misquoting Jesus: The Story Behind Who Changed the Bible, and Why*. New York: HarperOne.

Fales, Evan. 1976. 'Truth, Tradition, and Rationality', *Philosophy of the Social Sciences*, June: 97–113.

—— 1977. 'The Ontology of Social Roles', *Philosophy of the Social Sciences*, June: 139–61.

Helmer, Christine. 2002. 'Luther's Trinitarian Hermeneutic and the Old Testament', *Modern Theology*, 18: 49–73.

Hinson, E. Glenn. 1995. *The Church Triumphant*. Macon, Ga.: Mercer University Press.

Horsley, Richard A. (ed.). 1997. *Paul and Empire: Religion and Power in Roman Imperial Society*. Harrisburg, Pa.: Trinity Press International.

Kantorowicz, Ernst. 1957. *The King's Two Bodies: A Study in Medieval Political Theology*. Princeton, NJ: Princeton University Press.

McDonald, Lee. 2005. *The Formation of the Christian Canon*, 2nd edn. Peabody, Mass.: Hendrickson.

Marsman, Hennie. 2003. *Women in Ugarit and Israel*. Boston: Brill.

Mason, Rex. 1997. *Propaganda and Subversion in the Old Testament*. London: SPCK.

Mayes, Andrew D. H. 1979. *Deuteronomy*. London: Marshall, Morgan & Scott.

Oehler, Gustav Friedrich. 1883. *Theology of the Old Testament*, trans. G. E. Day. New York: Funk & Wagnalls.

Reuss, Eduard. 1881. *Die Geschichte der Heiligen Schriften Alten Testaments*. Braunsch-weig: C. A. Schwetschke.

Rowe, C. Kavin. 2002. 'Biblical Pressure and Trinitarian Hermeneutics', *Pro Ecclesia*, 11: 295–312.

Seitz, Christopher. 1996. 'Old Testament or Hebrew Bible? Some Theological Con-siderations', *Pro Ecclesia*, 5: 292–303.

—— 1997. 'On Not Changing Old Testament to Hebrew Bible', *Pro Ecclesia*, 6: 136–40.

—— 1998. 'In Accordance with the Scriptures', in *Word Without End*. Grand Rapids, Mich.: Eerdmans.

—— 2008. 'Accordance: The Scriptures of Israel as Eyewitness', *Nova et Vetera*, 6: 513–22.

Soulen, R. Kendall. 1999. 'YHWH the Triune God', *Modern Theology*, 15: 25–54.

Stern, Philip D. 1991. *The Biblical Herem: A Window on Israel's Religious Experience*. Atlanta: Scholars Press.

Weinfeld, Moshe. 1993. 'The Ban on the Canaanites in the Biblical Codes', in André Lemaire and Benedikt Otzen (eds.), *History and Traditions of Early Israel: Studies Presented to Eduard Nielsen May 8th 1993*. VT Supplement 50. New York: E. J. Brill.

Wellhausen, Julius. 1957. *Prolegomena to the History of Ancient Israel*, trans. J. S. Black and A. Menzies. Cleveland: World Publishing. 1st edn. 1878.

Wright, N. T. 1992. *The New Testament and the People of God*. Minneapolis: Fortress Press.

Yeago, D. 1993. 'The New Testament and the Nicene Dogma: A Contribution to the Recovery of Theological Exegesis', *Pro Ecclesia*, 3: 152–64.

Part IV

Concluding Remarks

Part A

Concluding Remarks

11

God's Struggles

Howard Wettstein

I am Y-H-V-H and there is none else;
I form light and create darkness,
Peace is my doing, and I create evil
I, Y-H-V-H do all these things.

(Isa. 45: 7)[1]

A person should always stand in awe of Heaven, in private as well as in public, and admit the truth, and seek the truth in his heart.

(Jewish morning prayer)

Public discussion of [religion] lurches uncomfortably between overconfident denial ('God' certainly does not exist, and anyway it's all His fault) and blind allegiance.

(Judt 2009)

The power of our religious traditions is a function, at least in part, of the edifying, morally elevating texts so central to them. Being ancient, however, these texts inevitably reflect—sometimes in shocking ways—the cultural settings from which they emerge. God, for example, is said in Tanak to command, or at least to allow, slavery, genocide, rape, and other assorted

---

This chapter derives from 'Concluding Remarks' I gave at the University of Notre Dame conference, 'My Ways Are Not Your Ways: The Character of the God of the Hebrew Bible'. I'm told by friendly critics that the written version does not quite capture the oral presentation, available at http://www.youtube.com/playlist?list=PLD28FAFBBD4463095.

[1] I use the transliterated letters of the Tetragrammaton name since the usual 'The Lord' obscures the fact that the term is a proper name (unvocalized); 'The Lord' and a proper name also differ dramatically with respect to distance and formality.

It is important to note that it is difficult to be precise in the translation of the crucial and final word of the penultimate line of the quotation from Isaiah, like other key words at focal points in Tanak. The word is used in many nuanced ways in Tanak (all designating something in the vicinity of evil). See CARM.org, for the reading 'calamity', as in natural evil.

horrors. Critics of religion often seize on these things, paying scant attention to the edifying and elevating; Defenders do the opposite.

The power of the ancient texts is not that of straightforward articulation, the way of many philosophical texts. Rather, their meanings are displayed by way of poetically infused narrative, and dramatic and mythological tropes. As with mythology, one does not want to put the stories through the wringer of the categorical imperative. Better to struggle with the dark side of God's world than to reject such ancient gifts.

How might one even begin to come to terms with divinely mandated moral horror? Given our reverence for these texts there are temptations here, most notably a tendency to minimize the moral awfulness or explain it away. At the Notre Dame Conference on the Hebrew Bible, as in the history of theology, there were many such defenses. Some seemed at the extreme: God, it was said, having granted the gift of life, a temporary gift, can justifiably withdraw it at will. There is, it would follow and it was urged, no issue at all about the death of good people. Being with God in heaven is, for all we know, a superior situation than life on earth, so that even the killing of babies, when divinely mandated, may not represent a morally significant problem. At lesser extremes were variations on familiar modes of theodicy.

Needless to say, and worth saying, not all the contributions by religiously committed contributors were along such lines. But those that were dominated, or so it seemed. Moreover, one had a sense that the Critics and many Defenders of traditional religion agreed on the general idea that some such defense is what traditional religion implicates. For the Critics such defenses provide ample reason for skepticism about the whole enterprise.

My aim here is to provide a very different sense of traditional religion, one that agrees with the Critics on the utter unacceptability of such defenses. The quotation from Isaiah at the head of this chapter speaks of a dark side to God's world; a part and parcel of creation, no mere surface appearance. This is less than a happy thought—to all of us, religiously committed or not. But it has the ring of truth.

Peter Van Inwagen points out[2] that Tanak is more like a library than a work, indeed one whose ethical ideas are under development, one that represents no single doctrine on many key notions. And this applies to my Isaiah-inspired view of evil and its place in creation. Such is clearly not the only attitude towards evil in Tanak, but it is one to which I want to focus attention.

---

[2] In his talk at the conference. See his chapter in this volume.

Our problem, though, is not just the dark side of creation, natural evil for example. It's difficult to read the text naively—a good thing in my view[3]—and not come away with a sense of a dark side to God. In the cases of *Amalek* and the *Akedah*, had we not seen such texts we likely would have denied their possibility. For God asks of us what is not only immoral, but a violation of something at the heart of what God presumably stands for, killing children for example.

Indeed, in the case of the *Akedah*—even more horrendous—God commands Abraham not only to violate a moral norm, one that resides close to Abraham's core. God commands Abraham to kill his child, his only child, his beloved child. If asked to do this, the last thing one (other than maybe Kant . . .) would naturally think about is the moral violation. (It helps here to have had children of one's own.) 'But it's my boy!,' we can imagine him screaming, to himself if not to God. Indeed the very language of the command seems to rub it in, to put it, so to speak, right in Abraham's face.

My emphasis here will be on the *Akedah* and also on the strange story of Job. These stories represent God's treatment not of His (or Israel's) enemies, but rather of His beloved, and so they have a special sting. God considers Abraham one with whom He is intimate,[4] and yet asks of him the unspeakable. God mandates the death of Job's children as an Accuser-inspired[5] test of this person whom God judges to be the most righteous on earth. Why is this not moral monstrosity?

Such a question, admittedly on the edge of blasphemy, seems a religious imperative. Let me selectively choose several biblical texts in support of this idea. I'll return below to my selectivity.

In Genesis 18, only a few chapters before the *Akedah*, God approaches Abraham with His plan to destroy Sodom and Gomorrah. Imagine Abraham's reaction; an intimidating situation, even terrifying, not to speak of confusing. For many of us, standing up to social pressure is difficult enough; standing up to God is unimaginable. And yet Abraham challenges God in the strongest moral terms. 'Heaven forbid that the judge of all the earth would punish the good along with the wicked.' Nor, as God begins to back down, does Abraham hesitate to repeat and renew the challenge.

---

[3] Such naive readings may not prove tenable in the end. And a religious tradition, almost like the courts in our legal tradition, may provide another reading of what, as it were, the constitution meant. But it is important to pay significant attention to what the text *seems* to say, to stay with the naive reading for a while.

[4] See Gen. 18: 19, where God refers to Abraham as (translating literally) one He has known, or perhaps one He has singled out. The verb, *la'daat*, suggests intimacy in biblical Hebrew.

[5] The Hebrew 'Satan' is, in context, not the fallen angel of the Christian tradition, but a kind of heavenly accuser, a heavenly investigator/prosecuting attorney, so to speak.

Perhaps God approaches Abraham in this way to allow Abraham to do just what he does. Perhaps this is part of Abraham's moral training. Nevertheless, Abraham's lack of care for his own safety, for his life after all, his being nothing less than appalled at God and unable to keep quiet about it, these things are no doubt part of why he is so revered by the tradition. And if one can say it, perhaps this is part of why he is revered by God, honored with intimacy.

At the end of the book of Job, God rebukes Job's ironically named 'Comforters'. They appropriately begin their visit with the bereft Job, sitting silently with him for a full week in the manner of Jewish mourning practices. Silence is difficult to sustain, however, and when the conversation begins, it quickly degenerates. They criticize Job in the manner of conventional religious thinking, ways that are all too familiar. God is just; so Job must be deserving of what's befallen him. He should repent and beg for God's understanding and forgiveness, and the like. We, the readers, know better, having been apprised at the beginning of the book of Job's innocence. What happens does so as a result of a challenge to God from 'the Accuser', a representation according to C. G. Jung of God's insecurity about Job's love. Jung's suggestion is irreverent, but hardly out of line with the text.

God eventually rebukes the Comforters; they, unlike Job, failed to tell the truth about God. This, I want to suggest, is an ethical moment of inestimable importance. God appears to be saying that the usual pietisms are false and objectionable, that Job's pre-Whirlwind near blasphemous remarks about God's injustice were well taken.

In selecting the passages from Genesis and Job I am, admittedly, being selective. Religious texts and even more so the larger traditions that house them allow for multiple moral emphases. One could as well pick texts that support a point of view very distant from my own. But this very fact also works against the Defenders, for whom God's authority can justify what looks to us morally horrendous. For it suggests that religious traditions of the sort known to us are too inclusive to provide a definitive foundation for the ethical life. One can cite too many contrary verses; one can cite widely divergent religious authorities. In the end, one is left with one's ethical good sense.

This is not to deny that one's religious tradition may help to form and develop one's ethical stance and character. There are multiple and exceedingly rich connections between religion and the ethical life. In selecting these passages about Abraham and Job, I bring to bear my own substantive ethical views. But those views have in part been formed, enhanced, developed by my contact with those and similar passages as well as by contact with religious models of the ethical life.

The religious perspective I have begun to sketch—it is here that I take issue with the sense apparently shared by the Critics and Defenders—reflects my own Jewish sensibility. This is hardly to suggest that there is a single Jewish view on these matters. Nor is it to suggest something uniquely Jewish. Better still if there are resonances in other traditions. But there is a distinctive flavor perhaps especially to the three passages I am about to explore.

To begin with a passage from the Babylonian Talmud, Tractate *B'rachot* (Blessings),[6] Rabbi Yochanan mentions God's prayer. The interlocutor—as shocked as you or I might be at such mention—immediately poses the question, 'And what does God pray?' He prays, we are told, that when His children are at issue, His attribute of mercy/nurture overwhelms His anger and His other attributes—presumably His desire for strict justice. But this is to suggest that it is no trivial matter even for God to subdue His anger, to allow His love to vanquish His demand for justice. In short, God struggles. This is an idea that is difficult to incorporate into the picture of religion shared by Critics and Defenders.

I move now to the book of Hosea, astounding in many respects. Its hyper-anthropomorphic talk of God would be blasphemous if not itself found in the holy text. The book begins with God telling the prophet to marry a whore. The idea appears to be—and this is of a piece with the tone of much of the book—that only in the context of such a marriage can the prophet understand what it is like for God to be wed, as it were, to the people Israel.

God, as reported by the prophet, seems to jump between extreme moods, at one moment longing powerfully and painfully for His beloved people; at another furious with her and promising to punish or destroy her and her lovers, the foreign gods.

At one moment (2: 16):

> Assuredly,
> I will speak coaxingly to her,
> And lead her through the wilderness,
> And speak to her tenderly,
> (2: 17) I will give her vineyards . . .

At another (2: 4):

> Rebuke your mother, rebuke her—
> For she is not My wife
> And I am not her husband—
> And let her put away her harlotry from between her breasts.
> (2.5) Else I will strip her naked
> And leave her as on the day she was born:
> Render her like desert land,
> And let her die of thirst.

---

[6] Folio 7a. The translation—really paraphrase—is my own but follows the text quite closely.

In the 1948 Academy Award winning film *The Best Years of our Lives,* a daughter who is suffering through a difficult relationship cries to her parents about the contrast between her own relationship and that of her parents. She remarks that her parents have always had one another; their intimacy was a constant source of untroubled support, this as opposed to her own situation. Her mother looks at her father, turns to her, and replies, 'If you only knew how many times we had to fall in love again.' The comment applies well to the intimacy between God and His people as depicted in Tanak and as understood and experienced in Jewish tradition.

Such is quite a different conception of loving and being loved by God than our usual one: grace on the part of God and adoration of perfection on our side. This is not to say that on the suggestion I am developing God's love for Israel and Israel's for God are one and the same. But the Bible's model moves us closer to a human love relationship. In neither direction does this sort of love presuppose that its object is perfect. God as depicted in Tanak is not the perfect being of later tradition. Even before we get to serious moral problems with God, He is spoken of as changing His mind, as angry and resentful, even petty at times, and subject to flattery, and the rest.

It is striking that the Song of Songs (or of Solomon), with its depiction of erotic love, was canonized and used by the religious traditions to model the relationship between God and the people Israel, or God and the Church, etc. We should, I think, not pass over the eroticism too quickly.[7] What does it mean to model— even as one model among others—the relationship between persons and God in this way? Seemingly important is the central role of our longing for intimacy with God, someone with whom we share our deepest longings, pains, and joys. There is also the suggestion of a certain longing on the part of God, for intimacy with His people, for sharing their love in the context of a transformed world.

I turn now to my final passage, from the rabbinic commentary *Midrash Rabbah* on the book of Lamentations, an attempt by the rabbis of the Talmud to bring Lamentations to bear on the destruction of the second Temple, their latest and by far greatest tragedy. (Lamentations itself was written some 650 years earlier, in connection with the destruction of the first Temple in 587 BCE.)

The aspects of divinity a literature emphasizes reflect salient features of the community's experience. Subject a community to great trial or triumph and its way of thinking about God may well alter or enlarge. The Temple's destruction accompanied by the prospect of an unending exile certainly qualifies as such a great trial. And the *Midrash* on Lamentations evidences an important theological development, an altered—but of course not histori-

---

[7] In my own tradition, it is often passed over instantaneously, as if (some actually make this suggestion) the erotic imagery was a mere superficial appearance, not deserving of focus.

cally discontinuous—perspective on God. God is, one might say, super-anthropomorphized.

Anthropomorphic depiction was of course characteristic of the Hebrew Bible.[8] Early in Genesis, for example, God is angry at our antics, even regretful that He initiated the human experiment. But these were the emotions of a being that was—despite the anthropomorphism—somehow wholly other, the awesome Creator of the universe in whose hands was its destruction, a somewhat remote purveyor of rage, passion, justice, and the rest.

It has been said that the biblical narrative is the history of God's learning that He cannot do it alone, that His plan crucially requires partnership with His human reflections. By the time of the *Midrash* on Lamentations, and in the perception of its authors, the lesson is well learned. Not only cannot he do it alone, the project is not going well.[9] And God's reaction reveals a new level of affective engagement and self-awareness. He suffers, weeps, even mourns. 'Woe is Me!' he cries in Proem 24, 'What have I done?'

Sometimes the *Midrash* sees God in maternal terms—or, more accurately, God, as the *Midrash* has it, sees him-/herself in such terms (Proem 22):

'Just as when you take away its young a sparrow is left solitary,' so spake the Holy One, blessed be He, 'I burnt my house, destroyed My city, exiled My children among the nations of the world, and I sit solitary.'

Sometimes the imagery is paternal: God is compared with a king who, enraged at his two sons, thrashes them and drives them away. The king afterward exclaims, 'The fault is with me, since I must have brought them up badly' (Proem 2). Indeed, not only does God mourn, God, it would seem, needs instruction in mourning from us.

The Holy one, blessed be He, said to Jeremiah, 'I am now like a man who had an only son, for whom he prepared a marriage canopy, but he dies under it. Feelest thou no anguish for Me and My children? Go summon Abraham, Isaac, and Jacob, and Moses from their sepulchres, for they know how to weep.' [10]

One aspect of this humanizing of the divine image, interestingly parallel to (roughly simultaneous) Christian developments,[11] is a new emphasis on

---

[8] See Wettstein 1997 for an exploration of the contrast between, on one hand, biblical and rabbinic anthropomorphic characterization, and, on the other, the anti-anthropomorphism of Greek philosophy-inspired medieval theology.

[9] This is to some extent true of the prophetic literature more generally. What is new here is a matter of degree and sustained emphasis.

[10] Proem 24. For more detail see my paper from which this discussion of the *midrash* is adapted, Wettstein 2002. For a more complete treatment see Mintz 1996.

[11] A key difference of course is that in Jewish thought, there is no suggestion of God becoming—or having an aspect that is—human in some more serious or literal sense.

divine vulnerability. God is, as it were, exposed to the elements to a degree scarcely predictable by what we knew of Him.

Closely related is what we might call divine approachability. God, in Genesis, is available to the patriarchs, and to some extent to the matriarchs. But the *Midrash* on Lamentations (in the continuation of Proem 24) imagines the three patriarchs—Abraham, Isaac, and Jacob—and Moses pleading with God for mercy. God, however, is unaffected; He cannot or will not comply. Eventually, He does promise to restore Israel to its place, but the promise is made not to the patriarchs or Moses. It is only mother Rachel who can move him. Rachel tells God that she knew of her father's plan to substitute Leah for her in marriage to Jacob. She attempted to foil the plan, but when that failed

I relented, suppressed my desire, and had pity upon my sister that she should not be exposed to shame . . . I delivered over to my sister all the signs which I had arranged with Jacob so that he should think that she was Rachel. More than that, I went beneath the bed upon which he lay with my sister; and when he spoke to her she remained silent and I made all the replies in order that he should not recognize my sister's voice. I did her a kindness, was not jealous of her, and did not expose her to shame. And if I, a creature of flesh and blood, formed of dust and ashes, was not envious of my rival and did not expose her to shame and contempt, why should You, a King who lives eternally and is merciful, be jealous of idolatry in which there is not reality, and exile my children and let them be slain by the sword . . .'

Forthwith, the mercy of the Holy One, blessed be He, was stirred, and He said, 'For your sake, Rachel, I will restore Israel to its place.'

It is interesting that Rachel does not argue on the grounds of justice. Nor does she appeal on the basis of her own merit, as do the patriarchs, Abraham, Isaac, and Jacob (earlier in Proem 24). Her appeal is more personal, predicated on issues of character.

My aim in this chapter is not to answer the central questions of this volume. I don't know how to do that, although I'll say a bit by way of speculation below. Instead I've attempted to alter our perspective in a way that puts those questions in a different light.

I want to return now to the *Akedah* and Job specifically to note some features common to both stories. These stories have a kind of resonance that defies time. We somehow feel that things haven't changed that much. Of course God does not ask us to sacrifice our children. But we, like Abraham, are put in situations that test us, or test our souls, situations— writ large and often small—in which we have to choose between incompatible but truly non-negotiable values. And while the mythological sounding text attributes Job's losses to God's wager with the Accuser, the fact is that awful things happen to people without apparent reason, often pretty obviously undeserved. And so we can feel and share Job's hurt and his eventual outrage. 'These things really happen,' the texts seem to speak to us; the sense that the universe treats us as if by a whim is familiar.

So there is a kind of truth, or universality, to these stories, right at the outset. I see a certain truth as well in the human heroes' responses. I use 'truth' here in a way that I don't have entirely under control. Perhaps it would be more cautious to say that both Abraham and Job, as I read the stories, are moral heroes; they exemplify ethical virtues of the first importance. And in the case of Job, God's revelation to him from the Whirlwind—I'll discuss it below—is at once a revelation to us, another measure of the truth I see in these stories.

My reading, though, is certainly controversial; to take the case of Abraham, some see mere obedience—ethically deficient—where I see ethical/spiritual valor. Job is often praised for his patience, actually rather short lived, and not the integrity, even spiritual stubbornness, which I will emphasize. What follows is a quick sketch of my readings of those texts.

Abraham, I want to propose, does *not* decide to obey God; not that he decides against it. Nor is this indecision. Abraham holds in his hands two incompatible non-negotiable loves, two non-negotiable commitments—commitments do not go any deeper than these—towards God and towards his son. Nor does Abraham, I'm imagining, have any conception of what it would mean to prioritize such commitments. The idea of making such a choice boggles the mind. There is almost something obscene about it.

The text, strikingly spare, invites us to imagine Abraham's reaction. How could he not have been feeling alone in the universe? It must have been a long and lonely night. As I imagine his response the next morning—all one can do is dwell in the language, letting it seep in—what he does is to proceed, to march resolutely ahead, his eyes fixed, together (the Hebrew *yachdav,* repeated several times, suggests intimate togetherness) with his beloved son.

Abraham's transcendent faith is exhibited in his ability to so march forward, not knowing where the path will lead, but ready to follow it, with confidence that he will know what to do when he has to.[12] To withstand any such an experience must be transformative. And *sometimes*, as the text perhaps suggests, one comes out the other end having survived that ordeal, loves intact, having grown in ways otherwise unavailable. I hope it is clear that I mean this as a comment on Abraham, and hardly a justification of God's command. If I am even roughly on track, there is universal significance here.

---

[12] I see this sort of faith as an important, if rare, human virtue. Attendant to it is the ability not to look too far ahead, not to anticipate the moment of decision.

Turning to Job, let's distinguish the core of the story from the very strange beginning—God and the Accuser—and the equally strange end—when Job is restored, a new family, riches, and the rest. The core is a classic tale: someone having had everything loses it all, hits bottom, finds God, and through God finds peace.

The peace Job finds seems in part a consequence of his spiritual straight-forwardness, his own deep commitments. In his stubborn responses to the Comforters, it is as if he were speaking about a love relationship and said things like, 'I don't understand. My love for her was boundless. She under-stood all that, and she clearly reciprocated. Until today. I am lost.'

When Job hits bottom—sitting on a pile of ashes, scratching his lesions with potsherd—God appears and Job is, as it were, taken on a strange journey to a new perception of reality. God, hardly in a soft and comforting mode or mood, somewhat strangely becomes a poet and equally strangely shares with Job the view from above, the view *sub specie aeternitatis*, God's own sense of his achievement. The vision—not to speak of the experience of God—is overwhelming. It inspires awe, and a strange comfort, the latter a consequence of seeing in a new perspective his own pain and the lack of justice in the world. He gets philosophical, one might say.[13]

Whatever one does with the thorny business of God's role in these 'tests', there is genuine moral and religious power in these stories. From my own perspective it would be a real loss to overlook that power in favor of an exclusive focus on what is so genuinely difficult—even appalling—God's moral role in subjecting his beloved to such tests, a topic to which I now turn.

The conception of love between people and God that I sketched above finds resonance in these two stories. Prayer experience is at its best an experience of intimacy, of sharing one's longings, pains, joys, and the rest. It is, however, a strange intimacy for our experience of the Other is through a glass darkly. There is here a religious idea—I mean one that derives not from philosophic reflection but (in my own tradition) from Tanak and Talmudic literature—that in thinking about or trying to understand God one is over one's head. Intimacy with God tends toward the *sui generis*.[14]

As I read these texts, neither Job nor Abraham knows quite what to make of God. In the case of Job this is easier to see; by the end of the Whirlwind he is overwhelmed, chastened by his lack of understanding how it all works. The text

---

[13] See Wettstein 1999, also on my website.

[14] I say 'tends towards the *sui generis*' since it may be that the phenomenon I'm discussing has a reflection in the sense of imperfect connection even with those people with whom we are most intimate. The topic deserves real scrutiny; the eroticism of the Song of Songs seems relevant here.

emphasizes no such thing in the case of Abraham. But his notorious silence in response to God's command to kill Isaac signals that he knows that this is not the time to argue with God. He knows that God knows that he, Abraham, will not understand; Abraham senses that what is appropriate here—as opposed to the case of Sodom and Gomorrah—is to follow the path and see where it leads. And reflecting more generally on the matter of understanding God's ways, we should not forget that Moses—closest of all to God according to the Bible—is sharply rejected in his request to see God's face.[15]

There is a folk fable, perhaps a piece of actual history, concerning the inmates at the Auschwitz concentration camp. As the story goes, they put God on trial for crimes against humanity and against his chosen people. The jury deliberates; God is found guilty. And then the group proceeds to its afternoon prayers. A focus on this story pays dividends for understanding the religious perspective I'm trying to elucidate.

A student of mine suggested recently that one would need some doctrinal understanding in order to pray responsibly. 'One needs to know to whom one is praying,' as she put it. My response was that religious experience may be otherwise. One prays; one achieves (sometimes) a sense of intimate contact. But exactly who or what 'stands on the other end' is another question, a matter well beyond us.

Religion, suggests William James, is in the end a matter of the gut rather than of the head. In this spirit, I want to suggest that religion's natural bedfellows are more the arts than the sciences. Religion, wrote Santayana, pursues wisdom through the imagination. It is productive not of a system of the world, a sort of super-physics or metaphysics, but of a way—a literature and set of related practices—to ennoble human life, to give meaning to and make meaning of our deepest hopes, fears, longings, and dreams.

A SPECULATIVE APPENDIX

Anthropomorphism is deeply entrenched in biblical literature, in the Talmud, not to speak of our religious lives. The rabbinic attitude to anthropomorphism, unlike that of the later philosophers, was dual: on one hand, we experience God in these anthropomorphically describable ways; at the same time, we experience Him as beyond all that. Such 'inconsistency', characteristic

---

[15] There is a tradition in Jewish commentary that Moses was asking to understand the problem of evil—the apparent lack of justice in God's world.

of the sort of literary theology we find in the Bible and Talmud, is disastrous if one wants a coherent theoretical theology.

But whatever one does with the thorny problem of biblical anthropomorphism, it is there and very prominent. God so presents himself, and not always in the best light. Indeed, it is striking how little the Bible seems interested in creating or protecting the image of a perfect being. It is especially striking by comparison with the works of philosophers and theologians.

What then, allowing ourselves speculation, might we make of God's treatment of Job and Abraham? One is inclined to smile at Jung's suggestion that the 'Satan', the Accuser in Job, represents God's insecurity about Job's love. At the same time, Israeli religious thinker David Hartman advances a related idea concerning language of Deuteronomy when God is speaking to the Israelites about their forthcoming entrance into the promised land. God, says Hartman, sounds a bit like a parent of a teenager about to leave for college. 'We were together from the time of the exodus,' God seems to be saying. 'I was with you, led the way, protected you. Will you remember Me—will you still love Me—when you are in your own land, not dependent upon Me for sustenance and protection?'

The idea that God is vulnerable is not new, not after the prophets and the *Midrash,* only a bit of which I made mention of above. Might these strange 'tests' of Job and Abraham be a function of God's as-it-were humanity? Perhaps.

If one can think of these stories not as history but as parables[16]—so that one doesn't have to ponder actual deaths and the like—another idea suggests itself. I will introduce this suggestion by way of another similarity between the Job story and the *Akedah.* The language of both stories, specifically, the description of God's initial command to Abraham and his mandates to the Accuser, are, to put it mildly, quite stark. It is as if the reader is invited to extreme discomfort and confusion, perhaps to outrage. It would not have been inappropriate for the writer to warn the reader: '*what you are about to hear will make your hair stand on edge.*'[17]

Perhaps the reader is encouraged to experience discomfort to the point of moral horror, to join Job pre-Whirlwind, to join Abraham in his reaction to

---

[16] Job reads like a parable; the *Akedah* less so. Maimonides, in the *Guide,* announces a highly controversial methodological principle that one might think to apply to the *Akedah.* Strikingly, and unexplained, he does not so apply it. The idea is that when a biblical text mentions an angel, what that text formulates is not a piece of history, but rather the vision of a prophet. So Maimonides, to very mixed reviews over time, interprets the story of Abraham and the three men/angels that visit him in Mamre. To apply this to the *Akedah*—an angel is indeed mentioned in the text—renders it a nightmarish vision of Abraham. It would remain a tremendously interesting vision, one whose messages are hardly mooted by its vision status.

[17] Thanks to Jeff Helmreich here.

God's plan for Sodom, to inquire about justice, to ask how God can be indifferent to the spiritual torture of His beloved Abraham, how He can be influenced by the Accuser in the face of what God knows about Job. Perhaps these texts are challenging us to ask hard questions that have no answers forthcoming. Why this would be is a speculative matter for another day.

These of course are the merest speculations. Here's another, from a very different direction. The Bible seems to sometimes attribute natural occurrences, the work of God's creation, to God. One quick example: Exodus speaks of God's hardening Pharaoh's heart, perhaps the outcome of natural processes, as when one sets out on a ill-chosen course of action and nevertheless finds sustenance and encouragement for that course. Perhaps then it is the universe that, as it were, tests us, killing our children, removing our riches, nullifying our accomplishments, putting us in a position where we must choose between alternatives, none of which can be abandoned virtually at the cost of our selves.

I don't have a settled view, or even something that approaches one. Job and the *Akedah*, however, virtually reek of truth for the reasons explored above. Better to suffer in confusion about God, an appropriate state for us if not a pleasurable one, than to forgo these stories.

REFERENCES

Judt, Tony. 2009. 'Leslie Kolakowski (1927–2009)', *New York Review of Books*, September 24.

Midrash Rabbah. 1983. London: Soncino Press.

Mintz, Alan. 1996. *Hurban: Responses to Catastrophe in Hebrew Literature*. Syracuse, NY: Syracuse University Press.

Wettstein, Howard. 1997. 'Doctrine', *Faith and Philosophy*. Also available at http://www.philosophy.ucr.edu/people/faculty/wettstein/index.html.

——1999. 'Against Theodicy', in *Proceedings of the Twentieth World Congress of Philosophy*. Also on my website.

Wettstein, Howard. 2002. 'Coming to Terms with Exile', in H. Wettstein (ed.), *Diasporas and Exiles*. Berkeley and Los Angeles: UC Press.

Index